"/07

16.99

8.50 used

TAKE
HEART

Compiled and Edited by
Diana Wallis

TAKE
HEART

Daily Devotions with the
Church's Great Preachers

kregel
PUBLICATIONS

Grand Rapids, MI 49501

To my pastor,
John White Jr.

Take Heart: Daily Devotions with the Church's Great Preachers

© 2001 by Diana Wallis

Published by Kregel Publications, a division of Kregel, Inc., P.O. Box 2607, Grand Rapids, MI 49501. For more information about Kregel Publications, visit our Web site: www.kregel.com.

Unless otherwise indicated, Scripture taken from the *Holy Bible: New International Version*®. © 1973, 1978, 1984 by International Bible Society. Used by permission of Zondervan Publishing House. All rights reserved.

Scripture quotations marked NASB are from the *New American Standard Bible*, © the Lockman Foundation 1960, 1962, 1963, 1968, 1971, 1972, 1973, 1975, 1977.

Scripture quotations marked NKJV are from *The New King James Version*. © 1979, 1980, 1982, Thomas Nelson, Inc., Publishers.

Scripture quotations marked ASV used by permission of Thomas Nelson, Inc., original publisher of the American Standard Version.

Scripture quotations marked KJV are from the King James version of the Holy Bible.

ISBN 0-8254-3945-0

Printed in the United States of America

1 2 3 / 05 04 03 02 01

Contents

Editor's Preface

Be strong and take heart and wait for the Lord.
—Psalm 27:14

When life is difficult, too difficult for platitudes, people need strong, honest words of encouragement. Christian truth possesses that kind of power, power that transcends the ages. The apostle Paul still speaks to us today; so does Moses. And the words of others—though not "inspired" as Scripture is inspired—speak to us, too—great preachers like George H. Morrison, C. H. Spurgeon, John Ker, and G. Campbell Morgan.

The preachers quoted in this volume weren't of the smile-God-loves-you variety. They didn't sugarcoat life. Take this, for example, from a sermon preached by Arthur John Gossip shortly after the death of his wife:

> I do not understand this life of ours, but still less can I comprehend how people in trouble and loss and bereavement can run away peevishly from the Christian faith. In God's name, run to what? Have we not lost enough without losing that too? If Christ is right—if, as he says, there are somehow, hidden away from our eyes as yet . . . wisdom and planning and kindness and love in these dark dispensations—then we can see them through. . . . Already some things have become very clear to me. This to begin, that the faith works, fulfills itself, is real, and that its most audacious promises are true. . . . Further, one becomes certain about immortality. You think that you believe in that. But wait till you have lowered your dearest into an open grave, and you will know what believing it means.[1]

When facing calamities large and small in our own lives, surely we can take heart from such testimony as that.

That the gospel is clearly proclaimed in these pages may seem superfluous in a book whose audience likely already believes in Christ. But, first, these preachers did, after all, proclaim the gospel. And second, the gospel is the great joy of believers. So be reminded, and meditate on the truths of it.

When these preachers lived on the earth they spoke the language of their day, using word forms and vocabulary that may, for the modern reader, obscure the message. Because the content of that message is of greater value than preserving archaic forms, I have modernized the language in many older sermons—replacing *thees* and *thous* and older styles and sometimes changing word order. Except where it is necessary to a particular sermon I have also replaced the King James Version and Revised Version texts with *The New International Version.*

These preached words are a part of our Christian heritage, and you will find the power of God in them still. I want to preserve them not because they are old but because they are true. It is our loss if we allow this part of our heritage to crumble to dust, forgotten, on out-of-the-way shelves. Let us carry with us that which is of value from our Christian history, that we may "be strong and take heart" as we go forward in the new millennium—still waiting for the Lord.

PART ONE

Winter

Grace grows best in the winter.

—Samuel Rutherford

You have never been this way before. . . .
Consecrate yourselves.

—Joshua 3:4–5

When the New Year steps up to greet us, it evokes a certain response within the heart.[2] We have reached an end that is also a beginning. Behind us is a common journey, before us an untrodden way. What, then, does this old story give us to hearten and guide us as we cross the threshold of the year?

We must sanctify ourselves. What that means is gathered from the words of Jesus: "For them I sanctify myself" (John 17:19). Facing the untrodden way, we are to dedicate ourselves again to God. We are to give ourselves to the duties of our calling with a fresh and unreserved surrender—no matter what our calling. The wonders of tomorrow depend on the sanctification of today—a new surrender here and now is the prelude to a wonderful experience, which ought to be borne in mind by those who are growing weary of their work and dreading the prospect of another year. The enthusiasm of youth may have departed, the strength we once enjoyed may have been weakened, the freshness may have been rubbed off things through the ceaseless handling of the years. But if, here and now, facing the unknown in our Lord's fashion we sanctify ourselves, tomorrow will be more wonderful than yesterday.

Israel sent on ahead the ark of God. It was the sign and symbol that the Lord was with them, and they sent it on ahead into the swollen river. In spite of the express command of Jesus, how we send our imaginings ahead! How we toss ourselves into a fever over the fears of the untrodden way! Fear is a poor hand at finding a place to wade across. Fear is a sorry bridge-builder. Fear drowns the music of today. It hears nothing but the rushing of the river. But Israel sent on the ark of God, and that made all the difference. With a fresh surrender of ourselves, with spirits receptive and responsive, with a conviction that God is ahead, ordering everything in perfect love, let us go forward with the banners flying, to the high adventure of another year, for we have not come this way before.

—George H. Morrison

You made both summer and winter.

—Psalm 74:17

It is easy to believe that God made the summertime.[3] Beauty is everywhere. The singing of the birds, the warmth of the sun, the amazing prodigality of life—these draw our hearts to the Giver of them all and make it easy to say, "You made summer." With winter it is different. It is not so easy to see the love of God there. There is a great deal of suffering in winter, for both the animals and for people. It may therefore aid the faith of some who are tempted to doubt the love of God in winter if I suggest some of winter's spiritual services.

One service of winter is to deepen our appreciation of the summer. We would be blind if summer were perpetual. We must feel the grip of winter, before we fully appreciate the summer. It is not the one who lives in bonnie Scotland who feels most deeply how beautiful Scotland is. It is the exile, yearning for the mountains and the glens. It is not the one with unbroken health who feels most deeply the value of health. That is realized when health is shattered.

Another service of winter is the larger demands it makes on the will. In summer it is comparatively easy to get out of bed at the appointed hour, for the earth is warm, the birds are singing, the light streams through open windows. But in winter, to fling the covers off and get up when it is dark and cold—that calls for a certain resolution, an instant demand on the will. Winter—when life is difficult and it takes some doing even to get up—is God's tonic for his children's will. Summer is languid; winter makes us resolute. We have to do things when we don't feel like doing them.

Another service of winter is to intensify the thought of home. The thought of home is sweetest and richest and most beautiful in the dark and cold of winter. We talk in the same breath of hearth and home, and it is in winter that the hearth is glowing. Now think of everything we and the nation owe to home. Home is the basis of national morality.

[A final] service of winter is how it stirs our hearts to charity. It unseals the springs of pity. It moves us with compassion for the destitute, and to be moved so is very Christlike.

Such thoughts as these in icy days, when we are tempted to doubt the love of God, make it easier to say with David, "You made . . . winter."

—George H. Morrison

I have seen something else under the sun: The race is not to
the swift or the battle to the strong.
—Ecclesiastes 9:11

Men might be swift, but they did not always win.[4] Armies might be strong, but they did not always triumph. There were incalculable powers abroad, balancing, adjusting, compensating, so that turn where one would in human affairs, there were unexpected and dramatic outcomes. You may call that chance, or you may take it from the other side and call it God. But whatever you call it, the fact remains that the rearranging and revising power is there.

This is true of Jesus Christ, the Man of Sorrows and acquainted with grief. I sometimes contrast the Man of Nazareth with the emperor who was reigning then, Tiberius. Tiberius was the most powerful person living, the ruler of all that was fairest in the world. There was no control to his power, no limit to his wealth, no barrier to his pleasures. On one of the most enchanting spots of earth he chose his home—a lovely island with a delicious climate. Wouldn't you be happy if all that were yours? Yet Pliny calls him the most gloomy of souls. Now think of Christ with nowhere to lay his head, despised and rejected, jeered at, crucified. Pay attention to his words about "my joy," "my peace" that the world cannot give and cannot take away. Who wins in that race for happiness and peace? Is it the mighty Caesar or the rejected Christ?

Let me suggest some of the moral values of this truth. First, it keeps us from discouragement and cheers us when the lights are dim. We can say in our weakness, I may still win my crown, for the battle is not always to the strong. Then, it weans us from pride and keeps us watchful, humble, and dependent. It is a strange world, rich in dramatic touches, and the battle is not always to the strong.

Lastly, it clears the ground for God and leaves a space to recognize him. If the strongest were sure of triumph in every battle there would be little room on the field for the divine. Whose is the arm that so upholds the weak that after the strife theirs is the cry of victory? So we return, we who were once so blind, with eyes that have been opened to see God, and now we know that just because *he* reigns, the battle is not always to the strong.

—George H. Morrison

The God of all grace . . . make you perfect.

—I Peter 5:IO KJV

The word that Peter uses for "make you perfect" is the same word [that] is used for mending the nets.[5] It is as if Peter had said, "The God of grace, whatever else he may do, will mend your nets for you."

Nets are often broken through encountering some jagged obstacle—caught by some obstruction in the deep and, clearing themselves free of it, are torn. It may be a piece of wreckage in the sea. It may be the sharp edge of some familiar reef that has been swept clear of its seaweed by the storm. But whatever it is, the net drags over it, is caught and torn, and, tearing itself free, it gapes disfigured like some wounded thing.

Are there no human lives like that? Maybe a hidden and surprising sin does it, maybe a sudden and overwhelming sorrow; it may be the ruin of a cherished friendship or the wreckage of a love that meant the world or some swift insight into another's baseness where we dreamed there was sincerity. In such an hour as that the net is torn. There is a tearing of the very heartstrings. Faith is shattered, and God is but a name, and life seems the shallowest of delusions. For always, when we lose our faith in people, there falls a shadow on our faith in God, so that the very stars seem to have no master, and goodness seems only the mockery of a dream.

The torn net entails missing the riches that are at hand on every side. And that was the pity of the useless net—all that was precious was so near at hand and yet might have been a thousand miles away.

We have sinned, and we have sinned greatly. We have done our very best to spoil our lives. We have wasted time and squandered opportunity and been unloving and utterly unworthy. Thanks be to God, in spite of all that—and of things that may be darker than that—the broken net is going to be mended. He forgives us completely, he is pledged to save us completely. Deeper than our deepest need are the infinite depths of his compassion. It is in such a faith that we give him our lives, which are so torn and ragged, assured that his grace will be sufficient for us and his power made perfect in our weakness. God's hands are powerful and can grasp tremendously when the wind is high and the waves are raging. But [his hands], too, with a delicacy infinite and with tenderness, can mend the broken net on life's shore.

—George H. Morrison

Some time later the brook dried up.

—1 Kings 17:7

The failure of the waters was meant, first, to deepen the prophet [Elijah's] sense of kinship.[6] He was drawn into a new communion with Israel in the very hour that Cherith ceased to flow. There had been no rain, and the whole land was parched—and all the time, in the little vale of Cherith, the coolness and murmuring of the stream. It was very comfortable, and it was very happy, but it is not thus that Jehovah makes his prophets. What people have got to suffer they must suffer. What people have to endure they must endure. And so, that he might be a brother among brothers and feel his kinship with his suffering nation, some time later the brook dried up.

That is still the secret of the failing brook—not because God is angry; it is because our Father wants us to be a family. One touch of nature makes us all akin, even if it is only a touch of common thirst, and there is many a brook that the Almighty dries so that we may cease from our pride and realize our kinship. There is no sympathy so deep and strong as the sympathy that springs out of a common suffering. Exclude a person from what others have to bear and you exclude him or her from the family heritage.

There are things, then, that it is hard to lose, but in God's sight it may be good to lose them. We grow more loving, more sympathetic, and more kind; life is fuller and richer and warmer than it once was. We were very superior and exclusive once, and the common people were odiously common—but some time later the brook dried up.

—George H. Morrison

Some time later the brook dried up.

—1 *Kings* 17:7

Elijah was taught by this event that in certain matters God makes no exceptions.[7] God has his chosen ones, but whatever they are chosen for, it is not to escape the heritage of tears. Now to be a prophet was a lofty calling. Therefore it was reasonable to expect that [Elijah] would have a little special care and would be guarded, as the favorite of God, from some of the ills that flesh is heir to. I have no doubt that Elijah had such thoughts. I believe indeed that they never wholly left him. God, when he dried up the waters of the Cherith, was teaching him how false it was to count on any exception as his right. Elijah had to learn that though he was God's messenger, he was not going to escape the common lot. Called with a heavenly calling in Christ Jesus, he had to suffer some things like the vilest reprobate.

Now that is a lesson we do well to learn, that in certain matters there are no exceptions. I had a visit from a friend the other day who was brokenhearted in unexpected grief. A little rivulet of life had made his meadow beautiful, when suddenly its music was no more. And "Oh," he said to me, "if I had been wicked— if I had been a rebel against God, I might have understood it, but it is hard to be dealt with thus when I have striven to serve him and tried to be true to him in home and business."

At the heart of his so bitter grief there was a thought that is common to us all. My friend was like Elijah at his stream, saying, "I am a prophet and it can never dry." And one of the hardest lessons we must learn is that the name and nature of our God is love, yet for the person who trusts and serves him best, there is to be no exception from the scourge.

—George H. Morrison

Some time later the brook dried up.

—1 Kings 17:7

The deepest lesson of the story is that the ceasing of the prophet's brook was the beginning of larger views of God.[8]

There is a faith that runs through the green fields of childhood, making everything it laps on fresh and beautiful. Yet while some never lose that faith, living in its gladness until the end, for most of us, some time later the brook dries up. There may be moral causes at the back of that. A vast deal of doubt runs down to moral grounds. But if we are earnest and truthful and if we trust and pray, there is nothing to sigh for in the failing brook. For the God whom we find again through many a struggle and the faith that we make ours by many a battle and the things that we wrestle for until break of day—although we may go limping ever after—these are our own for time and for eternity, and neither life nor death can take them from us.

And then there are the blessings we enjoy—our health, our prosperity, the love of those who love us. There are many people who never lose these blessings, moving beside still waters to the end. But there are others with whom it is not so. They have suffered terribly or had sharp and sore reverses. There was a day when they had everything they wanted, but it came to pass some time later that the brook dried up. I will not comfort them by any platitudes. I will only ask them, Has not God been nearer—has not religion been more to them since then? And if it has taken the failing of the stream to cast them utterly on the arm of God, if they have risen from an empty brook to drink of an ocean that is ever full—perhaps it was not in anger but in love that the waters ceased to be musical at Cherith.

—George H. Morrison

Give thanks in all circumstances.

—1 Thessalonians 5:18

Consider the value of thankfulness.[9]

It quells brooding. We are all prone, in certain moods, to complain of our lot. Everyone has at some time or other imagined that he or she has a particularly hard time in this world. It is to be hoped that in other moods we are ashamed of ourselves for such brooding. But how to prevent its recurrence? A valuable help will be the habit of thankfulness to God. Then if a brooding spirit arises, in the middle of some complaining sentence we will suddenly express thankfulness and perhaps laugh at ourselves for the folly of such brooding.

Thankfulness soothes distress. Those who are greatly afflicted—and not accustomed to be thankful—sometimes find the memory of past joys only an aggravation of present sorrow. It is otherwise with those who have learned to be habitually thankful. For these, the recollection of happier hours is still a comfort.

Thankfulness helps to allay anxiety. Notice what the apostle says to the Philippians: "Do not be anxious about anything, but in everything, by prayer and petition, with thanksgiving, present your requests to God. And the peace of God . . . will guard your hearts and your minds" (Phil. 4:6–7). Notice that we are to prevent anxiety by prayer as to the future with thanksgiving for the past.

Thankfulness cannot fail to deepen penitence. "God's kindness leads you toward repentance" (Rom. 2:4). When we are in the habit of thankfully recalling the kindnesses and mercies of our heavenly Father, we perceive more clearly and lament more earnestly the evil of sin against him, and what is more, this will strengthen us to turn from our sins to his blessed service.

Thankfulness brightens hope. "I love to think on mercies past, And future good implore." If we have been accustomed to set up milestones of God's mercy on the path of life, then every glance backward will help us to look forward with more of humble hope.

Thankfulness strengthens for endurance and exertion. We all know how much more easily and effectively those work who work cheerfully, and the very nutriment of cheerfulness is found in thankfulness as to the past and hope as to the future.

—John A. Broadus

Give thanks in all circumstances.
—1 Thessalonians 5:18

Be thankful to God for everything that is pleasant.[10] We so often speak about the religious benefits of affliction that we are in danger of overlooking the other side. It is a religious duty to enjoy every rightful pleasure of earthly existence. He who gave us these bodies desires that we should find life a pleasure.

We work best at what we enjoy. The young should enjoy what they are studying. [But] it is possible that by well-guided efforts they should learn to relish studies to which they were at first disinclined. I sometimes hear young married people say, "We are going to set up housekeeping, and then we can have what we like." I sometimes reply, "Yes, you may, but what is far more important and interesting—you will be apt to like what you have." To have what we like is, for the most part, an impossible dream; to like what we have is a possibility and not only a duty but a high privilege.

Be thankful to God for everything that is painful. That may be stating the matter too strongly. Notice that the apostle does not say, "For every circumstance give thanks"; he says, "Give thanks in all circumstances" (1 Thess. 5:18). That, surely, need not seem impossible. We may always be thankful that the situation is no worse. With some persons it has been worse. Let us always bless the Lord that, but for his special mercies, it would be worse with us today.

An unpublished anecdote about President Madison [relates that] the venerable ex-president suffered from many diseases and took a variety of medicines. A friend sent him a box of vegetable pills of his own production and begged to be informed whether they helped. In due time came back one of those carefully written and often felicitous notes for which Mr. Madison and Mr. Jefferson were both famous: "My dear friend, I thank you very much for the box of pills. I have taken them all, and while I cannot say that I am better since taking them, it is quite possible that I might have been worse if I had not taken them, and so I beg you to accept my sincere acknowledgments." Really, my friends, this is not a mere pleasantry. There is always something, known or unknown, but for which our condition might have been worse. And that something constitutes an occasion for gratitude.

—John A. Broadus

Give thanks in all circumstances.
—1 *Thessalonians* 5:18

It is common Christian philosophy that our sufferings may, through the grace of God, be the means of improving our characters.[11] Such is by no means a matter of course. Sufferings may be borne with gloom and brooding so as greatly to damage character. But devout souls may regard affliction as but a loving Father's discipline, meant for their highest good. There has never been a devout life that did not share this experience. To be exempt would, as the Bible declares, give proof that we are not children of God. Many of us could testify that the sorrows of life have, by God's blessing, done us good.

If we believe this to be true, and it is a belief clearly founded on Scripture, then can't we contrive, even amid the severest sufferings, to be thankful for the benefits of affliction?

Remember, too, our seasons of affliction make real to us divine compassion and sympathy. When you look with parental anguish on your own suffering child, then you know the meaning of those words, "As a father has compassion on his children, so the LORD has compassion on those who fear him" (Ps. 103:13). When you find the trials of life hard to bear, then it becomes sweet to remember that our High Priest can sympathize with our weaknesses, who was "tempted in every way, just as we are—yet was without sin" (Heb. 4:15). Thus affliction brings to mind views of the divine character, which otherwise we would never fully gain.

Besides all this, remember that the sufferings of this present life will but enhance the life to come. A thousand times have I remembered the text of my first funeral sermon, "There will be no more death or mourning or crying or pain, for the old order of things has passed away." These are the present things now—all around us and within us, but the time is coming when they will be the old order, quite passed away.

Skillful composers make use of discords in music. The jarring discord is solved and makes more sweet the harmony into which it passes. And oh! the time is coming when all the pains and pangs of this present life will seem to have been only a brief, discordant prelude to an everlasting harmony.

—John A. Broadus

Give thanks in all circumstances.

—1 Thessalonians 5:18

How may the habit of thankfulness be formed and maintained?[12]

If you wish to establish the habit of doing a certain thing, take pains to do that thing on every possible occasion and avoid everything inconsistent with it. If you wish to form the habit of thankfulness, just begin by being thankful—not next year but tonight; not for some great event or experience but for whatever has just occurred, whatever has been pleasant and, yes, for whatever has been painful. Find some special occasion for thanksgiving this very night. And then go on searching for material for gratitude and continuing to be thankful hour by hour, day by day. Thus the habit will be formed by a very law of human nature.

But remember that good habits cannot be maintained without attention. They require self-control, self-constraint. Isn't the habit of thankfulness worth taking pains to maintain? I once dined with Ole Bull, the celebrated violinist, and found him a man of generous soul, full of noble impulses and enthusiasm, rich with the experience of travel. And I was interested in a remark of his: "When I stop practicing one day, I see the difference; when I stop two days, my friends see the difference; when I stop a week, everybody sees the difference." Here was a man who by lifelong labor had cultivated a wonderful natural gift until he was probably the foremost of his time, and yet he could not afford to stop practicing for a single week or even for a single day. "They do it to get a crown that will not last; but we do it to get a crown that will last forever" (1 Cor. 9:25). Shall we shrink from vigilance and effort to keep up the habit of thankfulness to God?

I see many young persons present this evening. Won't some of you at once begin the exercise of continual thankfulness? Will you think over it, pray over it, labor to establish and maintain so beautiful and blessed a habit? What a help it will be to you amid all the struggles of youth and all the sorrows of age! And in far-coming years, when you are gray, when the preacher of this hour has long been forgotten, let us hope that you will still be gladly recommending to the young around you the habit of thankfulness.

—John A. Broadus

About midnight Paul and Silas were
praying and singing hymns to God, and the other
prisoners were listening to them.

—Acts 16:25

All of us exercise unconscious ministries.[13] When we never dream we are affecting anybody, we are touching others all the time. We sing at midnight because God is with us and prisoners in other cells are cheered.

We never know what we are doing when we do it. Like Faithful in the Valley of the Shadow, we lift our voices because our hearts are strong. And some poor Christian, stumbling on behind us also on the way to the Celestial City, thanks God and takes courage at the music. Be quite sure that the very humblest life is full of unconscious ministries. There is not a note of song we ever raise but the ear of some other prisoner will catch it. Words that we utter and then forget—a smile in passing, the clasp of hands in comradeship—have their work to do and will meet us in the dawn.

This unconscious helpfulness is one of the chief ministries of happiness. Happiness is sometimes selfishness, but happiness is sometimes service. The one who resolves at all costs to be happy is generally a very miserable person. In this world the things we set our hearts on are often the things we never get. When anyone is genuinely happy, then happiness is unconscious benediction.

The ones who can sing at midnight because God is with them are doing something for others all the time. To be happy when the shadows deepen and the cross is heavy is one of the finest of life's unconscious ministries.

I believe that much of our Christian service must always be of that unconscious character. I trust that when this life is over, you and I will each have the *well done.* That is the only thing worth living for, the only welcome that I want. But I have sometimes thought that the great surprise of the dawn will be the kind of thing for which it is the reward. Certain ministries of which I knew nothing as I went out and in among you will waken the trumpets on the other side.

People who do their best always do more, though they are haunted by the sense of failure. Be good and true, be patient, be resolute. Leave your usefulness for God to estimate. He will see to that you do not live in vain.

—George H. Morrison

I, the LORD *your God, am a jealous God.*

—Exodus 20:5

Jealousy is so associated with evil that we hesitate to attribute it to God.[14] And yet the Bible, which knows our human hearts and searches out the latent evil in them, assures us of the jealousy of God.

We begin to see the solution of this difficulty when we recall the connection of jealousy with love. Jealousy is the shadow cast by love. That is the difference between jealousy and envy. We may be envious of other people although it has never been our lot to love them. Jealousy is one side of love, though often a very dark and tragic side. It is along such lines that we begin to fathom the possibility of jealousy in God. For the God of the Bible in his essential nature is revealed to us as Love. And if that love flows out on humanity in an infinite and everlasting mercy, it also, if it is deep and mighty, can scarcely lack the attribute of jealousy.

For it is God alone who has the right to the undivided devotion of the creature. That is where human jealousy is evil. That is the source of all its bitter tragedy. It is the passionate claim of one poor human creature to the undivided devotion of another. And it is always selfish and forever wrong. No human heart is large or deep enough entirely to absorb another heart. We are all finite creatures at our highest, and one such creature cannot fill another. And so our jealousy tends to become sinful because it is our assertion of a claim that is proper to the infinity of God. For only God can satisfy the heart—even the poorest and the meanest heart. Only he can absorb it without wronging it, for in him we live and move and have our being. Only he has the full right to say in the highest spiritual interest of his children, "My child, give me your heart." The jealousy of God does not differ from human jealousy in this, that both are born of love—a love that cannot tolerate a rival. But human jealousy grows dark and terrible because it makes a claim that is impossible, and the jealousy of God makes [the claim] by right.

—George H. Morrison

I, the Lord *your God, am a jealous God.*

—Exodus 20:5

It is in the Bible, and the Bible only, that we meet with the thought of the jealousy of God.[15] That the unseen powers are envious of humans is an old concept. You light on it far back in ancient Greece; you detect it in a hundred superstitions. That the gods are envious and filled with a grudge against too great prosperity is one of the oldest conceptions of the mind. Such divine envy is wholly different from divine jealousy. [Envy] does not spring from a great pity; it springs from the malevolence of spite. And not until there had dawned on the world that truth so wonderful—that God is love—do you ever have the truth that God is jealous. It is the Bible and the Bible only that has convinced the world that God is love. And it is the very depth and splendor of that love, sealed in the gift of the Lord Jesus Christ, that has given us the jealousy of God.

Note that the same attitude is very evident in our Lord himself. No one can read the story of the Gospels, believing that God was incarnate in humanity, without awaking to the awful truth that the Lord our God is a jealous God. As surely as God will tolerate no rival, Jesus Christ would tolerate no rival. He makes a claim on the human heart of absolute and unconditional surrender. Even had we never heard from the Old Testament that there was such a thing as divine jealousy, we would conclude it from the life of Jesus. There were many things that Jesus tolerated that we would never have thought to find him tolerating. He bore with social abuses—with personal discourtesies—in a way that is sometimes hard to understand.

But there was one thing Jesus never tolerated, and that was the division of his empire. "I am the way and the truth and the life. No one comes to the Father except through me." That is either stupendous arrogance—or the jealousy of God.

A jealous God may be a dark conception, but a jealous God can never be indifferent. He loves with a love so burning and intense that he is passionately jealous for his people. And it was that great love, shown in a beauty that people had never dreamed of, that was at last revealed in the Lord Jesus Christ.

—George H. Morrison

[Nothing] will . . . separate us from the love of God.
—Romans 8:38

In his enumeration of things that might dim the love of God to us, the apostle mentions things present.[16] By things present he means the events and trials of the present day. The task in which we are presently engaged, the duties of the common day, the multitude of things we must get through before bed—these are apt to blind us to the great realities and to separate us from the love of God in Christ.

That separating power arises from the exceeding nearness of things present. Things that are very near command our vision and often lead to erroneous perspective. Each day brings its round of present duties. They absorb us, commanding every energy and, so doing, may blind us. In busy lives where near things tyrannize, we all require moments of withdrawal. To halt a moment and just to say, "God loves me," to halt a moment and say, "God is here," is a secret to mastering the separating power of things present.

Another element in that separating power is the difficulty of understanding present things. It is always easier to understand yesterday than to grasp the meaning of today. We begin to understand our past, its trials, its disappointments, and its illnesses, but such things are very hard to understand in their actual moment, and it is that, the difficulty of reading love in the dark characters of present things, which constitutes their separating power.

Another element of the separating power is found in the distraction of things present. "Life isn't a little bundle of big things: it's a big bundle of little things." What things escape us in our unending busyness! Peace and joy and self-control and the serenity that ought to mark the Christian. And sometimes that is lost which to lose is the tragedy of tragedies—the sense and certainty of love divine.

Of spiritual victory over present things, the one perfect example is our Lord. Never doubting the love of God in his darkest hour, through broken days, through never-ending calls, when there was not leisure so much as to eat, he mastered the separating power of things present. Do not forget he did all that for us. His victories were all achieved for us. In a deep sense we do not win our victories—we appropriate the victories of Christ.

—George H. Morrison

But a Samaritan . . . took pity on him.

—Luke 10:33

Our Lord, true poet that he was, had a great liking for pictorial teaching.[17] The scene, familiar to them all; the robbery, an occurrence they all dreaded; the ecclesiastics, [those] whom they knew so well; the Samaritan, [he] whom they all despised—these made a glowing, vivid picture that nobody but a master could have painted, and nobody but the Master ever did. It is a beautiful etching of benevolence, and as such it is immortal. But people have loved to find in this Samaritan a delineation of the Lord himself in his infinite compassion for humankind.

The Samaritan came just where the man was and handled him where he lay battered. How perfectly that touch applies to the Lord, the teller of the story!

Think of the Incarnation. It was the Son of God seeing human need and coming in mercy where humans were. Not speaking from high heaven, not casting down a scroll out of eternity. No, this is the glory of the Incarnation, that when people were bruised and battered by their sin, Christ, the Son of God, the good Samaritan, came just where they were. Show me where folk are lying ill at home, and I can show you Jesus there. Show me where hearts are crying out in darkness, "My God, why have you forsaken me?" and I can show you Jesus there. Where people have suffered, Jesus Christ has suffered. Where people have toiled, Jesus Christ has toiled. Where people have wept, Jesus Christ has wept. Where people have died, Jesus Christ has died. He took up our infirmities and carried our sorrows and made his grave with the wicked.

Christ was genial, kindly, and accessible, a lover of human haunts, the friend of publicans and sinners. Simon Peter was busy with his nets, and Christ came where he was. Matthew was seated at the tax collector's booth, and Christ came to him. The poor demoniac was in the graveyard and our good Samaritan came exactly where he was.

That is exactly what he is doing still. "Just As I Am" is a very gracious hymn, but I want someone to write me another hymn: "Just *where* I am, O Lamb of God, you come."

—George H. Morrison

The time has come for my departure.
—2 Timothy 4:6

A familiar and striking figure is used when Paul speaks of the time of his "departure."[18] The thought is found in most tongues. Death is a going away, or, as Peter calls it, an exodus. But the well-worn image receives new depth and sharpness of outline in Christianity. To those who have learned the meaning of Christ's resurrection and feed their souls on the hopes that it warrants, death is merely a change of place or state, an accident affecting locality and little more.

We have had plenty of changes before. Life has been one long series of departures. This is different from the others mainly in that it is the last and that to go away from this visible and fleeting show, where we wander aliens among things that have no true kindred with us, is to go home, where there will be no more pulling up the tent pegs and toiling across the deserts in monotonous change. How strong is the conviction, spoken in that name for death, that the essential life lasts on quite unaltered through it all! How slight the else formidable thing is made. We may change climates and for the stormy bleakness of life may have the long still days of heaven, but we do not change ourselves. We lose nothing worth keeping when we leave behind the body, as a dress not fitted for home, where we are going.

We only travel one more stage, though it is the last, and part of it is in pitchy darkness. Some pass over it as in a fiery chariot, like Paul and many a martyr. Some have to toil through it with slow steps and bleeding feet and fainting heart, but all may have a Brother with them and, holding his hand, may find that the journey is not so hard as they feared and the home, from which they shall remove no more, better than they hoped when they hoped the most.

—Alexander Maclaren

In my Father's house are many rooms; if it were not so,
I would have told you.

—John 14:2

Change in things around us is like fixity to the change that is in ourselves.[19] Old times are gone, old interests, old aims; the haunts, the friends, the faces of our youth—where are they? Gone, or so changed that we dare not think to recall them. Or, if we try, we cannot; they are so different, so far away they are shadows, like things in a dream. And we are changing within. There are few who can say the spring leaves are as green, the flowers as sweet, the summer days as long and sunny, the heart as open and free from distrust as when life was young.

There is indeed compensation for this, if we will seek it. If we have a home in God through Christ, it brings in something better than youthful brightness, the taste of which is like the wine of Christ's higher feast that makes the guests say, "The new is better."

But here, too, there is frequently change. The anchor of our hope loses its hold, our sense of pardon and peace may be broken, and the face of God may look dim and distant. The disciples who were in fellowship with Christ at the close of the week were, before another, scattered or hopelessly seeking him in his grave.

It is from such changes that the promise of Christ carries us. The permanence of the dwelling will ensure permanence in all that belongs to the dwellers in it, otherwise the home and the inhabitants would be out of harmony. There will be no wavering of faith, no waning of hope, no chill of love.

Here, change leaves some lost good behind it; there, change will take all its good things forward into fuller possession. "There remains, then, a Sabbath-rest for the people of God." We can rely on nothing else but his promise for the fulfillment of it. Sometimes it looks so strange, so unearthly, so utterly away from all the laws of nature and life as we see them here that it seems incredible. It is for faith, not for sight; for the trust of the heart, not for the telescope of science. Heaven is a state before it is a place. It is being in God, then with God. The locality will flow from the heart.

—John Ker

In my Father's house are many rooms; if it were not so,
I would have told you.

—John 14:2

It is the Father's house, a paternal home.[20] The Father is needed to make it a home in any sense; needed to give the heart rest either on earth or in heaven. Those who inquire into the facts and laws of the world and find no God in it have made themselves homeless. Those who have found human affection but no God beneath it have found only the shadow of a home. Thought and affection are shallow, short-lived things without him—the Father of our spirits—who sets the solidarity in families.

It is to teach us this that God has made a father's love the bond of a true human household. You recollect how Joseph, when he spoke with his brothers, could not rest until he had an answer to his question, "How is your aged father?" The good of the land of Egypt would have been empty and its glory gone without his father to look on and share it with him. It is not that love like this leads us to think of having a father in God; God himself, desiring to be our Father, has put this love into our hearts that it may reflect his own. Let a soul but once awake truly to the feeling of its misery, if it is orphaned in the universe—no pitying eye looking down on its solitude, no hand to guide its wanderings or hold it up in its weakness, no infinite heart to which it can bring its own when wounded and bleeding—let it see, or think it sees, that the world is fatherless and that there is no hope beyond the grave for those that are broken in their hearts and grieved in their minds, and I cannot understand how that soul would not be stricken with despair. If it were possible to enter heaven and find no Father there, heaven would be the grave of hope. But what will make the heavenly house a home is that it will have not friends and brothers and sisters only, but a Father whose presence will fill it and make itself felt in every pulse of every heart.

—John Ker

In my Father's house are many rooms; if it were not so,
I would have told you.

—John 14:2

If we were to think of every room in [the Father's house] having its four enclosing walls, each would have its inscription written by God's own hand.[21]

There are those who have often doubted their acceptance and forgiveness, who have walked in darkness and with difficulty stayed themselves on God, questioning whether they might not in the end be castaways; it stands inscribed, "Your many sins have been forgiven."

There are those who have felt all through life as if God were turned to be their enemy and were fighting against them. Their desires have been thwarted, their hearts pierced through and through with losses and crosses and cruel wounds, and failure upon failure has followed their plans. But it is written, "The LORD disciplines those he loves, as a father the son he delights in," and "In all things God works for the good of those who love him."

And there are those who have yearnings of heart to feel God's presence close and constant, to hear him and speak with him and be sure his is not, as some would say to them, a voice or a vision or a dream of their fond imagination. They have felt it at times so certain that they could say, "The LORD is the stronghold of my life—of whom shall I be afraid?" (Ps. 27:1). But clouds roll in on the assurance, and the voice seems far off or silent, as if it were among the trees of the garden, and it is toward evening, and there is doubt and fear. But it shall be "like the light of morning at sunrise on a cloudless morning, like the brightness after rain that brings the grass from the earth," and his name shall be written as the "Father of the heavenly lights, who does not change like shifting shadows." And the one who reads it shall say, "You are my Father, my God, the Rock my Savior." Here is hope and aim for stricken spirits and solitary hearts. There is a Father, there is a home. The sky is not empty, the world is not orphaned. Doubtless, you are our Father, our Redeemer.

—John Ker

In my Father's house are many rooms; if it were not so,
I would have told you.

—John 14:2

Our Lord has taught us to connect heaven with the thought of himself—"my" Father's house.[22] Heaven is the house of Christ's Father. It is as when an arch is built and last the keystone is put in that binds it all into one, or as when a palace has been raised with all its rooms and their furniture complete, but it is dark or dimly seen by lights carried from place to place. The sun arises, and by the central dome the light is poured into all the corridors and chambers. The Lord Jesus Christ is the sun of this house. If we think of its rooms and wonder where the final resting place will be, it is where Christ takes up his dwelling. His person is the place of heaven. If we think of its extent and variety, our imaginations might be bewildered and our souls chilled by boundless fields of knowledge, which stir the intellect and famish the heart. But where he is, knowledge becomes the wisdom of love—the daylight softened—and a heart beats in the universe, which throbs to its remotest and minutest fiber, for "in him was life, and that life was the light of men."

If we think of heaven in its unity of communion, it is in him that it is maintained and felt—at his throne, through his love—according to his prayer. And if we think of a Father in heaven, it is Christ who has revealed him. "No one has ever seen God, but God the One and Only, who is at the Father's side, has made him known" (John 1:18). Even in heaven, God cannot be seen by created eye; the pure in heart see him, but with the heart. For the human eye, it is Jesus Christ, the glorified God-man, who says in heaven as on earth, "Anyone who has seen me has seen the Father." He who gave us a corporeal nature and surrounded us with a material world has put into us the craving wish to approach him with our entire beings, soul, body, and spirit, and he has met the wish in the Son of God. In his person are enshrined the infinite attributes of God, so that finite creatures can look on them and comprehend them and see the Father in the Son. Thus God becomes open to human vision and accessible to human affection.

—John Ker

In my Father's house are many rooms; if it were not so,
I would have told you.

—John 14:2

It is Christ's Father's house because he is the way and the door to it.[23] "No one," he himself has said, "comes to the Father except through me." I know not of any heaven for human beings but that which the Lord Jesus has opened up and fitted and filled, and I know of no Father for them but the God and Father of our Lord and Savior Jesus Christ. None will ever reach it but that his foot led the way and his hand upheld their goings. It is because it is Christ's Father's house that new songs have been made for it and a new and peculiar joy created, joy among the angels for sinners that repent, joy among the saved that they have had wonderful deliverance, and joy in the heart of the Father himself—"For this son of mine was dead and is alive again; he was lost and is found." It is this that gives its deepest and highest meaning to the heaven of the Gospel; it is the heaven of the Redeemer.

Yet this truth, that the heavenly house has for its center the throne and cross of Christ, that it is the home of the pardoned and purified, makes it needful that a closing word should be spoken to be pondered by us all. Are you on the way to it, are you preparing for it? It is surely the most reasonable of all things to believe that someone cannot dwell in peace in God's house unless he or she is at peace with God himself and cannot enjoy the heaven of Christ without the mind of Christ. God cannot make you blessed by surrounding you with blessings. He cannot give someone heaven who will not have God himself. If, then you are refusing God, you are refusing God's heaven; if you will not have him in your heart, you can never look with loving confidence on his face. All deceptive dreams, all vain illusion about what God may do are scattered by this, that God has set heaven's door open to you, and you will not enter it; you are framing a heart and life within you that make misery sure by the most fixed of all laws, the law of the divine nature. He who has made heaven ready and who is the door to it is now at the door of your heart, ready to enter with pardon for all the past and divine help for all the future. Will you not receive him?

—John Ker

Suppose one of you has a hundred sheep and loses one of
them. Does he not leave the ninety-nine in the open
country and go after the lost sheep until he finds it?
—Luke 15:4

The love of Jesus, the Great Shepherd, is very practical and active.[24] There is a sheep lost, and the Lord regrets it, but his love does not spend itself in regrets; he arises and goes forth to seek and to save what was lost. The love of Jesus Christ is love not with words only, but in actions and in truth. He does not wait until the sheep is willing to return or until it makes some attempt to come back; no sooner is its lost estate known to the Shepherd than he starts off to find what was lost. The love of Jesus to the lost sheep is preeminent. He leaves the ninety-nine so that all his heart, his eye, his strength may be given to the one that has gone astray. O sweet love of Christ! Let us learn the love of Christ, that we may be wise in shepherdry. Let us not talk about our friends and say we love them, but let us show it by earnest, personal, speedy endeavors to do them good. Let us not wait until we see some goodness in them—until they seek after instruction. Long before they have a thought of coming home, let us be eager to grasp them, if by any means we may save some.

[The shepherd's] whole soul is in his eyes and ears until he finds it. This is a faint yet true picture of the Great Shepherd who came here to seek his flock. So the Evangelists have drawn him—always watchful, spending night and day in prayers and tears and entreaties, never to have a joy more until he finds the lost one.

Like the shepherd, there is no hesitating with Jesus. The sheep is lost, and the news is brought to the shepherd. He knows which way that stray sheep will go, and he is on its track at once, though he knows that he must mark that track with his blood. See the blessed shepherd pressing on: there is no pausing nor resting until he finds it.

—C. H. Spurgeon

Suppose one of you has a hundred sheep and loses one of them. Does he not leave the ninety-nine in the open country and go after the lost sheep until he finds it?
—Luke 15:4

If you look into that shepherd's face, there is no trace of anger.[25] It is all love and nothing else but love, before he finds and until he finds [the lost sheep], and you may be sure that careful tenderness will be in full action after he has found it.

And mark, for a shepherd there is no giving up. The sun has risen, and the sun has set, but as long as the shepherd can see and the sheep is still alive, he will pursue it until he finds it. He is impelled onward by irresistible love, and he must continue his weary search until he finds it. It was precisely so with our Lord Jesus Christ. When he came after you and after me, we ran from him, but he pursued us; we hid from him, but he discovered us.

He would not be turned away. The Lord Jesus has in hundreds and thousands of cases pursued sinners with unflagging mercy until he has found them. We are now his forever and ever, for he who has found us will never lose us. Blessed be his name.

If ever you are seeking the conversion of any, follow up until you find them. Do not be discouraged. Put up with a great many rebuffs and rebukes. Whisper to yourself, "I might well have put the Great Shepherd off from caring for me, and yet he was not turned aside. If he persevered with me even to the death, I may well persevere as long as I live in seeking and finding this soul." Persevere with loving entreaties! Until you bury your unsaved ones, do not consider them dead.

Live or die, or work or suffer, whether the time is short or long or the way is smooth or rough, let each one of you be bound to seek a soul until you find it. You will find it then, even as Christ found you.

—C. H. Spurgeon

And when he finds it, he joyfully puts it on his shoulders
and goes home. Then he calls his friends and neighbors
together and says, "Rejoice with me;
I have found my lost sheep."

—Luke 15:5–6

I wonder whether the sheep could see that the shepherd rejoiced.[26] I do not suppose that it could, but it could feel it. At any rate, I know that Christ has a way of saving us—oh, so gently, so lovingly, so gleefully, that he makes us happy in being saved. He saves us rejoicingly. It is a matter of thanksgiving to him when he gets hold of his lost sheep and gets it on his shoulders. It makes me glad to think that it is so.

We are not saved by a grudging Christ, who seems as if he were weary of us and must save us to get rid of us. He does not act with us as some rude surgeon might do who says, "I will attend to you directly, but I have plenty else to do, and you gratis patients are a trouble." Nor does he roughly set the bone. No; Jesus comes, and he molds the dislocated joint, and when he sets it—there is bliss even about the method of the setting. We look into his face, and we see that he puts his most tender sympathy into each movement. You know the different ways that workers have. Some kind of work one is soon sick of. The principle of division of labor is a very admirable one for the production of results on a large scale, but it is a miserable business for the worker to have to do the same thing over and over again, all day long, as if he or she were an automaton. The best work is done by the happy, joyful worker, and so it is with Christ. He does not save souls out of necessity—as though he would rather do something else if he might—but his very heart is in it, he rejoices to do it, and therefore he does it thoroughly, and he communicates his joy to us in the doing of it.

Notice that Jesus Christ loves other people to rejoice with him, so that, when he finds a sinner, he has so much love in his heart that his joy runs over. Let us catch the blessed infection. If you have just heard of somebody being saved, be glad about it because Jesus is glad.

—C. H. Spurgeon

*And when he finds it, he joyfully puts it on his shoulders
and goes home. Then he calls his friends and neighbors
together and says, "Rejoice with me;
I have found my lost sheep."*

—Luke 15:5–6

Heaven is a home.[27] Don't you like to think of it under that aspect? It is the home of Jesus, and if it is the home of Jesus, can any other home be equal to it?

Note that lost ones are known in heaven. I give you that thought more from the Greek than from the English here. "When he comes home, he calls together his friends and neighbors, saying to them, 'Rejoice with me, for I have found my sheep—the lost one.'" That is how it should run. It is as if the friends knew that one had been lost, and the loss had been deplored. Up there they know which are Christ's sheep and which are lost. Heaven is nearer earth than some of us dream. And there are more communications between earth and heaven than some folk dream, for here it is clear that when the shepherd came home he said to them, "I have found the sheep, the lost one." So they knew all about it.

Notice, next, that repentance is regarded as coming home. This sheep was not in heaven. No, but as soon as it had been brought into the fold it is described as repenting, and Jesus and the angels rejoice over it. If a person truly repents, and Christ saves that individual, it is clear that he or she never will be lost. A certain old proverb forbids us to count our chickens until they are hatched, and I do not think that angels would do so in the case of immortal souls. If they believed that repenting sinners might afterward be lost, they would not ring the marriage bells just yet, but they would wait a while to see how things went on. If converts can yet perish there is not one that the angels dare rejoice over, for if any child of God might fall away and perish, why not every one of us? If anyone falls from grace, I fear I shall.

I believe that where the Lord begins the good work of grace he will carry it on and perfect it: "My sheep listen to my voice. . . . I give them eternal life, and they shall never perish; no one can snatch them out of my hand." Now, if they have eternal life, it cannot come to an end, for eternal life is eternal, evidently; if they have eternal life, the Shepherd and his friends may justifiably sing. Sing away, angels!

—C. H. Spurgeon

One thing I do.

—Philippians 3:13

The first element [in the secret of Paul's incomparable life] is the element of wholehearted concentration.[28] "One thing I do"—not a dozen things, not even two things, but this one thing I do. No life can be very great or very happy or very useful without this element of concentration. Decision is energy, and energy is power, and power is confidence, and confidence to a remarkable degree contributes to success. Turn to any realm that you will, and the vital meaning of concentration stands out in all human life in the most striking fashion.

Take the business world. [Its] very watchwords magnify this element of concentration—*specialization* and *consolidation* and *incorporation.* The day for the jack-of-all-trades has passed. An individual must do one thing and do it with all his or her might. The day of the specialist has come.

When we look at the notable scientists, that truth of concentration seems to be written in their lives as with letters of living fire. Edison concentrated his energies in the realm of electricity and was constantly surprising the world by his marvelous discoveries.

When we come to the realm religious—this element of concentration there holds sway just as in these other realms. No one can serve two masters. Jesus stands above all humanity and says, "If you would be my disciple, I must come before father or mother or the dearest loved one of your life. I must come before your own business or your own property. I must come before your own life."

Many a Christian follows Christ afar off and limps and grovels in the Christian life, seeking to adjust in life to giving Christ some secondary place, and Christ will not have it. Concentration is a prime requisite in the victorious life anywhere.

—George W. Truett

*Forgetting what is behind and straining toward what is
ahead, I press on toward the goal to win the prize for which
God has called me heavenward in Christ Jesus.*
—Philippians 3:13–14

[Paul] cultivated a wise forgetfulness.[29]

And what are some of the things that we ought to forget? We ought to forget our blunders. How many blunders we all make! Learn how to make them bridges over which we will span the chasms and go to better days.

We are to learn how to forget our losses. In human life losses of all kinds come. No one is to whine and mope because losses come. We are to learn to get past them and to forget them.

We are to learn how to forget life's injuries. Refuse to let them rankle like poisons in the heart and thus vitiate every high thing that the spirit should hold most dear.

We are to learn how to forget our successes. There is danger in success. A person who can bear success can bear anything. Easier far can the human spirit bear adversity than it can bear prosperity, for the human spirit is lifted up. If we do not learn what success is for, the day comes for our undoing and our downfall and our defeat.

We are to learn how to forget our sorrows—and sooner or later these sorrows come to us, each and all. We are to take these sorrows to the great, refining, overruling Master and ask him so to dispose, so to rule and overrule in them and with them that we may come out of them all refined and disciplined, the better educated and more useful. You are to learn how to so have it woven into the warp and woof of your life that you will not be weaker and worse for the sorrow but will be richer and stronger and better because of such sorrow.

We are to learn how to forget our sins. If Paul had not learned how to forget his sins he would have been crippled utterly. Paul consented to the death of Stephen. Paul persecuted the church. Paul was a ringleader in sin. Paul seemed to run the whole gamut of sin. He called himself the chief of sinners, and perhaps he was. When we look at the debit side of our lives do our hearts faint within us? Mine faints within me. But then the Master of life says, "I will forgive their wickedness and will remember their sins no more."

—George W. Truett

Now these three remain: faith, hope and love.
But the greatest of these is love.

—1 Corinthians 13:13

What is the supreme good?[30] You have life before you. Once only can you live it. What is the noblest object of desire to covet?

We have been told that the greatest thing in the religious world is faith. Well, we were wrong. I have taken you, in [1 Corinthians 13] to Christianity at its source, and there we have seen, "the greatest of these is love." [Paul] says, "If I have a faith that can move mountains, but have not love, I am nothing."

Paul, in three short verses, gives us an amazing analysis of what this supreme thing is. By a multitude of small things and ordinary virtues, the supreme thing, the *summum bonum,* is made up.

The spectrum of love has nine ingredients:

- patience—"Love is patient."
- kindness—"Love is kind."
- generosity—"[Love] does not envy."
- humility—"[Love] does not boast, it is not proud."
- courtesy—"[Love] is not rude."
- unselfishness—"[Love] is not self-seeking."
- good temper—"[Love] is not easily angered."
- guilelessness—"[Love] keeps no record of wrongs."
- sincerity—"[Love] does not delight in evil but rejoices with the truth."

Observe that all are in relation to people, in relation to life, in relation to the known today and near tomorrow and not to the unknown eternity. Religion is not a strange or added thing but the inspiration of the secular life, the breathing of an eternal spirit through this temporal world.

Where love is, God is. Whoever lives in love lives in God. God is love. There-fore love—without distinction, without calculation, without procrastination. Lavish it on the poor, where it is very easy; especially on the rich, who often need it most; most of all on our equals, for whom perhaps we each do least of all. There is a difference between trying to please and giving pleasure. Give pleasure. Lose no chance of giving pleasure. For that is the ceaseless and anonymous triumph of a truly loving spirit.

—Henry Drummond

Now these three remain: faith, hope and love.
But the greatest of these is love.

—1 Corinthians 13:13

Isn't life full of opportunities for learning love?[31] Every man and woman every day has a thousand of them. The world is not a playground; it is a schoolroom. If people do not exercise their arms they develop no biceps muscles; if they do not exercise their souls, they acquire no muscle in the soul, no strength of character, no vigor of moral fiber nor beauty of spiritual growth. Love is not a thing of enthusiastic emotion. It is a rich, strong, vigorous expression of the whole, round Christian character—the Christlike nature in its fullest development. And the constituents of this great character are only to be built up by ceaseless practice.

Paul's reason for singling out love as the supreme possession is this: it lasts. "Love," urges Paul, "never fails."

Some think the time may come when two of these three things will also pass away—faith into sight, hope into fruition. Paul does not say so. But what is certain is that love must last. God, the eternal God, is love. Covet therefore that everlasting gift, that one thing which it is certain is going to stand, that one coinage that will be current in the universe when all the other coinages of the nations of the world will be useless and unhonored. You will give yourselves to many things—give yourselves to love. Let at least the first great object of our lives be to achieve the character—and it is the character of Christ—that is built around love.

How many of you will join me in reading this chapter once a week for the next three months? You might begin by reading it every day. Get these ingredients into your life. Then everything that you do is eternal. It is worth doing. It is worth giving time to.

It is the Son of Man before whom the nations of the world shall be gathered. It is in the presence of humanity that we shall be charged. And the spectacle itself, the mere sight of it, will silently judge each one. Be not deceived. The words that all of us shall one day hear sound not of theology but of life, not of churches and saints but of the hungry and the poor, not of creeds and doctrines but of shelter and clothing, not of Bibles and prayer books but of cups of cold water in the name of Christ. Everyone who loves is born of God.

—Henry Drummond

At home with the Lord.

—2 Corinthians 5:8

Deep in the human heart there is a homing instinct, profound, persistent, ineradicable, that we often ignore and might even deny.[32]

There is something in us that earth can never satisfy. It is common for people to say and to believe that if they only had this or that thing they would always be happy, and some of them die believing it. But the evidence of those who obtain the treasure does not bear them out. It satisfied for a little while—and then there was the old, persistent hunger again, clamorous as ever.

Earth does not satisfy us. I cannot help but feel that that is an impressive fact. I believe that there is in us a homesickness for heaven, that that ache which earth cannot satisfy can be satisfied by God, that all feel it, but only some understand it.

God has put in the heart of everyone of us a longing for himself. The mass of humanity does not understand it. People just know that there are times when they want to be quiet, times when they want to be alone, times when the calendar or the stars or death speaks to them. They hunger and they thirst—but for what?

It is part of the service of religion to make the hunger of our souls clear to us.

You may have lost your way, but don't lose your address. Don't deny that hunger in your soul. Don't say, "It isn't there; earth satisfies me; when this life is over I will have had all that I want of life."

The homesickness for God in your heart is a precious, divine gift. It won't make you less keen to serve others here below, but it will be a constant reminder to you that the most permanent dwelling earth provides is a tent, and at any time the word may come to draw the pegs. We are, indeed, strangers and pilgrims here below.

Here we sojourn; there we belong. You will work with zest and skill and thoroughness in all that concerns the outworking of God's purpose on this earth, and you will work the better because, by faith, you have the perfect always in view.

—William E. Sangster

In hell, where he was in torment, he looked up.
—Luke 16:23

At death we are going to lose something, each of us.[33] We are going to lose the physical. We are going to lose our possessions. Whatever may be our material wealth in this world, we may depend on it that the hands of the dead are not clutching hands. Our shrouds will have no pockets. Death will rob us of all that is material.

But there is one something that death cannot take away from us. It cannot rob us of ourselves. Yesterday I was myself. I will be myself still tomorrow. I will continue to be myself as long as heaven is heaven, as long as God is God.

In spite of this fact, however, there is a tremendously great tendency to believe that death will work a moral change, that you can lie down one moment self-centered, sin-conquered, godless—and by the mere act of dying, wake up the next moment holy, sinless, and Christlike. It is absolutely false. If Christ does not save you in the here and now, do not expect death to accomplish what he was unable to accomplish. If the blood of Jesus Christ cannot cleanse you from all sin, do not be so mad as to expect that cleansing at the hands of the undertaker, the shroud, and the coffin. Believe me that as death finds you, so you will be the instant after when you open your eyes in the world unseen.

The truth of the matter is that God has no way of getting anyone into heaven who has hell in his or her own heart. You cannot mix the living and the dead even in this life.

So the conclusion of the whole matter is this: Forever you are going to live. Forever you are going to be yourself. You are going to have to keep house with yourself for all eternity. Forever you are going to remember. Forever you are going to enjoy or suffer the destiny that you make for yourself while in this life. If it sounds foolish, remember it is the foolishness of him who spoke the way no one ever spoke. If it seems heartless, remember that it is the heartlessness of infinite love. Remember, too, that though some people are lost, no one needs to be lost. Everyone can be saved who will. This minute you can be saved if you will only be wise enough and brave enough to make a right choice. "Whoever comes to me I will never drive away." Will you come? Will you come now?

—Clovis Gillham Chappell

*If you have raced with men on foot and they have worn
you out, how can you compete with horses?*
—Jeremiah 12:5

Suppose that to you, as to Christ, it became evident that life was not to give what you expected, that your dreams were not to be granted, that yours was to be a steep and lonely road, that some tremendous sacrifice was to be asked of you, could you adjust to face it with a shadow of the Master's courage and the Master's calm?[34] There is no supposing in the matter. To you too, in your turn, someday, these things must come.

And when it does, nobody has the right to snivel or whimper as if something unique and inexplicable had befallen him or her. "Never morning wore to evening but some heart did break"—hearts just as sensitive as yours and mine. But when yours breaks, what then? It is a bit late in the day to be talking about insurance when your house is ablaze, somewhat tardy to be searching for something to bring you through when the test is on.

So many people's religion is a fair-weather affair. A little rain and it runs and crumbles; a touch of strain and it snaps. So long as God's will runs parallel to ours, we follow blithely. But the moment that they clash, that life grows difficult, that we do not understand—how apt faith is to fail us just when we have most need of it!

Well, what of you and me? If the small ills of life have frayed our faith and temper, what will we do in the roar and swirl of Jordan?

The essence of faith [is] a certain intrepidity of loyalty that can believe undauntedly [when] in the dark and that still trusts God, unshaken even when the evidence looks fairly damning. Do you think Christ always understood or found it easy? There was a day when he took God's will for him into his hand, turned it round, and looked at it: "Is this what you ask of me?" he said. Yes, and another day when, puzzled and uncertain, he cried out, "But is this really what you mean that I should give you, this here, this now?" Yes, and another still, when the waters roared through his soul, yet he would not turn back, fought his way to the farther bank and died, still believing in the God who seemed to have deserted him. That is why he is given a name that is above every name.

—Arthur John Gossip

If you have raced with men on foot and they have worn you out, how can you compete with horses?
—Jeremiah 12:5

I do not understand life, but still less can I comprehend how people in trouble and loss can run away from the Christian faith.[35] In God's name, run to what? Have we not lost enough without losing that too? If Christ is right—if there are, hidden from our eyes, wisdom and planning and kindness and love in these dark dispensations—then we can see them through. But if Christ was wrong, and all that is not so; if God set his foot on my home heedlessly, as I might tread on some insect in my path, haven't I the right to be angry? If Christ was right, and immortality and the dear hopes of which he speaks do really lie ahead, we can manage to make our way to them. But if it is not so, if there is nothing more, how dark the darkness grows! You people in the sunshine may believe the faith, but we in the shadow must believe it. We have nothing else!

[Out of loss and bereavement] already some things have become very clear to me. This to begin, that the faith works, fulfills itself, is real, and that its most audacious promises are true. The glorious assertions of the Scriptures are not mere suppositions and guesses. There is no *perhaps* about them. These splendid truths are flowers that human hands like ours plucked in the gardens of their actual experience. Why is the prophet so sure that God will comfort all hurt things? How did the psalmist know that those who are broken in their hearts and grieved in their minds, God heals? Because it had happened to them, because in their dark days they had felt his helpfulness and tenderness. And it is true. When we are cast into some fiery furnace we are never alone. "I will not leave you as orphans," said Christ. There is a presence with us, a comforter, a fortifier, who upholds and brings us through from hour to hour and day to day.

There is a marvelous picture in the National Gallery. Christ hangs on the cross, and at first, that is all one sees. But in the background, gradually there stands out another form, God's form; other hands support Christ, God's hands. The presence, the sufficiency, the sympathy of God grow very real, very sure, very wonderful!

—Arthur John Gossip

If you have raced with men on foot and they have worn
you out, how can you compete with horses?
—Jeremiah 12:5

[Out of loss and bereavement, some things have become clear.][36]

One becomes certain about immortality. You think that you believe in that. But wait till you have lowered your dearest into an open grave, and you will know what believing it means.

We Christian people are unchristian in our thoughts of death. We keep thinking of what it means to us, and that is all wrong!

In the New Testament, you hear very little of the families with that aching gap but a great deal about the saints in glory. And that is where our thoughts should dwell. Dare you compare the clumsy nothings our poor blundering love can give them here with what they must have yonder, where Christ himself has met them and has heaped on them, who can fathom, what happiness and glory?

In any case, are we to let our dearest be wrenched away by force? Or, seeing that it has to be, will we give them willingly and proudly, telling God that we prefer our loneliness rather than that they should miss one tittle of their rights? When the blow fell, that was the one thought that beat like a hammer in my brain. I felt I had lost her forever, that to all eternity she must shine far ahead of me, and my heart kept crying out, "I choose it, I choose it, do not for my sake deny her anything." I know, now, that I have not lost her. For love is not a thing one leaves behind. When we are young, heaven is vague. But as our friends gather there, it gains vividness and homeliness. And when our dearest have passed yonder, how real it grows, how near: Where your treasure is, there your heart will be also. It is not far. They are quite near. The communion of the saints is a tremendous and most blessed fact.

You need not be afraid of life. Our hearts are very frail, and there are places where the road is steep and lonely. But we have a wonderful God. And as Paul puts it in Romans 8:38–39, what can separate us from his love? Not death, he says immediately, pushing that aside at once as the most obvious impossibility.

No, not death, for standing in the roaring Jordan, cold to the heart with its dreadful chill and conscious of its terror, I, too, like Hopeful, can call back to you who one day will have to cross it, "Be of good cheer for I feel the bottom, and it is sound."

—Arthur John Gossip

*If you have raced with men on foot and they have worn
you out, how can you compete with horses?*

—Jeremiah 12:5

Yes, unbelievably they come.[37] You and I go our sunny ways and live our happy lives, and the rumors of terrors blow to us from a world so distant that it seems to have nothing to do with us; then, it happens.

You remember our Lord's story of two men who lived in the same village, went to the same synagogue, and one day, some kind of gale blew into their lives. In the one case, everything collapsed. For that unhappy soul had built on sand, and in his day of need, everything was undermined and vanished. But the other, though he, too, faced the emptiness, the loneliness, the pain, came through braver and stronger and mellower and nearer God. For he had built on the rock.

That has always been my chief difficulty about preaching. Thomas Carlyle said that the chirpy optimism of Emerson maddened him. "He seemed to me like a man, standing himself well back out of the least touch of the spray, who throws chatty observations on the beauty of the weather to a poor soul battling for his life in huge billows that are buffeting the breath and the life out of him, wrestling with mighty currents that keep sweeping him away." It did not help.

I, too, have had a happy life, and always when I have spoken of the gospel and the love of God and Christ's brave reading of this puzzling life, it has seemed that an easy answer lay ready to anybody who found these hard to credit. "Yes, yes," they might well say irritably, "if I stood in the sunshine where you are, no doubt I, too, could talk like that! But if your path ran over the cold moors, where the winds cut to the very bone, if you were sat down where I am, I wonder if you would be so absolutely sure?" We will listen to Jesus Christ—for he spoke from the darkness round the cross. We may not understand him or agree with him or obey him, but nobody can challenge his right to speak. But you! Wait until you stand in the rushing of the Jordan. And what will you say then?

I will tell you now. I know that we are warned in Job that the most drastic test of faith is not even these tremendous sorrows but a long purgatory of physical and mental agony. Still, I do not think that anyone will challenge my right to speak today. I always thought greatly of the Christian faith, but I think more of it now, far more.

—Arthur John Gossip

*"Lord, don't trouble yourself, for I do not deserve to have
you come under my roof. That is why I did not even
consider myself worthy to come to you. But say the word,
and my servant will be healed. . . ." When Jesus heard
this, . . . he said, "I tell you, I have not found such great
faith even in Israel."*

—Luke 7:6–7, 9

Observe the centurion's humble expressions.[38] Was it because he had had an insight into his own heart and was most unworthy in his own view?

When Christians make abject confessions, it is not that they are worse than others but that they see themselves in a clearer light. This centurion's unworthiness was not because he had been more vicious than others but because he saw what others did not see and felt what others had not felt.

Deep as was this man's contrition, overwhelming as was his sense of utter worthlessness, he did not doubt either the power or the willingness of Christ. He takes it for granted that such a one as Jesus must be willing to do all the good that is asked of him.

Nor is he at all dubious about our Lord's power. The palsy that afflicted the servant was a grievous one, but it did not stagger the centurion. He felt not only that Jesus could heal it completely and at once, but that he could heal it without moving a step.

My dear friends, especially you who are under concern of soul, you feel unworthy—that is not a mistaken feeling, you are so. You are much distressed by reason of this unworthiness, but if you knew more of it you might be more distressed still.

Beloved, it has come to this: you are so unworthy that you are shut out of every hope but Christ. If there is anything to be done for salvation, you cannot do it. If there is any fitness wanted, you have it not. Christ comes to you and tells you that there is not fitness wanted for coming to him but that if you will trust him he will save you. I think I hear you say, "My Lord, on your atonement I cast my guilty soul, persuaded that you are able to save even such a one as I am. I am so thoroughly persuaded of the goodness of your heart that I know you will not cast away this poor trembler who takes you to be my only ground of trust."

—C. H. Spurgeon

I did not even consider myself worthy to come to you.
—Luke 7:7

You are much more sinful than you think you are, much more unworthy than you know yourself to be.[39] Instead of attempting a soothing of your dark thoughts, I pray you believe that yours is a hopeless case apart from Christ. This disease is not skin deep. It lies in the source and fountain of your life and poisons your heart. The flames of hell must wrap themselves about you certainly unless Christ interposes to save you. You have not nor will you ever have merit of any sort. And more, you have no power to escape from your lost condition unaided by the Savior's hand. No words can exaggerate your deplorable condition, and no feelings can ever represent your real state in colors too alarming. You are not worthy that Christ should come to you. You are not worthy to draw near to Christ.

But—and here is a glorious contrast—never let this for a single moment interfere with your full belief that he who is God but who took our nature, who suffered in our stead on the cross, who now rules in heaven is able and willing to do for you immeasurably more than all you ask or imagine. Your inability does not prevent the working of his power. Your unworthiness cannot put fetters to his bounty or limits to his grace. You may be an ill-deserving sinner, but that is no reason why he should not pardon you. Jesus Christ is able and willing to save those who come to God through him. Your emptiness does not affect his fullness. Your weakness does not alter his power. Your inability does not diminish his omnipotence. Your undeserving does not restrain his love.

Your troubled hearts, your sense of your unworthiness should drive you to Christ. You are unworthy, but "Christ died for the ungodly" (Rom. 5:6). He gave himself for our—what? Excellences and virtues? No, he "gave himself for our sins" (Gal. 1:4), according to the Scriptures. We read that he "died for sins . . . the righteous for the"—righteous? No, "the righteous for the unrighteous" (1 Peter 3:18), to bring us to God. Gospel pharmacy is for the sick; gospel bread is for the hungry; gospel fountains are open to the unclean; gospel water is given to the thirsty. Let your huge and painful wants impel you to fly to Jesus. Let the vast cravings of your insatiable spirit compel you to go to him. Your unworthiness should act as a wing to bear you to Christ, the sinner's Savior.

—C. H. Spurgeon

[Moses] persevered because he saw him who is invisible.
—Hebrews 11:27

To endure is to accept the uncontrollable.[40] It is to pass through difficult hours free from any embittering of spirit, for to grow bitter is always to be beaten. We say what can't be cured must be endured, but that is hardly the endurance of the Scriptures. Paul and Silas in the prison at Philippi did not accept things in a joyless way. They were happy; they sang loudly. That is the endurance of the Scripture: acceptance with a note of triumph. Of that gracious and beautiful endurance the New Testament indicates three sources.

The first is *faith*. The apostle tells us to "take up the shield of faith" (Eph. 6:16). If we are to be guarded amid the blows and buffetings of life, there must be faith in the heart. If our darker hours have no meaning, if they are devoid of plan or purpose, if life is nothing but accident or chance, the highest a person can achieve is resignation. But if God is love, and if everything that comes to us arrives in the perfect ordering of the Father, then another frame of mind becomes possible. The person who believes that God is in the hard part is empowered to endure the hard part. Faith finds goodness in things evil.

Then, too, there is *love,* for love "always perseveres" (1 Cor. 13:7). Wherever there is love in the heart, there the power to endure. God is patient, says Saint Augustine, because he is eternal. But there is a deeper source of his patience than eternity. He is patient because he loves. And our Lord empowers his children to endure by the new love he kindles in their hearts. He shows them that God is eminently lovable. He reveals the lovable element in people. He sends into their hearts his Spirit, and the fruit of the Spirit is love.

Lastly there is *vision*. Moses "persevered because he saw him who is invisible." To see the invisible when skies are dark is to have power to win. Never was there endurance like the Master's. It was radiant with peace and joy. It did not falter even in Gethsemane. It was equal to the agony of Calvary. And inspiring, animating, and sustaining it was the vision of his Father's face. We too can practice that same presence. We can do it when life is very difficult. We can do it when the way is dark. We can do it when we cannot understand. And, doing it, we come to be so sure that underneath are the everlasting arms that endurance passes into joy.

—George H. Morrison

*My flesh and my heart may fail, but God is the strength of
my heart and my portion forever.*

—Psalm 73:26

I find in [Mary] the loneliness of love.[41] The mother of Jesus was the bride of loneliness. Had her husband, Joseph, been spared to her through the years, it might have been very different with Mary. She might have turned to him when things were difficult. But Joseph died when Jesus was a boy, and Mary was left utterly alone, to love and ponder and be brokenhearted. Other mothers could compare experiences, but that was what Mary of Nazareth could not do. Even to her family she dare not turn for sympathy, for they thought [Jesus] was beside himself. Because Christ was unutterably wonderful, Mary was unutterably lonely, and she was lonely because she loved him so.

Every mother knows something of that loneliness, as childhood reaches to manhood or to womanhood. There comes a day when the most perfect mother has to make room for others in her son's or daughter's heart. And you have to multiply all that ten thousand times into the absorbing passion of the Son of God if you would understand the loneliness of Mary. Not to be able to blast and blight his slanderers when they said he had a devil and was mad—to be utterly powerless to keep him silent when every word was ringing out his death-knell—and then to stand at the cross and see him nailed there and hear the exceeding bitter cry he cried—could any loneliness be worse than that? Love is the secret of the sweetest song, and love is the fountain of the deepest loneliness. Sooner or later in this shadowed world a loving mother is a lonely mother. And it is when you remember Mary's love for a Son who was as mysterious as God that you come to think of her, in all her glory, as perhaps the loneliest woman in the world.

—George H. Morrison

Then Thomas . . . said to the rest of the disciples, "Let us
also go, that we may die with him."

—John 11:16

I find in Thomas the loneliness of doubt.[42] Thomas is always a solitary figure, as doubters very generally are. You never think of Peter as being much alone—he was too ardent and impetuous for that. And you never think of John as wooing solitude with his so affectionate and sympathetic heart. But Thomas is always standing a little apart from cheerful interaction; he is solitary because he is a doubter. And on that evening of resurrection Sunday the disciples were gathered—and Thomas was not there. He was a lonely man that resurrection day, perhaps wandering amid the olives of Gethsemane, separated from all glad companionship, and separated because he was a doubter. Think of the gladness that filled these eager hearts when they whispered to one another, "Christ is risen." Then think of Thomas, wandering alone, hurrying from all sound of human voices. For him there was no fellowship that evening in the radiant light of resurrection glory; for him there was only the loneliness of doubt.

Amid the common ties of common life, [doubt] makes a solitude and calls it peace. And that is why when any person doubts God and thinks the heaven above the stars is tenantless, sooner or later he or she has a lonely heart. There are those who doubt because they are too lonely; there are more who are lonely just because they doubt. It takes the bond of faith to give us fellowship with child and husband, with comrade, and with Christ. And when faith crumbles and doubt lifts up its head, a man or woman may still be heroic in duty, but for that person, as for Thomas on resurrection evening, there is the anguish of the lonely heart. That is the very misery of doubt. It is the mother of the hungriest loneliness.

—George H. Morrison

The invalid replied, "I have no one to help me into the pool
when the water is stirred."
—John 5:7

I find in the man by the pool of Bethesda what I call city loneliness.[43] For thirty-eight years he had been crippled—and now he had no friend in the whole city. There is a loneliness of the moor and of the glen, where there is never a whisper except of the sighing wind. But there is a loneliness that is far worse than that: it is the loneliness of a great and crowded city. There may be someone who in our thronging streets is far more lonely than any Highland cottager; the man by the pool of Bethesda was like that. Round him was all the traffic of Jerusalem, and Jerusalem was a very busy city. And at the heart of all that stir and activity, without one single person to give a hand to him, there lay that lonely sufferer by the water. Where life is richest and relationships most varied and where pleasures flaunt themselves at every corner, it is possible to be more exquisitely lonely than in the solitary shelter of the glen.

I had a friend who went to America six years ago, and I will never forget what he once wrote me. He had spent a year or two in the far west of Canada and then had gone south and settled in the States. And he wrote me that the vast and silent prairie stretching away, endless, from his threshold, never so overwhelmed him with a sense of loneliness as did the tumultuous crowding of New York City. In the city where everyone was hurrying, and no one seemed to care a jot for him, he realized he was a lonely man. It may be that passing you tonight out in the lighted streets, and you so happy, there is someone who is heart weary for a friend.

—George H. Morrison

As soon as Judas had taken the bread, he went out.
And it was night.

—John 13:30

I find in [Judas] the loneliness of sin.[44] Having received the sop at the Last Supper, he went immediately out, and it was night. Why did he hurry from that little company? Nobody drove him from the supper table. Christ did not rise with clenched hands of loathing and hound him onto the bosom of the dark. In that brief hour everything is intense, and you see in a flash into the heart of things—into the infinite love of the Redeemer, into the infinite loneliness of sin.

We sometimes talk in our foolish way of social sins. We might as reasonably talk of gentle murder. There is no such thing in the world as social sin. Sin is the mightiest of antisocial forces. Sin is disruptive in its very nature. It shatters homes and disintegrates companionship. It raises barriers between classes and cleaves society down to its very deeps. Your little child goes singing through the house and jabbers to you of a hundred trifles. And then some day the child is strangely silent and shuns you and forgets the little songs. And then you know at once that there is something troubling that little conscience and that the one path to communion is confession. Sin separates the parent from the child. Sin separates the engaged from his or her beloved. We think that sin is going to make us happy, and in the end it only makes us lonely. From every company, from all society, from love and fellowship, from home and heaven, sin drives the sinner out into the night. Why did our Lord, in that so perfect parable, speak of the *one* sheep as going astray? Why not five of them—why not a score of them—where there were a hundred in the flock? It is one of those touches that reveal the Master that from one hundred he separated one, as teaching us the loneliness of sin. One coin, from all the cottage treasury; one sheep, from all the congregated flock; one son, off to a far land from all the dear companionship of home. So Judas, having received the sop, and the Devil having entered into him, went immediately out, and it was night.

This is a strange world, and that is invariably the way of it. Every sin you conquer in the battle helps you to a richer comradeship. Every sin you deliberately cling to is a mighty power in you making for loneliness, and to be lonely forever—that is hell.

—George H. Morrison

About the ninth hour Jesus cried out in a loud voice, "Eloi, Eloi, lama sabachthani?"—which means, "My God, my God, why have you forsaken me?" When some of those standing there heard this, they said, "He's calling Elijah."
—Matthew 27:46–47

I find in [Jesus Christ] the loneliness of grandeur.[45] Jesus was supremely lonely, because he was supremely great. There is a type of character with which we are all familiar that makes few demands on the love of others. It is severe. It aims at self-sufficiency. It will not lean hard on anyone. And while we may admire that type of character—and do so justly for it is often noble—we must remember it is not the character of Christ. It was the passion of Christ's heart that people should trust him. It was the yearning of his soul that people should love him. In those rare moments when he was understood, he was thrilled to the finest fiber of his being.

And it is when we think how people misunderstood him and were blind to all that he was and all he lived for that we realize the loneliness of Christ. To crave for love and, craving, not to find it, to have one's every action misinterpreted, to feel that one's dearest do not sympathize, to long for trust and to be met with scorn—for certain natures quivering with life there is no loneliness that can compare with that, and such was the loneliness of the Redeemer. I do not imagine that had you seen the Christ you would have said, "There goes a lonely man." The Pharisees never thought to call him lonely. They called him the friend of publicans and sinners. But the ecstasy of joy that filled his soul when one understood him and cried, "You are the Christ," betrays how unutterably lonely he had been. Was ever anyone misunderstood like this man? *"Eloi, Eloi, lama sabachthani?"*—and they thought he was calling for Elijah. It is only when you remember that, and all akin to it in the Evangel, that you come to feel how awful and unceasing must have been the loneliness of Christ.

—George H. Morrison

> *They have proved a comfort to me.*
> —Colossians 4:11

The word *comfort* in our text is interesting.[46] This is the only place where it occurs in the New Testament. The term is our English word *paregoric.* Now, *paregoric,* in Greek just as in English, is medicine.

Paregoric is a medicine that mitigates or alleviates pain. And what could be more delightful than the thought that there are men and women who are like that—they mitigate or alleviate our pain. Pain is one of the conditions of our being, something nobody escapes. All life is rich in pain—the pain of striving, the pain of being baffled, the pain of loneliness and incompleteness, the pain of being misunderstood.

People add to that pain, sometimes without meaning it. How often is the pain of life increased by those who mean well. But who has not numbered in his or her list of friends somebody whose Christlike ministry has been to alleviate pain? Such people were the apostle's paregoric. Such are the paregoric of us all—often humble people, not in the least distinguished and not at all conspicuous for intellect—yet somehow in the wear and tear of life, amid its crosses and its sorrows, mitigating and alleviating pain.

You can be a comfort to another though you never know anything about it. Just as the finest influence we exercise is often that of which we are unconscious, so the greatest comfort that we bring is often the comfort we know nothing of—not our preaching nor our words of cheer, but the way in which we bear ourselves in life when the burden is heavy and the sky is black. Let men or women behave gallantly, and behave so because they trust in God, when life is difficult, when things go wrong, when health is failing, when the grave is opened, and though they may never hear a whisper of it, there are others who are thanking God for them. Every sorrow borne in simple faith is helping others bear their sorrows. Every burden victoriously carried is helping men and women to be braver. Every cross, anxiety, foreboding, shining with the serenity of trust, comes like light to those who sit in darkness. Dear friend, if you walk in light and love, you are a comfort when you never know it. And other people, writing their letters, will put your name in, to your intense surprise, and say, "You were a comfort to me."

—George H. Morrison

*When he came to his senses, he said, "How many of my
father's hired men have food to spare, and here I am
starving to death!"*

—Luke 15:17

The prodigal was an exile in a far country.[47] The memory of his home filled his heart. It was not terror that struck the prodigal deep. It was home for which his poor soul was crying. He saw the farm among the hills, and the weary oxen coming home at eventide and the happy circle gathered round the fire and his father crying to heaven for the wanderer. [The prodigal's] sorrow was remembering happier things. He came to himself, and he was homesick.

Wickedness is not the homeland of the soul, and the unrest and the dissatisfaction of the wicked is the craving of the heart for home. We were not fashioned to be at home in sin. We bear the image of God, and God is goodness. The native air of this mysterious heart is the love and purity and joy of heaven. So when someone deliberately sins and all the time hungers for better things, it is not the hunger for an impossible ideal; it is the hunger of the soul for home. You can satisfy that hunger instantly. Out of the furthest country you may come home. God waits. Christ says, "Return this very hour."

We were made in goodness, and we were made for goodness, and we will always be dissatisfied, always homesick, if we are trying to live in any other land. [Thus,] people cover evil with a veil of goodness, longing to give a homelike touch to their surroundings. When people take the names of goodness and label their vices and their sins with them, when we use a kindly term for some habit or frailty that is most unkindly, it is the soul telling where it was born, confessing unconsciously that it is homesick and trying to give a homelike touch to the far country.

We can understand the loneliness of sin when we remember this homesickness of the soul. The individual who is homesick is always lonely. Sin is a power that makes for loneliness. Slowly but surely, if you live in sin, you drift into spiritual isolation. And the sins we call social sins, the sins that begin in fellowship and company, are the very sins that leave you at last utterly alone. That loneliness is homesickness of the soul. It is the heart craving for home again. If you are drifting away on a great sea of self-indulgence, God grant that, drawn by the love of Christ, you may come home.

—George H. Morrison

As the deer pants for streams of water,
so my soul pants for you, O God.

—Psalm 42:1

We often speak of heaven as our home, and in many senses that is true.[48] If in heaven we will meet again those whom we loved and lost, and if boys and girls will be playing in the streets of Zion, I have no doubt that heaven will be a home-like place. But in deeper senses heaven is not our home, or if it is, it is just because God is there. In the deepest sense our home is not heaven, but God.

O God, our help in ages past,
    Our hope for years to come,
Our shelter from the stormy blast,
    And our eternal home.

—Isaac Watts

God is the true home of the human soul.

Craving for God is one of the strangest facts in human history. You would have thought that in a world like this, full of color, music, and delight, humanity would be content without God. But the book of Psalms is filled with that passionate craving. And if the book of Psalms has lived through chance and change, cherished when ten thousand volumes are forgotten, it is largely because it gives a voice to this unappeased hunger. We do not crave for God because he is glorious or because he is sovereign. We are homesick—that is the meaning of it. We crave for God because he is our home.

Now this homesickness of the soul for God is one of our surest proofs of God. It is an argument more powerful than any that philosophy affords to convince me that there is a God. No one denies that souls still pant for God. And hearts today and here still thirst for him, as truly as the exiled psalmist did. And there cannot be homesickness without a home. All other arguments may fail me. When my mind is wearied and my memory tired, I forget them. But this one, knit with my heart, part and parcel of my truest humanity, survives all moods, is strong when I am weak, and brings me to the door of God my home.

I will arise and go to my Father. Thank God we need no money for that journey. Is there no one here who has been far away who is going to come home—to God—this very hour?

—George H. Morrison

> *Just as he was speaking, the rooster crowed. The Lord*
> *turned and looked straight at Peter. Then Peter remem-*
> *bered the word the Lord had spoken to him: "Before the*
> *rooster crows today, you will disown me three times." And*
> *he went outside and wept bitterly*
>
> —Luke 22:60–62

Our Lord's look at Peter was a revival of all Peter's looking to Jesus.[49] The Lord's look at Peter took effect because Peter was looking at the Lord. Do you catch it? If the Lord had turned and looked at Peter and Peter's back had been turned, that look would not have reached Peter nor affected him. The eyes met to produce the desired result. Notwithstanding all Peter's wanderings, he was anxious about his Lord and therefore looked to see what was done with him. Even while he warmed his hands at the fire, he kept looking into the inner hall. His eyes were constantly looking in the direction of the Lord Jesus. While he wandered about among the maids and serving men, talking to them—fool that he was— yet still he would steal a glance to see how it fared with the man he loved. He had not given up the habit of looking to his Lord. If he had not still, in a measure, looked to his Master, how would the look of Jesus have been observed by him? [Christ's] eye must look through your eye to get to your heart. The remainders of faith are the sparks among the ashes of piety, and the Lord blows on these to raise a fire. If you have given up the outward forms of religion, it is a grievous fault. But if you still inwardly look to the Crucified, there is something in you to work on, there is an eye that can receive the look of Jesus. Oh, that you who have this lingering faith in the Lord may now receive a look from him that will work in you a bitter, salutary, saving repentance, without which you can never be restored!

The whole process may not have occupied more than a second of time—"The Lord turned and looked straight at Peter"—less time to do than it takes to tell. Yet in that instant an endless work was done.

That look of Christ also opened the sluices of Peter's heart. He went out and wept bitterly. There was a gall in the tears he wept, for they were the washings of his bitter sorrow. Dear friends, if we have sinned with Peter, God grant us the grace to weep with Peter. Sin, even though it be forgiven, is a bitter thing.

—C. H. Spurgeon

> *Joseph of Arimathea, a prominent member of the Council,*
> *who was himself waiting for the kingdom of God, went*
> *boldly to Pilate and asked for Jesus' body. . . . So Joseph*
> *bought some linen cloth, took down the body, wrapped it in*
> *the linen, and placed it in a tomb cut out of rock.*
> —Mark 15:43, 46

The time had come when he must boldly act as Christ's disciple.[50]

I do not suppose that he fully understood the design of our Lord's death. He had some knowledge of it but not such a knowledge as we have now that the Spirit of God has appeared in all his fullness and taught us the meaning of the Cross.

Oh, listen, you that are not on his side openly, you who have never worn his livery nor manifestly entered his service. He died for you! Those wounds were all for you. That bloody sweat, of which you still may see the marks on the countenance of the Crucified, was all for you; for you the thirst and fever, for you the bowing of the head and breathing his last. Can you be ashamed to own him? Will you not endure rebuke and scorn for his dear sake who bore all this for you? Now speak from your soul and say, "He loved me and gave himself for me." If you cannot say that, you cannot be happy. But if you can, then what follows? Must you not love him and give yourself for him?

The Cross is a wondrous magnet, drawing to Jesus everyone of the true metal. It is as a banner lifted on high to which all who are loyal must rally. This fiery Cross, carried through all lands, will rouse the valiant and speed them to the field. Can you see your Lord suffering to the death for you—and then turn your back? If the Cross does not bring a person out, what will? If the spectacle of dying love does not quicken us into courageous affection for him, what can?

—C. H. Spurgeon

And when you have turned back, strengthen your brothers.
—Luke 22:32

Peter has gone astray, and he has been brought back.[51] He must have staggered the faith of the weaker disciples—Peter, who had been such a leader among them, was among the first to deny his Lord. Therefore, Peter, you must build what you have thrown down and bind up what you have torn! Go and tell these people how foolish and weak you were. Warn them not to imitate your example. Be more bold than anybody else, that you may in some measure undo the mischief that you have done.

Any of you who have been cold toward the Lord, you have wasted months, even years, in backsliding. Try to recover lost ground. If people have been staggered by your backsliding, look after them, try to bring them back and strengthen them. Ask their pardon and beg them to recover the strength of which you helped to rob them. This is the least that you can do. If almighty love has drawn you back, lay yourself out to do good to those who may have been harmed by your turning aside. Am I asking more of you than simple justice demands?

How can you better express your gratitude to God than by strengthening your weak brothers and sisters when you have been strengthened yourself? If God has restored our souls and made us strong again, then we ought to renew our zeal for the salvation of others. We ought to have a special eye to backsliders like us.

This becomes our duty because it is a part of the divine design. Let us never imagine that God's grace is given to us simply with an eye to ourselves. Grace neither begins nor ends with us. When God saved you, he did not save you for your own sake but for his own name's sake, that he might through you show his mercy to others. We are windows through which the light of heavenly knowledge is to shine on multitudes of eyes. The light is not for the windows themselves but for those to whom it comes through the windows.

If we have been restored let us look after our weak brothers and sisters, showing zeal for the honor and glory of our Lord. When we went astray we dishonored Christ. If others go astray they will do the same. Let us be watchful that we may prevent their being as foolish as we have been. Let us learn tenderness from our own experience and feel a deep concern for other believers.

—C. H. Spurgeon

*Simon, Simon, Satan has asked to sift you as wheat. But I
have prayed for you, Simon, that your faith may not fail.
And when you have turned back, strengthen your brothers.*
—Luke 22:31–32

Observe what came before the sifting and went with the sifting.[52] "But I have prayed for you." Not, your brothers have prayed for you; not, you have prayed for yourself. But I have prayed for you. Jesus, that master in the art of prayer, that mighty advocate above, assures us that he has already prayed for us. Before the temptation, "I have prayed for you." I foresaw all the danger in which you would be placed, and concerning that danger I have exercised my function as high priest and intercessor. What a comfort to any who are passing through deep waters! You only go where Jesus has gone before you with his intercession. Jesus has made provision for all your future in a prayer already presented: "I have prayed for you." You may be much comforted by the prayers of a minister or of some Christian who has power with God, but what are all such intercessions compared with the praying of your Lord? It were well to have Noah, Samuel, and Moses praying for us, but better far to have Jesus say, "I have prayed for you." Satan may have his sieve, but as long as Jesus wears his breastplate we will not be destroyed.

The object of the prayer of our Lord was "that your faith may not fail." He knows where the vital point lies, and there he holds the shield. As long as the Christian's faith is safe the Christian's self is safe. Faith is the standard-bearer in every spiritual conflict; if the standard-bearer fall, then it is an evil day. Therefore our Lord prays that the standard-bearer may never fail to hold up the banner in the midst of the fray: "I have prayed for you, Simon, that your faith may not fail." If faith fails, everything fails—patience, hope, love, joy. Faith is the root; if this is not in order, then the leafage of the soul, which shows itself in other graces, will soon begin to wither.

Learn a lesson from this, my friend—that you take care to commend your faith to your God. Do not begin to doubt because you are tempted—that is to lay bare your breast. Do not doubt because you are attacked—that is to loosen your harness. Believe still. "I had fainted," said David, "unless I had believed" (kjv). It must be one thing or the other with us. Believing or fainting, which shall it be?

—C. H. Spurgeon

"Woman," he said, "why are you crying?"
—John 20:15

Let us turn to the depth of Mary's love.[53] And how intensely she loved may be most surely gathered from her refusal to believe that he was lost. There was nothing more to be done; the grave was empty. Mary could not tear herself away but stood outside at the sepulcher weeping. There is a kind of love that faces facts, and it is a noble and courageous love. But there is an agony of love that hopes against hope and beats against all evidence. No one will ever doubt John's love to Jesus. No one will ever doubt the love of Simon. But the fact remains that on that Easter morning Peter and John went to their homes again, and only a woman lingered by the grave. She must linger and watch in the teeth of all the facts. Measured by a test like that, there is not a disciple who can match the love of Mary.

The unceasing wonder of it all is this, that to her *first* he should have showed himself, neither to John nor to Peter had there been a whisper—no moving of pierced feet across the garden—all that was kept for a woman who had been a sinner and out of whom there had been cast seven devils. It is very notable that the first word of Christ after he had risen from the dead was *Woman.* "Woman, why are you crying?"

That he should pass by Pilate and the people and his mother and John and James and Simon Peter, that he should show himself first and foremost to a woman who had nothing to her credit but her love, I tell you that even the genius of a Shakespeare could never have conceived a scene like that.

—George H. Morrison

You yourselves are God's temple and
God's Spirit lives in you.

—1 Corinthians 3:16

Doubtless the church is the kingdom, the home, the temple of the Spirit; but how?[54] The Spirit governing the church is not like a human monarch, controlling his or her subjects, so to speak, as a force above and outside them. The Spirit is not only an atmosphere in which the church's members move and breathe. He is not any merely external power or influence. The presence of the Spirit in the church is realized by his presence in the separate souls of her children. He is given without measure to the whole because he is given in a measure to each. Although he lives in souls because he lives in the church, yet the collective church is the temple of deity because the souls of regenerated Christians are already so many tenements in which the Heavenly Guest deigns to tarry and to bless.

The presence on which he insists is ultimately a presence in the individual. Such was to be the law of the messianic kingdom: each of its subjects was to be gifted with an inward presence of the Holy One.

The [Spirit's] presence carries with it the gift of a new nature, the nature of God's sinless Son. Along with this Spirit comes the gift of a new moral being, a new capacity and direction to the affections and the will, a clear perception of the truth by the renewed intelligence. And it becomes us today to remember that this gift dates from the morning of the first Christian Pentecost.

That intimate, absorbing, transforming gift of himself by God presupposes a recipient unlike all creatures that merely grow and feel, while they are incapable of reflective thought and self-determination. The human being, as an immortal spirit, is the temple of God. But how the divine Spirit enters into the human, who will say? But just so far as we bear constantly in mind the immateriality of our real selves can we understand the high privilege to which we are called in Christ. The presence of the Spirit, having its seat in the immortal human spirit, is inseparable from the presence of the incarnate Christ. This sanctification of the Christian's whole being radiates from the sanctification of the inmost self-consciousness, involving the self-dedication to God of that imperishable center of life, that "I," which is at the root of all feeling and all thought, which is each person's true, indivisible, inmost self.

—H. P. Liddon

Pray continually.

—1 Thessalonians 5:17

It is not necessary to pronounce many words.[55] To pray is to say, "Let your will be done." It is to form a good purpose, to raise your heart to God, to lament your weakness, to sigh at the recollection of your frequent disobedience. This prayer demands neither method nor science nor reasoning; it is not essential to quit your work; it is a simple movement of the heart toward its Creator and a desire that whatever you are doing you may do to his glory. The best of all prayers is to act with a pure intention and with a continual reference to the will of God. It depends much on ourselves whether our prayers are effective. It is not by a miracle but by a movement of the heart that we are benefited, by a submissive spirit.

Do not devote all your time to action, but reserve a certain portion of it for meditation on eternity. Jesus invited his disciples to go apart in a desert place and rest awhile. How much more necessary is it for us to approach the source of all virtue, that we may revive our declining faith and charity, when we return from busy lives, where people speak and act as if they had never known that there is a God! We should look on prayer as the remedy for our weakness, the rectifier of our faults. He who was without sin prayed constantly; how much more ought we, who are sinners, to be faithful in prayer!

That we feel God should bless our labors is another powerful motive to prayer. It often happens that all human help is vain. It is God alone who can aid us, and it does not require much faith to believe that it is less our exertions than the blessing of the Almighty that can give success to our wishes.

We must pray with attention. God listens to the voice of the heart, not to that of the lips. The whole heart must be engaged in prayer. Every human object must disappear from our minds. To whom should we speak with attention if not to God? This attention to prayer may be practiced with less difficulty than we imagine. True, the most faithful souls suffer from occasional involuntary distractions. But these unbidden wanderings of the mind ought not to trouble us; they may promote our perfection even more than the most sublime and affecting prayers, if we strive to overcome them and submit with humility to this experience of our infirmity.

—François de Salignac de la Mothe-Fénelon

When you come, bring the cloak that I left with
Carpus at Troas.

—2 Timothy 4:13

We are taught in this passage how similar one child of God is to another.[56] We look on Abraham, Isaac, and Jacob as being great and blessed—we think that they lived in a higher region than we do. We cannot think that if they had lived in these times they would have been Abraham, Isaac, and Jacob. We suppose that these are very bad days and that any great height of grace is not easily attainable. But if Abraham, Isaac, and Jacob had lived now, instead of being less, they would have been greater saints—for they only lived in the dawn, and we live in the noon. The apostles are called *Saint* Peter and *Saint* Paul. Thus they are set up on an elevated niche. If we had seen Peter and Paul, we would have thought them very ordinary people—wonderfully like ourselves. If we had gone into their daily lives and trials, we would have said, "You are superior to what I am in grace. But somehow you are people like me. I have a quick temper; so have you, Peter. I have a thorn in the flesh; so have you, Paul. I complain of rheumatism, and the apostle Paul, when aged, feels the cold and wants his cloak."

The Bible is not intended for transcendental, superelevated souls—it is an everyday book. These people were everyday people, only they had more grace, but we can get more grace as well. The fountain at which they drew is as full and free to us as to them. We only have to believe in their fashion and trust to Jesus in their way, and although our trials are the same as theirs, we will overcome.

I like to see religion brought out in everyday life. Tell me about the godliness of your shop, your counter, and your kitchen. Let me see how grace enables you to be patient in the cold or joyful in hunger or industrious in labor. Grace is no common thing, yet it shines best in common things. To preach a sermon or sing a hymn is a paltry thing compared with the power to suffer cold and hunger and nakedness for Christ's sake.

Courage then, fellow pilgrim, the road was not smoothed for Paul any more than it is for us. There was no royal road to heaven in those days other than there is now. They had to go through sloughs and bogs and mire as we do still. But they have gained the victory at last, and even so shall we.

—C. H. Spurgeon

Do not fret because of evil men or be envious of those who
do wrong; for like the grass they will soon wither, like green
plants they will soon die away. Trust in the LORD and do
good; . . . and enjoy safe pasture.

—Psalm 37:1–3

Do not envy [evil men].[57] Do not be troubled at their prosperity.

Do not imitate them. Do not by their happiness be provoked to practice the same wickedness to arrive to the same prosperity.

Do not be not sinfully impatient and do not quarrel with God because he has not allowed you the same measures of prosperity. Do not accuse him of injustice and cruelty because he afflicts the good and is indulgent to the wicked. Leave him to dispense his blessings according to his own mind.

Do not condemn the way of piety and religion. Do not think the worse of your profession because it is attended with affliction. The happiness [of the wicked] has no stability. It has, like grass, more of color and show than strength and substance. Grass nods this way and that with every wind. The mouth of a beast may pull it up, or the foot of a beast may tread it down; the scorching sun in summer or the fainting sun in winter will deface its complexion.

[Rather, have] faith. Trust in the Lord. This is a grace most fit to quell such impatience. The stronger the faith, the weaker the passion. Impatient motions are signs of a flagging faith. Many times people are ready to cast off their help in Jehovah and address to the God of Ekron multitudes of friends or riches. But trust in the Lord, in the promises of God, in the providence of God.

Obedience. Do good. Trust in God's promises and observance of his precepts must be linked together. It is but a pretended trust in God where there is a walking in the paths of wickedness. Let not the glitter of the world render you faint and feeble in a course of piety.

The keeping our station. Do good. Because the wicked flourish, do not therefore hide in a corner, but keep your sphere, run your race. "And enjoy safe pasture." Because people delight in that in which they trust, [turn] from all other objects of delight to God as the true object. "Delight yourself in the LORD"; place all your pleasure and joy in him. Trust is the spring of joy and of supplication. When we trust him for sustenance and preservation, we will receive them; so when we delight in seeking him, we will be answered by him.

—Stephen Charnock

*Delight yourself in the LORD and he will give you the
desires of your heart.*

—Psalm 37:4

Without cheerful seeking we cannot have a gracious answer.[58]

God will not give an answer to prayers that dishonor him. A flat and lumpish attitude is not for his honor. We do not read of lead employed about the temple but the purer and most glittering metals. God wants the most excellent service, because he is the most excellent Being. He wants the most delightful service, because he bestows the most delightful gifts. It is a dishonor to so great a majesty to put him off with low and dead-hearted services. It is not for the credit of our great Master to have his servants dejected in his work, as though God were a wilderness and the world a paradise.

Dull and lumpish prayer does not reach him and therefore cannot expect an answer. Such desires are as arrows that sink down at our feet; there is no force to carry them to heaven.

Lumpishness speaks an unwillingness that God should hear us. Any who coldly and dully put up a petition to a sovereign give the ruler good reason to think that they do not care for an answer. That farmer has no great mind to harvest who is lazy in tilling the ground and sowing the seed. How can we think God should delight to read over our petitions when we take so little delight in presenting them? God does not give mercy to an unwilling person. God makes his people willing. Dull spirits seek God as if they did not care if they find him; such attitudes either account God not real or their petitions unnecessary.

Without delight we are not fit to receive a mercy. Delight in a mercy wanted makes room for desire, and large desires make room for mercy. If no delight in begging, there will be no delight in enjoying. If there is no cheerfulness to enliven our prayers when we need a blessing, there will be little joy to enliven our praise when we receive a blessing. A weak, sickly stomach is not fit to be seated at a plentiful table. God will not send his mercies except to a soul who will welcome them. A cheerful soul is fit to receive the least and fit to receive the greatest mercy. Such individuals will more prize a little mercy than dull petitioners will prize a greater, because they have a sense of their needs. If Zacchaeus had not a great joy at the news of Christ's coming by his door, he would not have so readily entertained and welcomed him.

—Stephen Charnock

*As a father has compassion on his children, so the LORD has
compassion on those who fear him.*

—Psalm 103:13

In the former part of this psalm the psalmist sang of God's deeds of love, his gifts, his benefits, and his acts of kindness, but here he goes deeper into the divine motive and finds sweeter incentives to devout gratitude.[59] There is consolation in the fact that the heart of God is toward his people. He takes a warm interest in our welfare and has a feeling toward us of kindly, gentle affection—of such intensity that one of the highest forms of earthly love is here used to set forth the tender mercy of our God toward us.

It is an axiom in theology that God has no griefs—that he is "without parts or passions." But I inwardly demur to such statements. They seem inconsistent with the tone and tenor of Scripture, for he appears to take pleasure in his people and to be "angry" with their ill-manners. Surely, metaphors that are inspired must have a meaning that is instructive. If the Father's "heart yearns," if our Lord and Savior is "filled with compassion," and if the Holy Spirit is grieved, there must be something analogous to emotion in the attributes of the Most High.

At least he appears to sympathize with us, so that "in all their distress he too was distressed," and he pities us as a father has compassion on his children. "That is speaking in a human way," says somebody. True, and it is exactly the way I do speak. In no other way do I know how to speak, and until I learn to speak after the manner of angels you must pardon me and also the incapacity of my hearers to understand any other than human language.

Pity sympathizes with its objects, makes itself one with them. I believe in a God who can feel. As to Baal and the gods of the heathen, they may be passionless and without emotion or without anything that is akin to feeling. Not so do I find Jehovah to be described.

Believe it then, dear friends, with all your hearts, that God has kindly feelings toward those who fear him, such as a father has toward his children. This is a truth of which I feel jealous, and I do not wish to see it toned down.

—C. H. Spurgeon

As a father has compassion on his children, so the LORD has compassion on those who fear him.

—Psalm 103:13

There is a sentiment that is accepted by many Christians that God puts us to much sorrow, wisely and for our good, while his own heart is callous to our suffering, because he foresees the good that will come out of it.[60] An analogy might in that case be suggested between God and a skillful surgeon, who cuts to remove a cancer from the flesh. The surgeon would be too intent on the success of the operation to bestow much sympathy on the sufferings that will effect a permanent cure.

But I pray you not to think that it is exactly so with God. Of course, in a higher scale, he has all the wisdom of the physician, and he does view our afflictions in light of that hereafter when he will heal all our diseases and give us beauty instead of ashes, gladness instead of mourning, and a garment of praise instead of a spirit of despair. Still he does not steel his heart to the present trouble of his people, but, "As a father has compassion on his children, so the LORD has compassion on those who fear him."

The surgeon can look at the patient, while causing pain, with the intrepidity of one whose nerves cannot easily be shaken. But a father must leave the room, he cannot bear it; the mother cannot look on—they are carried away with the immediate distress. And so it is with God; even though his wisdom and foreknowledge enable him to see the end as well as the beginning, yet like a father feeling compassion for his children, so the Lord feels compassion for those who fear him. [The verse] is in the present tense and carries the idea of continuity: at this very moment he has compassion on those who fear him. Though he knows your trials will work for your good, yet he has compassion on you. Though he knows that there is sin in you, which may require discipline, yet he has compassion on you. Though he can hear the songs and glees that will ultimately come of your present sighs and griefs, yet still he has compassion on your groans and wails, for "he does not willingly bring affliction or grief to the children of men" (Lam. 3:33). In all our distresses and present griefs he takes his share; he has compassion for us as a father has compassion for his children.

—C. H. *Spurgeon*

As a father has compassion on his children, so the LORD *has compassion on those who fear him.*

—Psalm 103:13

Look at the text, believing in its meaning and not saying, "That is in a human way."[61] For there is no other manner in which we can speak and no other manner in which God himself can speak if he means us to understand.

Hear it first for your encouragement, and hear it next for your imitation. Hear it, that you may be encouraged; God is not unfeelingly afflicting you, but he feels compassion for you. Hear it that you may go into the world with a like compassionate eye. If you ever have to say a rough word in fidelity or are required to utter a rebuke, do it in the way your heavenly Father does, having compassion even if you have to blame and gently delivering the expostulation that it grieves you to have to deliver at all.

Observe that the pity of the Lord extends to *all* those who fear him. There are none who are not fit objects of his compassion—the very best and brightest of his saints, the brave heroes, the well-instructed fathers, the diligent workers; God has compassion for you. Take that home to yourselves, because there is a beautiful lesson of humility in so accounting ourselves as pitiable creatures in the eyes of the Lord, even when we are at our best estate. I have seen some brothers and sisters who really did not seem at all fit for pity, because they imagined that the very roots of sin had been eradicated out of their hearts. Their characters and their conduct were akin to perfection in their own estimation. They had lived many weeks without a sin, except some wandering thought, but they could hardly refer to that as a fault. I pity people who talk so; if they are God's children, all that God does with them is he has compassion for them, and well he may; for he says to himself, "Poor dear creatures; how little they know of themselves, and how different their estimate of perfection is from mine." He still feels compassion for them.

The biggest children he has, the children who are most like their Father and have learned most of Jesus, may come to this text and see themselves depicted in it—"As a father has compassion on his children, so the LORD has compassion on those who fear him."

—C. H. Spurgeon

As a father has compassion on his children, so the LORD has compassion on those who fear him.

—Psalm 103:13

The Lord has compassion on our *childish ignorance.*[62] He is not angry with us because we do not know everything, because the little we do know we mostly turn topsy-turvy, because what he has taught us we are apt to forget by reason of fickle memory; no, but he has compassion on us. A true father, when his children do not know, tells them, and if a child hasn't got it then, he tries again.

Does the father expect his child to know as much as he himself? Certainly not. And when the child makes mistakes at which others laugh, the father feels the affront and has compassion on his child, and he goes on to teach more. "Why did you tell your child that piece of information twenty times?" said one. Said the mother, "Because when I had told him nineteen times he did not know it, so I went on to twenty times." And that is how God does with us. To know him and to know something of the power of his resurrection and something of conformity to his death—these are lessons we are learning, with a sweet prospect of being taught yet more and more and never a fear of being dismissed because of our dullness.

A word of admonition before we go any further. Do not think that you do not have the privileges of children because you do not know as much as more experienced saints. Do not think our heavenly Father does not love you, that he will refrain from keeping his eye on you or cease to watch your growth in grace and in the knowledge of Christ until he has more fully instructed you. Do not condemn those of God's children who do not know as much as you do. You have not gotten far yet yourselves. Still, there is a tendency in some to say, "Why, this cannot be genuine grace, for it is accompanied with such little knowledge."

If that suspicion leads you to give more instruction, it is well, but if it leads you to set aside the uninstructed one, it is ill. In the church of God it is fit for us to have the same compassion for the ignorant as our heavenly Father has shown toward our ignorance, and we ought to have even more, since he has no ignorance of his own and we have much. Let us therefore be compassionate and full of pity toward those who as yet know only a little.

—C. H. Spurgeon

As a father has compassion on his children, so the LORD has compassion on those who fear him.

—Psalm 103:13

Our heavenly Father shows himself compassionate to us is *in our weakness.*[63] Children cannot do much, they have little strength, especially little children, too helpless to run alone. The mother does not despise, she rather dotes on the babe she has to carry because it cannot walk. Her heart is not hardened against her infant because the wee one is unable to help itself.

Our heavenly Father knows our weakness. Some of you know something of your own lack of strength; you are bowed down under a sense of your infirmity tonight. Do not let your weakness lead you into unbelief or mistrust of God. He knows our frame; he remembers that we are only dust. An infant's incapacity never excites a parent's ire. You, being evil, know how to be tender with your offspring. How much more will the Father of our spirits sympathize with our weakness?

If you have guided your class in their studies but cannot find anything instructive to teach them, or if you are a minister and the words fall frozen when you hoped they would fire volleys from your lips, there may be some solution for your weariness. If it is pure weakness—whether from the body or from the mind that you are weary, disorganized, depressed, and bowed down—do not think of self-reproach, but hear the text say, "As a father has compassion on his children, so the LORD has compassion on those who fear him; for he knows how we are formed, he remembers that we are dust."

Some seem to think we are made of cast iron; they would have us preach all day and all night. They make use of bitter language when some servant of Christ cannot, through physical or mental weakness, do all they want. A person in perfect health and strength may joyfully accomplish what another cannot even think of undertaking. So are God's servants misjudged by the sterner sort, but they are not misjudged by God, for he has compassion on the weakness of his people and blames them not. God sees the efforts of his servants. They would drive the church before them and pull the world behind them, if they could. And if they seem unable to do it, does he blame them? No, truly he has compassion on the weakness of those who fear him.

—C. H. Spurgeon

As a father has compassion on his children, so the LORD has
compassion on those who fear him.

—Psalm 103:13

In children there is something worse than ignorance and weakness, and that is their *childish follies*.[64] A father and mother will put up with a thousand little ways in their children that strangers would frown at. There are all sorts of excuses made on their behalf, and it is right enough that it should be so. It is not weakness in children, it is just childishness. And so parents bear with their children.

But oh, how our Father bears with us! We think we are very wise; it is highly probable that we are never such fools as when we think we are displaying our wisdom. We think we are pleasing God sometimes, and in that very act we are displeasing him, though we know it not. There are sins in our holy things—oh, how strange must some of the things that we do seem to our great God! We have gotten so accustomed to them, we put up with them in others, and others put up with them in us.

There is much about our doubts and fears that must be depressing to the mind of the Father. Do we doubt him? Do we distrust his promises? We try to make out that we do not, but if you sift it thoroughly, it comes to that. Oh, the Father knows that we do not mean it, that we shrink in an instant from calling him a liar, and if anybody else were to put forward the very doubt that we have been entertaining we would be horrified.

And I believe it is a part of our Father's compassion that he should thus look on us and often construe what we do in such a kind and tender way. You know how Jesus prayed for his murderers—"Father, forgive them, for they do not know what they are doing" (Luke 23:34). And the Son is very like the Father; our Father does the same with us, he forgives us because we do not know what we do. It was beautiful of our Lord even with Pilate to say, "The one who handed me over to you is guilty of a greater sin" (John 19:11). It was the best he could say for Pilate, that though his sin was great yet there was a greater.

And our Father has those kind thoughts ready, we may be sure, for his children's wild and wayward deeds; Jesus had them ready even for his most wicked adversaries. Yes, he has compassion on our follies and bears with us still.

—C. H. *Spurgeon*

As a father has compassion on his children, so the LORD *has compassion on those who fear him.*

—Psalm 103:13

Children have something worse than follies; *they have faults to be forgiven.*[65] Our Father has compassion for the faults of his children—he has provided for their cleansing, and he freely gives them use of that provision and readily forgives them their iniquities.

Good children, who have done wrong, are never satisfied until they get to their parents and ask their forgiveness. Some parents think it wise to withhold the forgiving word for a little time; so may our great Father, but as a rule isn't it wonderful how readily he forgives? He for a little time, perhaps, makes us smart under the sin for our good, but it is not often; as a rule, the kiss is on our cheek almost before the confession has left our lips.

Do you think that Peter ought to have been kept out of the church awhile after denying his Master with oaths and cursing? Perhaps he would have been if we had been consulted, but Jesus Christ, by a kind look or a gentle word, could set crooked things straight. So we see Peter in company with John and the rest of the disciples within two or three days of his committing that serious trespass. The Lord is very ready to forgive; it is the church that is unmerciful sometimes, but not the Master; he is ever willing to receive us when we come to him and to blot out our transgressions.

Come along, then, you who have erred and gone astray, you backsliders who are aware of sin; you who walked in the light only a few days ago and have gotten into the dark by some sad slip; yet come along—you are very ready to forgive your children, aren't you? Don't you remember, you who are too old to have them about the house, how readily in your younger days you caught up your little ones in your arms and said, "Dear child, don't cry anymore; you must not do it again, but Father fully forgives you this time"?

Just so your heavenly Father waits to catch you up, press you to his bosom and say, "I have loved you with an everlasting love" (Jer. 31:3), not with a love that can soon be set aside by your fault, therefore, again I will blot out your transgression and set your feet on a rock and strengthen you to sin no more. Oh, it is a sweet, sweet thought—our Father feels compassion for us in our faults!

—C. H. Spurgeon

As a father has compassion on his children, so the LORD has compassion on those who fear him.

—Psalm 103:13

A father's compassion tenderly *lifts up those who fall.*[66] When your child falls down, as children are very apt to do, especially when they first begin to walk, don't you pity them? Is there a nasty cut across the knee, and tears? The mother takes the child up in her arms, and she has some sponge and water to take the grit out of the wound, and she gives a kiss and makes it well. I know mothers have wondrous healing lips! And sometimes, when God's servants do really fall, it is very lamentable, it is very sad, and it is well that they should cry. It were a pity that they should be willing to lie in the mire, but when they are up again and begin crying, and the wound bleeds—well, let them not keep away from God, for as a father has compassion on his fallen child, so the Lord has compassion on those who fear him.

Have you come in here tonight with that cut knee of yours? I am sorry you have fallen, but I am glad that our blessed Master is willing to receive you still. Come and trust in him who is mighty to save, just as you did at first, and begin again tonight. Come along! Some of us have had to begin again many times. You do the same. If you are not a saint you are a sinner, and Jesus Christ came into the world to save sinners. Put your trust in him, and you will find restoration, and maybe through that very fall you will learn to be more careful, and from now on you will walk more uprightly, to his honor and glory.

—C. H. Spurgeon

As a father has compassion on his children, so the LORD has compassion on those who fear him.

—Psalm 103:13

How the compassion of a father comes out to his child in the matter of pain![67] With what exquisite *tenderness a child's pains are soothed by a parent!* It is very hard to stand by the bedside and see a dear child suffer. Haven't some of you felt that you would gladly take your children's pains if they might be restored? You have one dear one at home now, the tear is in your eye as I mention it—a life of suffering she has. Well, it may be others of you have children who have mental troubles; the body is healthy, but the little one has a fret and a worry. I hope you sometimes have seen your children weeping because of sin; it is a blessed grief, and the sooner it comes the better. In such a grief as that, as indeed in all others, I am quite sure you feel compassion for your children. So ever does your Father feel compassion for you.

Broken heart, God's heart is longing to heal you. Weeping for your transgressions, the Father longs to clasp you to his bosom. Tried child of God, you who are often despondent and always ailing, God would not send this to you if there were not a necessity for it, and in sending it he shares it as far as this text goes, and it goes blessedly far, for he feels compassion for you. Sometimes hardhearted persons do not pity those who suffer, and some forms of suffering do not awaken sympathy, but all the sufferings of God's people touch the heart of Jesus, and sympathy comes to them at once.

I know some of you say, "I am quite alone in the world, and I have much sorrow." Please revise that hard saying! You are like your Master, of whom it is written that he said, "You will leave me all alone. Yet I am not alone, for my Father is with me" (John 16:32). Your Father is with you. I wish you had some Christian friend to speak with you as a companion, but in the absence of such a social confidant "there is a friend who sticks closer than a brother" (Prov. 18:24), and there is One above who is a Father to you. Believe it; there is no poverty, there is no reproach, there is no sorrow of heart, there is no pain of body in this world among those who fear God but what the Lord sees it and knows all about it and has compassion on those who endure it.

—C. H. Spurgeon

As a father has compassion on his children, so the LORD has
compassion on those who fear him.

—Psalm 103:13

Our children have our pity when *anybody has wronged them.*[68] I have heard say that there are some men that you might insult, almost with impunity, and should you even give them a blow they would stop to ask the reason before showing any resentment. But if you put a hand on their children, you will see the father's blood come up into his face, and the most patient man will, all of a sudden, become the most passionate. There was a livid blue mark where you struck the child, and the father looks as though he could forgive you if that were on his own body, but on his child—no, that he cannot endure. He turns it over and over, and he cannot resist his indignation that his child should be carelessly made to suffer. The wrongs of children call fondly for redress in the ears of every sensitive man or woman, but they are sure to awake a thrilling echo in a father's heart.

"And will not God bring about justice for his chosen ones, who cry out to him day and night? . . . I tell you, he will see that they get justice, and quickly." There is no wrong done to his people but it is registered in God's archives. "Whoever touches you touches the apple of his eye." Christ seemed to sit still in heaven till he saw the blood of his saints shed, and then he stood up as in indignation when they stoned Stephen. You remember how he cries, "Saul, Saul, why do you persecute me?" It was he himself who suffered, though his saints were made to die. Leave, then, your wrongs with God. "'It is mine to avenge; I will repay,' says the Lord," and let your reply be always gentleness and kindness toward those who hate you, for righteousness' sake.

—C. H. Spurgeon

> *As a father has compassion on his children, so the LORD has*
> *compassion on those who fear him.*
>
> —Psalm 103:13

The father will have compassion on his children to *remove their dreads.*[69] Some people seem to take delight in frightening children with bogey stories so that they hardly dare go out at night, but a kind father, if he finds his children frightened so, explains it all to them—he does not like to see them blanched with fear or haunted with terror. It may be that some here present are suffering because they are afraid. Are any of you under a dread of some boding evil? Be sure of this: your heavenly Father feels compassion for you.

Some hymns speak of death as associated with pains and groans and agonizing strife. Very much of that is old bogey. How many of God's people have we seen die without pains or groans or dying strife! I remember one who all her lifetime was afraid of death; she retired as usual to bed one night, and when they went to call her in the morning, there she lay with a sweet smile on her face; she had gone to heaven in her sleep. It was evident she never knew anything about it.

Are God's people by their observation of other saints driven to conclude that death is always the terrible thing the world says it is? There may be some whom God puts to bed in the dark, as we sometimes do our children, but usually he takes the candle with him and sits and talks with his children till they fall asleep. And [when they] wake up, there they are among the angels. God kisses the souls of his saints out of their bodies.

Go to your heavenly Father and tell him you are frightened, and he has ways of taking away these fears. For though they may be ridiculous to some, a child's dreads are never too frivolous for the sympathy of a loving father, but he meets them as if there were some great reality in them and so sets them aside.

Whatever then your need, your woe, your grief, go to your Father and he will give you comfort. Believe from this night forward that God does pity all those who fear him, and whatever he sees of weakness in their nature and of sorrow in their lot he will help them. So may you find it now and evermore, for Christ's sake. Amen.

—C. H. Spurgeon

I trust in the mercy of God for ever and ever.
—Psalm 52:8 KJV

Mercy as an attribute of God is not to be confounded with mere goodness.[70] Goodness may demand the exercise of justice. Mercy asks that justice be set aside. Mercy pardons the guilty. Justice treats all according to their deserts. Desert is never the rule that guides mercy, while it is precisely the rule of justice. Thus, mercy is exercised only where there is guilt.

Mercy can be exercised no farther than one deserves punishment. If great punishment is deserved, great mercy can be shown; if endless punishment is due, there is then scope for infinite mercy.

None can properly be said to trust in the mercy of God unless they have committed crimes and are conscious of this fact. Justice protects the innocent, and they may appeal to it. But for the guilty, nothing remains but to trust in mercy. Trusting in mercy implies a heartfelt conviction of personal guilt.

Trust in mercy implies understanding what mercy is. Many confuse mercy with grace, considered as mere favor to the undeserving. Grace may be shown where there is no mercy, the term *mercy* being applied to the pardon of crime. We all know that God shows grace to all on earth. He makes his sun rise on the evil and on the good and sends his rain on the unrighteous as well as on the righteous. But to trust in this general favor is not trusting in the mercy of God. Mercy is pardon for the crimes of the guilty.

Trust in God's mercy implies a belief that he is merciful. We could not trust him if we had no such belief. This belief must lie at the foundation of trust. Faith, or belief, includes a committal of the soul to God and a trust in him.

Trusting in the mercy of God forever implies a conviction of deserving endless punishment. When therefore the psalmist trusts in the mercy of God forever he renounces all hope of being ever received to favor on the score of justice.

Trusting in mercy implies a cessation from all excuse making. The moment you trust in mercy, you give up all excuses, for these imply a reliance on God's justice. An excuse is nothing more nor less that an appeal to justice, a plea designed to justify our conduct. Trusting in mercy forever implies that we have ceased from all excuses forever.

—Charles G. Finney

If you know that he is righteous, you know that everyone
who does what is right is born of him.

—1 John 2:29

Righteousness is ours is by faith.[71] Perfect righteousness exists not, except in the angels—and scarcely in angels, if compared with God. Yet if there is any perfect righteousness of souls and spirits, it is in the angels. In them is perfect righteousness.

But in us [righteousness] has begun, by faith, by the Spirit. The beginning of our righteousness is the confession of sins. You have begun not to defend your sin; now you have made a beginning of righteousness, but it will be perfected in you when "death has been swallowed up in victory," when there will be no itching of lust, when there will be triumph over the enemy—then will there be perfect righteousness.

At present we are still fighting. We pummel and are pummeled, but who will conquer remains to be seen. And those conquer who presume not on their own strength but rely on God. The Devil is alone when he fights against us. If we are with God, we overcome the Devil, for if you fight alone with the Devil, you will be overcome.

He is a skillful enemy! Consider to what he has cast us down. That we are born mortal comes of this, that he in the first place cast down from Paradise our very original. What then is to be done, seeing he is so well practiced? Let the Almighty be invoked to your aid. Let him who cannot be overcome dwell in you, and you will securely overcome him who is accustomed to overcome those in whom God dwells not. For Adam being in Paradise despised the commandment of God as if he desired to be his own master, loath to be subject to the will of God, so he fell from that immortality, from that blessedness.

This is what the epistle would have us lay to heart, that we may overcome the Devil, but not of ourselves. "If you know that he is righteous," it says, "you know that every one who does what is right is born of him"—of God, of Christ. And in that he has said, "is born of him," he cheers us on. Already therefore, in that we are born of him, we are perfect.

—Augustine of Hippo

He who does what is sinful is of the devil, because the devil
has been sinning from the beginning.

—1 John 3:8

"Is of the devil"—you know what he means: imitates the Devil.[72] For the Devil made no one, fathered no one, created no one, but whoever imitates the Devil, that person, as if fathered by him, becomes a child of the Devil. In what sense are you a child of Abraham, not that Abraham fathered you? In the same sense as the Jews, the children of Abraham, not imitating the faith of Abraham, became children of the Devil; of the flesh of Abraham they were born, and the faith of Abraham they have not imitated. If then those who were thus born were put out of the inheritance because they did not imitate, you, who are not born of him, are made a child, and in this way shall be a child of Abraham by imitating him. And if you imitate the Devil in the way he became proud and impious against God, you will be a child of the Devil.

"The reason the Son of God appeared was to destroy the devil's work" (1 John 3:8). Now then, beloved, mark! All sinners are born of the Devil, as sinners. Adam was made by God, but when he consented to the Devil, he was born of the Devil, and he fathered all as he was himself. With lust itself we were born, even before we add our sins; from that condemnation we have our birth. For if we are born without any sin, why this running with infants to baptism that they may be released? Then mark well, friends, the two birth-stocks; Adam and Christ are two men, but one of them, a man that is human; the other, a Man that is God. By the man that is human we are sinners; by the Man that is God we are justified. That birth has cast down to death, this birth has raised up to life; that birth brings with it sin, this birth sets free from sin. For this purpose Christ came as human, to undo human sins. The reason the Son of God appeared was to destroy the Devil's work.

—Augustine of Hippo

We are confident, I say, and would prefer to be away from
the body and at home with the Lord.
—2 Corinthians 5:8

The souls of true saints, when they leave their bodies at death, go to be with Christ.[73] They are brought into perfect conformity to and union with him. Their spiritual conformity is begun while they are in the body, but when they see him as he is in heaven, then they become like him in another manner. That perfect sight will abolish all remains of deformity, disagreement, and sinful unlikeness, as all darkness is abolished before the blaze of the sun. It is impossible that the least degree of obscurity should remain before such light; so it is impossible the least degree of sin and spiritual deformity should remain before the beauty and glory of Christ. When saints see that Sun of righteousness, they themselves shine forth as little suns, without spot.

And then the saints' union with Christ is perfected. This also is begun in this world. The union of a heart to Christ is begun when that heart is drawn to Christ at conversion, and consequent to this a vital union is established with Christ, by which the believer becomes a living branch of the true vine, living by a communication of the vital juice of the root, and a member of Christ's mystical body, living by a communication of spiritual influences from the Head and by a kind of participation in Christ's own life. But while the saints are in the body, there is much remaining distance between Christ and them: there are remainders of alienation, and the union is very imperfect and so, consequently, is the communication of spiritual influences. There is much between Christ and believers to keep them apart—sin, temptation, a world of carnal objects to keep the soul from Christ and hinder a perfect coming together.

But when the soul leaves the body, all these clogs and hindrances will be removed, every separating wall will be broken down and every impediment taken out of the way, and all distance will cease. The heart will be wholly and forever bound to him by a perfect view of his glory. And the vital union will then be brought to perfection; the soul will live perfectly in and on Christ, being perfectly filled with his spirit and animated by his vital influences—living, as it were, only by Christ's life, without any remainder of spiritual death or carnal life.

—Jonathan Edwards

> *O worship the* LORD *in the beauty of holiness.*
> —Psalm 96:9 KJV

The word translated "beauty" here is somewhat rare.[74] It suggests honor or glory or beauty, an inherent quality, not something put on from without, but something revealed to the eye and appealing to the emotion and the mind as glorious and beautiful in itself, yet belonging essentially to the item with which we are brought into contact.

The psalmist is appealing to people to praise God, calling them to recognize his greatness, his glory, calling them to think of his power and majesty, urging them to answer the things their eyes see and their hearts feel by offering praise to him. In this call so poetic and full of beauty is revealed the meaning of worship, its condition and glory. "O worship the LORD." The supreme thing is worship. But how is worship to be rendered? "In the beauty of holiness." Wherever you find beauty, it is the outcome of holiness. Wherever you find beauty as the outcome of holiness, that beauty itself is incense, is worship. To live the life of holiness is to live the life of beauty, and that is to worship.

When Charles Kingsley lay dying, he said, "How beautiful God is!" We are almost startled by the word. We speak of his majesty. We speak of his might. We speak of his mercy, his holiness, his love. Yet there is nothing of God that he has made more conspicuous to us than his beauty. Every manifestation of God is full of beauty.

The beauty of God, blossoming in the daisy, blazing in the starry heavens—brings you back to my text, "O worship the LORD in the beauty of holiness." All the beauty of flowers, in form and color and perfume, are of God. All the beauty of the seasons—spring and summer and autumn and winter; all that is beautiful in human beings physically, mentally, spiritually, and all that is beautiful in the interrelation between people is of God.

God is a God of glory. God is a God of love. But he is also the God of beauty.

I stayed with a friend in Devonshire who brought from his greenhouse a spray of roses and put them under the microscope. And the more closely I looked, the more perfect they were. The beauty of God is revealed in the tiniest cell of the flower. God is very beautiful, and everything that is of God is essentially beautiful.

—G. Campbell Morgan

O worship the LORD *in the beauty of holiness.*

—Psalm 96:9 KJV

What is worship?[75] The essential meaning of the word is prostration, bowing down. Worship suggests the attitude that recognizes the throne, that recognizes superiority, that takes the low place of reverence in the presence of that which takes hold on the life and compels it. It is a word full of force, which constrains us and compels us to the attitude of reverence.

The word *worship* runs through the Bible, and the thought of worship is to be found from beginning to end. The thought of worship is the recognition of divine sufficiency, the recognition of our absolute dependence on the divine sufficiency, the confession that all we need in our lives we find in God. And the spoken answer to that conviction is worship. I worship in the presence of God as I recognize that in him I find everything that my life demands, that in myself I am incomplete. A sense of my need and his resource, a sense that my life finds its heights and its best and fulfills itself in relation to him produces the act and the attitude of worship. The attitude of worship is the attitude of a subject bent before a monarch; the attitude of a child yielding all its love to a parent; the attitude of the sheep that follows the shepherd and is content in all the pasturage that the shepherd appoints. It is the attitude of saying *yes* to everything that God says.

The height of worship is expressed in the use of two words that have never been translated, which remain on the page of the Holy Scriptures and in the common language of the church as they were in the language where they originated: "Hallelujah" and "Amen." When I have learned to say those two words with all my mind and heart and soul and being, I have found the highest place of worship and the fullest realization of my own life. Amen to his will, and Hallelujah, the offering of praise. I know it is but a simple symbol. I know it is only saying an old thing, but I address my own heart as much as any of you, and I say, Oh, soul of mine, have you learned to say "Amen" to him, and that on the basis of a deep and profound conviction of all his absolute perfection in government and method and providence? Can you say, as the quiet expression of a heart resting in the perfection of God, "Hallelujah" and "Amen"? Then that is worship, that is life.

—G. Campbell Morgan

They are still in the world, and I am coming to you.
Holy Father, protect them by the power of your name . . .
so that they may be one as we are one.

—John 17:11

This Scripture contains the first preparation of Christ for death, where he sets his house in order, prays for his people, and blesses them before he dies.[76] The love of Christ was ever tender and strong to his people, but the greatest demonstration of it was at parting, in two ways especially: in leaving support and comfort with them in his last heavenly sermon, in John 14 through 16, and in pouring out his soul to the Father for them in this heavenly prayer, chapter 17. In this prayer he gives them a sample of his intercession, which he was just then going to perform in heaven for them. Here his heart overflowed, for he was leaving them and going to the Father. The last words of a dying person are remarkable—how much more a dying Savior?

We have here Christ's petition in behalf of his people, not only those at that place, but all others that then did or afterwards would believe on him. And the sum of what he here requests for them is that his Father would protect them through his name, where you have both the mercy and the means of attaining it. The mercy is to be protected. Protecting implies danger, and there is a double danger anticipated in this request: danger in respect of sin and danger in respect of ruin and destruction. To both these the people of God lie open in this world.

The means of their preservation from both is the name, that is, the power of God. This name of the Lord is the strong tower that the righteous run to and are safe (Prov. 18:10). Alas! It is not your own strength or wisdom that keeps you, but you are kept by the mighty power of God. This protecting power of God does not, however, exclude our care and diligence but implies it. God keeps his people, and yet they are to keep themselves in God's love (Jude 21), to, above all else, guard their hearts (Prov. 4:23).

The arguments with which he urges and presses on this request are drawn partly from his own condition—within a very few hours he will be separated from them in regard to his corporeal presence; partly from their condition—"they are still in the world," that is, I must leave them in the midst of danger; and partly from the joint interest his Father and he himself had in them: Keep those you have given me.

—John Flavel

They are still in the world, and I am coming to you.
Holy Father, protect them by the power of your name . . .
so that they may be one as we are one.

—John 17:11

The preparations made by Christ for his death were the solemn recommendation of his friends to his Father, the institution of a commemorative sign to perpetuate and refresh the memory of his death in the hearts of his people, till he come again, and his pouring out his soul to God by prayer in the garden, which was the posture he chose to be found in when they apprehended him.[77]

The fatherly care and tender love of our Lord Jesus Christ was eminently displayed in that pleading prayer he poured out for his people at his parting with them. It belonged to the priest and father of the family to bless the rest, especially when he was to be separated from them by death. This was a rite in Israel. When good Jacob was grown old, and the time came that he would be gathered to his fathers, then he blessed Joseph and his sons, Ephraim and Manasseh, saying, "May the God before whom my fathers Abraham and Isaac walked, the God who has been my shepherd all my life to this day, the Angel who has delivered me from all harm—may he bless these boys" (Gen. 48:15–16). This was a prophetic and patriarchal blessing—not that Jacob could bless as God blesses. He could speak the words of blessing, but he knew that the effect, the real blessing itself, depended on God. Now when Jesus Christ comes to die, he will bless his children also and in this will reveal how much dear and tender love he has for them: "Having loved his own who were in the world, he now showed them the full extent of his love" (John 13:1). The last act of Christ in this world was an act of blessing (Luke 24:50–51).

—John Flavel

Holy Father, protect them by the power of your name . . .
so that they may be one as we are one.

—John 17:11

What were those mercies and special favors that Christ begged for his people when he was to die?[78]

The mercy of preservation both from sin and danger: "Protect them by the power of your name," which is explained, John 17:15, "My prayer is not that you take them out of the world but that you protect them from the evil one." We and the saints that are gone have reaped the fruit of this prayer. How else are our souls preserved amid temptations—assisted and aided by our own corruption? Surely, the preservation of the burning bush, of the three children amid the flames, of Daniel in the den of lions are not greater wonders than this.

The blessing of union among them. This he joins immediately with the first mercy of preservation and prays for it in the same breath, verse 11, "so that they may be one as we are one." Their union with one another is a special means to preserve them all.

That *"they may have the full measure of my joy within them"* (v. 13). He wanted to provide for their joy even when the hour of his greatest sorrow was at hand—he wanted not only to obtain joy for them, but full joy. It is as if he had said, "Father, I am to leave these dear ones in a world of troubles and perplexities; I know their hearts will be subject to discouragement. Let me obtain the restoratives of divine joy for them before I go. I would not only have them live, but live joyfully; provide, for fainting hours, reviving tonics."

And to maintain all these mercies, *"Sanctify them by the truth; your word is truth"* (v. 17), that is, more abundantly sanctified than yet they were, by a deeper establishment of gracious habits and principles in their hearts. This is a singular mercy in itself, to have holiness spreading itself over and through their souls. Nothing is more desirable. And it is also a singular help to their perseverance, union, and spiritual joy.

And lastly, as the complement and perfection of all desirable mercies, *that they may be with him where he is, to see his glory* (v. 24). This is the best and ultimate privilege they are capable of. The design of his coming down from heaven and returning there is to bring many sons and daughters to glory. Christ asks no trifles, no small things for his people. No mercies but the best that both worlds afford will satisfy him on their behalf.

—John Flavel

Holy Father, protect them by the power of your name . . .
so that they may be one as we are one.

—John 17:11

With what arguments does he plead with the Father for these mercies?[79]

The first is drawn from the joint interest that both he and his Father have in the persons for whom he prays, "All I have is yours, and all you have is mine" (v. 10), as if he would say, "Father, see and consider the persons I pray for, they are not aliens but Christians. Yes, they are your children as well as mine, the very ones on whom you have set your eternal love and in that love have given to me. Great is our interest in them, and interest draws care and tenderness. Everyone cares for his own, provides for and secures his own. Property, even among creatures, is fundamental to their labor, care, and watchfulness; they would not so much prize life, health, estates, or children if they were not their own. Lord, these are your own by many ties or titles. O therefore keep, comfort, sanctify, and save them, for they are yours." What a mighty plea is this! Surely, Christians, your intercessor is skillful in his work, your advocate lacks no eloquence or ability to plead for you.

The second argument, and that a powerful one, treads on the very heel of the former, "Glory has come to me through them"; "my glory and honor are infinitely dear to you; I know your heart is entirely on the exalting and glorifying of your Son. Now what glory have I in the world but what comes from my people? Others neither can nor will glorify me; no, I am daily blasphemed and dishonored by them. From these my active glory and praise in the world must rise. It is true, both you and I have glory from other creatures; the works that we have made and impress our power, wisdom, and goodness on thus glorify us, and we have honor from our very enemies accidentally, their very wrath will praise us. But for active and voluntary praise, where does this come from except from the people who were formed for that very purpose? Should these then go wrong and perish, where shall my glory be demonstrated and active, and from whom shall I expect it?" Here his property and his glory are pleaded with the Father to prevail for those mercies, and they are both great and valuable things with God. What dearer, what nearer to the heart of God?

—John Flavel

*I will remain in the world no longer, but they are still in the
world. . . . Father, protect them.*

—John 17:11

With what [further] arguments [does] he plead with the Father?[80]

He adds, in the beginning of John 17:11, a third argument in these words, "I will remain in the world no longer." Consider the sense of it as a proposition and the force of it as an argument. This proposition, "I will remain in the world no longer," is not to be taken universally as if in no sense Christ would be any more in this world but only as to his corporeal presence. This, which had been a comfort to them in all their troubles, was soon to be removed from his people.

And here lies the argument: "Father, consider the sadness and trouble I shall leave my poor children under. While I was with them I was sweet relief to their souls, whatever troubles they met. In all doubts, fears, and dangers, they could turn to me, and in their adversities and needs I supplied them. They had my counsels to direct them, my reproofs to correct them, and my comforts to support them. Yes, the very sight of me was unspeakable joy and refreshment to their souls. But now the hour has come, and I must go. All the comfort and benefit they had from my presence is ended, and except you make up all this to them another way, what will become of these children when their Father is gone? What will be the case of the poor sheep and tender lambs when the shepherd is struck?"

And yet, to move and engage the Father's care and love for them, he subjoins [a fourth] consideration in the very next words, "but they are still in the world." The world is a sinful, infecting, and unquiet place. And a hard thing it will be for such imperfect creatures to escape the pollutions of it, or if they do, yet the troubles, persecutions, and strong oppositions of it they can't escape. "Seeing therefore I must leave your children, those from whom the glory is to rise, in the midst of a world where they can neither move backward nor forward without danger of sin or ruin—since this is so, look after them, provide for them, and take special care for them all. Consider who they are and where I leave them. They are your children, left in a strange country; your sheep, in the midst of wolves; your precious treasure, among thieves."

—John Flavel

I am coming to you. Holy Father, protect them by the power of your name—the name you gave me.

—John 17:11

With what [final] arguments [does] he plead with the Father?[81]

He adds [a fifth] argument in the words, "I am coming to you." As his leaving them was an argument, so his going to the Father is a mighty argument also. There is much in these words, "I am coming to you"—"I, your beloved Son, in whom your soul delights; to whom you never denied anything. It is I who come to you, swimming through a bloody ocean. I come, treading every step to you in blood and unspeakable sufferings—all this for the sake of those dear ones I now pray for. Yes, the design and purpose of my coming to you is for them. I am coming to heaven in the capacity of an advocate to plead with you for them, my Father and their Father, my God and their God. Since I who am so dear come through such bitter pangs to you, so tenderhearted a Father, and all this on their account, since I now give them a little taste of that intercession work that I shall forever perform for them in heaven, Father, grant what I request. I know you will not deny me."

And [sixth,] to close up all, he tells the Father how careful he had been to observe and perform that trust which was committed to him: "While I was with them, I protected them and kept them safe by that name you gave me. None has been lost except the one doomed to destruction" (John 17:12).

And thus lies the argument: "You committed to me a certain number of souls. I undertook the trust and said, if any of these are lost, I will answer for them. In pursuing this trust I am now here on the earth in a body of flesh. I have been faithful. I have redeemed them" (for he speaks of that as finished and done which was now ready to be done). "I have kept them also and confirmed them until now, and now, Father, I commit them to your care. Do not let them fail now, do not let one of them perish."

Thus you see what a muscular, argumentative, pleading prayer Christ poured out to the Father for them at parting.

—John Flavel

I will remain in the world no longer, but they are still in the world, and I am coming to you. Holy Father, protect them by the power of your name—the name you gave me—so that they may be one as we are one.

—John 17:11

Why [did] Christ thus pray and plead with God for them when he was to die?[82] Certainly it was not because the Father was unwilling to grant the mercies he desired. No, the reasons of this great persistence are,

1. He foresaw a great trial then at hand and all the later trials of his people, as well. He knew their faith would be shaken by the approaching difficulties, when they would see their Shepherd struck and themselves scattered, the Son of man delivered into the hands of sinners and the Lord of life hang dead on the tree and sealed up in the grave. He foresaw what distresses his people would fall into between a busy Devil and bad hearts. Therefore he pleads with such persistence and ardency for them, that they might not go wrong.

2. He was now entering on his intercession work in heaven, and he desired in this prayer to give a sample of that part of his work before he left us, that we might understand what he would do for us when he was out of sight. It shows us what affections and dispositions he carried away with him and satisfies us that he who was so earnest with God on our behalf will not forget us or neglect our concerns in the other world. The intercession of Christ in heaven is carried much higher than this. Here he used prostrations of body, cries, and tears in his prayers; there, his intercession is carried in a more majestic way, befitting an exalted Jesus. But in this he left us special assistance to know the working of his heart, now in heaven, toward us.

3. And lastly, he would leave this as a standing monument of his fatherlike care and love to his people to the end of the world. And for this Christ delivered this prayer publicly, not withdrawing from the disciples to be private with God as he did in the garden. But he delivers it in their presence: "I say these things while I am still in the world" (John 17:13). And not only was it publicly delivered, but it was also recorded by John, that it might stand to all generations for a testimony of Christ's tender care and love to his people.

—John Flavel

I will remain in the world no longer, but they are still in the
world, and I am coming to you. Holy Father, protect them
by the power of your name—the name you gave me—so
that they may be one as we are one.

—John 17:11

How [does] this prayer give evidence of Christ's tender care and love to his people?[83]

1. His love and care was obvious in the choice of mercies for them. He does not pray for health, honor, long life, riches, and the like, but for their preservation from sin, spiritual joy in God, sanctification, and eternal glory. No mercies but the very best in God's treasure will content him. The rest he is content should be dispensed indiscriminately by providence, but these he will settle as a heritage on his children. See the love of Christ! Look over your spiritual inheritance in Christ, compare it with the richest, fairest, sweetest inheritance on earth, and see what poor things these are to yours.

2. He pleaded your concerns with God at a time when a world of sorrow surrounded him on every side, a cup of wrath mixed and ready to be delivered into his hand. At that very time when the clouds of wrath grew black, a storm coming such as he never felt before, one would have thought all his care, thoughts, and diligence would have been employed on his own account to mind his own sufferings. No, he forgets his own sorrows to mind our peace and comfort.

If Christ so amply showed his care and love for his people in this his parting hour, then we conclude the perseverance of the saints is unquestionable. Do you hear how he pleads! how he argues! how he chooses his words and sets them in order, how he winds up his spirit to the very highest pitch of zeal and fervency? Can such a Father deny the persistence and strong reasonings and pleading of such a Son? O, it can never be! He cannot deny him. Christ has the art and skill of prevailing with God. If the heart and hand of God were hard to be opened, yet this would open them, but when the Father himself loves us and is inclined to do us good, who can doubt of Christ's success?

Think on this when dangers surround your souls or bodies. When fears and doubts are multiplied within, think on that encouragement Christ gave to Peter, Luke 22:32: "I have prayed for you."

—John Flavel

*I will remain in the world no longer, but they are still in the
world, and I am coming to you. Holy Father, protect them
by the power of your name—the name you gave me—so
that they may be one as we are one.*

—John 17:11

Argumentative prayers are excellent prayers.[84] The strength of everything is in its joints; how strongly jointed, how sinewy was this prayer of Christ. Some think we need not argue and plead in prayer but only present the matter and let Christ plead with the Father—as if the choicest part of our prayers must be kept back because Christ presents our prayers to God. No, Christ's pleading is one thing, ours another; his and ours are not opposed but subordinate. His pleading does not destroy ours but makes it successful.

God calls us to plead with him: "Come now, let us reason together" (Isa. 1:18). God reasons with us by his word and providences outwardly and by his Spirit inwardly. We reason with him by framing (through the help of his Spirit) certain arguments, grounded on allowed principles, drawn from his nature, name, word, or works. What was Jacob's wrestling with the angel but his holy pleading and persistence with God? Let God frown, strike, or wound, a blessing Jacob came for and a blessing he will have; "I will not let you go," he said, "unless you bless me" (Gen. 32:26). His limbs, his life might go, but there is no going from Christ without a blessing. The Lord admires him and honors him to all generations.

We are not heard either for our much speaking or our excellent speaking; it is Christ's pleading in heaven that makes our pleading on earth effective. But surely when the Spirit of the Lord suggests proper arguments in prayer and helps the humble suppliant to press them home, when he helps us to weep and groan and plead, God is greatly delighted in such prayers. "I will surely make you prosper" (Gen. 32:12) is your own promise. This is pleasing to God, we can come to him crying, "Abba, Father, hear, forgive, pity, and help me. Am I not your child?"

To whom may a child be bold to go, with whom may a child have hope to succeed, if not with its father? The fathers of our flesh are full of tenderness and pity their children and know how to give good things to them. And is not the Father of spirits more full of tenderness, more full of pity? "Father, hear me." This is that kind of prayer which is melody in the ears of God.

—John Flavel

I will remain in the world no longer, but they are still in the
world, and I am coming to you. Holy Father, protect them
by the power of your name—the name you gave me—so
that they may be one as we are one.

—John 17:11

Look on dying Jesus, see how his care and love to his people flamed out when the time of his departure was at hand.[85] As we remember our relations every day and lay up prayers for them in the time of our health, so it becomes us to imitate Christ in our earnestness with God for them when we die. Though we die, our prayers do not die with us; they outlive us, and those we leave behind may reap the benefit of them when we are turned to dust.

I must profess that I have a high value for this mercy and bless the Lord who gave me a tender father who often poured out his soul to God for me. This stock of prayers and blessings left by him before the Lord I esteem above the fairest inheritance on earth. It is no small mercy to have thousands of prayers lying before the Lord, filed up in heaven for us. Surely our love should not grow cold when our breath does. Oh, that we would remember this duty in our lives and, if God give opportunity, fully discharge it when we die, considering, as Christ did, we will be no more in this world, but they are, in the midst of a defiled world—it is the last office of love that we will ever do for them.

Here we may see what high esteem and value Christ has of believers; this was the treasure that he could not quit, he could not die till he had secured it in a safe hand. "I am coming to you. Holy Father, protect them by the power of your name."

Surely believers are dear to Jesus Christ—and good reason, for he has paid dear for them. Let his last farewell speak for him, how he prized them. What is much on our hearts when we die is dear to us indeed. How dear should Jesus Christ be to us! Were we first and last upon his heart? Did he mind us, did he pray for us, did he so wrestle with God about us when the sorrows of death surrounded him? How much are we committed not only to love him and esteem him while we live, but to be in pangs of love for him when we feel the pangs of death upon us! The very last whisper of our departing souls should be this, Blessed be God for Jesus Christ.

—John Flavel

About midnight Paul and Silas were . . .
singing hymns to God.

—Acts 16:25

This story reveals that which is peculiarly Christian, the victory of the soul over adverse circumstances and the transmutation of opposing forces into allies.[86] Paul who sang that night, in paraphrase, says, "Tribulation works patience, therefore rejoice in tribulation." He says, "Troubles work an eternal glory that far outweighs them all, therefore we will rejoice in our troubles." He says, "Godly sorrow brings repentance." These are things from which the human soul shrinks—tribulation, troubles, sorrow. These things are made the allies of the soul, they work on behalf of the soul. This is the central truth concerning Christian experience: God compels all things to work together for good to those who love him.

The Christian does not say, "What cannot be cured must be endured." Christianity says, rather, that these things must be endured because they are part of the cure. They have the strange and mystic power to make whole and strong and so to lead on to victory and the final glory. Christianity is never the dour pessimism that submits. Christianity is optimism that cooperates with the process because it sees that, through suffering and weakness, joy and triumph must come.

Two men were in Philippi, in the inner prison, in the stocks, in suffering, in sorrow. But they were in God! Their supreme consciousness was not of the prison or the stocks or the pain but of God. They were not indifferent; pain was pain to them, but they realized how all these things were held in the grasp of the King of the perfect order, whom they knew as their Lord and Master, and, consequently, they sang praises.

All this took place at midnight. That accentuates the difficulty, the loneliness and weariness and pain. Yet the phrase is not really "at midnight." "*About* midnight"! To these men midnight was not a definite moment. Midnight is never a stopping place. It is coming, and lo! it is gone.

Midnight, that most terrible hour; but for these men there was no such actual time. It was about midnight, and then they sang, and they sang praises to God.

—G. Campbell Morgan

You are the light of the world.
A city on a hill cannot be hidden.

—Matthew 5:14

This passage of Scripture implies that there is a difference between Christians and other people.[87] It is a radical and permanent distinction as regards their principles of action.

The principles of Christian piety will be in fact developed in the life. By this I mean that those who are truly Christians in their hearts will be in their lives. Now that this will be the case it does not require many words to prove. For the nature of the change is such that it cannot but develop itself. Regeneration effects no direct revolution in the intellect, but it does in the heart—none in the essential stamina of the mind, but it does in the principles of action and in the volitions, desires, and preferences of the individual. Nor is it a slight change. It is so great as to make it proper to apply to it the terms *new creation, new birth,* and *life from the dead.* There is no other change in the human mind like it—none so deep, so thorough, so abiding. This is so clear in the Bible as to need no further proof.

The change in someone's religious views and feelings in regeneration is one that affects that individual not in any one department of life but in all. It is not a revolution whose effects we expect simply in the church or in the family, in the external conduct or in the abandonment of vices, but in all the appropriate circumstances of life. If a revolution like that exist, it will be seen. It will constitute that person a new creation in Christ Jesus.

The world is fitted to develop human principles. The whole arrangement of God's moral government is to show what humanity is and to make the sentence of the day of judgment be seen to be just. People are permitted to become learned, to see whether they are disposed to employ their learning for the welfare of the universe. They are permitted to accumulate wealth, that the native propensities of the heart may be brought out. Objects of fame, of ambition, of pleasure pass before the mind. It is not that God may know, but that a fair trial may be made. Before that trial, condemnation would appear to be unfair. When people have been fairly tried, when virtue and vice, honor and dishonor have been fairly brought before them, it is right that God should address them and say to each, "Bear that character with you to eternity."

—Albert Barnes

> *You are the light of the world.*
> *A city on a hill cannot be hidden.*
>
> —Matthew 5:14

The text is not, "You ought to be the light of the world," but you are; not that Christians should be like a city set on a hill, but an affirmation that they are such.[88] Though exhortations are addressed to Christians in the New Testament urging them to lives of faith, yet they are also addressed as actually putting forth the principles of piety and as true to their God and Savior. "You were once darkness, but now you are light in the Lord" (Eph. 5:8). Many Christians regard the Bible as filled with exhortations that they are not expected to comply with, rather than with statements of what the gospel actually accomplishes among them. God intended that the gospel should have effect, and in fact, the early effect of the gospel was such that Paul could address any church as actually demonstrating the change wrought by the Spirit of God. "You yourselves are our letter" (2 Cor. 3:2), said he to the church at Corinth, the living proof at once of the power of the gospel and of the effect of his ministry. We have fallen on different times. The language addressed to churches is not, "You are . . . ," but, "You ought to be," the consistent followers of the Lord Jesus."

True, the people whom Paul addressed had been heathen and therefore the change would be more obvious. But the ground of the address to the primitive Christians was not what they had been so much as what they then were. Besides, are a people nursed in heathenism—only yesterday degraded and sunk in abomination—to be addressed as actually in advance in Christian principles of the people of our times, trained from their earliest years in the principles of the Christian religion? Are we to expect more living demonstrations of the power of piety from the recovered populations of Athens, Corinth, and Rome than from the people of our times?

No, the gospel considers it as a matter of fact that we can appeal to you and to all Christians and say, "You are . . ."—not you ought to be—"the light of the world." We can address the language of obligation and of duty to the most degraded population on the globe; we can approach the profligate and the profane and the pagan with the language, "You ought to be humble followers of God." We can approach true Christians with the language of certainty and say, "You are the salt of the earth, you are the light of the world."

—Albert Barnes

You are the light of the world.
A city on a hill cannot be hidden.

—Matthew 5:14

No principle in the universe can be brought to bear with such weight as the gospel.[89] Nothing can develop the principles of humanity if not the gospel.

Law, philosophy, morals had failed to restrain and reform. But the gospel has been effective. Millions of women and men have been changed, redeemed, purified, saved. The gospel is powerful enough to overcome all the tendencies of sin. It will unclench the hands of greed, silence the blasphemer, make pure the corrupt heart, and stop the strut of the arrogant. There is not a grasp on gold or pleasure that the gospel has not the power to break. And there is not a sinner who, if he or she fairly comes under its dominion, will not become holy. Your strongest propensities it may subdue. Your proudest systems of morality it may destroy, and your most gigantic schemes of corruption it may demolish—for thousands of such sinners as you it has humbled, prostrated, changed into holy people.

No persecutors are secure that they can accomplish their schemes before they are seized by it. The band sent to arrest the Savior were awed, humbled, convinced by his eloquence, and returned, saying, "No one ever spoke the way this man does."

Now can it be that this mighty gospel—that is dismayed by no crime; that cowers before no propensities; that fears no titles, no splendor, no renown; that throws down arrogance as easily as the tempest does the proudest oak; that can enter any circle of corruption and shed peace around the profane and the scoffer and the drunkard; that carries its principles into the profoundest minds and sheds its humility into the proudest hearts—is it possible that it can exist and not be seen? Can it do all this—and no one know it? Can it live and act thus—and never be made visible?

Then may the light rest on the mountaintop and the vale—and no one see it. Then may the city lift its turrets to the clouds—and be invisible. Then may the ocean swell and surge on the shore—and no one be aware of commotion. It must, it will stand out in human view. If it accomplishes such changes, they will be seen, and if it ever grasps any human spirit, it must show its power in the life.

—Albert Barnes

You are the light of the world. A city on a hill cannot be hidden. . . . In the same way, let your light shine before men.

—Matthew 5:14, 16

Religion brings to life principles that are ultimately to have the ascendancy in the soul.[90] It calls up dormant powers—urges to conflict with the powers of darkness and bids us grapple with invisible and mighty foes. Let Christians contemplate the situation in which we are placed, and then let us ask whether this organization does not intend that our piety will be developed.

What is religion? It intends the subjugation of our natural propensities, the overcoming of our evil passions, the purification of our corrupt hearts, the discipline of wayward and rebellious minds. It demands that chastened and serious feeling should take the place of frivolity; prayer, the place of thoughtlessness; the love of God, the place of the love of fashion; and delight in devotion, the place of delight in amusement and ostentation. The nature of godliness is to stamp our lives in letters indelible, legible to all.

There is enough human opposition to all that is pure and humble to make it indispensable that a line be distinctly drawn between the friends and the foes of God. Christians have been a little band—a remnant amid humanity's tribes. We tread a world in possession of the enemies of God. Our very presence is a rebuke on human pursuits, our views a rejection of the opinions of others, our lives a living reminder of human folly and crime. There is not a single principle of your religion that the people of the world do not at heart hate. There is opposition enough to test Christian character and show what we are. It may meet you in the family—the eye of a father will criticize you for being a Christian, or the tongue of a brother will deride you for your serious piety. It may meet you in the circle of friends—the voice of professed affection will speak of you as superstitious for your regard for God. It may meet you in public and political life and subject the soul to a daily and constant test whether there is strength of devotion sufficient to avow the despised doctrines of the cross and to make them the governing principle of your life.

"Everyone who wants to live a godly life in Christ Jesus will be persecuted" (2 Tim. 3:12), and one design of persecution is to develop the strength of the Christian principle.

—Albert Barnes

You are the light of the world. . . . Let your light shine
before men, that they may see your good deeds and praise
your Father in heaven.

—Matthew 5:14, 16

There is enough affliction in the world to try the Christian.[91] Nor is there any of us who will not have trial, bereavement, and woe. God designs that there the Christian principle will triumph, fully equal to all the pains that we may endure. He varies those afflictions to bring us fully and fairly out. Now he takes away our health, to see how we will bear protracted disease. Now he removes our property, to see how we will bear the loss of an idol. Now he cuts down the child of our hopes and tries whether we will be still and know that he is God. Now he opens before our view our own death, to try whether we have confidence enough in him to commit our departing spirits to his unseen hand. In all these scenes, it is designed that our piety should shine forth, bright and burning.

God has placed us in a world exceptionally adapted to call forth the principles of the Christian—a world where, if those principles are not called forth, it is full proof that they do not exist.

Christians, you hold in your hands that gospel which will send peace around the globe—that gospel of God that can enlighten all nations, alleviate every sorrow, comfort every mourner, and change the outlook of every kingdom and tribe. Nor can you be inactive or undecided. Every time this great question is presented to you, in whatever form, it calls on you to act. Every plan of benevolence that is submitted to you affords an opportunity to test your character and will actually develop that character.

It was precisely this state of things that called forth the ardor of Paul. More, it was the view of the guilt and woes of suffering people that moved the Son of God with compassion and led to the self-denial of his ministry and the agonies of the garden and the cross.

I need not add that if human woes and dangers found their way to God's own Son, it is not to be wondered at that they should find their way also to all his followers. Can any be Christians whose hearts do not respond in this to the feelings of the Lord Jesus? If I have read the oracles of religion aright, they cannot.

—Albert Barnes

*You are the light of the world. . . . Let your light shine
before men, that they may see your good deeds and praise
your Father in heaven.*

—Matthew 5:14, 16

Every Christian is placed amid scenes that will bring out her or his character.[92]

You have a child unrenewed. That child will soon stand at the bar of God, will tread the deep profound of the eternal world, and will live forever. Need we put to Christian parents the question whether that child will live forever in heaven or in hell? There is much in the situation of that child to bring the Christian out and develop the character.

Or you have a parent who is not a Christian. Can there be anything so suited to call forth deep feeling in the youthful Christian as the sight of the venerable parent and the feeling that that parent is going unrenewed to the bar of God?

You are a brother or a sister or a friend. The leaden, slow-moving ages of eternity are before your unconverted friends, and what in all the universe is better suited than this to call forth all the Christian within you to holy effort to save those friends from eternal night?

You are members of a Christian church. Does it slumber? Are there hundreds who profess no interest in all that the Redeemer has done to save them? Are they unrenewed, unpardoned, unconcerned, and unalarmed? They go to eternity, and they appeal to you, Christian, to put forth all your efforts to save them from death.

You live in an age when your influence in the cause of revivals and Christian benevolence may be felt around the globe. The farthest pagan tribe, the foulest cell of guilt and filth and woe, the darkest dungeon of depravity may be reached by your aid. A revival of religion such as existed in the day of Pentecost might be felt in its influence in all this land and in every land.

The making visible of your Christian principles, my companion members of the church, is what the world demands and what the Savior who died asks of you. If his death will not do it, there are no motives in the universe that will. There is no other blood, there are no other groans, there can be no more such dying agonies.

—Albert Barnes

PART TWO

Spring

The bird on the branch, the lily in the meadow, the stag in the forest,
the fish in the sea, and countless joyful people sing: God is love!
But under all these sopranos, as it were a sustained bass part,
sounds the de profundis *of the sacrificed: God is love.*

—Søren Kierkegaard

The kernel of winter itself is spring, or a sleeping summer.

—George MacDonald
in "The Wow O' Rivven"

See how the lilies of the field grow.
—Matthew 6:28

Open your Old Testament and tell me the aspect of nature you most often find there.[1] It is not the world of sunshine and of flower. It is the world of vast and mighty things. We read of the waves that lift themselves to heaven and of the deep places of the unfathomed sea. The stormy wind is the chariot of God. Did thunder reverberate among the mountains? Did the earth reel and tremble in the earthquake? The Jew was awestruck, and worshipped and adored and said it was the voice of the Almighty.

Now turn to the teaching of the Man of Nazareth—"See how the lilies of the field grow." The kingdom of heaven is like the crash of thunder? Not so; the kingdom of heaven is like a mustard seed. It is no longer the things that tower aloft, it is no longer the things that shock or startle—it is not *these* that to the Man of Nazareth are richest in divine significance. It is the vineyard on the sunny hill; it is the lily waving in the field. It is things common and usual and silent that no one had had eyes to see before.

Now do you see the meaning of that change? It lies not in an altered thought of beauty but in an altered thought of the character of God. Tell me that God is the almighty King, and I look for his power in the war of elements. Tell me that his voice is that of Sinai, and it takes the grandest music of the hills to echo it. But tell me that God in heaven is my Father—that I am his child, and that he loves me dearly—and from that moment I look with other eyes on the sunshine and the streamlet and the flower. It is not in terrible or startling things that love delights to body itself forth. Never is love richer in revelation than when it consecrates all that is quiet and lowly. And it was because God was love to Jesus Christ that, when he went abroad into the world of nature, he saw God and his kingdom in the birds and in the thousand lilies of the field. The kind of God you really believe in determines mightily your thought of heaven. And the kind of God you really believe in determines mightily your thought of earth. And this is the gladness of the knowledge of God that has been given us by Christ our Savior, that it sets every common bush afire with him and finds him in every lily of the field.

—George H. Morrison

See how the lilies of the field grow.
—Matthew 6:28

Let me say one thing more that helps to illuminate the mind of Christ.[2] It is how often, when he speaks of nature, he deliberately brings people on the scene. Jesus is not a painter of still life. He loves to have living forms on the scene. He does not regard people as intrusions but always as the completion of the picture. When he walked abroad, he saw more than the lights and shadows of the fields. "A farmer went out to sow his seed"—somehow he could not rest until he had brought a living human being into the picture. And so when he wandered by the Sea of Galilee and watched the waters and listened to the waves, all that, however beautiful, could not content him until the fishers and their nets were in the picture. He could not listen to the chattering sparrows without seeing the human hands that bought and sold them. He could not look at the lilies of the field without seeing Solomon in all his glory.

And it all means that while the love of nature was one of the deepest passions in Christ's heart, it was not a love that led to isolation, but it found its crowning in the love of humanity. There is a way of loving nature that chills a little the feeling for humanity. But when someone loves nature as Jesus Christ loved nature, it will deepen and purify the springs of kinship and issue in service that is not less loyal because the music of hill and dale is in it.

—George H. Morrison

The stone, which was very large, had been rolled away.
—Mark 16:4

Make no effort to hide the fact.[3] Death is the great enigma of life. Humanly speaking, it is an insoluble mystery; it is the one secret of the universe that is kept, the silence that is never broken. Death is one of the rare things that can be predicted of all people, the common end to a path of glory or to a road of shame. To the weary and despairing it may come as a friend; the cynical and disillusioned may meet it with indifference; to the healthy and happy it may appear as a foe. But as friend or foe or cold companion, it comes to all. All our plans for the future are made subject to its approval. There is no earthly tie too sacred for death to loosen. It reduces the exalted and the lowly to the common denominator of dust.

Moreover, the mystery is as old as humanity. From the dimmest beginnings of history, we find people pondering the problem of the beyond. In the upward movement of the human race, we find people nursing their hopes on a variety of dreams and passing in turn from belief in a dim spirit life to the shadowy existence called Sheol and finally to the vision of a life fuller and grander than this. But it was still a mystery. These dreams were *dreams,* interesting speculations, but nothing more. Death was still "the undiscovered country from whose bourn no traveler returns" *(Hamlet).* This was the great stone that blocked the path of human aspiration. What certainty was there of the continuity of life? What modest individual could find in himself or in herself anything worthy to endure for all eternity? Of what abiding worth was love—even our highest—if it ended in the passionless calm of death?

Then came the first Easter day and—*the stone was rolled away!* That stone! Mark says it was very large. And now it is rolled away, for one traveler returned. Death is an abysmal cavern no more, but a tunnel with a golden light at the farther end. It is no more a blind alley but a thoroughfare, no more a cul-de-sac but a highway. The mystery is a mystery no more.

"And," says Paul, "if the Spirit of him who raised Jesus from the dead is living in you, he who raised Christ from the dead will also give life to your mortal bodies through his Spirit, who lives in you" (Rom. 8:11).

—William E. Sangster

> *The stone, which was very large, had been rolled away.*
> —Mark 16:4

Why was the stone rolled away?[4]

Surely it was not rolled away that the risen Lord might come out? Of whatever nature was his resurrection body, the Lord Jesus was independent of doors and indifferent to walls. And yet the stone was rolled away! I think I know why. It was not rolled away that he might come out but that they might go in. It was not part of the *fact*, it was merely a part of the *demonstration*. It was not the means of his exit but the means of their entrance. This it is that makes the resurrection more than a piece of history; it makes it also a pledge. This lifts it above the level of mere news and makes it a promise, for God rolled away the stone not that his Son might rise but that we might know he had risen, that we might steal into the empty tomb and see only "the place where they laid him" (Mark 16:6).

What did the rolled-away stone reveal?

Let us follow the women into the tomb. It is a great hole, you see, hewn in a rock. What? Do you shrink a little because it is a tomb? Did you say it makes you feel eerie?

Not here! Not in the Savior's tomb! It's empty! There's nothing to be seen, only the place where they laid him.

How calm and private that blessed sepulcher must have been after all the dreadful and shameful publicity of the Crucifixion. How quiet and still! How blessedly secluded. Jesus loved solitude, and he had no solitude between Gethsemane and the sepulcher. Working out the time is difficult, but it seems that eight hours after his arrest he was on the cross.

So as he hangs there—the noise, the dust, the pain, the thirst—and perhaps the incessant noise was not the least of his pangs; the crowds, the jeers, the curses, the sobbing women—and he hangs stark naked between earth and heaven.

"It is finished. Father, into your hands I commit my spirit" (John 19:30; Luke 23:46).

And then the sepulcher. Do you still think of a tomb as being cold and eerie? No! No! It is quiet and calm, and our crucified God rests for hours and hours on a cool bed of rock.

—William E. Sangster

*Though he was rich, yet for your sakes he became poor, so
that you through his poverty might become rich.*
—2 Corinthians 8:9

Note how clearly these opening words point to the magnificent riches of Jesus Christ: "though he was rich."[5] If we could take the sum total of all the wealth people have ever known and multiply it a thousandfold, all this would be a mere bagatelle compared with the depth of the riches over which our Lord, as the eternal God, held sway. He was rich in the resources of the entire universe, rich in the exercise of all power in heaven and in earth, in the control of constellations; rich in the directing of the tides, in the shaping of human affairs into history. He was rich in the adoration of the heavenly legions; rich in the glory and purity of his divine sinlessness; rich in truth, in wisdom, and in justice. But—praise his name!—he was rich in love, in mercy, in grace toward a corroding and decaying world that had spurned the guidance of God. So rich that, unfathomable as it may be, he showed compassion for human souls by the magnificence of the sacrifice of which our text speaks: "yet for your sakes he became poor."

We have made the cross the greatest of all human symbols. Yet how little we sometimes comprehend of the love of him who so impoverished himself and died on the accursed tree!

And what a death it was! No matter under what circumstances the Grim Reaper may come, there is always anguish when our loved ones are called home by God. But how more intense was our Savior's crucifixion!—one of the most excruciating tortures ever known.

On the cross, deserted by God and by humanity, is one who in his tortured body bears the crushing weight of all the sins that have ever been committed throughout history. Here, in the poverty of Christ, is the greatest spectacle of love that the human race has ever seen or ever will see. Here, with his divine arms outstretched as though he would embrace sinful humanity in its totality, is God's answer to the plea for the forgiveness of sins, for the power to counteract evil, for the ability to rise up over death. Here, in the abysmal poverty of Christ, is the magnificence of grace—pure, saving, sanctifying grace.

No one is excluded from this all-embracing "for your sakes." Here are the riches of Christ's invitation. "Come to me, all you who are weary and burdened, and I will give you rest."

—Walter A. Maier

A man's spirit sustains him in sickness,
but a crushed spirit who can bear?

—Proverbs 18:14

This world is not the Garden of Eden, and you cannot make it to be so.[6] It is like that garden in this respect, that the serpent is in it, and the trail of the serpent is over everything here.

[Thus,] everyone will have to bear a weakness of some sort or other. To bear that weakness is not difficult when the spirit is sound and strong. The spirit that will best bear weakness is, first of all, a gracious spirit worked in us by the Spirit of God. If you want to bear your trouble without complaining, if you want to sustain your burden without fainting, you must have the life of God within you, you must be born again, you must be in living union with him who is the Strong One and who, by the life that he implants within you, can give you from his own strength. I do not believe that anything but that which is divine will stand the wear and tear of this world's temptations and of this world's trials and troubles.

Further, I think that a sound spirit that can sustain weakness will be a spirit cleansed in the precious blood of Christ. "Conscience doth make cowards of us all" *(Hamlet),* and it is only when conscience is pacified by the application of the sprinkled blood that we are able to sustain our weaknesses. Haven't you sometimes felt that if you had to spend the rest of your life in a dungeon and to lie there, as John Bunyan would have said, till the moss grew on your eyelids, yet, as long as you were sure that you were cleansed from sin by the precious blood of Christ, you could bear it all? Take sin away and give me a spirit washed in the fountain filled with blood, and I can patiently go through anything and everything, the Lord being my Helper.

Next, a [sound] spirit exercises itself daily to a growing confidence in God. The spirit that is to sustain weakness is not a spirit of doubt and fear and mistrust. There is no power about such a spirit as that; it is like a body without bone or sinew or muscle. Strength lies in believing. Someone who can trust can work; someone who can trust can suffer.

I must also add my belief that no spirit can so well endure sickness, loss, trial, sorrow, as a perfectly consecrated spirit. The person who lives only for God's glory looks to see not how to comfort herself or himself but how to most successfully fight the Master's battles.

—C. H. Spurgeon

A man's spirit sustains him in sickness,
but a crushed spirit who can bear?
—Proverbs 18:14

Some have talked about having a crushed spirit.[7] One has been disappointed in love—sad, but a trial that can be endured. We have no right to love the creature so much as to make it our idol. Some have been disappointed in their ambition. But who are you that you should not be disappointed, and what are you that you should have everything your way? Surely, if the Lord were to deal with us according to our sins, we would have something to bear worse than the present disappointment. Do not, therefore, allow these things to destroy your peace. About such crushed hearts as these is a good deal of sin mingled with the sorrow, and a great deal of pride, a great deal of creature-worship and of idolatry. Depend on it, if you make an idol, and God loves you, he will break it.

A mother wore black for years after her child had been taken away; she had never forgiven her God for what he had done. Now this is an evil that is to be rebuked. I dare not comfort those whose spirits are crushed in this fashion. If they carry even their mourning too far, we must say to them, "Dear friend, isn't this rebellion against God? May this not be petulance instead of patience?" We may sorrow and be grieved when we lose our loved ones, for we are human, but we must moderate our sorrow and bow our wills to the will of the Lord, for aren't we also people of God?

Some have crushed spirits through the cruelty of people, the unkindness of children, the ingratitude of those they have helped. It is a terrible crushing when one who should have been your friend becomes your foe and when you, like your Lord, also have your Judas. We should cry to God to help us bear this trial, for after all, who are we that we should not be despised? The wise expect this kind of trial and, expecting it, are not disappointed when it comes.

Others have been crushed by sorrow. They have had affliction upon affliction, loss after loss, bereavement after bereavement. And we ought to feel these things. Still, every Christian should cry to God for strength to bear repeated losses and bereavements. If we yield to temptation and begin to complain of God for permitting such things to come on us, we will only wound ourselves all the more. Let us be submissive to the hand that wields the rod of correction.

—C. H. Spurgeon

A man's spirit sustains him in sickness,
but a crushed spirit who can bear?

—*Proverbs* 18:14

This is the kind of crushed spirit I mean.[8] When a soul is under a deep and terrible sense of sin—when the notion of what guilt is first comes clearly home, and the soul sees that God must be as certainly just as he is good, then discovers that it has angered infinite love, has provoked almighty grace, and has made its best Friend to be, necessarily, its most terrible foe. A person in such a condition will have a crushed spirit such as none can bear.

Sometimes the spirit is crushed by the fierce temptations of Satan. I hope that you do not at all understand what this means, but there are some who do. Satan tempts them to doubt, tempts them to sin, to blasphemy, even to curse God and die. That temptation brings a crushed spirit. God save you from it, if you have fallen under its terrible power!

A crushed spirit may also come through desertion by God. The believer has not walked carefully and has fallen into sin, and God has hidden his face. A true child of God has played with sin and has been brought back to the Lord but goes on with an aching heart and limping limbs. Some who were once very bright stars who have been for a while eclipsed will never be able to escape from a certain sense of darkness that is still on them. Therefore, beloved, be very careful that you do not backslide, for if you do, you will have a crushed spirit that you will not know how to bear.

I believe that some of God's children have crushed spirits entirely through mistake. I am always afraid of those who get certain wild notions into their heads, ideas that are not true, I mean. They are very happy while they hold those high notions, and they look down on others who do not go kite-flying or balloon-sailing as they do. I think to myself, sometimes, *How will they come down when their precious balloon bursts?* I have seen them believe this and believe that, which they were not warranted by the Scriptures to believe. But when you come down again, you will begin to condemn yourself for things that you need not condemn, and you will be distressed and miserable in your spirit because of a disappointment that you need never have had if you had walked humbly with your God. For my own part, I am content to abide in the old way, myself ever a poor, needy, helpless sinner, finding everything I need in Christ.

—C. H. *Spurgeon*

A man's spirit sustains him in sickness,
but a crushed spirit who can bear?
—Proverbs 18:14

How are we to avoid a crushed spirit so far as it is evil?[9]

First, if you are happy in the Lord and full of joy and confidence, avoid a crushed spirit by *never offending your conscience.* Labor with all your might to be true to the light that God has given you, to be true to your understanding of God's Word, and to follow the Lord with all your heart. Nothing will come to you in a time of sorrow, pain, and brokenness of spirit so sharply as a sense of sins of omission or sins of commission. When the light of God's presence is gone from you, you will begin sadly to say, "Why did I do this? Why didn't I do that?" Therefore, dear friends, endeavor to live in the time of your joy so that, if there ever should come times of depression, you may not have to remember neglected duties or willful wickedness.

[Second], if you would avoid a crushed spirit, *get a clear view of the gospel.* Spell [that glorious word *grace*] in your own soul—free, rich, sovereign grace—and know that you, a guilty, lost sinner, are saved as a sinner, that Jesus Christ came into the world to save sinners, that he died for the ungodly, and that your standing is not in yourself or in your own attainments but wholly and entirely in the finished work of the Lord Jesus Christ.

[Third], you will avoid a crushed spirit *by living very near to God.* The sheep that gets bitten by the wolf is the one that does not keep near the shepherd. It has often happened that, when I have been preaching, there has been somebody dreadfully hurt. Yes, even the Good Shepherd's dog bites sometimes. But if you had kept near the Shepherd, his dog would not have bitten you, for neither the dog nor the wolf will bite those who are near him. But if you get away from holy living and close communion with God, you may expect to get a crushed spirit.

So much, then, for the prevention, which is better than a cure. God help us all to make good use of it.

—C. H. Spurgeon

By his wounds we are healed.

—Isaiah 53:5

There is only One who can heal a crushed spirit.[10] If you would be healed of the bleeding wounds of your heart, flee to Christ. You did so once; do it again. Go to Christ now, though you may have gone to him a hundred times before.

One thing, however, I would say to one who has a really crushed heart. Remember Christ's sympathy with you. O you who are tossed with tempest and not comforted, your Lord's vessel is in the storm with you. Yes, he is in the vessel with you. There is not a pang that rends the believer's heart but he has felt it first. He drinks out of the cup with you. Is it very bitter? He had a cup full of it for every drop that you taste. This ought to comfort you. I know of no better remedy for the heart's trouble in a Christian than to feel, *My Master himself takes no better portion than that which he gives to me.*

Also let me recommend, as a choice remedy for a crushed spirit, an enlarged view of the love of God. I wish that some of you who have a crushed spirit would give God credit for being as kind as you are yourself. You would not permit your child to endure a needless pain if you could remove it; neither does God willingly bring affliction or grief to his children. He would not allow you to be cast down but would cheer and comfort you, if it was good for you. His delight is that you should be happy and joyful. Take the comfort that he has set before you in his Word; he has put it there on purpose for you. Dare to take it, and think well of God, and it will be well with your soul.

If this does not cure the evil, remember the great brevity of all your afflictions, after all. What if you are a child of God who even has to go to bed in the dark? You will wake up in the eternal daylight. What if, for the time being, you are in grief? You have had to suffer grief in all kinds of trials, and you will come out of it. You are not the first child of God who has been depressed or troubled. Yes, among the noblest men and women who ever lived there has been much of this kind of thing. Do not, therefore, think that you are quite alone in your sorrow. Bow your head and bear it, if it cannot be removed, for only a little while, and every cloud will be swept away, and you, in the cloudless sunlight, will behold your God. Meanwhile, his strength is sufficient for you. The Lord grant his comforts to you, for his Son Jesus Christ's sake!

—C. H. Spurgeon

*And I saw what looked like a sea of glass mixed with fire
and, standing beside the sea, those who had been victorious
over the sea.*

—Revelation 15:2

With all the mystery of the book of Revelation, one thing we are sure of: in it we have the summing up of the moral processes of all time.[11]

I speak only of moral contest, of this struggle with suffering and wickedness, of trial, of the state that earnest people, conscious of their own inner lives, know full well. What will be the end of it all?

I do not know in full what is intended by this term "the beast." I think it means in its largest sense the power of evil in all its earthly manifestations, all that is low and base and tries to drag down what is high and noble, all sin and temptation, so that "those who had been victorious over the beast" are those who have come out of sin holy and out of trial pure and, out of much tribulation, have entered the kingdom of heaven.

These will walk on "a sea of glass mixed with fire." The sea of glass—calm, clear, placid—evidently that is the symbol of repose, of rest, of peace. And fire, testing all things, consuming what is evil, purifying what is good, never resting a moment, never sparing pain; fire, all through the Bible, is the symbol of active trial of every sort, of struggle. The "sea of glass mixed with fire" is repose mingled with struggle. It is peace and rest and achievement, with the power of trial and suffering yet alive and working within it.

This is our doctrine: the permanent value of trial—that when you conquer your adversaries and your difficulties, it is not as if you never had encountered them. Your victory is colored with the hard struggle that won it. Your sea of glass is always mixed with fire, just as this peaceful crust of earth on which we live, with its wheat fields, vineyards, orchards, and flower beds is full still of the power of the convulsion that wrought it into its present shape, of the floods and volcanoes and glaciers that have rent it or drowned it or tortured it. Just so, the life that has been overturned and overturned by the strong hand of God, filled with the deep, revolutionary forces of suffering, and purified by the strong fires of temptation keeps its long discipline forever. There roots in that discipline the deepest growths of the most sunny and luxuriant spiritual life that it is ever able to attain.

—Phillips Brooks

Standing beside the sea, those who had been victorious
over the beast . . . held harps given them by God.
—*Revelation* 15:2

However much we recognize the value of trial, the variations in the effect of trial on character will perplex us.[12] We meet with so many people whose characters seem not to be elevated or fired but depressed and smothered by suffering. They come out of adversity with a loss of what was noblest and most attractive in them before. Some who were smooth and gracious in health become rough and peevish in sickness. Some who were cordial and liberal in wealth turn reserved and tight as poverty overtakes them. If trial kindles and stirs up some sluggish natures, on the other hand it quenches and subdues many vigorous and ardent hearts and sends them crushed to their graves. It seems as if trouble, trial, and suffering were in the world like the fabled river in Epirus, of which the legend ran that its waters kindled every unlighted torch that was dipped into them and quenched every torch that was lighted.

But however much difficulty this may give us in single cases, it fits in well with our general doctrine. For it makes trial a necessary element in all perfected character. If so much character goes to pieces at its first contact with suffering and struggle, then all the more we see the need of keeping struggle and suffering as tests of character.

In sickrooms, in prisons, in dreary unsympathetic homes, in stores where failure brooded like the first haze of coming eastern storms, everywhere people have suffered, to some among the sufferers this truth has come. They lifted up their heads and were strong. Life was a new thing to them. They were no longer the victims of a mistaking chance or of a malignant devil but the subjects of an educating God. They no longer just waited doggedly for the trouble to pass away. They did not know that it would ever pass away. If it ever did, it must go despoiled of its power. Whether it passed or stayed, that was not the point, but that the strength that was in it should pass into the sufferer who wrestled with it, that the fire should not only make the glass and then go out, leaving it cold and hard and brittle. The fire must abide in that glass that it has made, giving it forever its own warmth and life and elastic toughness. This is the great revelation of the permanent value of suffering.

—*Phillips Brooks*

And I saw what looked like a sea of glass mixed with fire
and, standing beside the sea, those who had been victorious
over the beast. . . . They held harps given them by God.
—Revelation 15:2

[This doctrine of the permanent value of suffering] touches all the variations of Christian feeling.[13] In almost every Christian's experience come times of despondency and gloom, when there seems to be a depletion of the spiritual life, when the fountains that used to burst with water are grown dry; when love is loveless, hope hopeless, and enthusiasm so dead that it is hard to believe that it ever lived. At such times, there is nothing for us to do but hold to the bare, rocky truths of our religion, as shipwrecked people hang to a ragged cliff when the waves and eddies try to sweep them back into the deep. The rough rock tears their hands, but still they cling.

And so the bare truths of God and Christ, of responsibility and eternity are stripped for the time of all dearness. Then when the tide returns, and we can [again] hold ourselves lightly, when faith grows easy and God and Christ and responsibility and eternity are once more glory and delight, then certainly there is something new in them, a new color, a new warmth. The soul has caught a new idea of God's love when it has not only been fed but rescued by him. The sheep has a new conception of its shepherd's care when it has not merely been made to lie down in green pastures but also hears the voice of him who had left the ninety-nine in the wilderness and gone after that which had wandered astray.

The same applies to doubt and belief. "Why do things seem so hard to me?" you say. There is a willful and an unwilling unbelief. If it is willful unbelief, the fault is yours. You must not complain that the sun does not shine because you shut your eyes. But if it is unwilling unbelief—if you really want the truth, if you are not afraid to submit to it as soon as you see it, and something in your constitution or circumstances or in the aspect of Christian truth that has been held out to you makes it difficult for you to grasp—you are not to be pitied. To climb the mountain on its hardest side, where its granite ribs press out most ruggedly to make your climbing difficult, where you must skirt chasms and clamber down and up ravines, all this has its compensation. You know the mountain better when you reach its top. It's a nobler and so a dearer thing.

—Phillips Brooks

And I saw what looked like a sea of glass mixed with fire
and, standing beside the sea, those who had been victorious
over the beast. . . . They held harps given them by God.
—Revelation 15:2

If you keep seeking the truth, then somewhere, here or in some better world, the truth will come to you, and when it comes, the peace and the serenity of it will be made vital with the energy of your long search.[14]

Simon Peter is forgiven, becomes the preacher of the first sermon, the converter of the first Gentiles, the champion of faith. But he is always the same Simon Peter who denied his Master and struggled with himself on the crucifixion night. Paul mounts to the third heaven, hears wonderful voices, sees unutterable things, but he never ceases to be the Paul who stood by at the stoning of Stephen. You and I come by Christ's grace into communion with God, but does the power of our conversion ever leave us?

Aren't we prodigals still, with the best robe and the ring and the fatted calf before us in our father's house, conscious that our filial love is full of the repentance that first made us turn homeward from among the swine? The saved world never can forget that it was once the lost world.

[And] isn't a "sea of glass mixed with fire" a graphic picture of rest pervaded with activity—of contemplation pervaded and kept alive by work and service? Heaven will not be idleness, not any mere dreaming over the spiritual repose that has been forever won, but active, tireless, earnest work—fresh, lively enthusiasm for the high labors that eternity will offer. These inspirations will play through our repose and make it more mighty in the service of God.

That life which we dream of in ourselves, we see in Jesus. Where was there ever gentleness so full of energy? What life so still [yet] so pervaded with untiring and restless power? Who ever knew the purposes for which he worked to be so sure, yet so labored for them as if they were uncertain?

As more and more we get the victory over the beast, we too, are lifted up to walk where he walked. For this, all trial, all suffering, and all struggle are sent. May God grant us all much of that grace through which we can be more than conquerors through him who loved us and so begin now to walk with him in white on the sea of glass mixed with fire.

—Phillips Brooks

There will be no more . . . pain.
—*Revelation 21:4*

Now to show you the place that pain has in our beings, there are some facts I want to bring before you.[15] And the first is that our capacity for pain is greater than our capacity for joy. You experience, for instance, a great joy. Does that prolong its sway through the long months? Don't you know how it exhausts itself and dies, as Shakespeare says, in its own too much? But now you experience great pain, and I never heard that that must exhaust itself—it may continue with someone for years. That means that our capacity for pain is deeper than our capacity for joy. It means that we are so fashioned by the Infinite that the undertone of life is one of sorrow. And I mention that to show you how human nature, when you come to understand it in the deeps, is in unison with the message of the Cross.

Another fact is that pain is at the root of life and growth. It is not through its pleasures but through its pains that the world is carried to the higher levels.

It is through suffering that we are born, and it is through suffering that we are fed. It is through agony that we have won our property; it is through blood that we have reached our freedom. It is through pain—pain infinite and unutterable, the pain that was endured by Christ on Calvary—that you and I are ransomed and redeemed. Now that is a fact, explain it how you will. I do not deny that pain may be a curse; remember that it is also a power. We owe our laws to it, and all our art. We owe to it our immortal books and our salvation. We owe to it the fact that we are here and able to look the problem in the face.

The third fact I note is that in every country and in every age people have looked on suffering and pain as something that was acceptable to God. It hints at something mysterious in pain. People feel instinctively that in the bearing of it there is some hope of fellowship with heaven. An instinct that is universal is something you do well not to despise.

—George H. Morrison

> *There will be no more . . . pain.*
> —Revelation 21:4

That leads me to touch on the purifying power of pain.[16] Now I am far from saying that pain always purifies. We have all known cases where it has not done so. We have known people who were hardened and embittered by the cup of suffering they had to drink. But who has not known some life that was transfigured not by the glad radiance of joy but by bearing the cross of pain? How many shallow people has pain deepened! How many hardening hearts has it made tender! How many has it checked, and checked effectively, when they were running headlong to their ruin! How many has it weaned from showy things, giving a vision that was fair and true, steadying them into a sweet sobriety as if something of the unseen were in their sight! Pain may warn us of the approach of evil. It is the alarm bell that nature rings. Pain may be used in the strong hand of God as a punishment of the sin we have committed. But never forget that far above such ministries, pain, when it is willingly accepted, is one of the choicest instruments of purifying that is wielded by the love of heaven. Fight against it and it shatters you. All the tools of God have double edges. Rebel against it as a thing of cruelty, and all the light of life may be destroyed. But take it up, absorb it in your life, weave it into the fabric of your being, and God will bring the blossom from the thorn.

One of the hardest questions in the world is why the innocent should have to suffer so. There is no perfect answer to that question, nor ever shall be on this side of the grave. But isn't there at least a partial answer in what I have been trying to say? If pain were a curse—and nothing but a curse—well might we doubt the justice on the throne, but if pain is a ladder to a better life, then light falls on the sufferings of the innocent. It is not the anger of heaven that is striking them. It may be the love of heaven that is blessing them.

There are always tears and blood on the steps that lead people heavenward, to where the angels are. Mark you, not by the fraction of a penny's weight does that lighten the guilt of anyone who causes suffering. It only shows us how the love of God can take the curse and turn it to a blessing.

—George H. Morrison

There will be no more . . . pain.
—Revelation 21:4

What has the gospel done to help us to bear pain?[17]

1. The gospel has quieted those questionings that are often sorer than the pain itself. It has helped us to believe that God is love, in the teeth of all the suffering in the world. Have you ever noticed about Jesus Christ that he was never perplexed by the great fact of pain? Death troubled him, for he was moved in spirit and troubled when he stood before the grave of Lazarus. But there is no trace that the dark fact of pain did so—yet was there ever one on earth so sensitive to pain as Jesus Christ? Here was someone who saw pain at its bitterest, yet not for an instant did he doubt his Father. Here was one who had to suffer terribly, yet, through all his sufferings, God loved him—it is these facts that, for the believing soul, silence the obstinate questionings forever. We may not see why we should have to suffer. We may not see why our loved ones have to suffer. Now we know in part and see in part. But we see Jesus, and that is enough for us. We see how he trusted. We know how he was loved. And knowing that, we may doubt many things, but we never can doubt the love of God again, nor Christ's promise never to leave us.

2. The gospel has helped us here by giving us the hope of immortality. It has set our pain in quite a new environment, that of an eternal hope. I wonder if you have ever thought of the place and power of hope in human suffering? Hope is mighty in all we have to bear. When once you get the glow of a great hope right in the heart of what you have to suffer, I tell you that that suffering is transfigured. It is just there that Jesus Christ steps in. He has brought immortality to light.

3. Christ has helped us to bear suffering by the medical science and skill he has inspired. And I close with that, just mentioning it because I am speaking on Hospital Sunday. As a simple matter of historical fact, our hospitals are in the world today not because people are tenderer of heart but because Jesus lived and Jesus died. Without Christ, we would have had no Florence Nightingale. Without Christ, we would never have had Lord Lister—think what that would have meant for countless sufferers! Tell me if you have ever realized what Jesus Christ has done for the community. If you have, go out and reverence him. Go out into the night and call him wonderful. Go out into the night and say, "God helping me, I will follow that leader to the end."

—George H. Morrison

Who among you fears the LORD and obeys the word of his
servant? Let him who walks in the dark, who has no light,
trust in the name of the LORD and rely on his God.
—Isaiah 50:10

Why do the friends of God pass down the vale of suffering, darkness, and tears?[18] There are some partial answers to which our attention may be called. I say, partial answers. They must be partial. The full-orbed and complete answer we must wait for, until we read it yonder in the golden glow of the land and life above.

For one thing, trouble, if rightly used, enables us to honor God. Trouble, then, is a trust, and we are thus to receive it. We understand about other things being trusts. If you have an education, you must answer for those superior attainments. There is the one who can sing so the hearts are enchanted by the music; that singer must answer for that gift. If you are rich, you must answer for it. Those who make money must answer for that capacity. Whatever our gifts or capacities, all of them are to be received as trusts from God, to be used in his name to help humanity. Now, along with other trusts comes trouble. Trouble is to be received, however it comes, as a trust, and we are to bear it, we are to meet it, we are to go through it, we are to face it like we ought, as a trust from God, to be used for the glory of his great name.

There was a time in my life when, for days and days, the only book I wanted to read was the book of Job. I read it through and through and through—that book of Job, that tells how the human heart is swept in its deepest depths of suffering and darkness, and yet how God blesses it, brings it up and out, and sets the soul again in the high place of safety and peace. Trouble rightly borne honors God. Be careful, when trouble comes, how you behave. No matter what the trouble is, no matter how it came about, God is dishonored if a Christian does not bear the fiery trial like he or she ought to bear it. You are being tested for God, and you will dishonor him outrageously or you will honor him gloriously, according to your behavior when trouble is on. Remember that.

If you carp, quibble, criticize, murmur, and are evil in your speech, oh, how you will dishonor God! Trouble rightly borne will surely honor God.

—George W. Truett

Who among you fears the LORD and obeys the word of his
servant? Let him who walks in the dark, who has no light,
trust in the name of the LORD and rely on his God.
—Isaiah 50:10

[Darkness and suffering and tears] furnish an occasion for God to bestow his grace.[19] If I may so put it, they give God a platform on which to stand and do his great work. For example, there is a lawyer, well trained in the schools, who has received a diploma and is ready for the noble calling. Now, if the lawyer is to evince skill in legal learning, that lawyer must have a case. Even so, the Lord Jesus Christ, if he is to show people what he can do for them in the black Fridays, in the darkest vales, in the most dreadful hour, then the hour of trouble and darkness must come, that he may come and extricate us from it.

[Trouble] is the strange way of preparing such a friend of God to be a helper of others as she or he otherwise never could have been. There is no teacher like experience. Paul says God "comforts us in all our troubles, so that we can comfort those in any trouble with the comfort we ourselves have received from God" (2 Cor. 1:4).

Oh, my friends, suffering is often the way by which we are fitted to help a broken, bruised, sinning, suffering world as we never otherwise could help it!

Many a time, [suffering] is necessary discipline for us in the building of our own characters. Mark you, God's great concern is for what we are, not what we seem to be, for our inner, deeper selves. Again and again, trouble is God's disciplinary teacher to give us the experience that will refine us, teach us, cleanse us, and fit us, that we may be and do in God's sight what he desires. You and I are the pupils at school, and God has many teachers. One of his teachers that comes robed in black is suffering, is trial, is deepest, darkest testing. David said, "It was good for me to be afflicted so that I might learn your decrees" (Ps. 119:71). Oh, we need, my friends, to be disenchanted! Ease is the bane of everything that is good. We need to be disenchanted, so that our trust will not be in the flesh nor in the world, but fixed firmly on the living God.

—George W. Truett

> *Who among you fears the* LORD *and obeys the word of his*
> *servant? Let him who walks in the dark, who has no light,*
> *trust in the name of the* LORD *and rely on his God.*
>
> —Isaiah 50:10

Some of you have been called to pass through deep troubles—fiery troubles.[20] You will fatally err if you go anywhere else but to God. There is your anchor. If you have an anchor, you do not keep it in the ship when you need to anchor the ship. You let it down. So our anchor is not in us at all. We are anchored to Christ. That anchor will hold. And if you do not fix firmly on God in the dark and trying day, you have serious cause to suspect whether you have ever really trusted him at all. Trust him in the dark day, because God's grace and promises are designed for dark days, just as great ships are built to withstand the stoutest storm that ever drives the seas. Why should you trust God on the dark and cloudy day? Because such a faith will glorify God. With your submission to God's will—patient, meek, and uncomplaining—if you will trust him like that, you will be a blessed witness for God.

Why are you to trust him on the dark and cloudy day? Because it will not always stay dark and cloudy, thank God! Sure are his promises that "weeping may remain for a night, but rejoicing comes in the morning" (Ps. 30:5). It will not stay dark. There comes a sweet, fair morning, tinted and glinted with all the favor of God, and you are to look forward to that morning, cling to him, and go your way, knowing that all will be well.

Take one step at a time, and then take another step, and then take another step, and he will bring you into the fair day, and you will sing with the poet:

> I would rather walk with Christ in the dark
>   Than to walk alone in the light.
> I would rather walk with him by faith
>   Than to walk by myself with sight.

Stay yourself on him today, and from this day forward cleave ever to him with unhesitating trust, and then you may sing with the psalmist that "the LORD will fulfill his purpose for [us]" (Ps. 138:8), because his mercy endures forever.

—George W. Truett

> *If you have raced with men on foot and they have worn*
> *you out, how can you compete with horses? If you stumble*
> *in safe country, how will you manage in the thickets*
> *by the Jordan?*
>
> —Jeremiah 12:5

Jeremiah is being hardened in the fire like a Damascus blade.[21] Depressed, sick with his failure in the city, he longs for the quiet village of his youth. He turns to home like a tired bird to its nest—to find in the nest a scorpion! His townspeople, his own family, dealt treacherously with him. He is not only without friends, but sees friends become foes.

This experience through which the prophet passes is a cruel one. But he never lets go of God. The complaint is not the seeming prosperity of the wicked but his own pain and sorrow and terrible adversity.

The complaint here is answered by a countercomplaint. Jeremiah's charge against God, of injustice, is met by God's charge against Jeremiah, of weakness. The "thickets by the Jordan" means the dangerous ground by the river. It is a jungle of tangled bush where wild beasts lurk. The answer to the complaint against the hardness of his lot is that it will be harder still. He has only been racing with men on foot so far—he will have to contend with horses—then he may have cause to speak of weariness. He has only been living in a land of peace so far—he will have to dwell in the jungle, and then he may talk of danger.

Does it seem an unfeeling answer? It was the answer Jeremiah needed. He needed to be braced, not pampered. He is taught the need of endurance. It is a strange cure for cowardice, a strange remedy for weakness, yet effective. The tear-stained face is lifted up, calm once more. God appeals to the strength in Jeremiah, not to the weakness. By God's grace I will fight, and fighting fall if need be. By God's grace I will contend even with horses, and I will go to the thickets by the Jordan. This was the result on Jeremiah, and it was the result required. Only a heroic soul could do the heroic work needed by Israel and by God, and it was the greatest heroism of all that was needed—the heroism of endurance.

Nothing worth doing can be done without iron resolution. It is the spirit that never knows defeat, that cannot be worn out, that has taken its stand and refuses to move. This is the "patience" about which the Bible is full, not the counterfeit that so often passes for patience, but the power to endure all things, to die—harder still sometimes to continue to live.

—Hugh Black

*If you have raced with men on foot and they have worn
you out, how can you compete with horses? If you stumble
in safe country, how will you manage in the thickets
by the Jordan?*

—Jeremiah 12:5

Christ's church has survived through her power to endure.[22] She was willing to give up anything to hold her ground, to pour out blood like water in order to take root. The mustard seed, planted with tears and watered with blood, gripped the soil, twining its roots round the rocks, and spread out its branches a little fuller.

It is a true parable of the church. It was given to them not only to believe in Christ, but also to suffer for his sake. When their persecutors thought they were scattered like chaff, it turned out that they were scattered like seed. The omnipotent power of Rome was impotent before such resolution. The church met the Empire and broke it, through the sheer power to endure.

It is the same secret of success for the individual spiritual life. Patience is the Christian's safety. Even if all else is lost, it saves the soul, the true life. It gives fiber to the character. It purifies the heart, as gold in the furnace.

What do we know of this heroic endurance? We are so easily dispirited, not only in Christian enterprise, but also in personal Christian endeavor. We are so soon tempted to give up. The Enemy is too hard to dislodge; sin in us is too stubborn; evil is too deeply rooted; the kingdom of heaven of our dreams is impossible. What are we here in this world for? To look for a soft place? To find an easy task? What have we done, the best of us, for God or for humanity? What have we endured for the dream's sake? What have we given up in our self-indulgent lives? What sacrifice have we ever made?

Must Jeremiah harden himself forever and stiffen himself always to endure? Must we resist forever the sins of our own hearts? Must we protest forever against the evil of the world? Forever, if need be! To begin to serve God is to serve him forever. It knows no cessation. Complaining dies in his presence.

If God sends someone to the thickets of Jordan, it is well. That individual will not go alone. A land of peace without God is a terror. The jungle of Jordan with God is peace.

—Hugh Black

It is by grace you have been saved, through faith.
—Ephesians 2:8

What do we mean by *grace?*[23] The old definition called it "the free, unmerited favor of God." On that definition I cannot improve. It means that at the heart of all true communion with God there lies this deep truth, that God himself took the initiative. He loves us better than we can ever love him. He loves us with a love that does not depend on any answering love of ours. We do not have to earn his love any more than we earned our mothers' love. We have only to receive it.

Always the initiative is from God! When you first came to him, you came because he first drew you. The very faith by which you lay hold of him is not of yourself, this also is a gift of God. Nor is it only in the beginning that your salvation is God's free gift. Every onward step you have made in your spiritual pilgrimage has been possible by some bestowing of his grace. Even the life of holiness, to which all the time he is seeking to bring you—the Christlike quality that he wants to repeat in all of his children—even that you do not have to achieve but to receive. It is a gift of God.

There is in us something that rejects the idea of this free and generous forgiving. Of course it is pride, the deadliest of all the deadly sins. Bernard Shaw may in some things, I suppose, be taken as an example of the modern mind. He says, "Forgiveness is a beggar's refuge. We must pay our debts." So speaks the modern world, but, my dear friends, we cannot pay our debts. We will never be able to pay our debts to God. As our spiritual predecessors saw so clearly, the only language that we can honestly use in the presence of our awful debt is this prayer:

> Just as I am, without one plea
> But that Thy blood was shed for me,
> And that Thou bidd'st me come to Thee,
> O Lamb of God, I come.
>
> —Charlotte Elliott

In response to this coming, the free, unmerited favor of God comes to us, cancels the debt, imputes the righteousness of Christ to sinners such as we are, and progressively, as we live with him, also imparts that righteousness.

It is a part of the Holy Spirit's work, too, to make us holy. He sets out not only to justify us, but to sanctify us, and all the time the whole work is by grace.

—William E. Sangster

It is by grace you have been saved, through faith.
—Ephesians 2:8

There are many definitions of *faith*.[24] It means to "trust." Faith is not merely an expression of belief. It is a venture of the whole personality in trusting One who is worthy.

Nor is it right to think, as some people do, that faith belongs only to religion. All life is by faith. When you board a bus you have faith, faith that the driver knows his or her job. When you go to a restaurant for a meal you have faith, faith that the food is wholesome and well cooked.

Even science proceeds largely by faith. No one can prove the great principles on which scientists proceed, such principles as the uniformity of nature and the conservation of energy. But to proceed at all, scientists must assume such basic principles. All business, too, is built on credit. The word *credit* is simply the Latin form of *trust*.

We find faith everywhere. But only in religion do we find it supremely. Just as in the scale of values nothing about a person is so precious as the soul, so faith through which that soul can be saved must ever be the supreme expression of human trust.

If you have never yet ventured on Christ, I plead with you to do so now. If you have already received a timid faith, I urge you to venture on him far more completely, to recognize that the real purpose of faith is to unite the person who believes with the person on whom he or she believes, and that only as you are united with Christ through faith can you have the quality of life that is the pure silver of eternity.

This is the glad, good news that the evangelists carried everywhere in the first century and that their true followers have echoed in all the centuries since.

—William E. Sangster

When you come, bring the cloak that I left
with Carpus at Troas.

—2 Timothy 4:13

How utterly forsaken the apostle was by his friends![25] If he had no cloak of his own, couldn't someone lend him one? Ten years before, the apostle was brought in chains along the Appian Way to Rome. Fifty miles before he reached Rome, members of the church came to meet him. When he came within twenty miles of the city, a still larger posse of the disciples came to escort him, so that the chained prisoner Paul went into Rome attended by all the believers in that city. But, ten years later, nobody comes to visit him. He is confined in prison, and they do not even know where he is, so Onesiphorus, when he comes to Rome, has to seek him out. People have so forgotten him and the church has so despised him that he is friendless. The Philippian church, ten years before, had made a collection for him when he was in prison. Now he is old, and no church remembers him. Poor soul, he served his God and worked himself down to poverty for the church's sake, yet the church has forsaken him! Oh! how great must have been the anguish of the loving heart of Paul at such ingratitude.

What patience does this teach to those similarly situated! Has it fallen to your lot to be forsaken by friends? Were there other times when your name was the symbol of popularity? And has it come to this now, that you are forgotten as dead, out of mind? In your greatest trials do you find your fewest friends? Have those who once loved and respected you fallen asleep in Jesus? And have others turned out to be hypocritical and untrue? What are you to do now? You are to remember this case of the apostle. It is put here for your comfort. He had to pass through as deep waters as any that your are called to ford, yet remember he says, "But the Lord stood at my side and gave me strength" (2 Tim. 4:17). So now, when people desert you, God will be your friend. This God is our God forever and ever—not in sunshiny weather only, but forever and ever. This God is your God in dark nights as well as in bright days. Go to him, spread your complaint before him. Murmur not. If Paul had to suffer desertion, you must not expect better usage. This is common to the saints. David had his Ahithophel, Christ his Judas, Paul his Demas, and can you expect to fare better than they? As you look at that old cloak, as it speaks of human ingratitude, be of good courage and wait on the Lord, for he will strengthen your heart.

—C. H. Spurgeon

For Thy name's sake, O LORD, pardon mine iniquity,
for it is great.

—Psalm 25:11 KJV

It is evident by some passages in this psalm that when it was penned it was a time of affliction and danger with David.[26] His distress makes him think of his sins and leads him to confess them and to cry to God for pardon, as is suitable in a time of affliction.

It is observable in the text what arguments the psalmist makes use of in pleading for pardon.

First, he pleads for pardon *for God's name's sake.* He has no expectation for pardon for the sake of any righteousness or worthiness of his or for any good deeds he had done or any compensation he had made for sins. If human righteousness could be a just plea, David would have had as much to plead as most.

Second, the psalmist pleads the *greatness of his sins* as an argument for mercy. He does not plead his own righteousness or the smallness of his sins. He does not say, "Pardon my iniquity, for I have done much good to counterbalance it," or "Pardon my iniquity, for it is small and you have no great reason to be angry with me." But, "Pardon my iniquity, for it is great." He enforces his prayer with this consideration, that his sins are very heinous.

But how could he make this a plea for pardon? Because the greater his iniquity was, the more need he had of pardon. It is as much as if he had said, "Pardon my iniquity, for it is so great that I cannot bear the punishment. My sin is so great that I am in need of pardon. My case will be very miserable unless you are pleased to pardon me." He makes use of the greatness of his sin to enforce his plea for pardon as someone would make use of the greatness of calamity in begging for relief. A beggar who begs for bread will plead the greatness of his poverty and necessity. And God allows such a plea as this, for he is moved to mercy toward us by nothing in us but the misery of our case. He does not pity sinners because they are worthy but because they need his pity.

—Jonathan Edwards

For Thy name's sake, O Lord, pardon mine iniquity,
for it is great.

—Psalm 25:11 KJV

The mercy of God is as sufficient for the pardon of the greatest sins as for the least because his mercy is infinite.[27] The infinite is as much above the great as it is above the small. If one of the least sins is not beyond the mercy of God, so neither are the greatest—or ten thousand of them.

The satisfaction of Christ is as sufficient for the removal of the greatest guilt as the least: "The blood of Jesus, his Son, purifies us from all sin" (1 John 1:7). All the sins of those who truly go to God for mercy are satisfied, for God is true who tells us so. If they are satisfied, surely it is not incredible that God should be ready to pardon them. It was a sufficient testimony of God's abhorrence of sin that he poured out his wrath on his own dear Son when he took the guilt of it on himself.

God may, through Christ, pardon the greatest sinner without any prejudice to the honor of his majesty. Let the contempt be ever so great, yet if so honorable a person as Christ undertakes to be a Mediator for the offender and suffers so much for that offender, it fully repairs the injury done to the Majesty of heaven and earth. The sufferings of Christ fully satisfy justice. The justice of God as the supreme Governor and Judge of the world requires the punishment of sin. The supreme Judge must judge the world according to a rule of justice. God does not show mercy as a judge but as a sovereign; therefore his exercise of mercy as a sovereign and his justice as a judge must be made consistent with one another. This is done by the sufferings of Christ, in which sin is punished fully and justice answered.

—Jonathan Edwards

> *For Thy name's sake, O Lord, pardon mine iniquity,*
> *for it is great.*
>
> —Psalm 25:11 KJV

Christ will not refuse to save the greatest sinners who in a right manner come to God for mercy, for this is his work.[28] It is his business to be a Savior of sinners. It is the work on which he came into the world, therefore he will not object to it. He did not come to call the righteous but sinners to repentance. Sin is the very evil that he came into the world to remedy. Therefore he will not object to anyone that he or she is very sinful. The more sinful the person, the more the need of Christ.

The whole ingenious plan of the way of salvation is to glorify the free grace of God. God had it on his heart from all eternity to glorify this virtue; that is the reason that the technique of saving sinners by Christ was conceived. The greatness of divine grace appears very much in this, that God by Christ saves the greatest offenders. The greater the guilt of any sinner is, the more glorious and wonderful is the grace shown in that sinner's pardon. It is the honor of Christ to save the greatest sinners when they come to him, as it is the honor of a physician to cure the most desperate diseases or wounds.

The invitations of the gospel are always in universal terms: If anyone is thirsty, let him come to me and drink; come to me, all you who are weary and burdened; whoever wishes, let him take the free gift of the water of life. So Christ promises, "Whoever comes to me I will never drive away" (John 6:37). This is the direction of Christ to his apostles after his resurrection: "Go into all the world and preach the good news to all creation. Whoever believes and is baptized will be saved" (Mark 16:15–16).

This teaching encourages sinners whose consciences are burdened with a sense of guilt immediately to go to God through Christ for mercy. If you go in the manner we have described, the arms of mercy are open to embrace you. You need not be at all the more fearful of going because of your sins, let them be ever so evil. Therefore, if your souls are burdened and you are distressed for fear of hell, you need not bear that burden and distress any longer. If you are only willing, you may freely come and unload yourselves and cast all your burdens on Christ and rest in him.

—Jonathan Edwards

*You have been faithful with a few things; I will put you
in charge of many things. Come and share your
master's happiness!*

—Matthew 25:21

It was very like our Lord to make fidelity the test of life.[29] Just as he took obscure and lowly people when he wanted to build a kingdom, so he took obscure and lowly virtues when he wanted to build character—not merely because they were obscure but because they were within the range of all, and his was to be a universal gospel. There is nothing dazzling in fidelity. It has no power to arrest the eye or to get chronicled in newspapers.

It is like him, too, to recognize that fidelity demands courage. In [this] parable, one man was not faithful. He buried his talent. And when the reckoning was taken, that man said *I was afraid.* His infidelity was fear. There is a courage of the battlefield, which is often a splendid thing. There is a courage needed for every adventure, whether in Africa or on Everest. But perhaps the finest courage is the quiet and steady courage of fidelity. To do things when you don't feel like doing them, to keep on keeping on, to get to duty through headache and through heartache. That is not a thing of the rare moment—it is carrying victory into the common day. And life is never victorious unless our common days are full of victories of which no one hears anything.

This was the courage of our Lord himself. Sometimes we forget how brave he was. We dwell on his tenderness, and in a world like this we can never dwell on his tenderness too much. But if we ignore his courage, we lose one of the appeals of Christ to youth, and to do that is pitiful. Did it take no courage to come down from heaven and become the tenant of a cottage? Did it take no courage to resist the Devil offering him the kingdoms of the world? To scorn delights and live laborious days, to take the long trail to Calvary, to set out for Jerusalem, where the cross was waiting and the crown of thorns—never was finer courage in the world. When we feel that we are missing things, when we are tempted to rebel at drudgery, we must remember him who took up his cross, daily, to the end.

Our Lord associates fidelity with joy: "Enter thou into the joy of thy lord" (Matt. 25:21 KJV). Only be faithful, and when the task is over and the morning breaks on the farther shore, you will enter into the joy of your Lord.

—George H. Morrison

*There is rejoicing in the presence of the angels of God over
one sinner who repents.*

—Luke 15:10

Our text teaches us the sympathy of the two worlds.[30] Imagine not that you are cut off from heaven! Do not think that there is a great gulf between you and the Father, across which his mercy cannot come and over which your prayers and faith can never leap. Believe that there is a bridge across that chasm, a road along which feet may travel. This world is not separated, for all creation is one body. The same great heart that beats in heaven beats on earth. The love of the eternal Father that cheers the celestial makes glad the terrestrial, too. Rest assured that though the celestial is one and the terrestrial is another, yet they are only another in appearance; they are the same. You are no stranger in a strange land—a houseless Joseph in the land of Egypt, shut out from his father and his [brothers], who still remain in the happy paradise of Canaan. No, your Father loves you still. There is a connection between you and him.

When a tear is wept by you, don't think that your Father does not see it. Your sigh is able to move the heart of Jehovah; your whisper can incline his ear to you; your prayer can stay his hands; your faith can move his arm. Do not think that God sits on high in eternal slumber, taking no account of you. Engraved on the Father's hand your name remains, and on his heart. He thought of you before the worlds were made. Before the channels of the sea were scooped or the mountains lifted their heads in the clouds, he thought of you. He thinks about you still. You move in him. In him you live and have your being.

Remember again that you are not only linked to the Godhead, but there is another in heaven with whom you have a strange yet near connection. In the center of the throne sits One who is your brother, allied to you by blood. The Son of God—eternal, equal with his Father—became the son of Mary. He was—is—bone of your bone and flesh of your flesh. Oh, poor, disconsolate mourner, Christ remembers you every hour. Your sighs are his sighs; your groans are his groans; your prayers are his prayers.

You live in him, and he lives in you, and because he lives you will also live.

—C. H. Spurgeon

*There is rejoicing in the presence of the angels of God over
one sinner who repents.*

—Luke 15:10

Never was husband nearer to his wife and never soul nearer to the body than Christ is to you.[31] Do not think that heaven and earth are divided. They are but two ships moored close to one another, and one short plank of death will enable you to step from one to the other. This ship, having done the coasting trade, the business of today, and full of the blackness of sorrow. That ship, all golden, with its ensign flying and its sails all spread, fair as the angel's wing. The ship of heaven is moored side by side with the ship of earth. Though this ship may rock and career, yet the golden ship of heaven sails by her side, never separated, always ready, so that when the hour comes, you may leap from the dark ship and step on the golden deck of that happy one on which you will sail forever.

There are other golden links besides this that bind the present to the future and time to eternity. This earth is heaven below, the next world is only heaven above. The spirits of the just made perfect are never far from you and me if we are lovers of Jesus. All those who have passed the flood still have communion with us.

Aren't the saints above us a cloud of witnesses? We are running in the plains and the glorified ones are looking down on us.

Our text assures us that the angels have communion with us. Bright spirits, firstborn children of God, oh, cherubim, seraphim, do you think of us?

Those angels of God are creatures mighty and strong, doing his commandments, heeding his Word. And do they take notice of us? Let the Scripture answer: "Are not all angels ministering spirits sent to serve those who will inherit salvation?" (Heb. 1:14). Yes, the brightest angels are but the servants of the saints.

There is a greater connection between earth and heaven than any of us dreamed. Let none of us think, when we look upward to the sky, that we are far from heaven.

Hail, bright spirits! Hail, angels! Hail, you who are redeemed! A few more hours or days or months, and we will join your happy throng. Until then, your fellowship, your compassion will ever be our comfort and consolation. And having weathered all storms of life, we will at last anchor with you within the port of everlasting peace.

—C. H. Spurgeon

*There is rejoicing in the presence of the angels of God over
one sinner who repents.*

—Luke 15:10

Why do angels sing over repentant sinners?[32]

In the first place, I think it is because they remember the days of Creation. You know, when God made this world and fixed the beams of the heavens in sockets of light, the morning stars sang together and the sons of God shouted for joy. As they saw star after star flying abroad like sparks from the great anvil of omnipotence, they began to sing. Every time they saw a new creature made on this little earth, they praised afresh. And over everything he made, they chanted evermore that sweet song, "Creator, you are to be magnified, for your mercy endures forever."

Now, when they see a sinner returning, they see the Creation over again, for repentance is a new creation. I don't know that, ever since the day when God made the world, with the exception of new hearts, the angels have seen God make anything else. He may, if he has so pleased, have made fresh worlds since that time. But perhaps the only instance of new creation they have ever seen since the first day is the creation of a new heart and a right spirit within the breast of a poor penitent sinner. Therefore they sing, because creation comes over again.

I don't doubt, too, that they sing because they see God's works afresh, shining in excellence. When God first made the world, he said of it, "It was very good" (Gen. 1:31). He could not say so now. There are many of you that God could not say that of. He would have to say the very reverse, "No, that is very bad, for the trail of the serpent has swept away your beauty, and that moral excellence which once dwelt in humanity has passed away." But when the sweet influences of the Spirit bring people to repentance and faith again, God looks on them and he says, "It is very good." For what his Spirit makes is like himself—good and holy and precious—and God smiles again over his twice-made creation and says once more, "It is very good." Then the angels begin again and praise his name whose works are always good and full of beauty.

—C. H. Spurgeon

> *There is rejoicing in the presence of the angels of God over*
> *one sinner who repents.*
>
> —Luke 15:10

Beloved, the angels sing over sinners who repent because they know what the poor sinners have escaped.[33] You and I can never imagine all the depths of hell. Shut out from us by a black veil of darkness, we cannot tell the horrors of that dismal dungeon of lost souls. But the angels know better than you or I could guess.

They know it. Not that they have felt it, but they remember that day when Satan and his angels rebelled against God. They know what hell is for they have looked within its jaws and have seen their own brothers fast enclosed within them. Therefore, when they see a sinner saved, they rejoice because there is one more soul escaped out of the mouth of the lion.

There is yet a better reason. The angels know what the joys of heaven are, and, therefore, they rejoice over one sinner that repents. We talk about pearly gates, golden streets, white robes, harps of gold, crowns of amaranth, and all that, but if an angel could speak to us of heaven, he would smile and say, "All these fine things are but child's talk. God has given you an alphabet in which you may learn the first rough letters of what heaven is. But what it is you do not know." You may talk, think, guess, and dream, but you can never measure the infinite heaven that God has provided for his children. Thus, when they see a soul saved and a sinner repenting, they clap their hands. They know that all those blessed mansions are yours, since all these sweet places of everlasting happiness are the exclusive inheritance of every sinner who repents.

You remember the occasion when the Lord met with you. Ah! little did you think what a commotion there was in heaven. If all the rulers of earth had marched in pageant through the streets with all their robes and jewelry and crowns and all their regalia, yet an angel would only have stopped to smile at those poor tawdry things. But over you—the vilest of the vile, the poorest of the poor, the most obscure and unknown—over you angelic wings were hovering, and concerning you it was said on earth and sung in heaven, "Hallelujah, for a child is born to God today."

—C. H. *Spurgeon*

Is there any God besides me?

—Isaiah 44:8

In the Christian view of God there are two attributes that it is not easy for the human reason to combine.[34] One of them we call the *transcendence* of God; to the other we give the name of *immanence.*

Now what do we mean by the divine transcendence? We mean that God is over all, blessed forever. We mean that apart from and above the universe there lives and reigns a personal Creator. We mean that were this world to be extinguished and were every living being to disappear, still would there be, eternal in the heavens, the Spirit whom we designate as God. Over against all created things, sustaining them and yet distinct from them, self-conscious in the silence of eternity and looking from without on all things made—it is to such a God, exalted over all, that we apply the attribute *transcendence.*

And what do we mean by the immanence of God? We mean the presence of the Almighty in creation. We mean that time and space and all their thousand occupants are but the garments that we see him by. Deep through the universe runs the thrill of life, and wherever that life is, there is God. His personal habits are the laws of nature; his love of beauty is seen in every valley. A God transcendent, like some consummate painter, adorns with his brush the lilies of the field; a God who is immanent breathes into the lilies, and they become the expression of himself. A God transcendent, like some master crafter, fashions the fowls of the air for flight; a God who is immanent lives in every bird and breaks the eternal silence in their song. A God transcendent, like some mighty sculptor, models with his deft hand the human form; a God who is immanent looks through human eyes and thinks in the thinking of the human brain.

Deny, reject, make light of God's transcendence, and you cut at the very roots of human progress. The immanence of God is a great truth to be grasped firmly by the believing soul, but to say that the immanence of God is everything is to be a traitor to tomorrow.

—George H. Morrison

Is there any God besides me?

—Isaiah 44:8

When we deny transcendence, we cease to have a God who is a person.[35] And the one thing that you blot out when you identify the Creator with his creatures is a God who will answer when his children speak. Sooner or later, all of us need the living God. In such hours, if we thought that there was no one on the throne who cared or knew, the burdens and the cares of life would grow insufferable, and we would be plunged into darkness.

But there cannot be a living God if God is only the Spirit of the universe. You can adore creation, but you cannot cry to it, "Father, I have sinned." We do not want to find ourselves divine in the great moments when we are most ourselves. We want to find the living God above us, who is ready to hear us when we call.

Being what we are, God is truly nearest when he is seated on his throne in heaven. I am not always nearest those around me except in a shallow and physical sense. Those who are nearest may be a thousand miles off, if they are the ones who love and understand me. And so with God in the altitude of heaven—if he knows and cares and understands and pities, then he is far nearer to my heart than if he were by my side. If his presence is interfused with setting suns, you seem to bring him under my very gaze. But if that is all—if he is nowhere else— if you must search for him beyond the universe in vain, then the divine is brought within our hail only to be banished far away. It is not *things* that can enter through the portals of the heart. It is personality, love, power. It is the influence of a living spirit. And all these you inevitably forfeit when you believe only in God's immanence; it robs the heart of the God for whom it craves, while it seems to bring him very near.

When you lose the personality of God, you lose the individuality of human beings. Faced by a sovereign and transcendent God, men and women were strengthened to do and to endure. When you lose that sense of the high God and merge him in the movement of his world you lose the presence that is so needed to draw us to our best. Slip the anchor of the living God, and you slip the anchor of accountability. And as that conception strengthens, the meaning of personality decays, and people forget much of their noblest heritage in Christ.

—George H. Morrison

Is there any God besides me?

—Isaiah 44:8

[The denial of transcendence] is certain to put our moral lives in jeopardy, for it destroys the distinction between good and evil.[36] The moral power of the cross of Christ has not only made goodness very beautiful. It has also made sin more sinful. No one can ever be a Christian who treats sin lightly. God demonstrates his own love for us in this: while we were still sinners, Christ died for us. The meaning of that love will grow or lessen according to our measurement of sin. When people have most deeply felt the wonder of the love of God in Christ, they have felt at the same time the guilt of sin.

It is just that moral heritage that is likely to be lost in the teaching of today. It is a bad thing to vilify humanity; I believe it is even worse to deify it. If the life of God is the life of the human race and the activity of God is human activity, where is your standard to tell that *this* is right and to say with authority that *that* is wrong? There is no law, with its divine "Thou shalt not." There is no atonement on the cross for guilt. There is no Spirit of a holy God to convince of sin. [An exclusive immanence] may be full of charm, but confusing good with evil saps the conscience.

The logical outcome is that might is right. A hero may be good, may be bad— the one essential is that a hero be strong. There is no room for the baffled and the fallen in a world whose god is only a stream of being that neither can pity nor can love.

Christ's revelation of God was that of fatherhood, and as long as we are true to that, we have a living and true God who meets the need of human hearts. There is transcendence in the thought of fatherhood—the sweet and perfect sovereignty of love. Above his children, strong and just and merciful, a refuge from the storm, there stands the Father. And in fatherhood no less is immanence, for the father's very life is in the child, and, in ways not less real because they are undefinable, father and child are one. All that is noblest in the thought of sovereignty, all that is fairest in the thought of immanence meets in that God whose name and nature have been revealed to us by and in the Lord. We beseech you, then, O God, show us your glory. Give us the spirit that cries, "Abba, Father." Then earth and humanity will not be less because the life of the divine is more.

—George H. Morrison

Run in such a way as to get the prize.
—1 Corinthians 9:24

These words were taken from a runner running for a wager, a very apt picture to set before the eyes of the saints of the Lord.[37] That is, do not only run, but be sure you win as well as run.

Beware of bypaths. Mind the path before you, turn neither to the right nor to the left. Even though the kingdom of heaven is the biggest city, yet usually those bypaths are most beaten; most travelers go those ways. Yet, it is in this case as it was with the harlot of Jericho; she had one scarlet thread tied in her window by which her house was known; so it is here. The scarlet streams of Christ's blood run throughout the way to the kingdom of heaven, but have a care you do not beguile yourself with a fancy. So that you may not be mistaken, consider, though it seem ever so pleasant, if you do not find that in the very middle of the road there is written with the heart-blood of Christ that he came into the world to save sinners and that we are justified though we are ungodly, shun that way. How easy a matter it is for the Devil to be too cunning for poor souls by calling his bypaths the way to the kingdom. How speedily, greedily, and by heaps do poor simple souls throw away themselves on it, especially if it is daubed over with a few external acts of morality. But it is because people do not know painted by-paths from the plain way to the kingdom of heaven. They have not yet learned the true Christ and what his righteousness is, neither have they a sense of their own insufficiency but are bold, proud, presumptuous, self-conceited.

Take heed that you do not have an ear open to everyone that calls after you as you are in your journey. People who run, if any call after them saying, "Do not go too fast and you will have my company with you," if they run for some great matter, they say, "I can't delay for you, I am running for a wager. If I win I am made, if I lose I am undone, therefore do not hinder me." Thus are those wise who run for corruptible things, and thus should you do, and you have more cause to do so than they, for they run for things that do not last, but you for an incorruptible glory. You will have enough that call after you—the Devil, sin, this world, worthless company, pleasures, profits, esteem in human society, ease, pomp, pride—crying "Do not leave me behind."

Have a care you do not let your ear open to the tempting, enticing, alluring, and soul-entangling flatteries of such sink-souls as these are.

—John Bunyan

> *Let him who walks in the dark, . . .*
> *trust in the name of the* LORD.
>
> —Isaiah 50:10

Some who are in my judgment among the very choicest of God's people nevertheless travel most of the way to heaven by night.[38] They do not rejoice in the light of God's countenance, though they trust in the shadow of his wings.

Darkness is an evil that the soul does not love, and by it all our faculties are tried. It is possible at times to even question the existence of God, though we still cling to him with desperate resolve.

At such times the Holy Spirit seems to suspend his comforting operations, and we read the Bible, and we are not cheered by the promises; we attend public services, and the bells of the sanctuary seem to have lost their music. The Holy Spirit is leaving us for awhile that we may know what poor things we are apart from him, and how useless are ordinances without his divine presence in them. Satan makes earnest use of his hour, and it is no fault of his that we do not die in the dark and utterly perish from the way.

Perhaps the worst feature of this darkness is that it is so bewildering. You have to walk, and yet your way is hidden. What simpletons we are to fancy that if we do not see a way of deliverance God does not see one either! If you have ever steamed up the Rhine, you have looked before you, and it has looked as if you could go no further; the river seemed to be a lake; great mountains and vast rocks blocked up all further advance. Suddenly there has been a turn in the stream, and at once a broad highway has been before you, inviting you to enter the heart of the country. Perhaps you are in one of those parts of the river of life where no progress appears possible.

What is there to trust to when you are in such a condition as that? Well, says the text, "Trust in the name of the LORD."

What is there to trust in the name of Jehovah? It is "I Am," and signifies his self-existence. This is a fine foundation for trust. Your friend is dead, but Jehovah is still living. Those who could have succored you have forsaken you, but he says, "I am with you."

The name of the Lord contains within it immutability. Here is a rock under your feet. If you trust in an unchanging God whose love and faithfulness and power cannot be diminished, then you have a glorious object for your faith to rest on!

—C. H. *Spurgeon*

*Let him who walks in the dark, who has no light, trust in
the name of the* LORD *and rely on his God.*

—Isaiah 50:10

We understand by the name the revealed character of God.[39] When you cannot see your way, then open this Book [the Bible] and try to find out what sort of God it is in whom you trust. See what he did in the ages past; see what he has promised to do in all time present. See his infinite love in the gift of his dear Son.

By the name of the Lord is also meant his dear Son, for it is in Jesus Christ that Jehovah has proclaimed his name. When it is dark around you and within you, then get to your Savior, and think of him and all his sorrow and his victory. As you hear his cries and perceive the flowing of his blood, you will gain comfort and joy such as will turn your darkness into day.

It is also good, dear friends, when you are thinking of the name of the Lord to remember that to you it signifies what you have seen of God in your own experience. This is his memorial, or name, to you. A grand thing it is, when at present you have no consolation, to recollect the consolation you enjoyed in years gone by. Oh, the days when he did help us! You said, "What a deliverance I have had! I will never doubt him again!" O poor stupid, you are doubting him now! But why? Jehovah is with you, therefore do not be afraid.

Furthermore, the text says, let him "rely on his God." Let him lean on his God, make God his stay, his prop, his rest. You have taken God to be your God, haven't you? If so, he has also taken you to be his own. There is a covenant between you: lean on that covenant. Lean wholly and fully on him who is your covenant God.

—C. H. Spurgeon

Let him who walks in the dark, who has no light, trust in
the name of the LORD and rely on his God.

—Isaiah 50:10

Why should we trust God at such times?[40] If you do not trust him now, you will have cause to suspect whether you ever did trust him at all. When your children were about you, and you were healthy, honored, and prospering, you said, "I have faith in God." Was it faith if it departs from you now that your children are buried and your home is desolate and you yourself are sick and old and poor? Was it faith in God at all? Was it only a cheerfulness that arose out of your surroundings? Fair-weather faith is a poor imitation of the real grace. I entreat you to be stalwart, for if you cannot do so, your strength is small, and your faith is questionable.

Do remember one thing more, that you and I, in times of darkness, may well trust in God, that he will not fail us, for our blessed Lord and Master was not spared the blackest midnight that ever fell on human mind, and he was exceedingly sorrowful, even to death. Do you expect that you will be treated better than the Head of the house?

What will come of it if we do trust in God in the dark?

In the first place, such a faith will glorify God. The cherubim and seraphim glorify God with their endless songs, but not more than a poor downcast soul can do when in its distress it casts itself on God alone.

It is true that very likely through this darkness of yours you will be humbled. Walking in darkness and seeing no light, you will form a very low idea of yourself, and this will be a superior blessing.

If you can trust God in your trial, you will prove and enjoy the power of prayer. The person who has never needed to pray cannot tell whether there is anything in prayer or not.

If in your darkness you will go to God and trust him, you will become an established Christian. Faith will make your nights the fruitful mothers of brighter days.

And let me close by saying that by and by we will come out into greater light than we have as yet hoped for.

Therefore be of good cheer, O you people of God who walk in darkness, for you will have a full reward.

—C. H. Spurgeon

He split the rocks in the desert and gave them water as
abundant as the seas.

—Psalm 78:15

[The psalmist] sees the Israelites crowding around the rock and saying in their hearts, "This cannot last long."[41] He sees them watching for the supply to fail, as, of course, coming from a rock it must soon do. And then he sees their wild surprise when it dawns on them that the stream is inexhaustible and is fed by channels they know nothing of, from boundless and unfathomable reservoirs. What the people crave for is a drink of water, and God in his mercy gives them their desire. But he fills their cups not from a little cistern but as if from some limitless ocean. And the psalmist knows that that is always true, for whenever the Almighty satisfies his creatures, he gives them drink as abundant as the seas.

Let us think for a moment of God's ways in providence—in the ordering and discipline of our lives. When we are young our joys are all our own; we never dream that others can have known them. When we are young we take our little sorrows as if there were no such sorrows in the world. And much of the bitterness of childish trial lies in its terrible sense of isolation, in the feeling that in the whole wide world there is no one who has had to suffer just like us. It seems as if God had cut a special channel for us out of which no other life had ever drunk. In joy and in grief, in sunshine and in shadow, we seem to move alone when we are children. But as life advances and our outlook broadens and we learn the stories of the lives around us, then we see that we are not alone but are being made to drink of the great depths. It is not by exceptional providences that we live. It is not by exceptional joys we are enriched. It is not by anything rare or strange or singular that we are fashioned under the hand of God. It is by sorrows that are as old as humanity, by trials that a thousand hearts have felt, by joys that are common as the wind is common that breathes on the palace and on the meanest street. By these things we live; by these we grow—by love and tears, by trials, by work, by death—by the things that link us all into a family, the things that are common to ten thousand hearts. And it is when we come to recognize that truth and to feel our comradeship in a common discipline that we say, as the psalmist said of Israel, he gave us "water as abundant as the seas."

—George H. Morrison

> *He split the rocks in the desert and gave them water as*
> *abundant as the seas.*
>
> —Psalm 78:15

Whenever the Almighty satisfies his creatures, he gives them drink as abundant as the seas.[42] Think of the Bible—an ancient book and yet intensely modern and practical. Think of the ages that have gone since it was written; think of the life we [now] live and of the stress and strain unknown in the quiet East; to me it is wonderful that the Bible should be of any use at all now and not have moved into the quiet of libraries to be the joy of the unworldly scholar.

But one thing is certain—the Bible meets the need of modern life. As a practical guide there is no book to touch it. There is not a problem you are called to face and not a duty you are called to do, there is not a cross you are compelled to carry and not a burden you are forced to bear but your strength for it all will be as the strength of ten—if you make a daily companion of your Bible.

The Bible never offers a drink from shallow waters. There, you do not find a set of petty maxims, but the everlasting love of God; you do not find any shallow views of sin, but a Lamb slain from the foundation of the world. And *that* is the secret of the Bible's permanence—when our little systems have ceased to be, for sin and sorrow and life and death and duty, it gives us drink "as abundant as the seas."

Think of Jesus in relation to his words. If ever words were as water to a thirsty world, surely it was the words that Jesus spoke. How simple they were and yet how deep! How tender and full of love and yet how searching! There are those whose lives so contradict their words that when you know the people you cannot listen to them. And there are those who are so much less than their own words that when you come to know them you are disappointed. But what people felt about Jesus Christ was this, that when all was uttered, the half was never told, for at the back of all his words there was *himself,* deeper unfathomably than his deepest speech. That is why the words of Christ will live even when heaven and earth have passed away. You can exhaust the cup or drain the goblet, but you cannot exhaust the spring fed from the deeps. And just because the words of Jesus Christ spring from the depths of that divine humanity, they will save and strengthen the obedient heart to the last recorded syllable of time.

—George H. Morrison

When he saw the crowds, he had compassion on them,
because they were harassed and helpless, like sheep with-
out a shepherd.

—Matthew 9:36

Every leader reveals the gift of constructive imagination.[43] A great bridge is a work of imagination just as certainly as a great poem. To the building up of our modern civilization there has gone far more than intellect and will; there has gone at every step of the advance what we describe as imaginative power.

But imagination is more than that; it is also a religious power of the highest order.

Ours is a historical religion. That is the strength and that is the glory of it. It is not begotten of abstraction; it is born of a historic revelation. Anything, then, that takes these facts of history and brings them near us and makes them real and living is doing a mighty service to the faith. That is just what imagination does. It answers the heart cry, "Sir, . . . we would like to see Jesus" (John 12:21). It takes us to Calvary and to Gethsemane and, withdrawing the veil, it says, "Here is the man!" (19:5). And so our faith is strengthened and refreshed because the past, in which our faith is rooted, leaps up in life, like the bones of Elisha's vision, under the power of imagination.

Then again, imagination is a religious power because there are few powers so helpful to compassion as the power of the imagination. We commonly assign many faults to lack of love, while all the time it is not lack of love, it is lack of imagination that creates them. A vast deal of people's callousness and cruelty and of their severe or unkindly judgment does not arise so much from lack of heart as from failure to understand imaginatively. A person who has no imagination is certain to be tactless. A person who has no imagination is an unsympathetic person. For at the back of sympathy and tact there is the power to grasp another's situation; the faculty that can realize another's thought or another's burden. Now it is not love that realizes that. Love's work begins when it is realized. The power that helps us to share another's feelings is largely the imaginative power. Hence every dramatist and every novelist who reaches and reveals us to ourselves is someone preeminently of imagination. And if at the back of all the truest sympathy there lies the power of the imagination, you see, do you not? how the imagination is a religious power of the highest order.

—George H. Morrison

*Thomas said to him, "My Lord and my God!" Then Jesus
told him, "Because you have seen me, you have believed;
blessed are those who have not seen and yet have believed."*
—John 20:28–29

Not only is imagination an aid to love.[44] It is also an aid to faith in the unseen. In imagination unseen realities draw very near. Like a breath of wind it plays on the mists till they scatter and show the everlasting hills. And so imagination, which is an aid to love, is also an aid to faith in the invisible, for it draws into something of visionary clearness the objects on which faith must always rest. Imagination is not faith, any more than it is love. But imagination may be their foster mother. Faith is the whole being turning Godward and coming to rest in the eternal certainties. The imagination is only a particular faculty or power of that being. No one is saved by imagination. It is a question if anyone is saved without it. Without its vivifying and realizing help, the task of faith is simply overwhelming. And therefore, because it wakes the sleeping past, because it helps to [compassion], because it helps to God, I want you to realize that the imagination is a religious power of the highest order.

Friends, among all the services of Christ to a world that he has redeemed and is redeeming, there are not many more notable and blessed than his quickening of the imagination. It would be much had he taught us perfect truth, but he has done more: he has shown us perfect beauty. He has given us a vision of such grace that it haunts the heart and will not let it go. It is that figure, so tender and so loving, so brave and patient, so silent, so unselfish, that has cast a spell on the imagination and through the imagination reached the heart. No worse curse can fall on a person than to have a corrupt imagination. There is no greater purifying power than an imagination that is pure. And the person who dwells in the communion of Christ has such a vision of what is fair and lovely that things unclean and bestial and base steal away into the forests of the night.

—George H. Morrison

*In him we have redemption through his blood, the forgive-
ness of sins, in accordance with the riches of God's grace
that he lavished on us.*

—Ephesians 1:7–8

I walked alone by the incoming sea.[45] I read the words of my text to the accompaniment of the roar and advance of the incoming tide. The onrush of the ocean seemed to get into the words. The grace of the Eternal was rolling toward the human race in a wealthy and glorious flood.

I am grateful for this comment of the ocean tide. I am grateful for its suggestion of energy in the ministry of grace. Grace is too commonly regarded as a pleasing sentiment, a soft disposition, a welcome feeling of favor entertained toward us by our God. [That] interpretation is ineffective. Grace is not the shimmering face of an illumined lake; it is the sunlit majesty of an advancing sea. It is a transcendent and ineffable force, the outgoing energies of the redeeming God washing against the polluted shores of human need.

Grace includes thought and purpose and good will and love. We do it wrong and therefore maim ourselves if we esteem it only as a perfumed sentiment, a favorable inclination, and not as a glorious energy moving toward the race with the fullness and majesty of the ocean tide. Wherever I turn in the Sacred Book I find the mystic energy at work. In every instance it works and energizes as an unspeakable force.

Let me cull a little handful of examples. "Let each one do just as he has purposed in his heart. . . . And God is able to make all grace abound to you" (2 Cor. 9:7–8 NASB). Do you catch the connection? Let each one *do,* for God will make grace abound. Grace is the dynamic of endeavor! "God our Father by his grace gave us good hope." We have good hope! The lamp is kept burning. The light does not die out. All the rooms are lit up. Grace is the nourisher of optimism. "It is good for our hearts to be strengthened by grace" (Heb. 13:9). Grace is the secret energy of a fortified will.

Grace does not flow from a half-reluctant and partially reconciled God, like the scanty and uncertain movements of a brook in time of drought. It comes in oceanic fullness. It comes in "his kindness, tolerance and patience" (Rom. 2:4), "in accordance with the riches of God's grace that he lavished on us."

—John Henry Jowett

In him we have redemption . . . in accordance with the
riches of God's grace that he lavished on us with all wisdom
and understanding.

—Ephesians 1:7–8

Grace is not a prevalent word in modern speech, and its rare occurrence may be explained by the partial disappearance of the word *sin* from our vocabulary.[46] If we exile the one we will not long retain the other. Grace haunts the place where pangs are endured and tears are shed because of the sense of indwelling sin.

Sin is a word whose meanings are like sharp fangs, and they bite deep. We are busy creating easier and less distressing phrases, phrases without teeth, that we can apply to our perversities without occasioning any pain.

Sin is inevitable, says prevalent philosophy, so long as we are bound to a physical body. But if people were to be stripped of their bodies, the realm of sin would still remain, envy would remain, and malice and wrath, and so would thought and desire and will. What philosophy and personal inclination are disposed to extenuate, the Christian religion seeks to deepen and revive. Its endeavor is not to abate the sense of sin but to drive the teeth into still more sensitive parts. There is no delicacy in the way in which it describes the natural conditions of my life. Its sentences are clear and uncompromising. Sin reigns in me. The guest has become the master and determines the arrangements of the house. He is my tyrant. I am dead in sin—not a boat with power to encounter adverse winds and to ride on the storm, but a piece of driftwood, its self-initiative and self-direction gone, the pitiless prey of the hostile wind and waves.

And now to this sin-burdened and sin-poisoned race there flows, in infinite plenitude, the riches of his grace. What are the contents of the gracious flood? When grace possesses the life, it brings a threefold power. It brings "redemption," the powers of liberation; it brings "wisdom," the power of illumination; it brings "understanding," the power of applying the illumination to the difficulties of life.

How do we come into the marvelous effluence of the grace of God? "*In him we have.*" That is the standing ground. I know no other. To be in him, in the Christ, is to be in the abiding place of this superlative energy. To be associated with the Savior by faith, in the fellowship of spiritual communion, is to dwell at the springs of eternal life.

—John Henry Jowett

*One day Naomi her mother-in-law said to her, "My
daughter, should I not try to find a home for you, where
you will be well provided for?"*

—Ruth 3:1

Two words in the chapter call for detailed explanation.[47] The first [is] *menuchah*.
Naomi said to Ruth, "My daughter, should I not try to find a home [or place of
rest, safety] for you, where you will be well provided for?"

The position of an unmarried woman in the ancient world was both perilous
and unhappy. Only in the house of a husband was a woman sure of safety, respect, honor. And consequently the Hebrews spoke of the husband's home as the
woman's *menuchah*, or place of rest, her secure haven from servitude, neglect,
and license.

In like manner, they regarded a hereditary possession of land as the *menuchah*,
or rest, of a nation. Thus Moses said to the children of Israel, "You have not yet
reached the resting place *[menuchah]* and the inheritance the LORD your God is
giving you" (Deut. 12:9); they had no haven of repose and freedom, no settled
and well-defended inheritance.

King Solomon was the first Hebrew chieftain who could bless God for the
gift of complete "rest" to his people. He could thankfully acknowledge that
the land had become the secure inheritance of the Hebrew race. And hence, at
the opening of the temple, he said, "Praise be to the LORD, who has given rest
[menuchah] to his people Israel just as he promised" (1 Kings 8:56).

The prophets rose to a still higher conception of and use of the word. For them,
God was the true rest, or *menuchah*, of humankind. And hence they predicted
that when God came, in the person of the Messiah, Paradise would return and
the whole world would enter into its true *menuchah*, its final and glorious "rest."
When the Messiah came, he invited the weary and burdened to come to him, on
the express ground that he was their *rest*, that in and with him they would find
such a haven of freedom and honorable repose as the Hebrew wife found in her
husband's home, such a rest as the Hebrew race found in the Promised Land when
it was wholly their own—no, such a rest as the prophets had taught them to look
and hope for only in God.

Naomi sets herself, with courage and hope, to find a *menuchah*, a haven of
rest and honor, for the daughter who had clung to her with a love so rare.

—Samuel Cox

One day Naomi her mother-in-law said to her, "My daughter, should I not try to find a home for you, where you will be well provided for?"

—Ruth 3:1

The second of the two notable words in this chapter is *goel*.[48] Like the word *menuchah*, it has a history in the Hebrew conception of the Messiah. According to its derivation, *goel* means "one who unlooses"—unlooses that which has been bound and restores it to its original position. Boaz was among the *goelim* of Naomi and Ruth.

We learn from the Pentateuch that there were three tragic contingencies in which the legal redeemer and avenger was bound to interpose—each of which was of much more frequent occurrence than the case recorded in the book of Ruth.

The Forfeited Inheritance. If an Israelite had sold his estate or any part of it, any of his near kin who was able to do so was commanded to purchase it, but when the trumpets announced the year of Jubilee, it reverted to its original owner.

Of whom can the Israelite alienated from his original inheritance be the type but of fallen humanity? All things were ours, but by our sin, we put them all into the hands of the Adversary, so that through our sin, the whole creation has been brought under the shadows of decay. And who can the *Goel* be but that divine Kinsman—bone of our bone and flesh of our flesh—who has redeemed and restored the inheritance we had forfeited? All things are made ours by his grace—if we are his—and when the trumpet will sound Jubilee, even the creation will be delivered from imperfection, out of "bondage to decay . . . into the glorious freedom of the children of God" (Rom. 8:21).

The Forfeited Liberty. To discharge a debt or to save himself from the last extremities of want, a Hebrew might sell himself either to a stranger or another Israelite. If he sold himself to an Israelite, he was treated not as a slave but as a hired servant and became free [in] the year of Jubilee. But if he sold himself to a foreigner, he became a slave, and in that case any of his kinsmen was permitted to interpose and to pay the price of his redemption.

The human race was sold under sin, led captive at the will of an alien and adverse spirit. Our freedom was gone; we were in bondage. And Christ has proved himself our *Goel* by giving himself a ransom for all, by redeeming us with his own precious blood.

—Samuel Cox

One day Naomi her mother-in-law said to her, "My
daughter, should I not try to find a home for you, where
you will be well provided for?"

—Ruth 3:1

There were three tragic contingencies in which the legal redeemer and avenger was bound to interpose.[49] [The third is] *The Forfeited Life.* The avenger of blood is the *goel* who, in virtue of his kinship, becomes an avenger of wrongs.

Even in him who was "gentle and humble in heart" (Matt. 11:29), we may find the avenging function of the Hebrew *goel.* Christ came to destroy as well as to redeem, to destroy that he might redeem. He, of whom the Hebrew avenger of blood was a type, pursued that great enemy of our souls. To avenge the world for all that it had suffered at the hands of evil, to redeem it from enslavement, he disarmed the powers of evil.

One feature of the *goel* comes out markedly, whatever [his] function—whether redeeming an alienated inheritance, restoring liberty to a captive, or hunting down a homicide. He is one of the nearest kin. *Kinship with the redeemed,* in short, *is an unvarying law and condition of redemption.* And this law holds of the divine *Goel.* No stranger could interpose for us, only one who is our nearest Kinsman. Hence the Son of God became the Son of Man.

In thus speaking of the redemption wrought by our divine Kinsman, it must not be supposed that we are playing with mere figures of speech. Under this image, we have presented to us the truths that have most profoundly entered our spiritual experience. No Hebrew who had been compelled to part with the fields he inherited from his fathers suffered a loss comparable with ours, when, by sin, we had lost the righteousness in which we were originally placed by the Father of our spirits. No Hebrew selling himself for a slave ever endured a bondage half so bitter and shameful as that into which we fell when, sold under sin, we sank into bondage to our own lusts. No deliverance wrought by a Hebrew *goel* is worthy to be compared to that by which Christ made it possible for us to possess a righteousness more stable and more perfect than that which we had cast away.

With a fervor and a triumph infinitely transcending that of Naomi, we may exclaim, "Praise be to the Lord, who this day has not left us without a Kinsman-Redeemer."

—Samuel Cox

"Look, I am about to die," Esau said. "What good is the
birthright to me?"

—Genesis 25:32

We cannot suppress a natural sympathy with Esau in this scene between the two brothers.[50] He seems as much sinned against as sinning, and in comparison with the cunning, crafty Jacob, he appears the better of the two. There is nothing of the selfishness, the trickery, that make his brother appear contemptible beside him.

Esau's good qualities are evident—bold and frank, free and generous, impulsive and capable of magnanimity, reckless and passionate. [But] being largely a creature of impulse, he was the plaything of animal passion, ready to satisfy desire without thought of consequences. Without self-control, without spiritual insight, judging things by immediate advantage, there was not in him depth of nature out of which a really noble character could be cut. This damning lack of self-control comes out in the transaction of the birthright. Coming from the hunt hungry, he finds Jacob cooking stew of lentils and asks for it. Ungovernable appetite makes him feel as if he would die if he did not get it.

The Bible writers speak of Esau with a certain contempt, and, with all our appreciation of his good natural qualities, we cannot help sharing in the contempt. The individual who has no self-control, who is swept away by every passion of the moment, who has no appreciation of higher and larger things, that individual is only a superior sort of animal—and not always very superior at that.

True self-control means willingness to resign the small for the sake of the great, the present for the future, the material for the spiritual, and that is what faith makes possible. Of course, Esau did not think he was losing the great by grasping at the small. At the moment, the birthright, because it was distant, appeared insignificant. He had no patience to wait, no faith to believe in the value of the [non]material, no self-restraint to keep him from surrender to present gratification.

[Impulsive] passion has no use for a far-off good. Temptation allures the eye, whispers in the ear, plucks by the elbow, offering satisfaction now. The birthright is a poor thing compared to the red stew.

It is the distortion of vision that passion produces, the exaggeration of the present that temptation creates, making the small look like the great and discrediting the value of the thing lost.

—Hugh Black

*"Look, I am about to die," Esau said. "What good is the
birthright to me?"*

—Genesis 25:32

The author of the epistle to the Hebrews calls Esau "a profane person" (KJV).[51] "Profane" does not mean blasphemous but simply secular, a person judging things by coarse, earthly standards, without spiritual aspiration or insight, feeling every sting of flesh keenly but with no sting of soul toward God.

It is not merely lack of self-control that Esau displays. It is also lack of appreciation of spiritual values. In a vague way he knew that the birthright meant a religious blessing, and in the grip of his temptation that looked to him as purely a sentiment, not to be seriously considered as on a par with a material advantage.

How easy it is to drift into the class of the profane, the secular persons as Esau, to have our spiritual sensitivities blunted, to lose our appreciation of things unseen, to be so taken up with the means of living that we forget life itself and the things that alone give it security and dignity! How easy, when soul wars with sense, to depreciate everything that is beyond sense and let the moral tone be relaxed! There is much cause for the apostle to warn us, "See that no one . . . is godless like Esau."

We too can despise our birthright by living far below our privileges and far below our spiritual opportunities. We have our birthright as children of God, born to an inheritance as joint heirs with Christ. We belong by essential nature not to the animal kingdom but to the kingdom of heaven, and when we forget it and live only with reference to the things of sense and time, we are disinheriting ourselves as Esau did. The secular temptation strikes a weak spot in all of us, suggesting that the spiritual life, God's love and holiness, the kingdom of heaven and his righteousness, the life of faith and prayer and communion are dim and shadowy things, as in the land that is very far off.

What profit the red stew if I lose my birthright? What profit the momentary gratification of even imperious passion if we are resigning the true life and losing the clear vision and the pure heart? What profit to make only provision for the flesh if of the flesh we reap only destruction? What profit the easy self-indulgence if we are bartering peace and love and holiness and joy? What profit if, in the insistence of appetite, men and women go like an ox to the slaughter, knowing not that it will cost them their lives? "So Esau despised his birthright" (Gen. 25:34).

—Hugh Black

Don't you know that you yourselves are God's temple and
that God's Spirit lives in you?
—1 Corinthians 3:16

God is as present with the lowest as with the highest forms of life: he is as present with the lowest animals, with every variety of plant, with rocks, with heavenly bodies, moving in their undeviating obedience to law through trackless space—as with glorified humans, as with archangels.[52] He cannot contract his illimitable being and make corners in his universe where he is not. And there are not degrees of his presence, although there are various modes of its manifestation. He is everywhere, in all the proper intensity and force of his being, simply because he is God.

Yet the apostle does not mean that the Corinthian Christians were only God's temple as being a part of his universe. For, obviously, people are differently related to the divine omnipresence from anything else in nature. People alone can feel it, can acknowledge it, can respond to it. Neither animal nor plant is conscious to divine contact; people, however, can know and adore their God by the homage of their intelligence and of their moral freedom, and thus the human soul is a temple of God in a distinct sense. It is a living temple, so designed and proportioned as even by their silent symmetry to show forth their Maker's praise.

Such is the original draft of the human soul; it was to be a true temple of God, nor even in its ruins is it altogether unvisited by him, not merely because God sustains all mental powers, but because God is strictly the author of all good thoughts and truths that heathens have reached, as he is the strength of all natural goodness that heathens have practiced.

Yet Saint Paul did not mean that the communicants of the church of Corinth were God's temple only in the same sense as the heathen priests and philosophers and prostitutes who thronged the neighboring temple of Aphrodite. The fallen human soul is in a condition of contradiction, not to rules laid down by God but to the very essence of his being, to those constituent moral truths that are rooted in God's eternal self-consciousness and that—God being what he is—could not be other than as they are. But to those who are alive in Jesus Christ, God manifests his presence by his Spirit, and this manifestation makes them his temples in a sense more intense than is possible for unregenerate souls.

—H. P. Liddon

Don't you know that you yourselves are God's temple and
that God's Spirit lives in you?
—1 Corinthians 3:16

Christians *are* the temple of God; the Spirit of God dwells in them.[53] The Day of Pentecost was not to be deemed a day apart; it was merely the first day of the Christian centuries. The tongues of fire might no longer be visible, but the gift that they symbolized would remain. The Spirit, being the Spirit of Christ, had made the life of Christ to be forever in Christendom nothing less than a reality of the present. Christians know themselves to be temples of the indwelling Presence. From the moral pressure of this conviction there is no escape except by a point-blank denial of it.

We need motives, strong motives, one and all of us. We need them for purposes of action and for purposes of dogged resistance. We need them to counteract all that gives way and depresses from within and to oppose all that would crush our wills into culpable acquiescence from without. A few primal truths, to us clear, indisputable, cogent, again and again examined and proved and burnished like well-prized weapons—these are assuredly part of the inner furniture of every Christian. And among these none is better than that of the text—the motive that appeals to the sanctity, the responsibility, the powers, the capabilities implied in that inward presence of the eternal Spirit, which is the great gift of the new covenant. In moments of moral surprise, in moments of unusual depression, in moments of a felt sense of isolation that threatens to take the heart out of us, in moments of spasmodic daring, when ordinary sanctions have, as it seems, lost their hold on us, it is well to fall back on the reassuring, tranquilizing, invigorating resources of such an appeal, "Don't you know that you yourselves are God's temple and that God's Spirit lives in you?" Let us emblazon these words, if not on the walls of our churches, yet at least within the sanctuary of that inner temple where the All-Seeing notes our opportunities for acquiring a clear vision and a firm grasp of truth and, still more, the use that we really make of it.

—H. P. Liddon

Why do you stand here looking into the sky?

—Acts 1:11

The angels' address is a rebuke to idle speculation in regions beyond the reach of human knowledge.[54] It is a warning against substituting that which is visionary for that which is real in religion.

[But] aren't we told that our citizenship is in heaven? Aren't we commanded to store up treasure in heaven? In what sense then can we be required to avert our gaze from heaven and to fix our eyes on the earth?

The circumstances of the apostles will supply us with a first answer. What was a fault in them will be a fault in us also. They were eager to know the exact time— the day and the hour—when their King would come and claim his kingdom. He had told them again and again that this knowledge was hidden from them. It was hidden even from the angels of heaven. And still, the last words that they address to their risen Lord ignore the warning; still the last answer that they receive from his lips is a rebuke for desiring to fathom the unfathomable. "It is not for you to know the times or dates the Father has set."

The subject has exercised a strong fascination over Christians in all ages. Again and again people have predicted the time of the Second Advent. Again and again their predictions have been falsified.

And the wrong done by this lawless speculation is not trifling. It impairs that attitude of patient waiting that is enjoined on the church. It substitutes a spasmodic, feverish watchfulness for the calm and continuous expectation that suits the children of God. It is chargeable with still more fatal consequences than these. It has bred disappointment, and from disappointment has sprung skepticism and from skepticism, mockery and unbelief. It has given occasion to the enemies of Christ to blaspheme. And the guilt lies in no small degree with the speculation of believers. Strange that it should have been so; strange that people should not perceive how each such prediction falsified is a confirmation of the Master's saying, "No one knows about that day or hour."

Spend no more time on speculations; they only absorb energy and paralyze action. Stand no more gazing up into heaven, but return from the mount of ascension to your everyday life. There, continue in prayer and supplication; there await in confidence that outpouring of the Spirit; there live and bear witness to Christ.

—J. B. Lightfoot

When they landed, they saw a fire of burning coals there
with fish on it, and some bread.

—John 21:9

Christ once more stands among the common things of life—the fire, the fish, the bread; a group of tired, hungry fishers—all common men.[55] And he is there to affirm that in his resurrection he had not broken his bond with humankind but strengthened it—wherever common life goes on there is Jesus still.

"Early in the morning, Jesus stood on the shore." Jesus speaks, and it is not of the mysteries of God, the secrets of the grave, but of nets and fishing—the simple concerns of simple people engaged in humble tasks.

We have forgotten the dignity of common life. We have not learned even the alphabet of Christ's gospel unless we have come to see that the only true *in*dignity in human life is sin, malevolence, and small-heartedness and that all life is dignified where there are love, purity, and piety in it.

We boast that a single human soul is of more value than all the splendors of matter, but our actions treat the boast as mere rhetoric. There is nothing so cheap as men and women—[ask] the lords of commerce. But Christ acted as though the boast were true. He deliberately inwove his life into all that is commonest in life. Where childhood is, there is Bethlehem; where sorrow is, there is Gethsemane; where death is, there is Calvary; where the laborer is, there is the poor man of Nazareth; where the beggar is, there is he who had no place to lay his head. The true dignity of life is this, that Christ is in all people, defaced, half-obliterated, but there, and the church that forgets this has neither impulse nor mandate for Christ's work among them. The moment Christ is shut up in a church he becomes the priest's Christ, the thinker's Christ, the devotee's Christ, but he ceases to be the people's Christ.

Lift up your eyes and see this risen Christ, a fisher on the shore, busy preparing a meal for hungry people. Unlock your church doors, let Christ go out among the common people; no, go yourselves, for it is here that he would have you be. Wherever there is toil, there is the Christ who toiled, and there you should be, with the kind glance, the warm hand-grasp, and the warmth of human kinship.

—William Dawson

He said, "Throw your net on the right side of the boat and
you will find some." When they did, they were unable to
haul the net in because of the large number of fish.
—John 21:6

They had toiled all night and caught nothing; isn't that a description of many human lives?[56] "Friends, haven't you any fish?" asks the quiet voice from the shore, and they answer, "No." All the heartbreak and disappointment of the world cry aloud in that confession. Oh, I could fill an hour with the mere recital of the names of great and famous people who have toiled through a long life and, as the last gray hour came over their dim sea of life, "brackish with the salt of human tears," have acknowledged with infinite bitterness that they have caught nothing. Surely here is some tragic mismanagement of the great business of living. Is it true of you that, after all the painful years, happiness is not yours? You have no meat, no food on which the heart feeds, no green pasture in the soul, no table in the wilderness, and the last gray day draws near and will find you still hungering for what life has never given you.

Learn, then, that Christ knows more about the proper management of your life than you do. "Throw your net on the right side of the boat," speaks that quiet voice from the shore. And you know what happened. And it is so still. Just because Christ stands among the common things of life, he knows most about life, and, above all, he knows where the golden fruit of happiness is found and where the secret wells of peace.

And to some of us whom God has called to be fishers of souls the issue is yet more solemn. We have the boat and the nets, all this elaborate organization of the church, but have we caught anything this year? Where is the catch of fish? Where are the women and men saved by our triumphant effort? Only lately have I found the right side of the ship; only lately have I discovered how easy it is to get the great catch of fish by simply going to work in Christ's way. Go for them— that is Christ's method. Compel them to come in. And if your experience is like mine, you will find that there is strangely little compulsion needed to bring people to Christ. I ask you whether you really want a great catch of fish, for you can have it if you want it. Christ knows the business better than you do, and if you will come out of the cloister of the church and seek the people in his spirit, I promise you that very soon you will not be able to drag the net for the multitude of fish.

—William Dawson

Jesus saith unto them, Come and dine.

—John 21:12 KJV

Notice Christ's fire was kindled before they came.[57] Christ's fish was already laid on it, and all they had to do was to come and dine. It is all you have to do, all the churches have to do. Didn't Christ put it so in the parable of the great supper? "Come, for everything is now ready" (Luke 14:17). Is not the last word of Scripture the great invitation? "The Spirit and the bride say, 'Come!' Whoever is thirsty, let him come; and whoever wishes, let him take the free gift of the water of life." When he says, "Come and dine," there is enough for each, enough for all, enough for evermore. The same voice speaks even now to your hunger-bitten soul, to your famished heart, "Come and dine" (see John 6:51).

And then there comes one last touch in the beautiful story. While these things happened, the day was breaking. Is there one of us long tossed on sunless seas of doubt, long conscious of failure and disappointment in life? Are there those of us whose sorrow lies deeper than that which is personal—sorrow over our failure in Christ's work, pain over a life's ministry for Christ that has known no victorious evangel? Turn your eyes from that barren sea to him who stands on the shore; he will yet make you a fisher of souls. Turn your eyes from that bleak, dark sea of wasted effort where you have fared so ill; it is always dark till Jesus comes, it is always light when he has come. And to each of us he says today, "I am the living bread that came down from heaven. If anyone eats of this bread, he will live forever."

"Come and dine." Will you come?

—William Dawson

*Peace I leave with you; my peace I give you. I do not give
to you as the world gives.*

—John 14:27

Peace is not apathy, not stagnation.[58] It is certainly not freedom from labor nor suspension of energy. The peace that Christ has left us is not only consistent with the manifold occupations, interests, cares of life, but through and in these we must seek it. Peace is not freedom from trial and suffering. In the same breath Christ offers to his disciples tribulation and peace—the one as accompanying the other, the one as the condition of the other. He holds out no escape from vexation, from misunderstanding, from lies, from persecution, from any of the thousand forms of evil that friend or foe may inflict. But he has promised to endow us with a spirit that will rise triumphant over all these things and bear us to a region of unbroken, perennial peace. Two worlds are ours: this lower world with its privations, its miseries, its distractions, its cares; that higher world into which we are even now translated by faith, where even now the tear is wiped from every eye, and there is no more death nor sorrow nor pain.

This promise flows directly from the revelation of God in the gospel: the consciousness of one all-powerful, all-comprehensive, presiding will is the first stage. And the recognition of this one God as our Father is the second stage. Only when we have learned to throw ourselves unconditionally on the all-embracing love of our Father in heaven will we find that complete satisfaction, that perfect peace that transcends all understanding.

And this lesson we learn through the incarnation of the Son. God taught us his love in the life and teaching of Christ; God sealed for us his love in the cross and passion and resurrection of Christ. Henceforth it is written in large letters, written right across the scroll of this world's history, so that people cannot choose but read. Christ has drawn us to the Father, has reconciled us to him, has folded us in the arms of his infinite love. Here alone our deepest yearnings are satisfied; here alone we find repose for our weary spirits, repose from distraction and anxiety and temptation, repose in all time of our tribulation, in all time of our wealth, in the hour of death, and in the day of judgment.

—J. B. Lightfoot

When you pray, say: "Father."

—Luke 11:2

The prayer Jesus taught his disciples begins with a new name for God.[59] "When you pray, say: 'Father.'"

In the Old Testament God is very seldom spoken of as Father, and when the name is used, it is always with reference to the nation of Israel and not to individuals. From Genesis to Malachi you will not find a single instance of an individual speaking of God as Father. Moses did not dare to use this name [or] David [or] Isaiah. It was left to Jesus Christ to tell us God's best and truest name. It was left to him to say, "When you pray, say: 'Father.'"

The secret hidden from the prophet and psalmist and seer is here declared to the world in this name *Father.* One of the chief ends for which Christ came to earth was to tell us this new name and so to bring sunshine into our souls and hope into our lives. In Bethlehem, in Nazareth, in Galilee, in the Garden of Gethsemane, on the cross of Calvary, Jesus was spelling out for us this new name, revealing to us that God is more than wisdom, more than power, more than justice—that God, above and beyond everything else, is love. So the very opening phrase of this "pearl of prayers" brings us the best news ever whispered into human ears. It tells us that love is at the heart of all things. It tells us that God is our Father and we are his children.

Is God Father to everybody? Yes, to everybody. He is Father to the humblest, the poorest, the most degraded. All belong to God's family, and on all some trace of the family likeness is to be seen. And though people sin, the Father still loves. That is what Jesus would teach us in the parable of the prodigal son. God is Father not only to the obedient son, but he is Father also to the son who has strayed. The Father's heart yearns for that wayward child, and when that son returns with penitent heart, it is the word "Father" that leaps to the prodigal's lips, and it is with the word "son" that the father welcomes him home again.

Yes, God is the Father of *all.* But all are not his children. People become his children only through Jesus Christ. Christ came into the world to show us the Father, to seek lost children and bring them back home again. Those who receive him into their hearts receive the Spirit of adoption. They speak the name *Father* with a new accent. It becomes to them invested with a richer and fuller meaning.

—J. D. Jones

When you pray, say: "Father."

—Luke 11:2

This new name, *Father,* Christ places at the very commencement of the model prayer.[60] This name is to be the very basis of our prayer. The psalmist asked himself this question one day: "Who may ascend the hill of the LORD? Who may stand in his holy place?" Who has the right to worship God and pray to him? And he proceeds to answer the question. "He who has clean hands and a pure heart, who does not lift up his soul to an idol or swear by what is false." But the psalmist's answer is one of blank despair. For who is there whose hands are clean? Who is there whose heart is pure? When we look on ourselves what do we see but sin! SIN! SIN! If we have to wait till our hands are clean and our hearts pure, we will never, never ascend the hill of the Lord or stand in his holy place. What right have I, sinful being, to pray? What warrant have I for coming boldly to the throne of grace? I have no right but that which this name gives. I have no warrant except that which the name *Father* supplies. That is my right—not that I have clean hands or a pure heart, but that I am a child, and he, the almighty God, is *my Father.* Lord of the universe? Yes. Maker of the worlds? Yes. King of Kings? Yes. But *my Father.* Let us preface every prayer with that blessed word. It is our claim on God.

This name is ours to use; the love implied in it is ours to enjoy. Not one of us need go through life alone; not one of us need be orphaned and poor; not one of us need carry a troubled, anxious heart. For Christ has taught us to see love on the throne and to call to the almighty and everlasting God, who faints not, neither is weary, "Our Father in heaven."

—J. D. Jones

Hallowed be your name.

—Luke 11:2

In the invocation, Jesus gave us a new name for God.[61] In the first petition, he teaches us to pray for grace to honor that new name of *Father* by thought and life.

Our first thoughts when we pray must be of God. Above all personal interest stands the glory of God. Before the prayer for daily bread, for forgiveness, for deliverance, comes the prayer that God may have the glory due to his name. [And] hallowing God's name means honoring the character of God that has been made known to us in Jesus Christ.

[We hallow God's name] *by cherishing worthy ideas of God.* We are sinning against this name *Father* when we think of God as harsh, cruel. You must cherish beautiful thoughts of God if you are to hallow his name. The deeper we penetrate into the nature of God, the more loving, the more gracious we will find him to be. Therefore press on to know him until you come to feel that in earth, in heaven, you want none but him.

[You hallow God's name] *by the trustfulness of your life.* A child cannot dishonor a father more than by fearing him, being suspicious about him, doubting his love. People sometimes complain of God's dealing with them. They have spoken as if God used them hardly, as if God had lost his love for them. They were dishonoring God's name, casting a slur on his character, forgetting that his nature is love and his name is Father. Those who, in spite of Calvary, think God can be unkind are doing insult to his love. We find ourselves in storms sometimes. In such storms we have the most glorious opportunities of hallowing God's name. Let us ask him for grace to honor his fatherhood by trusting him in the dark and cloudy day.

[We hallow God's name] *by our obedience.* Nothing is so dishonoring to God as profession without practice. Obey him. Obey him promptly, absolutely, willingly. That was how Jesus hallowed his Father's name. It was his food and drink to do God's will. He gave his Father full, absolute, glad obedience, so that in his prayer he could say to God, "I have brought you glory."

We try to put God off with a little outward respect, we bow at his name, we bend in prayer before him, we sing hymns to his praise, but better than all is the daily obedience of the life. Tomorrow in the shop, the office, the school, and the home, make it your food and drink to do the Father's will.

—J. D. Jones

Your kingdom come.

—Luke 11:2

The Bible is a book of hope.[62] It always speaks of a best that is still to be. We read of Eden, of a time when the world was free from pain and sadness, because humankind was free from sin. Their home was a garden, all nature served them, and God was their familiar friend. But we read on a chapter or two, and a change comes over the aspect of things. Eden disappears and has never been found since.

People lost everything by sin except *hope*. That note of hope, struck even in the story of the tragedy of the Fall, is the keynote of the Bible. The Bible is a book of the future and the springtime and the dawn. "Your kingdom come" is a prayer for the good time coming, for the golden age, for the better Eden. For the earth's golden age will come when God is King. Jesus means that we are to pray that God may reign here on the earth, that people here may acknowledge him as King, that life here may be regulated by his commands. This is not a prayer that we may be taken out of earth into heaven, but it is a prayer that heaven may come down to earth, so that earth itself may become heavenly.

In most people's minds the idea of a golden age is associated with the name of some king. The Israelites associated it with the name of David. For [the] British, romance gathers round the time of Arthur and his Knights of the Round Table. And as a matter of fact, the world's good time is inseparably connected with the coming of a King and the establishment of a kingdom. But the kingdom is no earthly royalty, and the King is no David or Arthur. The kingdom is the kingdom of God, and the name of the King is Jesus. When that kingdom is established, when that King is enthroned, a better Eden will be here than the Eden we have lost.

But, isn't God King now? Isn't the world his? That is true! But that kingship rests on God's creatorship. God wants to be king in Jesus Christ, in virtue not of his power but of his love. He wants people to obey him not because they are afraid of him but because they love him. "*Your* kingdom come." Whose kingdom is it? It is our *Father's* kingdom—a kingdom of love! God wants to be King not because he is Creator, but because he is Father. It is for this kingdom we pray.

"Your kingdom come," in my own heart, over all the world, and in every department of life.

—J. D. Jones

"You are Simon the son of Jonah. You shall be called
Cephas" (which is translated, A Stone).
—John 1:42 NKJV

When the disciples found that miraculous draught of fishes enclosed in their nets, it was only on Peter's soul that there flashed a new sense of the holiness and majesty of Christ, and of the whole apostolic company he was the only one to fall at Christ's feet and cry, "Go away from me, Lord; I am a sinful man!"[63] When after those hard sayings in Capernaum the crowds were deserting Jesus Christ, he turned to his disciples with the pathetic, heartbreaking question, "Do you also want to go away?" (NKJV). It was to Peter's generous and loving soul that there came the great and immortal answer, "Lord, to whom shall we go? You have the words of eternal life." And when again, in Ceasarea, Christ made that wistful inquiry, "Who do you say I am?" it was the inspired Peter who made that high reply, "The Christ of God."

Yes, when I read of the incident on the lake and the answer in Capernaum and the confession in Caesarea, I do not wonder that the first place among the Twelve was given to a man of such insight and vision and rapture as this.

But there are other passages in the Gospels that, when I read, I marvel that Peter was among the Twelve at all. When I come across those passages in which Peter begins to boast, when I read of his presuming to correct and rebuke the Christ, when I read about his sleeping in the garden, when I read of that terrible and shameful episode in the judgment hall, I marvel that instead of coming down to us as the prince and chief of the apostles, Peter, the denier and the blasphemer, did not make his bed with Judas the betrayer in the lowest hell.

Is it possible, you say, for one to see the glory of the Lord on the mount and then to forsake him in the garden? Is it possible for one to confess Christ in Caesarea and then forswear him in the judgment hall? Yes, it is quite possible. Gaze steadily and bravely into that awful abyss, your own heart, and you will know it is quite possible. For in your own heart you will see both heaven and hell, aspirations and desires born of God and hideous lusts of foulnesses that issue from the pit. Yes, I will be very bold to say we can parallel Peter's history by our own. Heaven and hell contended for the mastery in Peter's heart long ago; heaven and hell are contending for the mastery in our divided and distracted souls today.

—J. D. Jones

*"You are Simon the son of Jonah. You shall be called
Cephas" (which is translated, A Stone).*

—John 1:42 NKJV

I [can] not discover a more beautiful illustration of the charity and hopefulness
of our blessed Lord than I find in his first words to Peter.[64] For when Simon came
to him that day he was anything but a rock. He was a man of sand that day and
for many a day after that. It took a lifetime to turn Simon into Peter—to turn
the man of sand into the man of rock.

It is the man of sand who ran away in the garden and who denied Christ. But
in the book of the Acts, on the day of Pentecost, at the temple gate called Beautiful, before the Sanhedrin—he is Peter, the Rock.

And this first I get from Simon Peter's history: a new and subduing idea of the
forgiving grace of Christ. Friends may cast you off, parents may disown you, but
there is mercy with Jesus Christ. Men and women laden with iniquities, sinning
and sinning and sinning again, I know of One who has not despaired of you; I
know of One whose patience has not failed. Come to Peter's Savior.

And this second thing I learn from Peter's story. I get a new idea of the restoring power of Christ. To turn Simon—the unstable, unreliable, vacillating Simon—
into a rock! What a work was that! There is not a person, however wicked and
broken and helpless, that Jesus cannot restore.

And Peter's chief virtue, his saving grace, was his love. Peter loved the Lord
with all the strength of his eager, impetuous heart. It was love that made him
leave all and follow him at the first. It was mistaken love—but still love—that
would have saved Christ from the Via Dolorosa. It was love that made him say at
the supper, in his own impulsive way, "You shall never wash my feet," and then,
when he knew what the act signified, "Not just my feet but my hands and my
head as well!" Yes, whatever charges may be brought against Peter, this at any
rate may be said in his favor: he loved his Lord with a deep, passionate, enthusiastic love.

Do you love the Lord Jesus Christ? Can you say as did Peter, "Lord, you know
all things; you know that I love you"? Then blessed are you and when you leave
this earth the gates of the city will open to welcome you and the trumpets will
sound for you on the other side.

—J. D. Jones

The glorious appearing of our great God and Savior,
Jesus Christ, who gave himself for us to redeem us
from all wickedness.

—Titus 2:13–14

[Paul] believed the Lord Jesus Christ to be truly human, but he also believed him to be God.[65] There is no appearing of God the Father. It is of that second person of the Trinity who has already once appeared and who will appear a second time in the latter days. It was Paul's delight to extol the Lord who once was crucified in weakness. He calls him here the *great* God, thus specially dwelling on his power, dominion, and glory. This is the more remarkable because he immediately goes on to say, "who gave himself for us to redeem us from all wickedness." He who surrendered life itself, who was stripped of all honor and glory and entered the utmost depths of humiliation, was assuredly the great God. If you take away the deity of Christ, what in the gospel is left that is worth preaching? No one but the great God is equal to the work of being our Savior.

Paul believed also in a great redemption: "who gave himself for us to redeem us from all wickedness." That word *redemption* sounds in my ears like a silver bell. We are ransomed, purchased back from slavery—and at an immeasurable price, not merely by the obedience, the suffering, nor even the death of Christ, but by Christ's giving himself for us. The splendor of the gospel lies in the redeeming sacrifice of the Son of God. It is the gem of all the gospel gems.

Paul looked, [too], on the appearing of the Savior as a display of the grace of God. He says, "The grace of God that brings salvation has appeared to all men." It is not a private vision of God to a favored prophet but an open declaration of the grace of God to every creature under heaven—a display of the grace of God to all eyes that are open to behold it. When the Lord Jesus Christ came to Bethlehem and when he closed a perfect life by death on Calvary, he manifested the grace of God more gloriously than has been done by creation or providence. This is the clearest revelation of the mercy of God. In the Redeemer we see the unveiling of the Father's face—the laying bare of the divine heart. This was given us not because of any deservings on our part; it is a fullness of free, rich, undeserved grace. The grace of God has been made manifest to the entire universe in the appearing of Jesus Christ our Lord.

—C. H. *Spurgeon*

The grace of God . . . teaches us . . . to live . . . upright and godly lives in this present age, while we wait for the blessed hope—the glorious appearing of our great God and Savior, Jesus Christ.

—Titus 2:11–13

We live in an interval between two appearings of the Lord.[66] We are divided from the past by the words *Bethlehem, Gethsemane, Calvary.* All the rest of time is before Christ, and the chief landmark in all time to us is the wondrous life of him who is the light of the world.

We look forward to a second appearing—of glory rather than of grace. Our Lord, in the fullness of time, will descend from heaven with a loud command, with the voice of the archangel, with the trumpet of God. This is the terminus of the present age. We look from *anno Domini,* in which he came the first time, to that greater *anno Domini,* or year of our Lord, in which he will come a second time in all the splendor of his power to reign in righteousness and break the powers of evil.

Behind us is our trust; before us is our hope. Behind us is the Son of God in humiliation; before us is the great God our Savior in his glory.

We are living between the two beacons of the divine appearings. We have everything to hope for in the last appearing, as we have everything to trust to in the first appearing. We wait with patient hope throughout that weary interval. Paul calls it "this present age." This marks its fleeting nature. It is present now, but it will not be present long. We look to the things that are not seen and not present as being real and eternal. We traverse an enemy's country—there is no rest for us by the way.

Already I have given you the best argument for a holy life. If before you blazes the splendor of the Second Advent and behind you burns the everlasting light of the Redeemer's first appearing, what manner of people ought you to be! If indeed, you are but journeying through this present world, do not permit your hearts to be defiled with its sins.

Put on therefore the "armor of light" (Rom. 13:12). What a grand expression! Helmet of light, breastplate of light, shoes of light—everything of light. What a knight must one be who is clad in light! Like a wall of fire, the Lord's appearings are around you; there ought to be a special glory of holiness in the midst. That is the position of the righteous, and it furnishes a call to holiness.

—C. H. *Spurgeon*

Jesus Christ . . . gave himself for us to redeem us from all wickedness and to purify for himself a people that are his very own, eager to do what is good.

—Titus 2:13–14

[Jesus Christ] gave himself for us with these two objects: first, redemption, that he might redeem us from iniquity, that he might break the bonds of sin and cast the cords of depravity far from us.[67] He died—don't forget that—died that your sins might die, died that every lust might be dragged into captivity. He gave himself for you that you might give yourselves for him.

[Second], he died that he might purify us—purify us to himself. How clean we must be if we are to be clean to him! The holy Jesus will only commune with that which he has purified after the manner of his own nature—purified to himself. He has purified us to be his own people, his choice portion. Saints are Christ's crown jewels, his very own. He carries his people as lambs in his bosom. He engraves their names on his heart. They are the inheritance to which he is the heir, and he values them more than all the universe. He would lose everything else rather than lose one of them. He desires that you who are being disciplined by his grace should know that you are altogether his. You are Christ's men and women. You are each one to feel, "I do not belong to the world. I do not belong to myself. I belong only to Christ, set aside by him for himself only, and his I will be." The silver and the gold are his, and the cattle on a thousand hills are his, but he makes small account of them; "the LORD's portion is his people" (Deut 32:9).

The apostle says that we are to be "eager to do good." Would to God that all Christians were disciplined by grace until they became eager to do good! We are not only to approve of good works and speak for good works, but we are to be red-hot for them. We are to be on fire for everything that is right and true. We may not be content to be quiet and inoffensive, but we are to be eager to do good. There is plenty of fuel in the church; what is wanted is fire. Many respectable people are doing as little as they can for any good cause. This will never do. We must wake up. Oh, that all of us were ardent, fervent, zealous! Come, Holy Spirit, and kindle us! We may not go about to get this by our own efforts and energies, but God will work it by his grace. Grace given us in Christ is the fountainhead of all holy impulse. O heavenly grace, come like a flood at this time and bear us right away!

—C. H. *Spurgeon*

My meditation of him shall be sweet.
—Psalm 104:34 KJV

It is simple fact.[68] There is a heaven, whether we reach it or not. There is a vision of God, whether it ever dilate and enrapture our eyes or not. God is infinite blessedness and glory, and no good being can see him without partaking of it. The more clear and full our vision, the more overwhelming and boundless is the influx of heaven into us. We may know something of this here on earth. The more we meditate on God and divine things, the happier we will become in our own minds.

In the saints' everlasting rest, there is an unending contemplation and sight of God. Who of us are certain that we will not turn away when we find that this, and this alone, is heaven. For this vision of God, this sight of him face-to-face, this contemplation of his perfections is the substance of paradise.

Meditation on God and divine things elevates, sanctifies, and blesses. But though this Christian habit produces such great and good fruits, there is probably no duty that is more neglected. We find it easier to read our Bibles than to ponder on them, easier to listen to preaching than to digest it, easier to respond to the calls of benevolence and engage in external service in the church than to go into our closets. And isn't this the secret of the faint and sickly life in our souls? Do you think that if we often entered the presence of God and obtained a view of things unseen and eternal, earthly temptation would have such a strong power over us? Do you think that if we received every day a distinct and bold impression from the attributes of God, we would be so distant from him in our hearts? Can't we trace our neglect of duty, our lukewarm feelings, and our great worldliness of heart to our lack of the vision of God?

The success of Christians mainly depends on habitual communion with God. No spasmodic resolutions can be a substitute for it. If holy communion and prayer are interrupted, we will surely fall into sin. In this world of continual temptation and lethargic consciences, we need to be awakened and awed by the splendor of God's holy face. But we cannot see that amidst the vapors and smoke of everyday life. We must go into our closets and close the door and pray to our Father who sees what is done in secret. Then will we know how power to resist temptation comes from companionship with God. Then we will know what a Sabbath that soul enjoys who looks long and steadily at the divine perfections.

—William G. T. Shedd

My meditation of him shall be sweet.
—Psalm 104:34 KJV

Will the eagle that has soared in the open sky, that has gazed into the sun, endure to dwell in the dark cavern of the bat?[69] If the vision of God were glorious to our minds, wouldn't a return to the things of earth be reluctant?

It should, therefore, be a diligent practice to meditate on God and divine things. But the inclination is greatly lacking. The avocations of our daily lives do not require the whole of our mental energy and reflection. Time should be set apart and used for this sole purpose. It is startling to consider how much of our lives pass without any thought of God, without any recognition of his presence and his character. And how much of [life] might be spent in sweet and profitable meditation. Wouldn't thought on God steal through and suffuse all our other thinking, as sunset does the evening sky, giving a pure and saintly hue to all our feelings and pervading our entire experience?

It is still not so easy and pleasant as it ought to be to walk with God. It is still too difficult for us to be happy in heaven. A foundation for heaven in our own minds is required in order to enjoy the heaven that is on high. That rational being who does not practice the meditations and enjoy the experiences of heaven will not be at home there and, therefore, will not go there. Is it supposable that a soul who never here on earth contemplated the divine character with pleasure will see that character in eternity, in peace and joy? Is it supposable that a human spirit filled with self-seeking and worldliness, destitute of devout and adoring meditations, will be taken among seraphim and cherubim when taken out of time? We will know then what we really love and what we really loathe. For whatever we think of with most relish here in time we will think of with most relish in eternity. Those who love to think of wealth and fame and sensual pleasure will think of wealth and fame and sensual pleasure in eternity. But those who, in any degree, love to think of God and Christ will think of God and Christ in eternity— where all such thought is music and peace and rest.

If our meditation on God is sweet here, it will be sweeter in eternity. And then our blessedness will be certain and secure, for no spirit can be made unblessed in any part of God's vast dominions, if it really finds joy in the contemplation of the ever-present God.

—William G. T. Shedd

> *Now my heart is troubled, and what shall I say? "Father,*
> *save me from this hour"?*
>
> —John 12:27

The first thing Christianity does to the problem of suffering is to heighten and accentuate the difficulty of it.[70] In fact, it is precisely our Christian faith that creates the problem. Only to the believer is suffering a mystery. For only Christians say, "God is love"; therefore it is only they who have in their hands and hearts the terrible task of squaring the dark, tragic things in life with such a daring declaration of faith.

We must reject the solution that all suffering comes from God. God has created his world in such a way that sin and suffering are possibilities. But to hold, as some good people do, that God is the direct and immediate cause of everything that happens and, therefore, the cause of all the evil things that happen—that kind of rigid determinism, that almost mechanical predestination—affronts our moral sense and makes nonsense of the fact of human freedom.

We must equally reject the doctrine that all suffering is due to sin. Sin produces suffering in one form or another. Indeed, sin and folly and bungling and selfishness are responsible for a vast amount of suffering in the world today. But it is not true that all suffering is due to sin, as if someone's troubles were punishments, indications of some flaw in her or his character.

> Now there were some present at that time who told Jesus about the Galileans whose blood Pilate had mixed with their sacrifices. Jesus answered, "Do you think that these Galileans were worse sinners than all the other Galileans because they suffered this way? I tell you, no!" (Luke 13:1–3)

That is plain enough. Here you have it, on the authority of Jesus, that it is a false simplification to say that all suffering is due to sin.

What, then, are we to say? The search for a solution must be continued. It may be, of course, that we will find there is no complete and final answer to the mystery of suffering. We may be led to conclude that there will always, to the very end of the day, be need for an act of sheer naked faith. If that is so, we need not be ashamed. Faith requires no apology. And, if faith in God creates the problem, it is surely understandable that faith in God is going to answer it.

—James S. Stewart

Even in darkness light dawns for the upright.
—Psalm 112:4

If someone inquired, "Do you see the answer to the riddle of life and the mystery of sorrow?" we would answer "No, I do not see it."[71] But if the inquirer went on to ask, "Do you see any points of light, any places where the mystery is not quite so dark?" some of us would reply, "I think I do." Consider now some of these beams of light. For the darkness in which we walk is not impenetrable gloom, and the night—thank God—has stars.

The first beam of light is the *goodness of unbending law.* Even though the physical laws of the universe may work out tragically for people, yet if we could choose to live in a world without these laws, our predicament would be infinitely worse.

Sometimes it would facilitate things vastly if the laws of nature would bend back and let us dodge them. We all wish feverishly that they would do that sometimes. And yet, what kind of universe would it be in which nature were erratic and capricious? It would be a madhouse of a world.

The second beam of light is what the apostle Paul described as *our membership of one another.* If one person plays the fool, a dozen or a score or a thousand may be ruined. If one country breaks faith, the whole world may be plunged in cataclysm. But over against it you have to set this compensating consideration, that our mutual interdependence—which is responsible for so much of the sheer tragedy of life, is also responsible for life's greatest glory.

Think what you owe to this perilous fact of belonging to the human community. You cannot share the blessings and shirk the risks.

The third beam of light is *the wisdom of the divine impartiality.*

Most of us would say that the real crux of the whole problem of evil, the cruel sting of the thing, is the absolutely indiscriminate way in which trouble aims its blows with appalling indifference at those who deserve them and at those who do not deserve them in the least.

If a Christian escaped the troubles that visit other folk, if religion "got you off," religion would become a commercial transaction. And that would be the ruin of religion and character forever. No, far better that troubles should come and the heavens crash and fall than that righteousness should be sought for any reason except for righteousness' sake alone.

—James S. Stewart

> *Even in darkness light dawns for the upright.*
>
> —Psalm 112:4

There is a fourth beam of light, the awakening of the human conscience.[72]

One main function of the face of the suffering that we encounter all around us is to be a perpetual challenge to us to be cooperating with a burden-bearing God and to be giving ourselves in consecrated service for the healing of this broken earth.

If poverty, unemployment, and war were the will of God, there would be no call for us to stir a finger to remove the sufferings they bring. But if these things are not the will of God at all but simply the product of human bungling and selfishness and sin, and if, accordingly, God's mind and program for the race is that [these things] should one day be banished from the earth, then clearly we are not meant to lie down under them.

He means us to be the agents of his purpose and the channels of his providence to one another.

Yet we admit quite frankly that if these gleams of light were the sum-total of the comfort to be offered, one would hardly have the heart to dwell on it at all. For what men and women want most in the hour of trouble is not an answer to a problem but a power to carry them through. And, indeed, even if the best and most completely satisfying solution of the mystery of suffering were available, that would not alter the fact that the actual suffering itself—the grim reality in experience—would still be there to be endured.

So we begin to see that there is a deeper question. The ultimate demand is not "Why has this happened to me?" but "How, seeing it has happened, am I to face it?" And when you see that, suddenly the New Testament comes right in. The New Testament is not much concerned about Why? But it is desperately and magnificently concerned about How? It does not offer you a theory and an explanation—it offers you a power and a victory.

Now we must press right in, until we reach the Holy Place, and there we shall see, coming forth to meet us, God's answer—when we lift our eyes and gaze on a cross.

—James S. Stewart

Although he was a son, he learned obedience
from what he suffered.

—Hebrews 5:8

There is a fifth light that flashes out before us.[73] It is the gift that suffering brings to character, the contribution trouble makes to the molding and shaping and beautifying of the soul. Even of Jesus it stands written that "he learned obedience from what he suffered."

It takes a world with trouble in it to make possible some of the finest qualities of life. You do not need to be an art connoisseur to realize that it is an essential of a good picture that in it there should be shadow as well as light. Now life is like that. If there were no risk and danger in life, where would fortitude and chivalry be? If there were no suffering, would there be compassion? If there were no discipline and hardship, would we ever learn patience and endurance?

It takes a world with trouble in it to satisfy the human demand for a dangerous universe. The passion for adventure haunts the human spirit. There is that in us which craves risk.

It takes a world with trouble in it to train people for their high calling as children of God and to carve on the soul the profile of Christ.

Who are those whose names stand on the dramatic roll-call of the faithful in the Epistle to the Hebrews? Are they people whose days were happy and unclouded and serene? "They were stoned; they were sawed in two; they were put to death by the sword. They went about in sheepskins and goatskins, destitute, persecuted and mistreated. . . . They wandered in deserts and mountains, and in caves and holes in the ground." That, declares the New Testament, has been in every age faith's grim heredity! And it is not from sheltered ways and quiet, sequestered paths; it is from a thousand crosses that the cry ascends—"Hallelujah! For our Lord God Almighty reigns" (Rev. 19:6).

—James S. Stewart

Although he was a son, he learned obedience
from what he suffered.

—Hebrews 5:8

If some recording angel were to visit all our homes today, and we were asked to name the experiences that have blessed and taught us most, surely that angel's book would tell of enrichment brought by God's gifts of love, home, nature, and the beauty of the world; but page after page would tell how trouble, difficulty, bereavement, disappointment—all the things that hurt and leave a mark—had brought blessing by imparting new depth, new insight, to the soul.[74] And these words that stand written of God's firstborn child, Jesus, God himself may be using as he looks on others of his children: "Although he was a son, he learned obedience from what he suffered."

Isn't this the great transfiguring discovery, that pain can be creative? You do not just have to bear it negatively; you can use it positively. By the grace of God, you can compel the darkest, bitterest experiences to yield up hidden treasures of sweetness and light. Do not think the trials and troubles are meaningless; one day you are going to look into the face of God and thank him for every sorrow and for every tear you ever shed. The true Christian reaction to suffering and sorrow takes difficulties as a God-given opportunity and regards troubles as a sacred trust and wears the thorns as a crown.

Let this be added—that the loveliest thing of all about the creative attitude toward suffering is that not only do you develop your own character, but you become a source of blessing and of strength to others.

There is nothing on earth more beautiful to see than suffering transmuted into love. To say that the bitter cup can be drunk heroically is no more than every brave man or woman knows already, but to say that one soul's hurt and suffering can distill out life and strength and healing for others—that is the everlasting miracle.

"Yes," someone will say, "but how am I to do it? I see now that suffering is not so much a problem to be explained as a challenge to be met, but how am I to meet it?"

The only answer that can ultimately suffice is God incarnate on a cross, facing there the worst that suffering and evil have ever done on the earth. For still he comes to us, this Christ victorious over all the mystery of suffering and evil, and offers to make his triumph ours.

—James S. Stewart

In all these things we are more than conquerors.
—Romans 8:37

Why should a Roman gallows, and the strange Man who hung there, haunt the imagination and the conscience of our race?[75]

It is because humankind, in the depths of the spirit, has always been conscious that in that Cross, God has spoken, and eternity has intersected history. We know that, past all our attempts to answer the problem of evil and suffering, here is *God's* answer. Here, if anywhere, is the clue to solve the riddle [of life and the mystery of sorrow].

It is not the fact of suffering that baffles us, for we can see that we need it; it is the frightful excess of the thing that seems so cruel and senseless. If God intends human sanctification, why couldn't he have thought out some kindlier way?

There is still another difficulty. We talk about suffering producing character. But it does not always have that effect. The beneficent influence of pain does not work automatically! In different lives, suffering produces different effects. One man loses his wife, and the loss makes him more tender and gentle. Another faces the same loss, and it makes him hard and sullen. One woman has a great sorrow, and it turns her to God. Another [has] a similar experience, and she is never seen inside a church again.

Trouble, in itself, is neither positive nor negative. It is neutral; whether it is going to become positive or negative depends on the human reaction. Some have the grace to use it creatively, forcing trouble to yield up its hidden blessing. But we do not always rise to that. How often our negative reaction balks even his will to bless!

This fact emerges—that our main concern with suffering is not to find an explanation; it is to find a victory. It is to lay hold on a power. Even if you possessed the answer to the riddle, had it written down to the last detail and could say, "There is the full and final explanation of the problem of pain," that would not be enough, would it? For the pain itself would still have to be borne. That is the real demand of the human spirit—not the explaining of this thing, but grace and help to bear it. *And that is why God gave us Christ.*

On every page of your New Testament the living God comes toward you, and he holds in his hands not the answer to the questions of the mind but something better and diviner: a liberating, reinforcing power for the soul!

—James S. Stewart

In all these things we are more than conquerors through him who loved us.

—Romans 8:37

What does the Cross tell about the fact of suffering?[76] It tells you that *God is in it with you.* When I grasp that the sufferer hanging there is God incarnate, then my heart answers those who speak of a remote, spectator God, "You are wrong! In every pang that rends the heart of man, woman, or little child, God has a share."

What is the Christian answer to the mystery of suffering? Not an explanation but a reinforcing presence—Christ to stand beside you through the darkness, Christ's companionship to make the dark experience sacred. "Even though I walk through the valley of the shadow of death, I will fear no evil, for you are with me."

How different suffering becomes to those who have seen that vision! It is not just that God knows and sympathizes with you in your troubles. He is *in* you. And therefore your sufferings are his suffering, your sorrow his sorrow. Now that is true of all God's creatures. Just think what God's burden of suffering must be when the pains of all the world are in his heart! No one who has once grasped this will ever again rail at providence for being unkind. All our accusations and complainings are silenced before the agony of God.

But remember this: if God shares your suffering, it is also true that you share his redemptive activity and his victory. "By his wounds we are healed." Thus, suffering gives you a chance to cooperate with God. Every soul that takes its personal griefs and troubles and offers these up on the altar alongside the sacrifice of Jesus is sharing constructively in that eternal passion of God. It is as though God said, in the day of darkness, "Here, my child, is something you can do for me!"

The real healers of human wounds are those whose own peace has been bought at a price, behind whose understanding and compassion there lies some memory of a valley of shadow, a lonely way, a wrestling in the dark.

If from one soul's hurt and conflict, the balm of healing and of peace can thus be distilled out for others, if pain can be transmuted into power, if, under Christ, our sacrifices can be made creative and redemptive—shall we still rail at life when it grows hard, and brood its cruelty and injustice? "Therefore I will boast all the more gladly about my weaknesses, that Christ's power may rest on me" (2 Cor. 12:9).

—James S. Stewart

In all these things we are more than conquerors through
him who loved us.

—Romans 8:37

God is in it with you, and you are in it with God—that is the message of the Cross on the mystery of suffering.[77] And that message means victory. The crucified figure of Christ looks, at first glance, pathetically like defeat. It looks like the climax of all the pathos of the world. But you do not see the Cross aright at first glance. You have to gaze and gaze again. And those who do that make a marvelous discovery. They see, not Christ the pain-drenched sufferer, but Christ the mighty victor. They see the blackest tragedy of this earth becoming earth's most dazzling triumph.

Isn't there a wonderful sense of mastery right through the passion narrative? "No one takes [my life] from me, but I lay it down of my own accord. I have authority to lay it down and authority to take it up again" (John 10:18). Isn't there royalty in that? See him marching to Jerusalem. Mark well his serenity through the last terrible days. Watch his bearing before Pilate. See him on the cross refusing the drug they offered. Hear the shout that broke on the darkness: "It is finished!" Is that defeat? Yes, it is, but not Christ's defeat—certainly not that! But the defeat of suffering. The defeat of the mystery of evil and of all the dark tragic powers of life—and Christ's victory! You are King of glory, O Christ—Conqueror renowned!

"But what has all this to do with me?" you ask.

Surely the answer is clear. If evil at its worst has already been met and mastered, if God has turned suffering's most awful triumph into uttermost defeat—if that in fact has happened, and on that scale, are you to say it cannot happen on the infinitely lesser scale of your own life, by union with Christ through faith? If you will only open your nature to the invasion of Christ's Spirit, you will do as he did. "In all these things"—these desolating, heartbreaking things that happen to us, these physical pains, these mental agonies, these spiritual midnights of the soul—"we are more than conquerors," not through our own valor or stoic resolution, not through a creed or code or philosophy, but "through him who loved us."

That is the only answer to the mystery of suffering, and the answer is a question: Will you let God reign? The answer is not a theory. It is a life. It is a dedicated spirit, a fully surrendered soul. May that answer be ours!

—James S. Stewart

> *Then all the disciples deserted him and fled.*
> —Matthew 26:56

Judged by any human standard, the life of Christ had proved a misadventure and a mistake.[78] Amid the Hosannas of an admiring throng, he entered the Holy City, the acknowledged King of Israel. Then came the end. The populace turned against him. His own disciples deserted him. He was left alone—amidst the insults of the judgment hall, in the agonies of the Cross. Could any failure be more complete?

Failure is inevitable. Success is not the rule of human life. It is the rare exception. The path of life is strewn with the corpses of magnificent projects and brilliant hopes crushed and trampled under foot.

If failure is inevitable, how can we turn it to account? What are its special uses?

Failure is a discipline. As a test of strength and as a test of faith alike it is without a rival.

[Have you] felt enthusiasm burning in your heart? You tried and failed, and your faith deserted you. You felt that you were left alone; you did not feel that the Father was with you. You appropriated the one-half of Christ's experience, the sense of failure; you did not appropriate the other and the essential half, the persistence of faith. There was in you then, there is in you now, if you will only believe it, a power that can defy failure, a power that must be victorious, because it is a power of God and not of your own.

The life of Christ was the most stunning failure, followed by the most stunning triumph that the world has ever seen.

This is the example of all examples. God's purpose cannot fail. Whatever is honest, whatever is lovely, whatever is pure, whatever is truthful has vitality that no time can obliterate and no antagonism can subdue. Believe this and no failure will be a failure to you. It will only be a triumph deferred. The pains that you have spent in reclaiming that poor outcast are not thrown away, though you see no immediate fruits. The seeds of morality and goodness that you have sown in that wayward child are not lost, though the soil seems hard and barren now. You may not live to see it. Your life may be pronounced a failure. Dare to face this possibility. But your work cannot die. Think of Christ, your Master. Trust God, who is one, and not the world because it is many. "This is the victory that has overcome the world, even our faith" (1 John 5:4).

—J. B. Lightfoot

And [Peter] went outside and wept bitterly. . . . Then
[Judas] went away and hanged himself.
—Matthew 26:75; 27:5

Simon of Bethsaida and Judas of Kerioth had possessed all things in common: common opportunities, common associations, common trials and dangers.[79] They had witnessed the same works and listened to the same words. They had lived in the same Presence. They had received the same revelation of the same Father from the same hallowed lips. Altogether it might have been thought that their characters must have been cast in the same mold. From what then came this difference?

From what but in the use or misuse of that mysterious, that fatal, that magnificent gift of God to humanity—free will?

Both were tempted. Both yielded to the temptation. The same night was fatal to the one and to the other. Just at this moment it might have seemed as if there were little to choose between Peter and Judas. How is it then that Peter rises again, while Judas sinks down, sinks suddenly, sinks irretrievably, sinks forever?

It was not what Judas had *done* but what Judas had *become* that prevented his rising. His guilt was great, but God's mercy is greater. His guilt was great, but God's pardon does not nicely calculate less or more.

Faith and hope are the two requisites without which restoration is impossible—faith in God and hope for the future. With these is life-giving repentance; without these is crushing remorse.

As long as we look only to ourselves, pardon seems wholly beyond our reach. There is nothing in our own hearts, nothing in our past lives that suggests it. It is well that we should grieve over our sins; it is not well that we should give ourselves up to overmuch self-dissection. Our failings must be our stepping-stones; they must not be our stumbling blocks. We cannot suffer them to cripple our energies or to bar our path. But this will always be the case so long as our gaze is directed solely within. For here we find only feebleness, only vacillation, only ignorance, only failure and sin. Our strength, our consolation, our renewal are elsewhere. It is only when our hearts go forth in faith to God the all wise and almighty, God the merciful, God our Father that the pardon comes, that the pure heart is made and the steadfast spirit renewed within us. This faith Judas did not realize. He knew God only as an avenging judge. He did not know him as a loving Father.

—J. B. Lightfoot

And [Peter] went outside and wept bitterly. . . . Then
[Judas] went away and hanged himself.
—Matthew 26:75; 27:5

The concentration on self is a denial of faith.[80] The concentration on the past is an exclusion of hope. Judas could not face the future. The past had been an utter failure. Yet the future was all before him; the future was uncompromised. The two great preachers of the Gospel were destined to be Peter the denier of Christ and Paul the persecutor of Christ. Why should not Judas the betrayer of Christ have made up the triad? Why not—except that having lost faith he had lost hope also.

Hope is the reflection of God's mercy; hope is the echo of God's love. Hope is energy, hope is strength, hope is life. Without hope, sorrow for sin will lead only to ruin. We have no time to brood over the errors of the past, while the hours are hurrying relentlessly by. Have you been tempted? Have you yielded? Have you sinned? Then go out from the scene of your temptation, as Peter went out, and weep bitter tears of repentance before God. But having done this, return, return at once and strengthen your brothers and sisters. In active charity for others, in devoted service to God is the truest safeguard against the suicidal promptings of remorse. Be the foremost to bear witness of him to an unbelieving world—the foremost in zeal, the foremost in danger, the foremost to do and to suffer. The past is beyond recall. Put it behind you. The future is full of magnificent opportunities. Be energetic, be courageous, be hopeful. In the agony of your contrition, from the depths of your despair, listen to the divine voice that summons you: "Let the dead bury their own dead"—dead opportunities, dead regrets, dead failures, yes, even dead sins—and "follow me" (Matt. 8:22; cf. Luke 9:60).

—J. B. Lightfoot

Jesus replied, "Have I not chosen you, the Twelve? Yet one
of you is a devil!" (He meant Judas . . . who, though one of
the Twelve, was later to betray him.)
—John 6:70–71

We are confronted with the archtraitor himself, whose name is [for] all generations branded with infamy.[81] For he betrayed the friend who was the very per-
sonification of love; he betrayed the cause in which the eternal interests of
humanity are bound up; he betrayed the country, the kingdom of heaven, where
we all aspire to dwell.

When [Judas] was chosen, he was worthy of the choice; there was in him perhaps the making of a Saint Peter or a Saint John. Can we suppose that he alone
made no sacrifices, suffered no privations, met with no reproaches during those
three years in which he followed the Master? All this while, Judas was on his trial,
as we are on our trial. He was not compelled by an irresistible fate to act worthily
of his calling; he was free to make his election between good and evil; he rejected
the good, and he chose the evil.

[Christ's] little company was not intended to be perfect. Otherwise it would
have conveyed no lessons to us. It had its coward in Peter, its skeptic in Thomas,
and it had also its traitor in Judas.

Had he not heard [Jesus] as he denounced the worries of this life and the
deceitfulness of wealth? Amidst all distractions, through every discouragement,
Judas had remained, had persevered, had listened—and yet he was a traitor.

And hadn't he also witnessed those works that were the very credentials of
[Jesus'] messianic claims? Hadn't he been present when those five thousand were
fed on the few loaves in Galilee? Hadn't he seen the lame walk and the dumb
speak and the lepers cleansed? and yet he was a traitor.

[Judas] had allowed one vile passion to grow unchecked in his heart. His office as treasurer of the little company had given him opportunities of indulging
this passion. He had yielded and so fell.

When people placed in positions favorable to the development of the higher
self do nevertheless give rein to some vicious tendency within, the vice seems to
gain strength by this very fact. It can only be indulged by resistance to the good
influences about them, and resistance always gives compactness and force, always
braces the capacity, whether for good or for evil.

—J. B. Lightfoot

Jesus replied, "Have I not chosen you, the Twelve? Yet one of you is a devil!" (He meant Judas . . . who, though one of the Twelve, was later to betray him.)
—John 6:70–71

It is the often-told tale of a single sin springing up and luxuriating in secret, till in its rank growth it has twined itself around the fibers of the heart and choked and killed with its poisonous embrace whatever there was of pure and noble and good in the soul.[82] [Judas] had, as everyone whether good or bad has in some form or other, an evil tendency in his heart. Here was his trial; here might have been his moral education. But he made it his master, and it plunged him in headlong ruin. There was, first of all, the pleasure of fingering the coin; then there was the desire of accumulating; then there was the reluctant hand and the grudging heart in distributing alms; then there was the silent appropriation of some trifling sum as indemnification for a real or imagined personal loss; then there was the first unmistakable act of petty fraud—and so it went on and on, until the disciple became the thief, the trusted became the traitor, the apostle of Christ [became] the son of perdition.

For there was no external check on him. The moral checks—the influences, the companionships, the divine presence—ought to have been more than a compensation for the absence of material checks. The incomings and the outgoings of the common purse were alike precarious. There was no balancing of ledgers, no auditing of accounts in the little company. No one knew what was received and what was spent. Each trusted and each was trusted by the other.

Up to the time of his fall Judas had been avaricious, miserly, fraudulent. Let us use the plain language of the Evangelist, he had been a thief. But a traitor, an archtraitor—this was far from his thoughts.

The opportunity came.

The end we know. He flung back the accursed coin, the seal of his guilt, to those who had tempted to the fatal act. He could not bear the light, could not bear life, could not bear himself.

Only his history remains as a warning to us how the greatest spiritual privileges may be neutralized by the indulgence of one illicit passion, and the life that is lived in the face of the unclouded sun may set at last in the night of despair.
—J. B. Lightfoot

No one can hold back his hand or say to him:
"What have you done?"

—Daniel 4:35

God has reigned from the first day; God shall reign when days are gone.[83] Everywhere he is the reigning God—reigning when Pharaoh said, "Who is the LORD, that I should obey him?" reigning when scribe and Pharisee, Jew and Roman, nailed his only-begotten Son to the cross; reigning amid all the calamities that sweep the globe, as much as he will be in the golden days of peace. Never is the throne vacant, never is the scepter laid aside. Your monarch has not yielded his sword to a superior foe, you do not have to search for another leader. In the person of his dear Son he walks among our golden lampstands and holds our stars in his right hand.

Here is our comfort; it is right that God should have this might, because he always uses his might with strictest rectitude. God cannot will to do anything unjust, ungenerous, unkind—ungodlike. No laws bind him as they bind us, but he is a law to himself. There is "Thou shalt," and "Thou shalt not," for me, for you, but who will attempt to be legislator to the King of kings? God is love. God is holiness. God is the law. God is love, and, doing as he wills, he wills to love. God is holy, and, doing as he wills, he wills holiness, he wills justice, he wills truth. It is not for me to unriddle the enigmas of the Infinite—he will explain himself. I am not so impertinent as to be his apologist; he will clear himself. I am not called to vindicate his character. "Will not the Judge of all the earth do right?" (Gen. 18:25). What folly to hold up a candle to show the brightness of the sun! How much more foolish to attempt to defend the thrice-holy Jehovah! Let him speak for himself if he will deign to contend with you.

How wise to be at one with him! He invites you to come. He might have commanded you to depart. If he is on our side, who can be against us? How this should help you that suffer! If God does it all, and nothing happens apart from God, even human wickedness and cruelty being still overruled by him, you readily may submit. It is your God who is in it all, your Father God, the infinitely good. If we can bow before his crushing strokes and feel that if the crushing of us by the weight of his hand will bring him honor we are content, this is true faith. Give us grace enough, O Lord, never to fail in our loyalty but to be your faithful servants even to suffering's bitterest end.

—C. H. Spurgeon

O daughter, consider and give ear: . . . The king is en-
thralled by your beauty; honor him, for he is your lord.
—Psalm 45:10–11

This psalm is called the song of loves, the most pure and spiritual loves, namely, those that are between Christ and his church.[84]

If you are married to Christ, you know and speak with him. You will endeavor to promote his interest and advance his name in the world. Surely this is the only desirable marriage, and the Lord Jesus Christ is the only lover who is worth seeking after.

Do you desire one who is great? He is the glory of heaven, admired by angels, dreaded by devils, and adored by saints. For you to be married to so great a king—what honor will you have by this marriage?

Do you desire one who is rich? The fullness of the earth belongs to Christ. You will share in his riches, and you will hereafter be admitted to glory and will live with this Jesus to all eternity.

Do you desire one who is wise? There is none comparable to Christ for wisdom. His knowledge is infinite, and his wisdom is correspondent to it. And if you are married to Christ, he will guide and counsel you.

Do you desire one who is potent, who may defend you against your enemies and all the insults and reproaches of the Pharisees of this generation? There is none who can equal Christ in power, for the Lord Jesus Christ has all power.

Do you desire one who is good? There is none like Christ. Others may have some goodness, but it is imperfect; Christ is full of goodness and in him dwells no evil.

Do you desire one who is beautiful? Christ is the most lovely person of all others in the world.

Do you desire one who can love you? None can love you like Christ.

For you who are married to him, he underwent death on the cross; can you hear this and not be concerned to think that the blessed Jesus underwent this for such sinful creatures as you and I? Surely, then, none is so deserving as the Lord Jesus Christ for you to engage yourselves to; if you are married to Christ he is yours, all that he is, all that he has; you will have his heart and share in the choicest expressions of his love.

The Lord Jesus Christ implores you to be his spouse. We ministers have a commission to invite you, in his name, to this very thing.

—George Whitefield

Jehovah of hosts is with us; the God of Jacob is our refuge.
—Psalm 46:7, 11 ASV

"Jehovah of hosts," the unpronounceable name, the incommunicable name, the name that stood as the sign and symbol of the infinite things of God.[85] Jehovah was the name that most forcefully gave expression to the facts concerning God that were beyond human comprehension—his absoluteness, without beginning, without end, without counsel taken, without forethought—for there was no thought before him—Jehovah.

This phrase, "Jehovah of hosts," teaches us that Jehovah is absolute, sufficient, and superior. It declares to us that God is the Lord of the heavens and all their inhabitants.

As the phrase passes our lips we are amid the eternal expanse, the unfallen intelligences—the vision of any one of which would blind us. And suddenly we move to the earth. The stars grow dim until they are but flecks [in the] night; the angels pass from our vision and we are on one small planet, in one small country looking into the face of one lonely man—Jacob. The psalmist says that the God who is the God of all the hosts is the God of that individual, as surely and positively interested in that one speck of thinking life as in all the unfallen intelligences of the upper spaces—as surely and as positively committed to that man as to all the order of the infinite universe.

Of all people for astute, hard-driving meanness, recommend to me Jacob. But God is "the God of Jacob." Oh, my soul, here find your comfort! I do not know whether it helps you, but it helps me. He is the God of Jacob, mean as Jacob was. This is the thing on which my faith fastens. Was that man such a person as I am? The longer I live the more astonished I am at that infinite grace that found me and loves me and keeps me. The meanness that lurks within, the possibilities of evil that I have discovered make me ask, "Will God look at me?" He is "the God of Jacob." He was his God and loved him notwithstanding all his meanness, led him, told him where to rest his head.

Notwithstanding the failure and wreckage of this life, despite that it is anything but what God meant it to be, that in its attempts to create its own destiny has led itself into blight and vain ambition, yet the inspiring word comes to me—"the God of Jacob." He has created us, and we have broken all his laws, but he is our God still and broods over us tenderly, our folly notwithstanding.
—G. Campbell Morgan

Jehovah of hosts is with us; the God of Jacob is our refuge.
—Psalm 46:7, 11 asv

The God of the stars will fight for me against the foes that hinder me as I climb toward the home of God.[86] He will command the whole universe for the making of a soul. Do you doubt me? Then let me remind you that for the purchase of my soul and yours, for our reconciliation and redemption, he gave one supreme gift that was infinitely superior to all the stars—the One by whose word they were made and in whose might they have consisted through the ages. He gave him for the remaking of my broken, spoiled life. The stars, the host of God if need be, will be pressed into the service of the making of the saint and into the service of the saints as they go forth in toil for God.

What did he do for Jacob? Think of his history. See at what infinite pains God was to make something out of him. Oh, the patience of God!

And he went down over the Jabbok, and God met with him and crippled him to make him. It was a wonderful night, only do not let us misinterpret it. Do not talk as though Jacob wrestled with God and overcame him. It is not true. With strong crying and tears he said, "I will not let you go unless you bless me" (Gen. 32:26). It was a voice choked with sorrow, the voice of someone being beaten, being crippled, in the last agony of despair as he went down beneath the pressure of that mysterious hand. He won when he was beaten; he triumphed when he yielded, and God never let him alone until, that night, by crippling him he broke him.

Oh, you who are conscious of your own weakness, you who are conscious of the evil within you that baffles, beats, and spoils you, "the God of Jacob is our refuge." When the only pillow we have is a hard, unsympathetic stone, he will open his heaven so that his hosts may teach us that those with us are more than those who are against us, and he will put his hands on us and, it may be, wound us, but the wounding is only for the deeper healing.

Oh, dear heart, tried as by fire, sing while the fire burns, sing while the pain is hot. If you trust him, he breaks to make, he cripples to crown. By God's grace we go on, not thinking of resigning or giving this fight or anything up except sin. "The LORD of hosts," marshaling all for our making, "is with us." We will follow, we will trust, we will fight—God helping us.

—G. Campbell Morgan

He is not the God of the dead, but of the living.
—Mark 12:27

In the Bible, the *nature* of the life to come is not so clear as the *fact* of the life to come.[87] Yet we are not left without hint as to what the nature of that life will be.

The Bible tells us that our personalities persist, go on. The Sadducees, who did not believe in angel or spirit or resurrection, once came to Jesus with that question about the seven-times-married woman who had survived all her husbands. The Sadducees wanted to know whose wife she would be in the Resurrection. Jesus told them that they misconceived the nature of the Resurrection and the future life. He reminded them of what God said to Moses at the burning bush: "Have you not read, . . . 'I am the God of Abraham, the God of Isaac, and the God of Jacob.' God is not the God of the dead but of the living." Personality, the you, the me, goes on.

The Bible tells us that the future life will be a life of great power and endowment—the "powers of the coming age." Paul said our bodies in the life to come will be like the resurrection body of Christ. If so, what an organ of expression we will have and what a platform of existence on which to stand!

Since we are to have so wonderful an organ of life and expression, it follows that we will have some great and high use for such a body and such a spirit. Here in this life all the noblest human work is done in connection with ignorance, suffering, sorrow, vice, and sin. But one day all those things are to pass away. What, then, will be the work of redeemed souls? What has Moses been doing since God buried him on Nebo's lonely mountain? What has Elijah been doing since the day he went up to heaven in a whirlwind? That we must leave to the infinite resources of God.

Further, the Bible tells us that the life to come will be a life of holiness. This we learn from one of those great "no mores" with which the Bible describes the heavenly life: no more sea of separation, no more night, no more fear, no more tears, and no more curse—that is, no more sin. We will do naturally and gladly what God wills. Then, with every evil cast out, clothed and in our right minds, we will stand before the Creator as God designed us at the beginning when he said, "Let us make man in our image."

—Clarence E. Macartney

> *Worship the* Lord *in the splendor of his holiness.*
>
> —Psalm 96:9

Worship consists in the finding of my own life and the yielding of it wholly to God for the fulfillment of his purpose.[88] That is worship!

You say, "Would you tell us to find our lives? Didn't Jesus say we must lose them?" Yes, "whoever finds his life will lose it," but he did not finish there: "whoever loses his life for my sake will find it" (Matt. 10:39), not another life, not a new life, not a new order of life—not an angel's life, for instance, but his or her own life. The Cross is necessary, restraint is necessary, sacrifice is necessary, self-denial is necessary, but these things are all preliminary.

And so if the Cross is absolutely necessary, and it is—your cross, my cross, my individual dying to the ambitions of selfish desire, all that is necessary—but beyond it, life. What life? My life. The new creation is but the finding of the meaning of and the fulfillment of the purposes of the first creation. "Worship the Lord in the splendor of his holiness." Discover his law, answer his law, walk in the way of his appointing. Let him who made you lead out all the facts of your life to the fulfillment of his purpose, and then your whole life is worship.

This [church] service is but a pause in which in word and attitude we give expression to life's inner song. And if there is no such inner song, there is no worship here. The outward acts are the least important parts of our worship. If I have not been worshiping God for the last six days, I cannot worship him this morning. If there has been no song through my life to God, I am not prepared to sing his praise. The worship of the sanctuary is wholly meaningless and valueless except as it is preceded by and prepared for by the worship of the life.

And it is in the service of a life, not specific acts done as apart from the life, not because I teach in Sunday school or preach here, that I worship. I may preach here today and never worship. But because my life is found in his law, is answering his call, responsive to his provision and arrangement, so, almost without knowing it, my life has become a song, a praise, an anthem. So I worship! I join the angels and all nature in worship when I become what God intends I should be.

And so I pray that when the service is over, and Sunday has passed, we may know that in the shop, in the home and marketplace, in all the toil of the commonplaces, we can worship the Lord in the splendor of his holiness.

—G. Campbell Morgan

In that case the offense of the cross has been abolished.
—*Galatians 5:11*

Paul lovingly yearned over the Jews.[89] When we remember that deep longing we realize what the Cross meant for Paul. For the great stumbling block for the Jews—the offense that made the gospel of Christ smell rank to them—was the Cross. That was the one theme Paul would not ignore.

There is a great lesson there for all who are trying to advance Christ's kingdom. The more eager they are to have people saved, the more willing they are to go all lengths to meet them. And that is right, but remember, there are a few facts we cannot yield, though they run counter to the whole spirit of the age. It were better to empty a church and preach the Cross than to fill it by keeping silent like a coward. It were better to fail as Paul failed with the Jews than to succeed by being a traitor to the Cross.

The Cross was offensive to the Jews just because it shattered every dream they ever dreamed. They had prayed for and had dreamed of their Messiah, and he was to come in power as a conqueror. Then—in the place of the triumph—there comes Calvary. In place of the Christ victorious comes Christ crucified. And was this the Messiah who was to trample Rome, pierced in hands and feet by Roman nails? To the Jews a stumbling block—you cannot wonder at it, when every hope they had formed was contradicted.

[The] offense of Calvary is just as powerful now as it was then. If I know anything about the ideals people cherish now and about the hopes that reign in ten thousand hearts, they are as antagonistic to the Cross as was the Jewish ideal of Messiah. Written across Calvary is sacrifice; written across this age of ours is pleasure. On the lips of Christ are the stern words, *I must die.* On the lips of this age of ours, *I must enjoy.* When I think of the passion to be rich and the judgment of everything by money standards, of the desire at all costs to be happy, of the frivolity, of the worship of success—and then contrast it with the scene on the hill, I know that the offense of Calvary has not ceased. A stumbling block to Jews—to far more than the Jews—to a pleasure-loving world and a dead church. Therefore say nothing about it. Let it be. Make everything interesting, pleasant, easy. Then the offence of the Cross has been abolished—and with it the power of the gospel.

—George H. Morrison

In that case the offense of the cross has been abolished.
—Galatians 5:11

The cross was an offense to the Jews because it swept away much that they took a pride in.[90] If there was any meaning in Calvary at all, some of their most cherished things were valueless. The Jews were preeminently a religious people, and this is always one peril of religious people—to take the things that lead to God and let the heart grow centered on them. There was the ceremonial law, for instance, with its scrupulous abhorrence of defilements. And there were the sacrifices and the feasts and festivals and journeys to Jerusalem. And there was the temple, that magnificent building, sign of their hope and symbol of their unity. Let this be said, that if they were proud, they were proud of worthy things. It is better to be proud of law and temple than to be proud of battleship and millionaire. Yet all that pride was swept away like autumn leaves—if there was any meaning in the Cross. No more would people's eyes turn to Jerusalem, no more would sacrifices fill the altars, no more was there room for ceremonial law, if the Son of God had died on the tree. And it was this crushing into the very dust of all that was dearest to the Jewish heart that was so bitter an offense of Calvary.

Today, has that stumbling block been removed? This is still the offense of Calvary—it cuts at the root of so much that we are proud of. There hangs the Redeemer saying, "No one comes to the Father except through me" (John 14:6).

Here is the offense of the cross in cultured ages: it is that people must go with empty hands, knowing our utter need of the pardoning mercy of Almighty God. We like a little toil and sweat. We measure the value of most things by all that it has cost us to procure them. And Calvary costs us nothing, though it cost God everything. The love and the life of it are freely offered, and to a commercial age there is something suspicious and offensive there. Ah, people, if I preached salvation by good works, how it would appeal to many an eager heart. I do not believe that if you do your best, all is well for time and for eternity. But I do believe—

> Not the labors of my hands
> Can fulfil Thy law's demands; . . .
> Thou must save, and Thou alone.
> —Augustus M. Toplady

—George H. Morrison

In that case the offense of the cross has been abolished.
—Galatians 5:11

The Cross was an offense to the Jews because it obliterated national distinctions.[91] It leveled those social barriers that were of such untold worth in Jewish eyes. They had had the bittersweet privilege of being lonely, and, being lonely, they had been ennobled; they were a chosen nation. The covenants were theirs, theirs were the promises. The knowledge of the one true God was theirs, [and] there rose in the Jewish mind a certain contempt for all the other human nations. They had no envy of the art of Greece. They were not awed by the majesty of Rome. Greeks and Romans were but Gentiles.

Then came the Cross. It leveled all distinctions; it burst through all barriers of nationality. There was neither Jew nor Greek, slave nor free, male nor female, but all were one in Christ. Let wild savages from the farthest west come to the cross of Christ pleading for mercy, and they had nothing less to do, and nothing more, than the proudest Jew who was a child of Abraham. One feels the insult of it all, how it left the Jews defenseless. All they had clung to was gone, their vineyard walls were shattered. And this tremendous leveling of distinctions—to the proud, reserved, and lonely people—was no small part of the offense of Calvary.

I would not have you imagine that Christ disregards all personal distinctions. If I sent you away harboring the thought that all who come to Christ get the same treatment, I would have done him an unutterable wrong. In everything he did, Christ was original, yet in no sphere was he so strikingly original as in the way he handled those who came to him. There is always some touch, some word, some discipline that tells of an individual understanding. But in spite of all that and recognizing that, this is the "scandal" of the Cross, that there every distinction is obliterated, and people must be saved as lost or not at all.

The brightest heart here needs pardon and peace with God in Christ as much as the wildest prodigal in Glasgow. Accept it. It is freely offered you. Say, "You, O Christ, are all I need." And then, just as the wilderness will blossom, so will the offense of the Cross become its glory.

—George H. Morrison

I am the LORD, *who heals you.*

—Exodus 15:26

The Lord our God will heal our spirits as he healed Marah.[92] First, he made the people know how bitter Marah was. There was no healing for that water till they had tasted it and discovered that it was too brackish to be endured, but after they knew its bitterness, then the Lord made it sweet to them. So is it with your sin. It must become more and more bitter to you, [making] you feel that you cannot live on anything that is in yourself. God's way is first to wound and then to heal. He begins by making Marah to be Marah ["bitter"], and afterwards he makes it sweet.

Next, there was prayer offered. I do not know whether any of the people possessed faith in God, but if so, they had a prayerless faith, and God does not work in answer to prayerless faith. Some think it useless to pray because they feel sure of having the blessing. Putting aside prayer is dangerous business. If there is not the daily cry to God for blessing and for keeping and for sanctification, the mercy will not come. Healing does not come to a prayerless faith. God will only hear you when you pray. Faith must pour itself out in prayer before the blessing will be poured into the soul. Moses cried, and he obtained the blessing; the people did not cry, and they would have been in a bad way had it not been for Moses. We must come to crying and praying before we will receive sanctification, which is the making whole of our spirits.

Marah became sweet through the introduction of something outside of itself— a tree. I know a tree that, if put into the soul, will sweeten all its thoughts and desires, that tree on which Jesus died and shed his blood for our sin.

If the merit of the Cross is imputed to you and the spirit of the Cross is introduced into your nature, then you will find a marvelous change of your entire nature. You were full of vice, so the Crucified One will make you full of virtue. You were bitter toward God, so you will be sweet to him, and even Christ will be refreshed as he drinks of your love, as he drinks of your trust, as he drinks of your joy in him. Where all was acrid and poisonous, everything will become pure and refreshing. We must first experience bitterness, then cry out in prayer, then yield an obedient faith that puts the tree into the stream, and then the divine power will be put forth on us by him who says, "I am the LORD, who heals you."

—C. H. Spurgeon

I am the LORD, *who heals you.*

—Exodus 15:26

The task of turning Marah sweet was very difficult.[93] No human power could have achieved it; even so, changing human nature is impossible to us. We must be born again, born of God. There was no turning Marah sweet by any means in the reach of Moses or the myriad that came with him out of Egypt. This wonder must come from Jehovah's hand. So the change of human nature is a thing beyond all human might. Who can make his or her own heart clean? God must work this marvel. We must be born again from above, or else we will remain bitter to the end.

Yet the work was very easy to God. How simple a thing it was to cast a tree into the bitter water and find it sweet at once. Even so, it is an easy thing to God to make you a new heart and a right spirit and thus to incline you to everything that is right and good. If I had to make myself holy I must despair, and if I had to make myself perfect and keep myself so it would never be done, but the Lord Jehovah can do it—and has already begun to do it. Simple faith in Jesus Christ, the putting of the Cross into the stream, does it all and so effectively that there is no return of bitterness—the heart remains sweet and pure before the living God.

The task was completely accomplished. As the people freely drank of Marah, so God will complete in me the change of my nature. Paul says he is "confident of this, that he who began a good work in you will carry it on to completion until the day of Christ." The Lord has not begun to sweeten us with the intent of leaving us in a half-healed condition, but he will continue the process till we are without defilement, made pure and right in his sight.

This work glorifies God. If the change of Marah's water made the people praise God, much more will the change of nature make us adore him forever. We are going to be exalted to the highest place in the universe next to God. Humanity— poor, sinful humanity—is to be so changed as to be able to stand side by side with Christ. The tendency to pride would be very strong, except that we will always recollect what we used to be and what power has made us what we are. This will make it safe for God to glorify his people.

—C. H. Spurgeon

PART THREE

Summer

Then sing ye Birds, sing, sing a joyous song!
And let the young Lambs bound
As to the tabor's sound!
We in thought will join your throng.
—William Wordsworth in "Intimations of Immortality"

I have ventured . . . this many summers in a sea of glory.
—William Shakespeare

You will have a covenant with the stones of the field.
—Job 5:23

In these long June days when the world is so fresh and green, our thoughts turn instinctively to the ministry of nature.[1] June is so fresh, so sweet, so full of light, so throbbing and thrilling with love and hope and joy that the dullest and most world-weary heart beats a little faster at the touch of its mystic fingers. There is always an element of surprise in June. It is always a new thing, fresh and unexpected. We have it annually since our childhood, yet when it comes again it is as a stranger from the glory. That is one mark of the genius of God—his gifts come so regularly, yet they never weary. They reach us a thousand times, but the thousand and first time they are still wonderful, surprising, touched with dew.

What does it mean, "You will have a covenant with the stones of the field"? Eliphaz is talking—not of everybody—he is talking of the person who trusts in God. He is describing the one who is at peace with God and who has entered into a covenant with the Almighty. And what he says is, "Are you in league with heaven? Then with the very stones you will be in league. Are you at peace with God in your own heart? Then you are on new terms with every bird and beast and flower." That is to say that people's attitude toward nature and all the meaning that nature may convey to them depends on their spiritual and moral state. It is not so much by the eye as by the heart that the book of this summer world must be interpreted. Let people live basely and in defiance of God, let them mock at these moral laws that are our safeguard, then somehow there will be no runes on any rock for them; they will be out of harmony with tree and flower and summer. But let people be reverent and lowly and pure in heart and tender, let them be at peace with that Jehovah who delights in love—then in the covenant of comradeship June will unfold her secrets to them, and they will read sermons in the stones of the field. It is not the artistic nature, it is the moral nature that holds the key to the ministry of summer. To be out of touch with God and God's ideal is to be out of touch with everything, but to be spiritually in league with God is to be in league with the stones of the field.

—George H. Morrison

You will have a covenant with the stones of the field.
—*Job* 5:23

This vital connection of the outward world with the grandeur or the debasement of human moral nature is one of the great and neglected truths of Scripture.[2] From the story of Eden with its idyllic environment, through the Fall with its curse of thistles and of thorns, on to the last picture of a new-created earth that will be in harmony with new-created humanity, everywhere the Word of God shows us the kinship between nature and human moral life. Think of what Paul says: "The whole creation has been groaning as in the pains of childbirth right up to the present time." That is the Bible outlook on the world. The world is not a mere stage for a brief play. It is lit by our triumphs, shadowed by our guilt, touched by our sorrows, watered by our tears. By every right thing we do it is made richer. It grows meaner and poorer by every sin we sin. It is ourselves that are impressed upon the world. It is the story of our own hearts we read in nature. We talk of the voices of the winds and waves, but the voices are only the echo of our souls. And that is why, when you get a soul like Christ's, infinitely beautiful and filled like a chalice with God, the meanest flower that blows has got a glory with which even the glory of Solomon cannot be compared.

We quicken or deaden everything we see by the life we live and the sins that we commit. For a bad man or woman there is really no summer, just as there is really no heaven.

What this summer will mean to you and how you will enjoy it is, after all, a moral and spiritual question. To be at peace with God is to be at peace with nature, and to love God is to see traces of him everywhere. As is my heart with God so is the world of this fresh June to me.

—George H. Morrison

Yet he saved them for his name's sake.

—Psalm 106:8

By the name of God we may understand his being, God himself: "this glorious and awesome name—the LORD your God" (Deut. 28:58).[3] To save for his name's sake is to save for his own sake.

By the name of God we may understand his authority, that is, his absolute right and power to do what he pleases with his own creatures. "My purpose will stand, and I will do all that I please" (Isa. 46:10). When he saves for his name's sake, he saves for the sake of his sovereign will and pleasure and for showing his own absolute authority.

By the name of God we may understand the Christ of God, for in our Lord Jesus Christ is the whole name and authority of God. When he pardons for his name's sake, he pardons for Christ's sake. God has done and will do much for Christ, because his name is in him, and in him he is well pleased and reconciled.

By the name of God we are to understand the attributes of God. I will mention some of these.

His power is his name, and for the sake of that he saves: "He saved them for his name's sake, to make his mighty power known." We cannot want more than he can give; we cannot pray for as much as he can bestow; we are not able to think what he can do. God's power is a part of his name that faith may take hold of for salvation and flee to.

When he saves for his name's sake, he saves for his *mercy's* sake: "May your mercy come quickly to meet us, . . . for the glory of your name; deliver us and forgive our sins" (Ps. 79:8–9).

God, in saving sinners through Christ, has such a regard to his name as a God of infinite *wisdom* that in this method of salvation, the manifold wisdom of God is shown (Eph. 3:10).

His truth and faithfulness is one of the capital letters of his name: "abounding in . . . faithfulness" (Exod. 34:5–6). And how often did God remember his promise toward Israel? In saving sinners through Christ, God's truthfulness is displayed in fulfilling the law on the Surety in the place of the sinner, in fulfilling the promises of the gospel, and in fulfilling the promises made to Christ of seeing his offspring upon his giving his life a guilt offering for sin (Isa. 53:10).

—Ralph Erskine

Yet he saved them for his name's sake.

—Psalm 106:8

By the name of God we are to understand the attributes of God.[4] I will mention [more] of these.

His justice is another part of his name for the sake of which he saves and works salvation. The justice of God may be viewed as either retributive or vindictive. Retributive justice may be viewed in the saints themselves. They are sinners, yet because [they are] objects of promised mercy in Christ Jesus he saves and delivers [them] for his righteousness' and justice' sake. He also saves for the sake of vindictive justice, because it has gotten full satisfaction: "God presented him as a sacrifice of atonement. . . . He did this to demonstrate his justice" (Rom. 3:25). It is ordinary for people to seek to be saved for his mercy's sake. But believing justice satisfied and God reconciled in Christ should make the soul seek to be saved in and through Christ the atonement. In Christ that name of God, Justice, has more glorious satisfaction than ever it will have in the damnation of sinners. In punishing sin in the Surety, God's vindictive justice is so cleared and vindicated that when he pardons sin through Christ, he is as just as he is merciful.

His holiness is a part of his name for the sake of which he saves. This is declared to be his name: "The high and lofty One . . . whose name is holy" (Isa. 57:15). For the sake of this he pities and saves: "It is not for your sake, O house of Israel, that I am going to do these things, but for the sake of my holy name" (Ezek. 36:22).

The *providence of God* is a part of his name—his watchful care over his people. He rules and overrules all for their good.

The name of God is the very thing by which he makes himself known, whether in his attributes, ordinances, words, or works. He has made himself known by his works of creation and providence—but a thousand times more clearly in the work of redemption and salvation. In these appear some perfection of the divine nature that would not have been displayed in case the first covenant had stood. Therefore, while Satan thought to have deleted the name of God written upon the creature at first—see how infinite wisdom counteracts him and makes that the occasion of making God's name more known than before!

—*Ralph Erskine*

Yet he saved them for his name's sake.
—Psalm 106:8

"For his name's sake," signifies his making his name the ALL of our salvation.[5] Thus God designed to show himself to be all in all. More particularly,

For God to save for his name's sake is to make his name the *motive* for which he saves. What moved him to save any guilty sinner? It is his name, his own mercy, his own grace, his own pity and compassion, his own love.

For God to save for his name's sake is to make his name the *reason* why he saves. Though his name is the motive, yet some may think there is some reason drawn from the creature—that it was [God's] foresight of faith and good works, that he foresaw some would be better than others and for this reason he would save them. But the Word of God says otherwise. God loves sinners because he loves them. His sovereign mercy is the cause of his showing mercy; "I will have mercy on whom I have mercy" (Rom. 9:15).

To save for his name's sake is to make his name the *substance* of their salvation—his name itself is their salvation. Those he saves have not only salvation from him, but in him. Christ, therefore, who calls us to look to him and be saved, is himself the salvation of the sinner. "My eyes have seen your salvation," said old Simeon (Luke 2:30). Christ is not only the helper, but the help itself.

To save for his name's sake is to make his name the *means* of salvation. "There is no other name under heaven given to men by which we must be saved" (Acts 4:12).

To save for his name's sake is to make his name the *measure* of our salvation; he will, therefore, save as far as his name and honor is engaged by promise to Christ or to his people in Christ.

To save for his name's sake is to make his name the *goal* of our salvation. The great goal he proposes in saving is the praise of his grace, Ephesians 1:6—the praise of his wisdom, power, holiness, justice, goodness, and truth. This is the great purpose of God in his work of saving sinners. Christ's grand prayer, when he was accomplishing the work of our salvation and redemption, was, "Father, glorify your name!" And here let us pause a little and admire the great design that God had in saving for his name's sake.

—Ralph Erskine

Yet he saved them for his name's sake.

—Psalm 106:8

In saving for his name's sake, God designs the *manifestation* of his name—that his name may be known, declared, published, and proclaimed.[6]

In saving for his name's sake, he designs the *vindication* of his name. The world is filled with harsh thoughts of God, as if he were either unjust or unmerciful; therefore, in saving for his name's sake, he will vindicate his name.

In saving for his name's sake, he designs the *exaltation* of his name: "I will be exalted among the nations, I will be exalted in the earth" (Ps. 46:10). He designs that the right hand of the Lord should be exalted in doing mighty things (Ps. 118:16). Why has God exalted Christ to his right hand except that his name may be exalted in him? "Who, being in very nature God, did not consider equality with God something to be grasped, . . . that at the name [or, in the name] of Jesus every knee should bow, in heaven and on earth and under the earth" (Phil. 2:6, 10).

In saving sinners for his name's sake, he designs the *pleasure* of his name, that his name should not only be exalted but delighted in. God being infinitely pleased in Christ, he takes pleasure in giving out of his goodness through him.

In saving sinners for his name's sake, he designs the *aggrandizing* of his name. His name should not only be glorified and exalted, but magnified to the highest, according to the song of the angels: "Glory to God in the highest, and on earth peace to men on whom his favor rests" (Luke 2:14). His name is magnified to the highest in this way of salvation through Christ. Damnation is only the lowest way in which God glorifies himself, [but] sinners may fall in love with that way in which God is glorified and magnified to the highest.

In saving sinners for his name's sake, he designs the *eternalizing* of his name, that his name may be celebrated with hallelujahs of praise to all eternity. Christ, the Savior, was set up from everlasting, that the sinner saved by God in him might praise him to everlasting. And his ransomed will come to Zion with everlasting songs, saying, "Praise and glory and wisdom and thanks and honor and power and strength be to our God for ever and ever" (Rev. 7:12).

—Ralph Erskine

Yet he saved them for his name's sake.

—Psalm 106:8

What is imported in this "Yet," in God's saving *notwithstanding?*[7] The text is speaking of impediments on the sinner's part. God saved Israel here, notwithstanding dreadful sins. God can save you with an everlasting salvation, notwithstanding the most grievous provocations that you have been guilty of and the greatest impediments that you have laid in the way.

He can save for his name's sake, notwithstanding *grievous guilt and heinous transgressions.* Thus his name is declared to be a God forgiving wickedness, rebellion, and sin. You see mercy courting you, notwithstanding this very objection.

He can save for his name's sake, notwithstanding *long continuance in sin.* Mercy follows you with many a "how long, how long": "How long will these people treat me with contempt? How long will they refuse to believe in me?" (Num. 14:11).

He can save for his name's sake, notwithstanding *many apostasies and backslidings.* "Let the wicked forsake his way and the evil man his thoughts. Let him turn to the LORD, and he will have mercy on him, and to our God, for he will freely pardon" (Isa. 55:7).

He can save for his name's sake, notwithstanding *enormous neglect and contempt of God* until now. See Isaiah 43:25, "I, even I, am he who blots out your transgressions, for my own sake, and remembers your sins no more."

He can save for his name's sake, notwithstanding *grievous, rebellious hardness and contrariness.* "He kept on in his willful ways. I have seen his ways, but I will heal him; I will guide him and restore comfort to him" (Isa. 57:17–18).

He can save for his name's sake, notwithstanding *outward afflictions and poor circumstances* in the world. Though you are an outcast and nobody cares for you, he may save you for his name's sake, for he "gathers the exiles of Israel" (Isa. 56:8).

He can save for his name's sake, notwithstanding *degradation, unworthiness, and pollution,* for there is a fountain opened. "On that day a fountain will be opened to the house of David and to the inhabitants of Jerusalem, to cleanse them from sin and impurity" (Zech. 13:1).

—Ralph Erskine

Yet he saved them for his name's sake.

—Psalm 106:8

God can save you [for his name's sake] notwithstanding *the most grievous provocations* that till now you have been guilty of and the greatest impediments that you have laid in the way.[8]

He can save for his name's sake, notwithstanding *gross darkness and fearful ignorance.* "It is written in the Prophets: 'They will all be taught by God'" (John 6:45).

He can save for his name's sake, notwithstanding *long refusals, resisting many calls, and slighting many opportunities* "All day long I have held out my hands to a disobedient and obstinate people" (Rom. 10:21). After all these refusals, he is yet standing with open arms to receive all comers.

He can save for his name's sake notwithstanding *unparalleled wickedness.* What if there is no sinner like you? Nevertheless, he can save for his name's sake—because there is no Savior like him. If your unbelieving heart suggests there is no salvation for you, let Micah 7:18 be an answer: "Who is a God like you, who pardons sin?"

In a word, he can save for his name's sake, notwithstanding the highest mountains of sin or misery that seem to be in the way, notwithstanding hardness of heart and innumerable plagues of heart, atheism, unbelief, deadness, and security. The God who works for his name's sake can take away the heart of stone and give the heart of flesh, can out of stones raise up children for Abraham. He can save, for his name's sake, notwithstanding nameless maladies, nameless objections that no minister in the world can mention, far less remove. Maybe the obstacles in the way of your salvation are out of human sight, but they are in God's sight, and the omniscient God who knows them is the omnipotent God who can remove them and save for his name's sake.

But some poor soul may think, *I doubt his will.* Why? Why is God now telling you what he can do except to remove your bad thoughts of him and to manifest his goodwill toward you—he is more willing to save than you are willing to be saved. If you are willing, you are more than welcome to him for all the salvation he can work for you. It is his will to save you, notwithstanding of thousands and millions of objections in the way.

—Ralph Erskine

Yet he saved them for his name's sake.

—Psalm 106:8

[Here are] some reasons why God saves for his name's sake.[9]

1. If he did not, he would save none of Adam's race. The best saints on earth cannot deserve mercy; the salvation of the most righteous is an act of grace. He could save none, if he did not save them for his name's sake.

2. He saves for his name's sake that sinners may hope in his name, that they may turn to him and call on him for mercy. Could not God be more feared if he had no mercy and forgiveness? True; humanity, in that case, could fear as devils do—despairingly—but not with any penitential fear. None could trust in his name, if he did not save for his name's sake.

3. He saves for his name's sake that sinners may adore his name, that they may admire his mercy. O wonder-working God who can show mercy when nothing is deserved but misery!

4. He saves for his name's sake so that sinners who will not flee to his name may be left inexcusable in their sins. The glory of God's justice will be conspicuous in those who have slighted his mercy.

5. He saves for his name's sake because it is the only fit way for us to be saved. If God should offer to save us for our own sakes, for our righteousness' sake—we might think God were mocking us, because we have nothing but sin and hell about us, and our best righteousness deserves damnation. But when he offers salvation for his own name's sake, then it appears to be a fit offer. We cannot think God is mocking us—would he thus affront himself when his own name is the ground of faith laid before us?

6. He saves for his name's sake because it is the only way of salvation suitable to his infinite excellence—God's glory requires that no salvation should be found except in his name. Why has he told us of mercy in the new covenant? Why has he told us that justice itself is on the sinner's side, inasmuch as he can be justified in forgiving sinners? Why has he displayed so much wisdom in judgment and mercy—wisdom in punishing sin and yet saving the sinner? Why? So that he might be glorified, that human pride might be brought down and arrogance laid low and that the Lord alone may be exalted. This way of saving suits his nature.

—Ralph Erskine

Yet he saved them for his name's sake.

—Psalm 106:8

When God saves sinners or a sinful people, he does it for his name's sake notwithstanding their provocations by which they forfeit his help and deserve destruction.[10] Learn, by way of caution, the following particulars:

1. This doctrine yields no encouragement to sin, though God saves sinners for his name's sake; the current of his providence, the current of his Word, the current of his dealing, all declare his enmity at sin. What is there in the Word that can encourage us in sin? All the threatenings of the law say, in effect, if you regard the wrath of God, beware of sin. All the commands of the law say, if you regard the authority of God, beware of sin. All the promises of the gospel say, if you regard the grace, love, and mercy of God, beware of sin. God's saving for his name's sake says, if you regard the great name of God, beware of sin. The great salvation that he exhibits for his name's sake is salvation from sin. To make this an encouragement to sin is to affront his name, to abuse it, to profane it, and to take it in vain.

2. Do not think that God will deliver any from eternal damnation who have gone to hell, or save them for his name's sake; no, by no means. Those who die out of Christ are lost forever.

By way of exhortation to all sinners in general, does God save for his name's sake and with that "yet"—a notwithstanding of innumerable sins? Then let sinners hope in his name and fly to his name for salvation.

You will find no object of faith in yourself. Then, sinner, his word, which you are called to take hold of, is his name; it is that by which he makes himself known. And in going to him for salvation, (1) let his name be your motive, for thus you will glorify his name; (2) let his name be your tower, to which you fly for salvation; (3) let his name be the measure of your hope—how much he will be glorified in saving you, so much let your hope and expectation go forth that he will do so; (4) let his name be your plea and argument, "O save for your name's sake. Glorify your name." Cast anchor here, and you will ride out all storms and be eternally safe.

—Ralph Erskine

Yet he saved them for his name's sake.
—Psalm 106:8

By way of exhortation to believers, O admire his goodness, admire his name.[11] He knows all your sins against him and against his name, yet he shows mercy. Let sin against so good a God be abhorred; let his goodness lead you to repentance more and more. Praise him for his mercy, truth, faithfulness. Credit all mercy you meet with to his name, and do your best to meet reasons for God's name to be more and more glorified, on his using his name for your help. For though sinners have a ground of hope that he *may* do for his name's sake, yet saints have a ground of hope that he *will* do for his name's sake. His name is pledged.

He has a name suiting every need. Do you need wonders to be wrought for you? His name is Wonderful; look to him so to do, for his name's sake. Do you need counsel and direction? His name is the Counselor. Do you have mighty enemies to debate? His name is the mighty God; ask him to exert his power for his name's sake. Do you need his fatherly pity? His name is the everlasting Father. Plead his pity, for his name's sake. Do you need peace external, internal, or eternal? His name is the Prince of Peace; seek, for his name's sake, that he may create peace. Do you need healing? His name is *Jehovah-Rophi,* the Lord the healer and physician. Do you need pardon? His name is *Jehovah-Tsidkenu,* the Lord our righteousness. Do you need defense and protection? His name is *Jehovah-Nissi,* the Lord your banner. Seek, for his name's sake, that his banner of love and grace may be spread over you. Do you need provision in extreme want? His name is *Jehovah-Jireh,* the Lord will provide. Do you need his presence? His name is *Jehovah-Shammah,* the Lord is there; *Immanuel,* God with us. Do you need audience of prayer? His name is the Hearer of prayer. Do you need strength? His name is the Strength of Israel. Do you need comfort? His name is the Consolation of Israel. Do you need shelter? His name is the City of Refuge. Have you nothing and need all? His name is All in All. He has a name suitable for your supply; he has wisdom to guide you and power to keep you, mercy to pity you, truth to shield you, holiness to sanctify you, righteousness to justify you, grace to adorn you, and glory to crown you. Trust in his name, who saves for his name's sake.

—Ralph Erskine

> *"My food," said Jesus, "is to do the will*
> *of him who sent me."*
>
> —John 4:34

When we turn to the word of Jesus Christ we discover that neither thought nor feeling is laid as the foundation of religion.[12] Christ had no quarrel with the human intellect. He recognized its wonder and its power. His own intellectual life was far too rich for him to be a traitor to the brain. Nor was Christ the enemy of human feeling. He never made light of the most tender emotion. He who wept beside the grave of Lazarus could never be the antagonist of tears. But in the teaching of Christ it is not thought nor feeling that is the wellspring of personal religion. The wellspring is in the region of the will. It is *there* that one must pass from death to life. It is *there* the path of piety begins. The first thing is the dedication of the will, the response of a free individual to a great God, the yielding of self to that imperious claim made by the loving Father in the heavens: "Seek first his kingdom and his righteousness."

With Christ there was no compulsion of the will except the compulsion of overmastering love. Do not wait then, I beg of you, as if a day were coming when you *must* be good. Do not think that the hour will ever strike when you will be swept irresistibly into the kingdom. At the last it is a matter of decision.

Think of the relationship of will to fellowship—our spiritual fellowship with our Redeemer. That friendship is not based on mutual feeling; it is based, according to Christ, on mutual will. "Whoever does the will of my Father in heaven is my brother and sister and mother." It is not a question, then, of what you know, if you are to be a brother or sister of the Lord. The one that does the will—though it is often sore, though the way is dark, and though the wind is chill—whoever does the will of my Father in heaven is my brother and sister and mother. That means that on dedication of the will depends all communion with Jesus Christ. And if communion with him is true religion—the truest and purest the world has ever known—you see how it does not rest on thought or feeling but has its wellspring in the surrendered will. Religion founded on feeling is unstable. A religion of intellect is cold and hard. Total surrender is what Christ demands, and in it lies the secret of all peace.

—George H. Morrison

Come to me, all you who are weary and burdened . . . and
you will find rest for your souls. For my yoke is easy and
my burden is light.

—Matthew 11:28–30

The invitations of the gospel are addressed to all; the Good News is to be preached to all creation.[13] God commands all people to repent; he promises that whoever believes in Jesus shall have eternal life—"the free gift of the water of life" (Rev. 22:17).

And it is worth observing that the gospel invitations are so varied. The same bountiful and gracious Being who suits the blessings of his providence to our various wants also adapts the invitations of his mercy to our varied characters and conditions. Are people enemies to God? They are invited to be reconciled. Have they hearts harder than a millstone? He offers to take away the stone and give a heart of flesh. Are they rushing madly along the way that leads to death? He calls upon them to turn, "Turn! Turn . . . ! Why will you die?" (Ezek. 33:11). Are people hungering? He tells them of the bread that came down from heaven. Are they thirsty? He calls them to the water of life. And are they burdened with sin? He invites them to come to Jesus for rest. It is those who are bowed down beneath a load of sin who are here especially invited to come to Jesus.

Sin is a grievous burden, and no one can feel its weight without wishing to be relieved of it. Aren't there many among you who have often felt heavy with the load of your transgressions and the burden of your sinfulness? If you do not all feel so, it is because your perceptions are blunted, you do not see things as they are. You have been servants of sin for a long time—haven't you found it a hard master? You have been wearing the yoke of Satan these many years—haven't you found that his yoke is indeed galling and grievous? How many things you have done at his bidding that you knew to be wrong? How often you have stifled the voice of your conscience and listened to the suggestions of the Tempter! How often you have toiled to gratify sinful desires and found that, still, the craving was left unfilled!

Let all, then, who are burdened with sin and sinfulness, who long to know how their transgressions may be forgiven and their souls saved, all who are inquiring what they must do, let them hear the gracious words of the text, "Come to me."

—John A. Broadus

Come to me, all you who are weary and burdened . . . and
you will find rest for your souls. For my yoke is easy and
my burden is light.

—Matthew 11:28–30

What has sin done for you that you should desire it?[14] It brought death and woe into the world. It has filled the earth with suffering and sorrow. It has made it necessary that Jesus, the only-begotten Son of God, should suffer and die to make atonement for it. It has brought on you much unhappiness now and many fears for the future. By your sins you have incurred the just anger of him who made you—already they rise mountain high, and still you go on in your sinfulness, "storing up wrath against yourself for the day of God's wrath" (Rom. 2:5). You shudder when you think of death, you tremble when you think of God, for you know well that you are not prepared to die, that you cannot meet your Maker and Judge in peace. And not only has sin brought on you all these sufferings and fears, but you cannot rid yourself of it.

It has made you unhappy, filling you with craving, unsatisfied desires; it has bound you with cords you cannot burst; it has brought on you the indignation and wrath of almighty God, which you cannot atone for. Isn't it then a burden of which you would like to be relieved? If so, hear the Savior's own invitation and go to him. He will take off the heavy load that crushes you, and you will find rest for your souls. He will intercede in your behalf before God, he will take away your guilt by the sacrifice he has offered, he will wash away all your iniquity and cleanse you from your sin.

Do you fear that God is angry with you and will not hear your prayer? It is true, God is angry with the wicked, and the sacrifice of the wicked is detestable to the Lord. You may not mock the offended majesty of God by going to him in your own name and trusting in your own righteousness. But you may go to Jesus— you are invited to go to him. He is the appointed mediator between God and you. Go and ask him to intercede for you. And then through him draw near to the throne of grace. Make mention of his merits, plead his atoning sacrifice, rely wholly on what he has done, and God's anger is turned away—he will hear, he will pardon, and your soul will live. If then you are burdened with a sense of your unworthiness, go to Jesus, and you will not go in vain.

—John A. Broadus

Come to me, all you who are weary and burdened,
and I will give you rest. Take my yoke upon you and learn
from me, for I am gentle and humble in heart, and you will
find rest for your souls. For my yoke is easy and my
burden is light.

—Matthew 11:28–30

This familiar passage of Scripture contains one of the most precious among the many precious invitations of our compassionate Redeemer.[15]

The Savior invites to him all "who are weary and burdened." In this he doubtless referred partly to the burden of ceremonies and observances that the scribes and Pharisees imposed on their followers. Such persons, then, borne down beneath the burden of the ceremonial law, are here invited to the Savior. But he refers likewise to all who are burdened with sin. All such are invited to him, with the promise that he will give them rest from their labor and relief from their load. They wear the galling yoke of sin and Satan, and he bids them take his yoke upon them.

Wearing the yoke of another is an expression often employed in Scripture to denote subjection to that other. The figure is taken, of course, from beasts of burden, being applied then to all who are the laboring servants of a master. Jesus is bidding those who have been the slaves of sin to be his servants; those who have been subject to Satan, to take him, instead, as their King.

He recommends himself not only as King and Master, but as teacher too. The gospel is frequently and properly represented as something to be learned; people need to be taught the way of salvation. These lessons of salvation must be obtained from the great teacher, Jesus.

And when he says, "I am gentle and humble in heart," the Savior means that he is fit to be a teacher. In order to win the hearts of pupils, the better to make them love to learn and love what they do learn, a teacher must unite to other qualities a certain gentleness and kindliness. And when our Savior bids people learn from him, he encourages the timid and fearful to come to him by telling them that he is gentle and humble in heart, mild and loving, that he will be kind to them, and they need not fear. He will not be rough and overbearing and arrogant. He is humble and affectionate and kind.

—John A. Broadus

Come to me, all you who are weary and burdened,
and I will give you rest. Take my yoke upon you and learn
from me, for I am gentle and humble in heart, and you will
find rest for your souls. For my yoke is easy and my
burden is light.

—Matthew 11:28–30

We may learn from these words the character of the lessons, as well as of the teacher.[16] It is the knowledge of himself that Jesus will give, and as he is gentle and humble, so those who go to learn from him will be taught lessons of gentleness, lessons of humility. "Take my yoke upon you and learn from me"; you need not fear to make me your teacher, "for I am gentle and humble in heart and you shall find rest for your souls." He promises to free them from their grievous toils, to relieve them of their heavy burdens, to give them rest.

To appreciate fully the expressiveness of this figure, you must imagine yourself bearing a heavy burden, a weight you can hardly sustain, and after bearing it till you are almost crushed to the ground, you throw it off and rest. There are few things so delightful as this rest to one who has been heavily burdened. And suppose the burden is clinging to you, bound with cords you cannot sever, though you are bowed down under the load and vainly striving to throw it off. Then one offers, if you go to him, to loose the bonds and take away the burden and let you rest—how sweet would be the thought! How quickly, how joyfully, how thankfully, you would run to him!

It is impossible that people should be without subjection to some higher power; by our very nature we look up to some being that is above us. All who are not subject to God are the subjects of Satan, and those who wish to be delivered from the dominion of the Evil One must find such deliverance in having God himself for their King, as he intended they should when he made them. Accordingly, when the Savior offers to give rest, he bids them take his yoke upon them and learn from him. And then he concludes the invitation by encouraging them to believe that this exchange will be good and pleasant; they labor under the galling yoke of Satan and are burdened with the grievous weight of sin, but his yoke is easy. His burden is light.

—John A. Broadus

*Come to me, all you who are weary and burdened, . . . for
I am gentle and humble in heart, and you shall find rest for
your souls.*

—Matthew 11:28–29

All that labor with whatever toil, all that are heavy laden with whatever burden may take this invitation as addressed to them.[17] "You call burdened souls to you, and such, O Lord, am I." Whatever it is that bears you down—the consciousness of sin, the terror of judgment, distressing doubts, or many and diverse temptations—whatever else may torment your soul and weigh down your spirit, this invitation is for you. If you are burdened with affliction or sorrow or fearful apprehension, if you bear any burden, you are invited to Jesus. "Come to me."

It would be natural enough to inquire, "What is meant by going to Jesus? Suppose I feel myself to be burdened and want to seek relief, how shall I go to Jesus for rest?"

Go to him as people [did] when he was on earth. It is true that the case is somewhat different now. We cannot now go to Jesus as a man living somewhere among us. But it is only a change from sight to faith—from a moving of the body to a moving of the thoughts and affections. It may be thought a great privation that we cannot go somewhere, as they did then, and find him. But isn't it, on the other hand, a great privilege that we need not now go anywhere, we may always find him here? He is everywhere and as much in one place as another. People have often forgotten this great and consoling and gladdening truth. Many a weary pilgrimage has been made in centuries past to the Holy Land in the hope that forgiveness of sin and peace of conscience, which could not be found at home, might be found there. It is pleasant and may do the heart good to stand where Jesus stood, to weep where he wept on Olivet, to pray where he prayed in Gethsemane, but he is here now as well as there. Wherever you seek him, there he may be found "For where two or three come together in my name, there am I with them." Wherever there is a tear of penitence or a sigh of godly sorrow, wherever there is earnest prayer to him or the desire to pray felt in the heart, Jesus is there to see and to hear and to answer.

—John A. Broadus

*Come to me, all you who are weary and burdened, . . . for
I am gentle and humble in heart, and you shall find rest for
your souls.*

—*Matthew* 11:28–29

We can always find him where we are.[18] And since this is so, go to him as people did when he was on earth. Many testify that they have gone and been heard, and none [have] been sent away empty—go, and you too will hear him say, "Your sins are forgiven." Go with the same humility the Syrophoenician woman felt when she pleaded that the dogs, though they should not eat the children's food, might yet have the crumbs that fell under the table—and that she, though a Gentile, might yet have some humble share in salvation. Go with all the earnestness the poor blind man felt. He heard that Jesus was passing, and none could hinder him from crying, "Son of David, have mercy on me!" And when the Savior commanded him to be called, they said to him, "Cheer up! On your feet! He's calling you." Even so, my hearer, Jesus commands you to be called, as you sit in your spiritual blindness. Just as Bartimaeus threw aside his cloak that nothing might hinder him and went eagerly to Jesus, so you go at once to him and ask that you may receive your sight. You too shall hear him say, "Go, your faith has healed you."

And go to Jesus just as you are. Do not wait to be ready—don't think of being prepared, don't dream of being fit to go. The readiness, the preparation, the fitness—all must be his gift. How wrong to put off your going to him till you have that which he alone can give! You are a burdened sinner—isn't it so? Jesus invites you, "Come to me." Do you say you are not sorry for sin as you ought to be? I know you are not. But go to Jesus and ask that he will help you to repent. If you have no faith, ask that he will give you faith. All must come from him. Let him be your Savior and your all.

You shall find rest. He will not send you away. He came into the world to save sinners—he suffered and died to save sinners—he invited burdened sinners to him. Then take this invitation to yourself—go to Jesus, and your soul shall live. "The Spirit and the bride say, 'Come!' And let him who hears say, 'Come!' Whoever is thirsty, let him come; and whoever wishes, let him take the free gift of the water of life" (Rev. 22:17).

—John A. Broadus

Christ . . . the wisdom of God.
—1 Corinthians 1:24

Our age is eager in its pursuit of knowledge.[19] It professes to be a truth-loving and a truth-seeking age. It is quite awake to science and thoroughly in love with its marvels. It has obtained insight into the processes of that which is called "nature." It has witnessed one substance, and another and another, yielding up their hidden wonders. It has seen earth and sea and air giving out their treasures, and it has wrung the deepest secrets from every region of being. It has taken possession of unreclaimed territory and covered the waste places of former days with verdure and fragrance and beauty.

Its fields of discovery lie all around us, near and far. Wherever it has turned its steps, it has found stores of truth. What a profundity of miracle there is contained in every ray of light, every drop of dew, every pebble of the brook, every fragment of rock, every blade of grass. What an exemplification of order and law there is revealed in every natural process—the motion of earth and sun and stars, the flow of tides, the rush of the breeze, the braiding of the rainbow on the cloud, the change of seasons, the springing, growth, blossoming, and fruit-bearing of flower and shrub and tree!

These are the works of God, the laws of God, the daily miracles of God. In all of them wisdom is seen, divine wisdom—wisdom as profound as it is perfect, as incomprehensible as it is glorious, as magnificent in its minuteness as in its vastness—in the grain of sand as in the mighty mountain, in the blush of the unnoticed desert flower as in the splendor of a new-lighted star.

In all this there is wisdom, wisdom that we do well to study. Yet all these are only parts, mere fragments, and, even when gathered together, they still form only the minutest portion of a whole, whose dimensions are vaster than the created universe—a whole of which nothing less than the infinity of Godhead is the measure. There is some proportion between a drop and the ocean, between the stream and the fountain, between a beam and the sun, between a moment and a million of ages, but there is no proportion between the fragments of wisdom that lie scattered over creation and the great whole, which can be contained in no treasure-house except that which is infinite and divine.

—Horatius Bonar

Christ . . . the wisdom of God.
                    —1 Corinthians 1:24

While in all the regions of creation may be seen portions of this wisdom [of God], only in the Son of God—in Christ Jesus, the incarnate Word—is the mighty whole contained.[20] He, and he only, is "the wisdom of God."

By the expression, "the wisdom of God," is not merely meant that Christ is wise but something more comprehensive. To say that he is infinitely wise is one thing, but to say that he is the wisdom of God is another. We say of the Father, he is infinitely wise, but we cannot say of him, he is the wisdom of God. Of the Son alone can this be said. He is infinitely wise, and he is the wisdom of God.

All that is in God, all that can come forth out of God is contained in Christ. He is the full representative of the invisible and incomprehensible Jehovah. He is the brightness of Jehovah's glory and the express image of his person. In the works of creation God has displayed portions of his wisdom, but in Christ he put forth the whole of it, so it can be said of Christ, he is the wisdom of God. Thus, the knowledge of Christ not only transcends all other knowledge, but includes them all; the study of this embodiment of all that is in God is not only superior to but embraces all other studies. Here, we cannot see how Christ could be the discovery of all science, all nature, all things in heaven and earth; hereafter we shall find it so.

Wisdom is one of the last things that we connect with the name of Christ. We connect with that name salvation, pardon, righteousness, love—but not wisdom. Yet it is wisdom that God especially associates with Christ, "in whom are hidden all the treasures of wisdom and knowledge." He is perfection, but specially the perfection of wisdom, so that, while each perfection is in him, it is in him in such a way as to demonstrate the wisdom of God. Holiness is in him, but in such a way as to show forth not only itself, but wisdom as well. Each perfection becomes thus not merely a display of itself, but an illustration or embodiment of wisdom.

It is this wisdom that says, "The LORD brought me forth as the first of his works, before his deeds of old. I was appointed from eternity, from the beginning, before the world began."

—Horatius Bonar

Christ . . . the wisdom of God.

—1 Corinthians 1:24

The divine and the human—these, in themselves and in their union, make up [the] Son of God and Son of Man, the "wisdom of God."[21] Both retain their distinct properties, unchanged by the union. [But] human wisdom can comprehend neither human nature nor God's, nor adjust the connection between them without confounding both.

God takes another way. All that is glorious in the Godhead and all that is excellent in humanity is gathered into one person and fully exhibited in him. The heavenly becomes earthly, yet both are preserved. The Creator becomes the creature, yet, though conjoined in one person, remain distinct. The Eternal becomes a being of time, yet continues eternal. The Infinite becomes finite, yet abides infinite. The Immortal becomes mortal, yet continues immortal.

The two parts of the universe are linked by a new tie—by incarnation. Earth now knows what Godhead is, by its coming down and dwelling here; heaven knows what humanity is, by the human nature at God's right hand in the person of the Christ.

It is union only at a single point—one body and one soul in which the Godhead is united. So the incarnation of Christ is the mooring of the whole nature to the fountainhead of life and being.

It was not with one particular stage of our being that this union was formed but with all, from the moment of conception to the grave. He enters the womb and begins life where we begin it, thus joining himself to us at the commencement of human existence, weaving the first, invisible thread of mortal life into his own Godhead. He is made of a woman, and that links him to woman and woman to him, in everlasting bonds. He is a man, and that links him to man and man to him, in eternal union. He was an infant, and that links infancy to him and him to infancy. He was a child, a boy, a youth, and that links childhood, boyhood, youth to him and him to them. He united himself to us at these different points, consecrating these steps of human development.

What a marvel of wisdom is here. What treasures of knowledge are thus spread out before heaven and earth! Truly he is *the* wisdom of God!

—Horatius Bonar

To grasp how wide and long and high and deep is the love
of Christ, and to know this love that surpasses knowledge
—Ephesians 3:18–19

Stand still and admire and wonder at the love of Jesus Christ to sinners—that Christ would rather die for us than for the angels.[22] They were creatures of a more noble extract and in all probability might have brought greater revenues of glory to God; yet that Christ should pass by those golden vessels and make us vessels of glory—what amazing and astonishing love is this! This is the envy of devils and the admiration of angels and saints.

The angels were more honorable and excellent creatures than we. They were celestial spirits; we, earthly bodies, dust and ashes. They were immediate attendants on God; we, servants of his in the lower house of this world and remote from his glorious presence. Their work was to sing hallelujahs, songs of praise to God in the heavenly paradise; ours, to dress the Garden of Eden, which was only an earthly paradise. They sinned only once and only in thought, as is commonly thought, but Adam sinned in thought by lusting, in deed by tasting, and in word by excusing. Why didn't Christ suffer for their sins as well as for ours? Or, if for any, why not for theirs rather than ours? We move this question not as being curious to search your secret counsels, O Lord, but that we may more admire the love of Christ, that surpasses knowledge.

The apostle, in admiration of Christ's love, affirms it to surpass knowledge—that God, who is the eternal Being, should love the human when it had scarcely a being (Prov. 8:30–31), that he should be enamored with deformity, that he should pity us when no eye pitied us. Such was Christ's transcendent love that our extreme misery could not abate it. The deplorableness of our condition only heightened the flame of Christ's love. It is as high as heaven—who can reach it? It is as low as hell—who can understand it? Such is his perfect, matchless love to fallen people. That Christ's love should extend to the ungodly, to sinners, to enemies who were in rebellion against him (Rom. 5:6, 8, 10)—yes, not only so, but that he should hug them in his arms, lodge them in his bosom, dandle them on his knees—is the highest refinement of love (Isa. 66:11–13).

—Thomas Brooks

To grasp how wide and long and high and deep is the love
of Christ, and to know this love that surpasses knowledge
—Ephesians 3:18–19

That Christ should come from the eternal bosom of his Father to a region of sorrow and death (John 1:18); that God should be made flesh, the Creator made a creature (Isa. 53:4); that he who filled heaven should be cradled in a manger (John 17:5); that the God of strength should be weary; that the judge of all flesh should be condemned; that the God of life should be put to death (John 19:41); that he who had the keys of hell and death should lie imprisoned in the sepulchre of another, having in his lifetime nowhere to lay his head nor, after death, to lay his body (John 19:41–42)—and all this for fallen, miserable human beings— is beyond the thoughts of created natures.[23] The sharp, the universal, and the continual sufferings of our Lord Jesus Christ, from the cradle to the cross, above all other things speaks out the transcendent love of Jesus Christ to sinners. That matchless wrath of an angry God that was so terribly impressed on the soul of Christ quickly sapped his natural strength, yet all this wrath he patiently underwent that sinners might be saved and that he might bring "many sons to glory" (Heb. 2:10).

Oh, wonder of love! Love is submissive, it enables to suffer. So it was love that made our dear Lord Jesus lay down his life to save us from hell and to bring us to heaven. Oh, love unspeakable!

Christ's love is like his name, and that is Wonderful (Isa. 9:6), so wonderful that it is above all creatures, beyond all measure, contrary to all nature. It is above all creatures, for it is above the angels and therefore above all others. It is beyond all measure, for time did not begin it, and time shall never end it; place does not bound it, sin does not exceed it, understandings cannot conceive it. And it is contrary to all nature, for what nature can love where it is hated? can forgive where it is provoked? can offer reconciliation where it receives wrong? What nature can heap up kindness on contempt, favor on ingratitude, mercy on sin? And yet Christ's love has led him to all this, so that well may we spend all our days in admiring and adoring this wonderful love and be always captivated with the thoughts of it.

—Thomas Brooks

*They did not love their lives so much
as to shrink from death.*

—Revelation 12:11

See that you love the Lord Jesus Christ with a superlative love, with an overtopping love.[24] None have suffered so much for you as Christ; none can suffer so much for you as Christ.

There is no love but a superlative love that is suitable to the sufferings of Jesus. Love him above your lusts, above your family, above the world, above all your outward contentments and enjoyments. Love him above your very lives, for thus the saints of old have loved our Lord Jesus Christ—with an overtopping love.

"Let fire, racks, pulleys," said Ignatius, "and all the torments of hell come upon me, so I may win Christ."

Love made Jerome say, "O my Savior, did you die for love of me? a love sadder than death, but to me a death more lovely than love itself. I cannot live, love you, and be longer from you."

Sufferings for Christ are the saints' greatest glory: "Your cruelty is our glory," said Tertullian.

Certainly the more Christ has suffered for us, the dearer Christ should be to us. The bitterer his sufferings have been for us, the sweeter his love should be to us and the more conspicuous should be our love to him. Let him be your manna, your tree of life, your morning star.

Oh, that our hearts were more affected with the sufferings of Christ! Oh, the infinite love of Christ, that he would leave his Father's bosom and come down from heaven so that he might carry you up to heaven; that he who was a Son would take the form of a servant; that you of slaves would be made sons and daughters, of enemies would be made friends, of heirs of wrath would be made heirs of God and joint-heirs with Christ; that to save us from everlasting ruin, Christ would stop at nothing, be willing to be made flesh, to be tempted, deserted, persecuted, and to die on a cross!

Oh, when will the sufferings of a dear and tenderhearted Savior kindle such a flame of love as will still be breaking forth in our words and in our ways, to the praise and glory of free grace? Oh, that the sufferings of a loving Jesus might at last make us all faint with love (Song 2:5)!

—Thomas Brooks

Delight yourself in the Lord.

—Psalm 37:4

This delight springs from the Spirit of God.[25] Not a spark of fire on your own hearth is able to kindle this spiritual delight; it is the Holy Spirit who breathes such a heavenly heat into our affections. The Spirit is the fire that kindles the soul, the spring that moves the watch, the wind that drives the ship. The swiftest ship with spread sails will be only sluggish in its motion unless the wind fills its sails; without this Spirit we are in a weak and sickly condition, our breath short, a heavy and troublesome asthma upon us. "When I called, you answered me; you made me bold and stouthearted" (Ps. 138:3). Just as prayer is the work of the Spirit in the heart, so delight in prayer owes itself to the same author.

[This delight springs] from grace. The Spirit kindles and gives us the oil of grace to make the lamp burn clear. There is not only need of fire to kindle the lamp but of oil to preserve the flame. Natural people may have their affections kindled in a way of common working, but they will soon faint and die, as the flame of cotton will dim and vanish if there is no oil to nourish it.

[Delight in the Lord springs] from a good conscience. Guilt will come trembling and with a sad face into the presence of God's majesty. A guilty child cannot with cheerfulness come into a displeased parent's presence. A soul smoked with hell cannot with delight approach heaven. Guilty souls, in regard of the injury they have done to God, will be afraid to come, and in regard of the soot of sin with which they are defiled and the blackness they have contracted, they will be ashamed to come. They know that by their sins they would provoke his anger—not allure his love. A soul under conscience of sin cannot look up to God. Nor will God with favor look down on it. Jonah was asleep after his sin and was outdone in readiness to pray even by idolaters. The mariners jogged him but could not get him, that we read of, to call on that God whom he had offended. Where there is corruption, the sparks of sin will kindle that tinder and weaken a spiritual delight.

—Stephen Charnock

> *Delight yourself in the* Lord.
>
> —Psalm 37:4

[This delight springs] from a holy and frequent familiarity with God.[26] Where there is a great familiarity there is a great delight. There is more swiftness in going to a God with whom we are acquainted than to a God to whom we are strangers. I go to a God whose goodness I have tasted, with whom I have often met in prayer.

[Delight in the Lord springs] from hopes of receiving. There cannot be motion where there is paralysis of doubts. How full of delight must that soul be who can plead a promise and can show God his own bond—when it can be pleaded not only as a favor to appeal to his mercy, but in some sense a debt to appeal to his truth and righteousness! We carry a covenant of grace with us for ourselves and a promise of security and perpetuity for the church. On this account we have more cause of motion to God than the ancient believers had. Fear motivated them under the law; love motivates us under the gospel. Those who have arguments of God's own framing to plead with him cannot but delight in prayer—God cannot deny his own arguments and reasonings. Little comfort can be sucked from a *perhaps.* But when we seek promised mercies, God's faithfulness to his promise puts the mercy past a *perhaps.* We go to a God who desires our presence more than we desire his assistance.

[Delight in the Lord springs] from a recognition of former mercies. If manna is rained down, it not only takes our thoughts off Egyptian garlic but quickens our desires for a second shower. A sense of God's majesty will make us lose our showy self-satisfaction. A sense of God's love will make us lose our lumpishness. We may return with merry hearts when God accepts our prayers. The doves will readily fly to the windows where they have formerly found shelter and the beggar to the door where he has often received alms. "Because he turned his ear to hear me, I will call on him as long as I live" (Ps. 116:2). I have found refuge with God before; I have found my wants supplied, my soul raised, my temptations checked, my doubts answered, and my prayers accepted; therefore I will repeat my appeals with cheerfulness.

—Stephen Charnock

> Delight yourself in the Lord and he will give you the
> desires of your heart.
>
> —Psalm 37:4

The highest step of delight is a silencing of desire and the banquet of the soul on its desired object.[27]

But there is a [less lofty] delight.

Delight in desires. There is a cheerfulness in labor as well as in attainment. The desire of Canaan made the good Israelites cheerful in the wilderness. There is a beginning delight in motion but a consummate delight in rest and fulfillment.

Delight in hopes. Desired happiness affects the soul—much more, expected happiness. "We rejoice in the hope of the glory of God" (Rom. 5:2). Joy is the natural consequence of a well-grounded hope. There may be joy in title as well as in possession.

Delight in contemplation. The consideration and serious thoughts of heaven affect a gracious heart and fill it with pleasure, though that heart is in a wilderness. The near approach to a desired good much affects the heart. Moses was surely more pleased with the sight of Canaan from Pisgah than with the hopes of it in the desert. A traveler's delight is more raised when nearest the journey's end, and a hungry stomach has a greater joy when it sees the food approaching that must satisfy the appetite. As the union with the object is nearer, so the delight is stronger. Now the delight the soul has in duty is not a delight of fulfillment but of desire, hope, or contemplation—a delight of the journey, not of the home.

Now this delight in prayer *is an inward and hearty delight,* seated in the heart. As God is hearty in offering mercy, so is the soul in petitioning for it. There is a harmony between God and the heart. Those purposes that God has in giving are a Christian's purpose in asking. The more our hearts are in the requests, the more God's heart is in the grants. The emphasis of mercy is *God's whole heart* and *whole soul* in it (Jer. 32:41). So the emphasis of duty is the Christian's whole heart and whole soul. As without God's cheerful answering, a gracious soul would not relish a mercy, so without our hearty asking God does not relish our prayers.

—Stephen Charnock

Delight yourself in the LORD and he will give you the desires of your heart.

—Psalm 37:4

[This delight in prayer] is a delight in God, who is the object of prayer.[28] The glory of God—communion with him, enjoyment of him—is the great goal of believers in their prayers. Such delight in prayer is only a spark of the delight that the soul has in the object of prayer. God is the center, in whom the soul rests, and the goal that the soul aims at. According to our perceptions of God are our desires for him; when we see him as the chief good, we will desire him and delight in him as the chief good. There must first be a delight in God before there can be a spiritual delight or a constancy in duty. Delight is a grace, and, as faith, desire, and love have God for their object, so does this. And according to the strength of our delight in the object or purpose is the strength of our delight in the means of attainment. When we delight in God as glorious, we will delight to honor him; when we regard him as good, we will delight to pursue and enjoy him and delight in that which brings us into communion with him. Those who rejoice in God will rejoice in every approach to him. "The joy of the LORD is your strength" (Neh. 8:10). The more joy in God, the more strength to go to him. The lack of this is the reason of our snail-like motion to him. We have no sweet thoughts of God and therefore no mind to converse with him. We cannot judge our delight in prayer to be right if we do not have a delight in God—natural men and women may have a delight in prayer when they have corrupt and selfish ends. They may have a delight in a duty as it is a means, according to their understanding, to gain their purpose, as Balaam and Balak offered their sacrifice cheerfully, hoping to ingratiate themselves with God and to have liberty to curse his people.

—Stephen Charnock

> *Delight yourself in the Lord and he will give you the*
> *desires of your heart.*
>
> —Psalm 37:4

This delight in prayer is a *delight in the precepts and promises of God, which are the ground and rules of prayer.*[29] First, David delights in God's testimonies and then calls on him with his whole heart. A gracious heart must first delight in precepts and promises before it can turn them into prayers, for prayer is nothing else but presenting God with his own promise, desiring that which he has promised to us. No one was more cheerful in prayer than David, because no one was more rejoicing in the statutes of God. God's statutes were David's songs (Ps. 119:54). And the divine Word was sweeter to him than honey. If our hearts do not leap at divine promises, we are likely to have drowsy souls in desiring them. If our eyes are not on the delicacies God sets before us, our desires cannot be strong for him. If we have no delight in the rich legacies of God, how can we sue for them? If we do not delight in the covenant of grace, we will not delight in prayers for grace. The hopes of reward made Moses valiant in suffering, and the joy set before Christ made him so cheerful in enduring the shame (Heb. 12:1–2).

A delight in prayer itself. A Christian's heart is—in secret—transported into heaven. There is a delight in coming near God and warming the soul by the fire of his love.

The angels are cheerful in the act of praise; their work is their glory. Holy souls so delight in this duty that if there were no command, no promise, they would be stepping into God's courts. They do not think it a good day that passes without some communion with God. David would have taken up his lodgings in the courts of God and regards it as the only blessedness (Ps. 65:4). And so great a delight he had in being in God's presence that he envies the birds the happiness of building their nests near God's tabernacle. There is a delight in the holiness of prayer; natural men or women under some troubles may delight in God's comforting and easing presence—but not in his sanctifying presence. They may delight to pray to God as a storehouse to supply their wants—but not as a refiner's fire to purge away their dross. Prayer, as praise, is a melody to God in the heart (Eph. 5:19). And the soul loves to be fingering the instrument and touching the strings.

—Stephen Charnock

*Delight yourself in the LORD and he will give you the
desires of your heart.*

—Psalm 37:4

[This delight in prayer is] *a delight in the things asked.*[30] This heavenly cheerfulness is most in heavenly things. What delight others have in asking worldly goods, a gracious heart has in begging the light of God's face. Souls cannot be dull in prayer who seriously consider they pray for no less than heaven and happiness, no less than the glory of the great God. A gracious person is never weary of spiritual things, as people are never weary of the sun; though spiritual things are enjoyed every day, yet we long for them to rise again. From this delight in the matter of prayer, the saints have redoubled and repeated their petitions and redoubled the *Amen* at the end of prayer, to show the great affections to those things they have asked. The soul loves to think of those things the heart is set on, and frequent thoughts express a delight.

[Delight in prayer is] *a delight in those graces and affections that are exercised in prayer.* A gracious heart is most delighted with that prayer in which grace has been more stirring, and gracious affections have been boiling over. The soul desires not only to speak to God, but to make melody to God; the heart is the instrument, but graces are the strings, and prayer is touching them, and therefore the soul is more displeased with the flagging of its graces than with missing an answer. There may be a delight in gifts, in a person's own gifts, in the gifts of another, in the pomp and varnish of devotion, but a delight in exercising spiritual graces is an ingredient in this true delight. The Pharisees are marked by Christ to make long prayers, self-glorifying in an outward bravery of words, as if they were playing the courtiers with God and complimenting him; the publican had a short prayer but more grace: "God, have mercy on me, a sinner." There is reliance and humility. A gracious heart labors to bring flaming affections, and if it cannot bring flaming grace, it will bring smoking grace; Christians desire the preparation of their hearts as well as the answer of their prayers.

—Stephen Charnock

*Though it linger, wait for it; it will certainly come
and will not delay.*

—Habakkuk 2:3

Faith, hope, love, these are great gifts.[31] Yet not all of them together will bring you through with honor. For that, something more is needed. Remember, says Saint Anthony, of all the virtues, perseverance alone wins the crown. Have you the courage that, checked and beaten back, can hold its ground and never think of giving way? For that is often what I need in those who would serve me, says God. Though it linger, wait.

"We all thought," said Baxter, speaking of the Civil War, "that one battle would end it, but we were all very much mistaken." And so most of us expected that our spiritual lives would move on much faster than they have. We knew we had certain temptations, but we were going to knock them on the head and put an end to that; yet perhaps some of them visit us to this day. We were aware that we were prone to this and that sin and weakness. But Christ would break them for us. Yet, perhaps, some of them persist.

We saw the glory of life as Christ led it, and our hearts ran out to that eagerly. But it has proved difficult to weave our characters into his likeness! We too have need of Paul's prayer for his friends—that our faith may become a thing of power. For it seems sometimes curiously ineffective, doesn't it?

Perhaps you are haunted by a feeling that after all your faith and efforts you are painfully little changed, that if Christ were really in your life surely there would be more to show. Look, your heart cries, how it was in his time! Everywhere he went were extraordinary happenings, there for all to see. But I, what can I show?

Into a liquid is dropped one drop, a second, and there is no result—another and another—and then one more, precisely like the rest, and all of a sudden everything is changed! And day by day doggedly we pray and hope and toil and believe. And what is there to show for it? Not much, to outward appearance. Yet, is far more going on than our eyes see? And one day, one other prayer, one other ordinary act of ordinary faith, one more looking toward Jesus Christ, may bring the long process to its culmination, and we waken satisfied because we are in his likeness—at last!

—Arthur John Gossip

Though it linger, wait for it; it will certainly come
and will not delay.

—Habakkuk 2:3

Sudden or slow, dramatic or invisible, "it will certainly come."[32]

And, says the prophet, it "will not delay." That is the fear that often haunts us. That "too late" is a grievous reality, a grim and fearful fact of life.

Often that is what we feel about ourselves. Once we might have really closed with Christ and taken what he offers us. But now the character is fixed, our habits are settled, the channels are cut that the rivers must run in to the end. It is too late. And there is dreadful truth in that.

"Are you still sleeping?" said the Master sadly, the glorious office he had offered his friends left unaccepted; sleep on, it does not matter now. The chance is lost, the opportunity is past, sleep on!

Every failure, in a way, is irremediable. Always our record must be by that amount less than it might and should and could have been. And we look wistfully across at Christ and then sadly enough at what we are. That is what I might have been, and this is what I am; that is what I was offered, and this is what I chose! Fool that I was, but now—it is too late.

But the whole point of the gospel is that, in one glorious way, it is not yet too late for anyone. If you have not seen that in Christ, have you seen Christ at all? Always he faced the poorest, the most soiled and tangled life with the sure confidence that even yet it could be righted; yes, and he would do it now. And how often and how strangely he was justified in cases that looked just impossible! Aye, and why should he not be so in you and me? It is to us, remember, to plain ordinary folk like you and me that he gives his bewildering promises; it is on us he makes his staggering claims; it is for us he prays those astounding prayers of his with their tremendous hopes! To that, then, he feels even yet we can attain.

No, it is not too late, even for you and me, to throw ourselves on Jesus Christ, really to take, really to use that strange power that he offers and so really grow into his blessed likeness, not too late for God's dream of us to come really true.

Up! up! and back into the thick of things with steady hearts and quiet eyes. And, even though it linger, wait for it; it will certainly come and will not delay.

—Arthur John Gossip

My lover is mine and I am his.

—Song of Songs 2:16

In this Song of Songs we see the love of Christ and his church.[33] There is a conjugal union between Christ and believers.

It is a natural union. This all people have, Christ having taken human nature on him. But if there is no more than this natural union, it will give little comfort. Thousands are damned though Christ is united to their human nature.

It is a sacred union. By this we are mystically united to Christ. The union with Christ is not personal. If Christ's essence were transfused into the person of a believer, then it would follow that all that a believer does should be meritorious.

But the union between Christ and a saint is

contractual. "My lover is mine." God the Father gives the bride, God the Son receives the bride, God the Holy Spirit ties the knot in marriage—he knits our wills to Christ and Christ's love to us.

effective. Christ unites himself to his spouse by his graces and influences. Christ makes himself one with the spouse by conveying his image and stamping the impress of his own holiness on her.

spiritual. It is hard to describe how the soul is united to the body and how Christ is united to the soul. But though this union is spiritual, it is real. Things in nature often work imperceptibly; so the union between Christ and the soul, though it is imperceptible to the eye of reason, is still real.

Before this union with Christ, however, there must be a separation. The heart must be separated from all other lovers. So there must be a leaving of our former sins, a breaking off the old league with hell before we can be united to Christ. There must be a divorce before a union.

The purpose of our conjugal union with Christ is twofold:

Cohabitation. This is one purpose of marriage, to live together "that Christ may dwell in your hearts" (Eph. 3:17). It is not enough to pay Christ a few visits in his ordinances; we must dwell on the thoughts of Christ. Married persons should not live apart.

Fruit bearing. The spouse bears the fruit of the Spirit: "love, joy, peace, patience, kindness, goodness, faithfulness, gentleness and self-control" (Gal. 5:22–23). Barrenness is a shame in Christ's spouse.

—Thomas Watson

My lover is mine and I am his.

—Song of Songs 2:16

This marriage union with Christ is the most noble and excellent union.[34]

There is a closer union in this holy marriage than there can be in any other. In other marriages, two make one flesh, but Christ and the believer make one spirit. "He who unites himself with the Lord is one with him in spirit" (1 Cor. 6:17). The joy that flows from the mystic union is inexpressible and glorious (1 Peter 1:8).

This union with Christ never ceases. Other marriages are soon at an end. Death cuts asunder the marriage knot, but this conjugal union is eternal. You who are once Christ's spouse will never again be a widow. "I will betroth you to me forever" (Hos. 2:19).

In this life there is only the contract. The glorious completing and solemnizing of the marriage is reserved for heaven. There is the wedding supper of the Lamb (Rev. 19:9). "And so we will be with the Lord forever" (1 Thess. 4:17). So death merely begins our marriage with Christ.

Have we chosen Christ to set our love on, and is this choice founded on knowledge? Have we consented to the match? It is not enough that Christ is willing to have us, but are we willing to have him? God does not so force salvation on us that we shall have Christ whether we want to or not. We must consent to have him. Many approve of Christ but do not give their consent. And this consent must be pure and genuine. We consent to have him for his own worth and excellence.

Have we taken Christ? Faith is the bond of the union. Christ is joined to us by his Spirit, and we are joined to him by faith. Faith ties the marriage knot.

Have we given ourselves to Christ? Thus the spouse in the text says, "I am his," as if she had said, "All I have is for the use and service of Christ." Have we made a surrender? Have we given up our names and wills to Christ? When the Devil solicits by a temptation, do we say, "We are not our own, we are Christ's; our tongues are his, we must not defile them with oaths; our bodies are his temple, we must not pollute them with sin"? If it is so, it is a sign that the Holy Spirit has produced this blessed union between Christ and us.

—Thomas Watson

*This is a profound mystery—but I am talking about Christ
and the church.*

—Ephesians 5:32

Saints are married, united to Christ, who is the best husband, "outstanding among ten thousand" (Song 5:10).[35]

Christ is a husband who cannot be paralleled

for tender care. The spouse cannot be as considerate of her own soul as Christ is considerate of her. If she wanders out of the way, he guides her. If she stumbles, he holds her hand. If she falls, he raises her. If she is sad, he comforts her with promises.

for ardent affection. No husband loves like Christ. He has given real demonstrations of his love to his spouse. He has sent her a love letter—his Word—and he has given her a love token—his Spirit.

Christ loves more than any other husband:

He puts richer clothes on his bride. "He has clothed me with garments of salvation . . . a robe of righteousness" (Isa. 61:10). [Because of] this robe, God looks on us as if we had not sinned and we are reputed righteous—as righteous as Christ, "so that in him we might become the righteousness of God" (2 Cor. 5:21).

He gives his bride not only his golden garments but his image. Christ imparts "the splendor of his holiness" (Ps. 29:2). "The splendor I had given you made your beauty perfect" (Ezek. 16:14). Christ never thinks he has loved his spouse enough till he can see his own face in her.

Christ discharges those debts that no other husband can. Our sins are the worst debts we owe. If all the angels contributed money, they could not pay one of these debts, but Christ frees us from these. He says to justice what Paul said concerning Onesimus: "If he has done you any wrong or owes you anything, charge it to me" (Philem. 18).

Christ has suffered more for his spouse than any husband ever did for a wife. He suffered poverty and scandal. He who crowned the heavens with stars was himself crowned with thorns. He was regardless of his life; he leaped into the sea of his Father's wrath to save his spouse from drowning.

Christ's love does not end with his life. He loves his spouse forever. Well may the apostle call it "this love that surpasses knowledge" (Eph. 3:19).

—Thomas Watson

This is a profound mystery—but I am talking about Christ
and the church.

—Ephesians 5:32

There is a conjugal union between Christ and believers. From that we may draw many inferences.[36]

See the dignity of all true believers. They are joined in marriage with Christ. There is not only assimilation but union—they are not only like Christ but one with Christ. When a king marries a beggar, by virtue of the union she is made of the blood royal. So the godly are divinely united to Christ, who is King of Kings and Lord of Lords. By virtue of this sacred union the saints are given distinction above the angels. Christ is the Lord of the angels but not their husband.

See how rich believers are. They have married into the crown of heaven, and by virtue of the union all Christ's riches go to them. Christ communicates his graces, and he communicates his privileges—justification, glorification. He settles a kingdom on his spouse as her inheritance (Heb. 12:28). This is a key to the apostle's riddle, "having nothing, and yet possessing everything" (2 Cor. 6:10). By virtue of the marriage union, the saints have an interest in all Christ's riches.

See how fearful a sin it is to abuse the saints. It is an injury done to Christ, for believers are spiritually one with him: "Saul, Saul, why do you persecute me?" (Acts 9:4). When the body was wounded, the Head, in heaven, cried out. In this sense, people crucify Christ afresh, because what is done to his members is done to him. Will a king tolerate having his treasure rifled, his crown thrown in the dust, his queen beheaded? The saints are the apple of Christ's eye, and let those who strike at his eye answer for it.

See the reason why the saints so rejoice in the Word and sacrament, because here they meet with their husband, Christ. The wife desires to be in the presence of her husband. The Lord's Supper is nothing other than a pledge and token of that eternal communion which the saints will have with Christ in heaven. Then he will take the spouse to his bosom. If Christ is so sweet in an ordinance, when we have only short glances and dark glimpses of him by faith, oh, then, how delightful and captivating will his presence be in heaven when we see him face-to-face and are forever in his loving embraces!

—Thomas Watson

My lover is mine and I am his.

—Song of Songs 2:16

This mystic union affords much comfort to believers in several cases.[37]

In the case of the disrespect and unkindness of the world. Though we live in an unkind world, we have a kind husband. The Father's love to Christ is the pattern of Christ's love to his spouse. This love of Christ as far exceeds all created love as the sun outshines the light of a torch. Though the world hates me, Christ still loves me.

In the case of weakness of grace. You are the spouse of Christ, and he will bear with you as the weaker vessel. Will a husband divorce his wife because she is weak and sickly? This is the spouse's comfort when she is weak. Her Husband can infuse strength into her: "My God has been my strength" (Isa. 49:5).

In the case of death. When believers die, they go to their husband. When a woman is engaged, she longs for the day of marriage. After the saints' funerals, their marriage begins. God is wise; he lets us meet with changes and troubles here so that he may wean us from the world and make us long for death. When the soul is divorced from the body, it is married to Christ.

In the case of passing sentence at the day of judgment. O Christian, your husband will be your judge. If the Devil brings indictments against you, Christ will obliterate your sins in his blood. Christ cannot pass sentence against his spouse without passing it against himself, for Christ and believers are one. Oh, what a comfort this is!

In the case of the saints' suffering. The church of God is exposed in this life to many injuries, but she has a husband in heaven who is mindful of her. Now it is a time of mourning with the spouse because the Bridegroom is absent. But shortly she will end her mourning. Christ "will swallow up death forever. The Sovereign LORD will wipe away the tears from all faces" (Isa. 25:8). Christ will comfort his spouse. He will solace her with his love; he will take away the cup of trembling and give her the cup of consolation. She will forget all her sorrows, being called into the banqueting house of heaven and having the banner of Christ's love displayed over her.

—Thomas Watson

My lover is mine and I am his.

—Song of Songs 2:16

Let me press [the first duty] on those who have this marriage union with Christ:[38]

Rejoice in your husband, Christ. Has Christ honored you by taking you into the marriage relationship and making you one with himself? This calls for joy. By virtue of the union, believers are sharers with Christ in his riches. It was a custom among the Romans when the wife was brought home for her to receive the keys of her husband's house, intimating that the treasure and custody of the house was now committed to her. When Christ brings his bride home to those glorious rooms that he has gone ahead to prepare for her (John 14:2), he will hand over the keys of his treasure to her, and she shall be as rich as heaven can make her.

Christians, let the times be ever so sad, you may rejoice in your spiritual betrothals. "Though the fig tree does not bud and there are no grapes on the vines, though the olive crop fails and the fields produce no food, though there are no sheep in the pen and no cattle in the stalls, yet I will rejoice in the LORD, I will be joyful in God my Savior" (Hab. 3:17–18). Let me tell you, it is a sin not to rejoice. You disparage your husband, Christ. When a wife is always sighing and weeping, what will others say? "This woman has a bad husband." Is this the fruit of Christ's love to you, to reflect dishonor on him? A melancholy spouse saddens Christ's heart. I do not deny that Christians should grieve for sins of daily occurrence, but to be always weeping (as if they mourned without hope) is dishonorable to the marriage relationship. "Rejoice in the Lord always" (Phil. 4:4). Rejoicing brings credit to your husband. Christ loves a cheerful bride, and indeed the very purpose of God's making us sad is to make us rejoice. We sow in tears, so that we may reap in joy. The excessive sadness and contrition of the godly will make others afraid to embrace Christ. They will begin to question whether there is that satisfactory joy in religion which is claimed. Oh, you saints of God, do not forget consolation; let others see that you do not regret your choice. It is joy that puts liveliness and activity into a Christian: "The joy of the LORD is your strength" (Neh. 8:10). The soul is swiftest in duty when it is carried on the wings of joy.

—Thomas Watson

My lover is mine and I am his.
—Song of Songs 2:16

Let me press [two more] duties on those who have this marriage union with Christ.[39]

1. Adorn this marriage relationship, so that you may be a crown to your husband.

Wear a veil. We read of the spouse's veil (Song 5:7). This veil is humility.

Put on your jewels. These are the graces that for their luster are compared to rows of jewels and chains of gold (Song 1:10 KJV). These precious jewels distinguish Christ's bride from strangers.

Behave as becomes Christ's spouse in chastity. Be chaste in your judgments; do not defile yourselves with error. Error corrupts the mind (1 Tim. 6:5). It is one of Satan's devices first to defile the judgment, then the conscience.

Behave as becomes Christ's spouse in sanctity. It is not for Christ's spouse to behave like harlots. An exposed body and impure speech do not become a saint. Christ's bride must shine forth in gospel purity, so though we can bring Christ no dowry, yet he expects us to keep ourselves pure.

2. Love your husband, Christ (Song 2:5). Love him though he is reproached and persecuted. A wife loves her husband when [he is] in prison. To kindle your love toward Christ, consider

Nothing else is fit for you to love. If Christ is your husband, it is not fit to have other lovers who would make Christ grow jealous.

He is worthy of your love. He is unparalleled in beauty: "altogether lovely" (Song 5:16).

How fervent is Christ's love toward you! He loves you in your worst condition, he loves you in affliction. He loves you notwithstanding your fears and blemishes. The saints' infirmities cannot wholly remove Christ's love from them. Oh, then, how the spouse should delight in her love to Christ! This will be the excellence of heaven: Our love will then be like the sun in its full strength.

—Thomas Watson

And he brought him to Jesus.

—John 1:42

While people sketch out imaginary designs, they frequently miss actual opportunities.[40] They would not build because they could not erect a palace. They therefore shiver in the winter's cold. They were not content to do a little and therefore did nothing.

Andrew was a commonplace disciple, a man of average capacity, and an ordinary believer. Yet Andrew became a useful minister, and thus the servants of Jesus Christ are not excused from endeavoring to extend the boundaries of his kingdom by saying, "I have no remarkable talent or singular ability." If you are only like a firefly's lamp, do not hide your light, for there is an eye predestined to see by your light, a heart ordained to find comfort by your faint gleam.

Awake and render service to the lover of your souls. Make no excuse, for no excuse can be valid from those who are bought with so great a price. Your business requires so much of your thoughts—I know it does. Then use your business in such a way as to serve God. There must be some opportunities for aiming at conversions. If you can reach but one, do not let that one remain unsought. Time is hastening and people are perishing. The world is growing old in sin.

O that I had the power to stir the hearts and souls of all other Christians by a description of this huge city wallowing in iniquity, by a picture of cemeteries fattening on corpses, by a portrayal of that lake of fire to which multitudes yearly descend. O that I could set before you the Redeemer on the cross dying to ransom souls! O that I could depict the heaven that sinners lose and their remorse when they shall find themselves self-excluded!

To bring people to Jesus—let this be your aim and mine! Not to bring them to baptism nor to the church building nor to adopt our form of worship, but to bring them to his dear feet who alone can say, "Your many sins are forgiven. Go in peace."

As we believe Jesus is the very center of the Christian religion, those who do not have Christ do not have true godliness. Determine in your spirit that you will never cease to labor for them until you have reason to believe that they are trusting in Jesus, loving Jesus, in the hope that they shall be conformed to the image of Jesus and dwell with him, world without end.

—C. H. Spurgeon

Do not store up for yourselves treasures on earth.
—Matthew 6:19

"Man is a mere phantom as he goes to and fro: he bustles about, but only in vain; he heaps up wealth, not knowing who will get it" (Ps. 39:6).[41] What is more mad, more unhappy? All day long you are harassed by labor, all night agitated by fear. That your coffer may be filled with money, your soul is in a fever of anxiety.

You bustle about in vain. Suppose that all your undertakings succeed. You bustle about, not fruitlessly indeed—still in vain. You are heaping up treasure and do not know for whom you gather it. For yourself?—you, who must die so soon? For your children?—those who must die so soon? It is a great futility—ones who must soon die lay up for those who must soon die also.

Let us then give ear to Jesus Christ: "Do not store up for yourselves treasures on earth. . . . But store up for yourselves treasures in heaven. . . . For where your treasure is, there your heart will be also." What more do you wait for?

The voice of prediction is, "Heaven and earth will pass away" (Matt. 24:35). The voice of warning is, "Do not store up for yourselves treasures on earth." If then you believe God in his prediction, if you do not despise his warning, let what he says be done. You will not lose what you have given away but will follow what you have only sent ahead of you. What you have on earth—with anxiety—you shall possess in heaven free from care. Transport your goods, then. I am giving you counsel for keeping, not for losing. "You will have," says he, "treasure in heaven. Then come, follow me" (Matt. 19:21), that I may bring you to your treasure.

If what we have must be transported, let us transfer it to that place from where we cannot lose it. What are the poor to whom we give but our carriers, by whom we convey our goods from earth to heaven? Give then—you are only giving to your carriers. "How," say you, "do they carry it to heaven? For I see that they make an end of it by eating." No doubt they carry it not by keeping it but by making it their food. Have you forgotten? "Whatever," says Christ, "you did for one of the least of these brothers of mine, you did for me." He has received it who gave you something to give. He has received it who, in the end, will give his own self to you.

—Augustine of Hippo

Do not store up for yourselves treasures on earth.
—Matthew 6:19

At the end of the world, when our Lord Jesus Christ comes to judge, he will gather all nations before him.[42] To those on his right he will say, "Come, . . . take your inheritance, the kingdom prepared for you since the creation of the world" (Matt. 25:34). But to those on the left, "Depart from me . . . into the eternal fire prepared for the devil and his angels" (v. 41).

Why so great a reward or so great a punishment? Why will the first receive the kingdom? "For I was hungry, and you gave me something to eat" (v. 35). Why will the others depart into eternal fire? "For I was hungry, and you gave me nothing to eat" (v. 42). Those who receive the kingdom gave as good and faithful Christians. Had they not done so, this barrenness would surely not have accorded with their good lives. Maybe they were chaste, not drunkards, and kept themselves from evil works. Yet if they had not added good works, they would have remained barren. For they would have kept, "Turn from evil," but they would not have kept, "and do good" (Ps. 34:14; 1 Peter 3:11).

Give away your earthly bread and knock for the heavenly! How will the Lord give to you who do not give to those in need? [Others] are in need before you, and you are in need before Another. Do then to others as you would have done to you. Though he is the Lord and doesn't need our goods, yet that we might do something for him, he has submitted to be hungry in his poor.

John said to those who came to him, "You brood of vipers! Who warned you to flee from the coming wrath? Produce fruit in keeping with repentance" (Luke 3:7–8). The crowd asked him, "What should we do then?" (v. 10). That is, what are these fruits that you exhort us to bring forth? He said, "The man with two tunics should share with him who has none, and the one who has food should do the same" (v. 11). What other meaning then can it have when he said, "Every tree that does not produce good fruit will be cut down and thrown into the fire" (v. 9), but the same that they on the left will hear, "Depart from me. . . . For I was hungry and you gave me nothing to eat." It is only a small matter to depart from sins, if you neglect to cure what is past. If then you will be heard when you pray for pardon of your sins, forgive, and it will be forgiven you; give, and it will be given you.

—Augustine of Hippo

> By faith Moses, when he had grown up, refused to be
> known as the son of Pharaoh's daughter. He chose
> to be mistreated along with the people of God rather
> than to enjoy the pleasures of sin for a short time.
> He regarded disgrace for the sake of Christ as
> of greater value than the treasures of Egypt,
> because he was looking ahead to his reward.
> —Hebrews 11:24–26

As though [the writer of Hebrews] said, "No one of you has left a palace . . . nor such treasures, nor, when you might have been a king's son, have you despised this, as Moses did."[43] And that he did not simply leave, [the writer] expressed by saying, he "refused," that is, he hated, he turned away. For when heaven was set before him, it was needless to admire an Egyptian palace.

And [the writer] did not say Moses regarded heaven and the things in heaven of greater value than the treasures of Egypt but—what? Disgrace for the sake of Christ he counted better than being at ease, and this itself was reward.

"He chose to be mistreated along with the people of God rather than to enjoy the pleasures of sin for a short time." He called unwillingness to be mistreated with the rest "sin." If then he counted it sin not to be ready to be mistreated with the rest, it follows that suffering must be a great good, since he threw himself into it from the royal palace.

But this he did seeing some great things before him. "He regarded disgrace for the sake of Christ of greater value than the treasures of Egypt." What is "disgrace for the sake of Christ"? It is being disgraced in such ways as that [which] Christ endured, or that [which Moses] endured for Christ's sake. It is disgrace for the sake of Christ when you are reproached by those of your own family or by those whom you are benefiting.

In these words [the writer of Hebrews] encouraged [his readers], by showing that even Christ suffered these things, and Moses also, two illustrious persons. But neither did the one send forth lightning nor the other feel any [anger], but he was reviled and endured all things. Since therefore it was probable that [the readers] also would bear such things and would long for the reward, [the writer] says that even Christ and Moses had suffered the like. So then ease is [the reward] of sin, but to be disgraced, of Christ. For what then do you wish? Disgrace for the sake of Christ, or ease?

—John Chrysostom

*[Moses] regarded disgrace for the sake of Christ as of
greater value than the treasures of Egypt, because he was
looking ahead to his reward.*

—Hebrews 11:26

If we too always see God with our minds, if we always think in remembrance of him, all things will appear endurable to us, all things will appear tolerable.[44] For if people, remembering one whom they love, are roused in spirit and elevated in thought and bear all things easily, we who remember him who loves us in deed, when will we feel anything painful, or dread anything fearful or dangerous? When will we be of cowardly spirit? Never.

Things appear difficult to us because we do not remember God as we ought, because we do not carry him about always in our thoughts. For great is the effect of God's remembrance and great also of his being remembered by us. The result of the one is that we choose good things, of the other that we accomplish them and bring them to their purpose.

Therefore let us also, as being in Babylon, [remember him]. For although we are not sitting among warlike foes, yet we are among enemies. For some indeed were sitting as captives, but others did not even feel their captivity, as Daniel, as the three children, who became in that very country more glorious even than the king who had carried them captive. Do you see how great virtue is? When they were in actual captivity he waited on them as masters. He therefore was the captive rather than they. Do you see that the really splendid things are those that relate to God, whereas human things are a shadow? The king knew not, it seems, that he was leading away masters for himself and that he cast into the furnace those whom he was about to worship.

Let us fear God, beloved; even should we be in captivity, we are more glorious than all rulers. Let the fear of God be present with us and nothing will be grievous, even though you speak of poverty or disease, of captivity or slavery, or of any other grievous thing. Even these very things will themselves work together for us the other way. These men were captives, and the king worshiped them.

—John Chrysostom

I pray for them.

—John 17:9

Jesus was speaking immediately of the little company of men who were right around him, the disciples.[45] On the evening before the crucifixion he said, "I pray for them," but a little later he said, "My prayer is not for them alone. I pray also for those who will believe in me through their message, that all of them may be one" (John 17:20–21). Through them and their word the circle would continue to widen until it would embrace all that would ever become believers in him.

I invite you to take this prayer in John 17 as an idea of what sort of things the Lord Jesus Christ is asking for [right] now in your behalf. Oh, the Savior who always lives prays for you and me, knowing us better than we know ourselves.

Notice this *first petition:* "My prayer is not that you take them out of the world but that you protect them from the evil one" (v. 15). What a common mistake it is to think that the only object Jesus Christ has with reference to the human race is to gather a few of us out of this world and carry us to the better world. But he was going out of the world, and his heart longed after those who had been with him. They wondered why they could not go with him, and one even said, in self-confident fervor, "I will lay down my life for you" (John 13:37). Many good people think hard of themselves because they do not want to die. I have heard such persons say, "Ah, me! I am so unwilling to die! I think anyone who loves God ought to be willing to die." Well, that is against nature. It is impossible; it is wrong. The Lord Jesus Christ proposes not merely to rescue some souls from this world, but to rescue them *in* this world and make them live in this world as they were meant to live, by the help of his grace. This world belongs to him, and he proposes to help those—all that will come to him—that are thus oppressed by sin to live a life such as they should live.

Elijah lay under a juniper tree in the desert and requested that he might die. In answer to his prayer, an angel came with food that he might eat and lie down and sleep again, and getting up might go work in God's service. Often when people are whining that they do not want to live, what they really need is food and sleep and exercise so that they may be ready to serve God.

—John A. Broadus

Sanctify them by the truth; your word is truth.
—John 17:17

The second petition.[46] You observe Jesus does not merely pray that they may be kept from evil, but that they may be made holy. Piety is not a mere negative thing. The Ten Commandments, I know, are all in negative form, "thou shalt not." Even so, Christianity reveals that this is but one side and that the nobler and more glorious side of piety is that we must not merely try to keep from doing wrong but try to do right. Jesus prays not simply that they may be kept from evil but that they may be made holy. Do you want to be holy? You should desire to be holy! Anyhow, Jesus wishes that for you, and he prays, "Make them holy—make them holy through your truth; your word is truth."

It is truth that makes people holy. Earth's unholiness began with a lie that people believed and so went headlong to ruin. Truth is the lifeblood of piety. Truth is the medicine for the soul's disease. Nobody is ever made holy except through truth. Blessed be God, it often works its healing work though sadly mingled with error. The truth may still work its healing, saving, sanctifying work. "Your word is truth." We know that word, and we may use it as the means of becoming holy.

Regard the Bible as that which we are to use as the means of becoming holy. Regard the Bible as the means of making you better, of making you good. Use the Bible for that purpose. I know how it is, many times you do not love to read your Bible. The truth is, you take up your newspaper a second time and go on looking for something else in it when the Bible is lying neglected by your side. Then when you do take the Bible, you feel that it is rather dull reading. Learn to regard the Bible more as the means of making you holy. When you read it in private or hear it read in public, regard it as the great means of making you better, of strengthening you, of correcting your faults, of helping you to know your duty and helping you to do your duty. Fill your heart and mind full of the teachings of God's Word, hoping it will make you better. You will take more interest in hearing the preacher read it from the pulpit and explain and impress on you its teachings, if you listen with the idea, "How I hope this will help me!" So in private read the Bible with the thought, "How I pray that this may do me good." Please remember this suggestion and act on it!

—John A. Broadus

I pray also for those who will believe in me through their
message, that all of them may be one, Father.
—John 17:20–21

The third petition.[47] I see Jesus Christ standing in that night hour with his little company of eleven. He sends his thoughts down the years to dwell on those who would believe on him, and his heart went out toward them, praying "that all of them may be one." Jesus Christ bends now from the mediator's throne with endless solicitude for every human heart that looks lovingly up to him, knowing them all, the sheep of his flock on earth, and praying still "that all of them may be one."

You expect me to contrast with this prayer the divisions of the Christian world. But I will not. The prayer is answered—imperfectly, certainly—and so is that other prayer, "Sanctify them." You may deem it strange that Jesus prayed that his people might be holy, and they are so unholy, yet you do not say his prayer is not answered. So with this other prayer; Christ's true people are one. All who truly trust in Jesus Christ are more one than they know, and in proportion as they are united to the Redeemer, they are united with each other.

This prayer will be more fully answered in the same way as the previous prayer—by the truth. The more gospel truth we know and believe and live by, the more we will be one. One of the problems of our day is to know how to cling to gospel truth in kindliness toward those who differ from us as to what is gospel truth.

Many people are possessed with the idea that everything must be given up to outward union. They have so liberalized the Christian faith that they say there is no assured truth; one thing is as true as another. Other people set their heads on certain views of truth until there is not anything in their view but those particular tenets that distinguish them from other Christians.

Now it is a fact that people are made better only by truth and that Christians will be made more thoroughly one through truth, and it is folly to sacrifice truth for the sake of outward union. The problem is how to maintain devotion to God's truth and yet deal in all loving-kindness and affection and cooperation with all who love our Lord Jesus Christ in sincerity. You say it is hard to do both of these things! Of course, it is hard to do anything well, always hard to do right and to do good, with this poor human nature of ours.

—John A. Broadus

*Father, I want those you have given me to be with me
where I am, and to see my glory, the glory you
have given me.*

—John 17:24

I mention *one more petition.*[48] They had beheld his humiliation, those who accompanied him, and he longed that they might be with him to behold his glory. He offers the same prayer for all that would believe on him through their word.

There are two reasons why Jesus Christ made this petition. He asked it partly for his own sake. Did you never imagine that he was sad at leaving his disciples? You know that they were sad, but wasn't he? Did you never suppose that he longs to have those who love him more immediately with him? He said to his disciples, "Do not let your hearts be troubled. Trust in God; trust also in me" (John 14:1), and it will all be well. "I am going . . . to prepare a place for you. And . . . I will come back and take you to be with me" (vv. 2–3). He says it not only to comfort them, but more than they know perhaps, he says it to comfort his own heart also. And so Jesus said, "I want those you have given me to be with me where I am." He wants to have his people with him.

But the other reason is more obvious to us; he made the prayer for their sake. He makes the prayer for our sake, "I want those you have given me to be with me where I am, and to see my glory." To be with him is to be delivered from all the infirmities and imperfections and conflicts of this earthly life. I do not suppose we could bear all this if it were not for the fact that it is to end—and to end in victory. I suppose we would give up the struggling effort to do right and to do good in this world were it not for the assurance that we will at last be conquerors and "more than conquerors through him who loved us" (Rom. 8:37). To be with him will be to be with all who have loved us and who have gone before us to him. To be with him is to be free from all sin, and safe. Safe! O my soul, safe from all temptation to sin. To be with him is to behold his glory.

So the Savior prays for us, and how grateful we are. Let us strive to fulfill his petitions that one day we may be with him.

—John A. Broadus

The Father loves the Son and has placed
everything in his hands.

—John 3:35

That everything is in Christ's hands will be evident from the following demonstrations.[49]

All good things in the world are only shadows of what is in Christ. Outward riches are but a shadow of the unsearchable riches of Christ. Outward life is only a shadow of him who is the way, the truth, and the life. Outward liberty is only a shadow of that freedom which is to be had in Christ, "If the Son sets you free, you will be free indeed" (John 8:36), meaning that no freedom is freedom indeed and in truth but this. Outward rest is only a shadow of the rest that is to be had in him: "Come to me, . . . and I will give you rest" (Matt. 11:28). The sun in the sky is only a shadow of the Sun of righteousness and of his glory. Rivers and fountains are only shadows of his fullness who is the fountain of living waters. Plants and trees are only a shadow of the foliage of him who is the tree of life. All things that have any excellence in them are only shadows of him in whom all worthwhile qualities come to a common center. All the stars are only shadows of him who is the bright and morning Star.

If Christ can supply all wants, then everything must be in his hands, [and] so it is, he can supply all wants: "My God will meet all your needs according to his glorious riches in Christ Jesus" (Phil. 4:19). Whatever you suffer from, there is in Christ that which can supply and support. Do you suffer from desertion? Then, he says, "Never will I leave you; never will I forsake you" (Heb. 13:5). Do you suffer from corruption and bondage to sin? It is he who says, "Sin shall not be your master" (Rom. 6:14). Do you suffer from temptation? It is he who, as "the God of peace will . . . crush Satan under your feet" (Rom. 16:20) and says, "My grace is sufficient for you" (2 Cor. 12:9). Do you suffer from weakness? It is he who says, "My power is made perfect in weakness" (v. 9). Do you suffer from affliction, inward or outward? "A righteous man may have many troubles, but the LORD delivers him from them all" (Ps. 34:19). Do you suffer from fears of public calamities? It is said of him, "He will be their peace" (Mic. 5:5). Do you suffer from the fears of death? It is he who says, "I will redeem them from death. Where, O death, are your plagues? Where, O grave, is your destruction?" (Hos. 13:14).

—Ralph Erskine

The Father loves the Son and has placed
everything in his hands.

—John 3:35

If Christ can satisfy all the desires, suit all the conditions, and answer all the objections of sinners, then he must have everything, [and] so it is.[50]

He can *satisfy all desires* of sinners, for everything desirable is in him. Is wisdom desirable? In him "are hidden all the treasures of wisdom and knowledge" (Col. 2:3). "Wisdom has built her house" (Prov. 9:1); it is in the plural, *wisdoms.* Christ is a compound of wisdom.

There is no condition you can be in but he has a promise suited to it, so that in Christ there is what *suits all cases,* for the promises are the veins where the blood and fullness of Christ run.

Are you wandering? Christ says, I am the way. Are you in darkness? Christ says, I am the light of the world. Are you guilty? Christ is the Lord our righteousness. Are you polluted? Christ says he is the fountain opened for sin and for uncleanness. Are you dejected? Christ will send the Comforter. Do you need direction? Christ is the wonderful Counselor, and he says, "I will lead the blind by ways they have not known" (Isa. 42:16).

Christ can *answer all objections.* If anyone says, "Alas! I am lost," then Christ says, "I came to seek and to save what was lost." Says another, "I am a great sinner." Well, Christ says, "I have not come to call the righteous, but sinners" (Matt. 9:13). Cries another, "I cannot turn from sin." It is Christ's work to turn you "from darkness to light, and from the power of Satan to God" (Acts 26:18).

"But I have no might or ability to go to Christ." It is answered, "He gives strength to the weary and increases the power of the weak" (Isa. 40:29). He is the author of faith. "Oh! but I have sinned to the uttermost." Why, then, he tells you he is able to save to the uttermost. "Alas! I am wayward." It is answered, "I will heal their waywardness and love them freely" (Hos. 14:4).

Whatever the objection is, he can answer it; whatever the case is, he can remedy it; whatever the desire is, he can satisfy it. Why, then, everything must be in his hands, and no wonder, for all the treasures of divine plenty and fullness are in his hands.

—Ralph Erskine

*The Father loves the Son and has placed
everything in his hands.*

—John 3:35

The next thing proposed was, in order to enlarge our faith, to speak of the extent of this store and treasure that Christ has, the Father having placed everything in his hands.[51]

If everything is in his hands, then all the attributes of God are in him. There is nothing that the Father has, except his personality, but the Son has, as Mediator; "All that belongs to the Father is mine" (John 16:15). Here then is an ocean where you and I may dive forever and never get to the bottom.

Having everything, he has all the wisdom of God: "In whom are hidden all the treasures of wisdom and knowledge" (Col. 2:3). Poor, foolish sinner, who has no wisdom, knowledge, nor understanding, here is a treasure for you—Christ, "who has become for us wisdom from God" (1 Cor. 1:30).

Having everything, he has all the power of God: "We preach Christ crucified: a stumbling block to Jews and foolishness to Gentiles, but to those whom God has called, both Jews and Greeks, Christ the power of God and the wisdom of God" (vv. 23–24).

Poor feeble soul, who can do nothing, here is a good bargain for you to take hold of; it is he who can work in you both to will and do. You are not called to come to Christ except by the power of Christ, which is the power of God. You are to receive him who can give you power to receive him. Having everything, he has all the holiness of God; he is said to be made by God our sanctification, and surely here is an immense fountain of sanctity, the infinite holiness of God. O poor, vile polluted sinner, who has lost the image of God by the fall of the first Adam and the deficiency of his holiness, here is a better head and husband for you, in whom is all the fullness of the deity, that you may be given fullness in him.

—Ralph Erskine

> *The Father loves the Son and has placed*
> *everything in his hands.*
>
> —John 3:35

Having everything, [Christ] has all the justice of God and all the righteousness of God in him.[52] You shall, in Christ, be more righteous in God's sight than ever you were guilty in his sight—yes, you shall be the very righteousness of God in him. You shall not only be justified but find God to be just in justifying you, because the justice of God is in Christ, and it is satisfied, glorified, in him.

Having everything, he has all the mercy of God in his hands; all the infinite love, pity, and compassion of God. What is Christ but the love of God in flesh and blood? "This is how God showed his love among us: He sent his one and only Son into the world that we might live through him. This is love: not that we loved God, but that he loved us and sent his Son as an atoning sacrifice for our sins" (1 John 4:9–10). Do you wish to find mercy in the moment of death and mercy at the great day? Know that there is no mercy to be expected from God's hands unless you look to his mercy in the hands of Christ, for he will never show mercy at the expense of his justice, and it is only in Christ that mercy and justice meet and embrace.

Having everything, he has all the faithfulness and truth of God. O, faithless and unfaithful sinner, who has many times lied to the God of truth—would you have your falsehood all done away and swallowed up in the truth of God and your salvation secured notwithstanding your falsehood? Here is a pillar on which you may stand fixed, amidst all changes, whether in your outward lot or your inward frame, for, "All men are like grass . . . but the word of our God stands forever" (Isa. 40:6, 8). The truth of God stands unalterably the same.

In a word, having everything, [Christ] has all the fullness of God in his hands. "For God was pleased to have all his fullness dwell in him" (Col. 1:19). Not only all the attributes of God, but all the fullness of all the divine attributes—not only the wisdom of God, but all the fullness of divine wisdom; not only the power of God, but all the fullness of divine power; all the fullness of divine holiness; divine righteousness; divine mercy; divine faithfulness; divine authority—not only is God in him, but all the fullness of the deity. Poor empty sinner! Here are unsearchable riches, everlasting salvation for you.

—Ralph Erskine

*The Father loves the Son and has placed
everything in his hands.*

—John 3:35

Let us come to and believe in this glorious One.[53] For a stimulus to action, consider, is it possible that we can desire a better pattern to follow in trusting in Christ than his eternal Father, who has entrusted him with everything? "Here is my servant, whom I uphold" (Isa. 42:1), or, as the word signifies, "my servant, whom I trust." Isn't it best loving whom God loves and trusting whom he trusts?

Consider, too, that those who believe cannot miss salvation, for it is in the hands of Christ to give to all comers. Those who do not believe cannot escape damnation, for, "How shall we escape if we ignore such a great salvation?" (Heb. 2:3)—so great a Savior, who has everything in his hands?

His Father crowned Christ with this honor, so you cannot put more honor on the Father or on Christ than by putting everything you have in his hands and going to him for everything you stand in need of. When you go to him and make use of this treasure, you join with his Father in putting a crown of glory on his head.

Consider for reason to look to this Jesus that everything is placed in Christ's hands so that he may give it out to you. Why has our Lord Jesus received gifts, even the gift of everything? He "gave gifts to men" (Eph. 4:8).

Do not say, then, "It cannot be for me"; yes, it is for you. Let faith say, "It is for me—for me—that everything was placed in Christ's hands."

It is not possible that he will keep all closed in his hands and give out nothing. No; it stands on his honor as Mediator; it stands on his credit as the church's treasurer and the Father's trustee to give from that treasure of grace and fullness that is given to him for our behalf. He would not be faithful to his trust if he would give out none of that treasure to poor sinners. When unbelief says, "Oh! He will give out nothing to me," let faith step in and say, "I hope he will give to me from his fullness, because his name is Faithful and True." And here is a door of faith even for sinners who are yet unbelievers, that there is a glorious and sweet necessity lying on Christ to give from his grace and fullness to human sinners— and why not to you?

—Ralph Erskine

> *The Father loves the Son and has placed*
> *everything in his hands.*
>
> —John 3:35

We are told, "He had to go through Samaria" (John 4:4)."[54] The purpose was to give from his grace to a poor, sinful harlot there. Was there a blessed necessity for his suffering at Jerusalem? Yes: "Did not the Christ have to suffer these things and then enter his glory?" (Luke 24:26). Even so, there is a blessed necessity for his applying the beneficial power of his death and sufferings, by pouring out his Spirit and communicating his grace for that purpose.

Consider, that though Christ is exalted to this honor and majesty of having everything placed in his hands, yet it is not possible that he would be therefore proud and disdainful, so as not to regard the case of poor sinners, for quite the contrary is the truth. Because he is thus honored, therefore he humbles himself. Read his mind on this with wonder and admiration: "Jesus knew that the Father had put all things under his power, and that he had come from God and was returning to God; so he . . . began to wash his disciples' feet, drying them with the towel that was wrapped around him" (John 13:3–5). What was the reason, then, that Christ stooped down to wash his disciples' feet? Because he knew the Father had put everything in his hands. Was he therefore proud? No, he was therefore humble.

There is a twofold humiliation of Christ. First, he humbled himself to come down into human nature and shed his blood for us. Secondly, being exalted, he humbles himself to come down into our hearts, our filthy hearts, and wash them in his blood.

He is exalted for this very purpose: to pardon and purge guilty and polluted sinners. As high and honorable as he is, he thinks it his honor to give out grace. He knows that the lower he stoops the higher will he be honored in the hearts of his people. I appeal to all believing hearts—the lower that he condescended to you—didn't your hearts exalt him the more and wonder at his glory? O sinner, then, do not think he is too high to look down toward you. The higher he is, the lower he stoops, and therefore the higher you believe he is, the more hope you may have of his pity and favor toward you, and the more you see is placed in his hands, the more do you expect to get out of his hands; faith has the more footing.

—Ralph Erskine

*God did this so that men would seek him and perhaps
reach out for him and find him, though he is not far from
each one of us.*

—Acts 17:27

Saint Paul is preaching on Mars Hill to the Athenians.[55] We hear a great deal about the tact of that discourse. The power of his tact was really love. He felt for those people, so he said to them what they needed. Never were people on the brink of so many of the highest things—and missed them—as these Athenians. They felt all the mystery of life. They built their altar to the unknown god. They were always on the brink of faith, without believing; always touched by spirituality, yet with their feet set on the material and carnal.

Two views [could] be taken by one who looked on their darkness. Easy enough it is to be contemptuous; to condemn as frivolous this life that walked on the brink of earnestness and yet was never earnest. But it is possible to be impressed with reverence and pity that left no room for contempt, reverence for the people who came so near to so much and pity for the people who missed it so sadly. The second thought is the thought of the best and wisest and divinest—the thought of Saint Paul and of Jesus Christ.

What makes the difference between these two views? People who look on others' puzzled lives with reverence and pity see God there behind the lives they are looking at. People who look at others' restless lives with contempt see no God there, but [only] vain and aimless dissatisfaction. If there is no God, whose life and presence, dimly felt, is making people toss and complain, then their tossing and complaining is a contemptible thing. If there is a God to whom they belong, whom they feel through the thinnest of veils, whom they feel even when they do not know that it is he whom they feel—then their restlessness, their hope, their dreams and doubts become solemn and significant.

And this is just what Saint Paul tells the Athenians. He says, "You are restless and discontented. Your restlessness, your impatience, your discontent, however petty the forms it takes, is solemn and not petty to me, because of what it means. It means that God is not far from every one of you."

Oh, what a revelation that was! What a preaching that was that day on Mars Hill!

—Phillips Brooks

God did this so that men would seek him and perhaps reach out for him and find him, though he is not far from each one of us.

—Acts 17:27

What Saint Paul said to the people of Athens Christ says to everybody, to you and me and all these multitudes.[56] He comes to you and says it: You are restless, always on the brink of something that you never reach, always on the point of grasping something that eludes you, always haunted by something that makes it impossible for you to settle down into absolute rest. I tell you what it means. It is God with you. It is Immanuel. His presence it is that will not let you be at peace. You don't see him, but he is close by you. You never will have peace until you do see him and turn to him to find the peace that he will not let you find away from him. "Come to me, . . . and I will give you rest" (Matt. 11:28). That was the revelation of the Incarnation. Listen, how across all the centuries you can hear the Savior giving that revelation, that interpretation of their own troubled lives to multitudes; now to Nicodemus, now to the Samaritan woman, now to Pontius Pilate, and all along, every day, to his disciples by what they saw from hour to hour of his peace in his Father.

Listen again. Hear Christ giving the same revelation today, and ask yourself this: "If it were true, if God in his perfection, with his perfect standards in himself, with his perfect hopes for me, God in his complete holiness and his complete love—if he were here close to me, only separated from me by the thin veil of my blindness, wouldn't it explain everything in my life?" There is the everlasting question, my dear friends, to which there is only one answer. What else can explain this mysterious, bewildering, fluttering, hoping, fearing, dreaming, dreading, waiting, human life—what but this, which is the Incarnation truth, that God from whom this life came is always close to it, that he is always doing what he can do for it, even when people do not see him, and that he cannot do for them all his love would do only because of the veil that hangs between him and them? "Not far from each one of us"—there is the secret of our lives—weak and wicked because we will not live with God; restless, unable to be at peace in our weakness and wickedness, because God is not far from us.

—Phillips Brooks

He spoke, and it came to be; he commanded,
and it stood firm.

—Psalm 33:9

The power of God appears in raising up a church to himself in spite of all his enemies.[57] For there were many and great difficulties in the way, such as gross and detestable idolatry. The princes of the world thought themselves obliged to prevent the introduction of a new religion, for fear that their empires should be in danger or the greatness and majesty of them impaired. If we consider the means by which the gospel was propagated, the divine power will evidently appear. The persons employed in this great work were a few illiterate fishers, with a publican and a tentmaker, without authority to force people to obedience and without eloquence to enforce the belief of the doctrines they taught. Yet this doctrine prevailed, and the gospel had wonderful success through all the parts of the then-known world. How could this possibly be, without a mighty operation of the power of God on human hearts?

The power of God appears in preserving, defending, and supporting his church under the trouble and persecution that were raised against it: "The gates of Hades will not overcome it" (Matt. 16:18). The most flourishing monarchies have decayed and wasted, and the strongest kingdoms have been broken in pieces, yet the church has been preserved to this very day. God has displayed his power in the preservation of his church and people, notwithstanding all the rage, power, and malice of their enemies.

The power of God appears in the conversion of the elect. O what a mighty power quells the lusts and stubbornness of the heart, demolishes the strongholds of sin in the soul, routs all the armies of corrupt nature, and makes the obstinate and rebellious will strike sail to Christ! The power of God that is exerted here is greater than there was in the creation of the world. For when God made the world, he met with no opposition; but when he comes to convert a sinner, he meets with all the opposition that the Devil and a corrupt heart can make against him. God wrought only one miracle in the creation, but there are many miracles wrought in conversion. The blind is made to see, the dead raised, and the deaf hears the voice of the Son of God. O the infinite power of Jehovah! In this work the mighty arm of the Lord in revealed.

—Thomas Boston

He spoke, and it came to be; he commanded,
and it stood firm.

—Psalm 33:9

The power of God appears in preserving the souls of believers amidst the many dangers to which they are exposed and bringing them safely to glory.[58] They have many enemies without: a legion of subtle and powerful devils, a wicked and ensnaring world. They have many strong lusts and corruptions within, and their graces are but weak, in their infancy while they are here. It [is a] wonder how they are preserved. But the apostle tells us that they "through faith are shielded by God's power" until salvation (1 Peter 1:5). Indwelling corruption would soon quench grace in their hearts if that grace were not kept alive by a divine power. But Christ's power moderates the violence of temptations, supports his people under them, [and] defeats the power of Satan.

The power of God appears in the redemption of sinners by Jesus Christ. Thus in Scripture Christ is called the power as well as the wisdom of God. This is the most admirable work that God ever brought forth in the world.

More particularly, *the power of God shines in Christ's miraculous conception in the womb of a virgin.* The power of the Highest overshadowed her (Luke 1:35), and by a creative act framed the humanity of Christ of the substance of the virgin's body and united it to the divinity. If God will accomplish that stupendous wonder, much more will he rescue his people from their adversaries.

The power of God shines in uniting the divine and human nature in the person of Christ, without any confusion of the two natures or changing the one into the other. One nature does not swallow up another and make a third distinct from both. But they are distinct and yet united; the properties of each nature are preserved entire. What a wonder of power that two natures, divine and human, infinitely distant, should meet together in a personal conjunction! Here the Creator and the creature are miraculously allied in the same being. Here a God of unmixed blessedness is linked personally with a man of perpetual sorrows. That is an admirable expression, "The Word became flesh" (John 1:14). Nothing less than an omnipotent power could bring about what an infinite and incomprehensible wisdom projected in this matter.

—Thomas Boston

He spoke, and it came to be; he commanded,
and it stood firm.

—Psalm 33:9

[The power of God appears] in supporting the human nature of Christ and keeping it from sinking under the terrible weight of divine wrath that came on him for our sins and in making him victorious over the Devil and all the powers of darkness.[59] His human nature could not possibly have borne up under the wrath of God and the curse of the law nor held out under such fearful contests with the powers of hell and the world, if it had not been upheld by infinite power. Thus, his Father says concerning him: "Here is my servant, whom I uphold" (Isa. 42:1).

The divine power appeared in raising Christ from the dead (Eph. 1:19). The unlocking the belly of the whale for the deliverance of Jonah, the rescue of Daniel from the den of lions and restraining the fire from burning the three children were striking declarations of the divine power and were foreshadows of the resurrection of our Redeemer. But all these are nothing to what is represented by them, for these showed a power over natural causes and curbing of beasts and restraining of elements. But in the resurrection of Christ, God exercised a power over himself and quenched the flames of his own wrath, which was hotter than millions of Nebuchadnezzar's furnaces. He unlocked the prison doors in which the curses of the law had lodged our Savior, stronger than the belly and ribs of a leviathan. How admirable it was that he should be raised from under the curse of the law and the infinite weight of our sins and brought forth with success and glory after his sharp encounter with the powers of hell! In this the power of God was gloriously manifested. Hence he is said to be raised from the dead "through the glory of the Father," and "declared with power to be the Son of God by his resurrection from the dead" (Rom. 1:4). All the miraculous proofs by which God acknowledged him for his Son during his life were ineffective without this. If he had remained in the grave, it had been reasonable to believe him only an ordinary person and that his death had been the just punishment of his presumption in calling himself the Son of God. But his resurrection from the dead was the most illustrious and convincing evidence that really he was what he declared himself to be.

—Thomas Boston

Open my eyes that I may see wonderful things in your law.
—Psalm 119:18

True wonder is never dispelled by what we know.[60]

That alone is genuine wonder—the wonder not of ignorance but of knowledge, the wonder that does not vanish when we know but grows and deepens with everything we know. It was the wonder of the apostle Paul. It was the wonder in the heart of Jesus. And it is the wonder we will feel forever in the perfected knowledge of eternity.

It is not knowledge, then, that is the foe of wonder; it is something far more commonplace than that. The blight that wilts our faculty of wonder is the familiarity that begets contempt. Someone has said that if all the stars were to cease shining for a hundred years and then were suddenly to flash on again, there is not an eye on earth but would be lifted heavenward and not a heart but would break forth in praise to God. But the stars were there when we were little children, and they will be shining in the heavens tonight. And to us the spectacle is so familiar that we have lost the wonder of it all. Live forty years in such a world as this and a certain blindness falls on the eyes. And therefore the need that when the evening falls, the morning breaks, and the summer comes again, we should pray as the psalmist prayed so long ago, "Lord, open my eyes that I may see."

May I say in passing that all great experiences tend to recreate the sense of wonder? Sickness, sorrow, death, conversion have a way of bringing new wonder into everything. And I suggest that in the will of God, which is as merciful as it is wise, that recreating of the sense of wonder may be one purpose of many an hour of discipline.

—George H. Morrison

Open my eyes that I may see wonderful things in your law.
—Psalm 119:18

In all the great experiences of the soul, none is greater than genuine conversion, and it recreates the faculty of wonder.[61] That is how the rod of God is sometimes sweet and blessed as the dew. It touches the dusty lanes of life, and they sparkle as on a morning in the May time. The world is never more beautiful or fresh, nor life more wonderful, nor loved ones dearer than after a season when the sky was darkened and we thought that everything was over.

The gospel, steadily and surely, has deepened the sense of wonder in humankind.

Our Christian faith has added to the mystery of everything. There is not a common word that we can use—*sin, life, death, love,* or *duty*—but has become a thousand times more awful since Jesus moved across the fields of Galilee. For the pagan, life was a brief journey; for the Christian, it is the prelude to eternity. For the pagan, death was a forgetting; for the Christian, it is heaven or it is hell. For the old pagan, sin was folly; for the Christian, sin is an infinitely guilty thing in the eyes of a holy God. It is a religion of joy and peace and power. And yet at the heart of a peace too deep for words is a mystery that humankind can never fathom. In the presence of a mystery like that, one can only wonder. We must cease speaking, we must bow. We must say to our hearts, *Keep silence before God.* And that is what the faith of Christ has done and is doing. It has recreated wonder by the mystery that it has found in common words like *sin* and *life* and *death* and *love* and *duty.*

Our Christian faith has shown us love at the heart of everything. And wherever love is, whether in heaven or earth, wonder is never far away. That little child asleep in its mother's arms is an ordinary little mortal. But to its mother, it is a wonderful child because she loves it so. And so with Christ—once we have learned to love him and to experience his love to us, there falls a newness of wonder on everything. I know that God is power—but he may be power and still leave me cold. I know that God is justice—and yet infinite justice can never win my heart. God is love, the world is made in love, and every touch of his hand on me is love—and immediately I cry in adoration, "He will be called Wonderful!"

—George H. Morrison

In my Father's house are many rooms.

—John 14:2

The disciples seemed sorrowful at the news of Christ's going away, but Christ comforts them that in his Father's house where he was going there was room for them too.[62] When the disciples perceived that Christ was going away, they expressed a desire to go with him. Peter asked him where he went, that he might follow. Christ told him that he could not follow him now, but that he would follow him afterwards. But Peter said, "Lord, why can't I follow you now?" (John 13:37). Christ signifies that he was going home to his Father's house, and he encourages the disciples that they will be with him there in due time, in that there was a room provided not only for them, but for all that would ever believe in him to the end of the world, and though he went before, he only went to prepare a place for those who would follow.

Yes, there is room in this house of God for great numbers, for all people who are or ever will be: "Sir, . . . what you ordered has been done, but there is still room" (Luke 14:22).

It is not with the heavenly temple as it often is with houses of public worship in this world, that they fill up and become too small and scanty for those that would meet in them, so that there is not convenient room for all. The disciples demonstrated a great desire to be where Christ was, and Christ therefore, to encourage them that it would be as they desired, tells them that in his Father's house where he was going were many rooms, that is, room enough for them.

There is mercy enough in God to admit an innumerable multitude into heaven. There is mercy enough for all, and there is merit enough in Christ to purchase heavenly happiness for millions of millions, for all the human race that ever were, are, or will be. And there is a sufficiency in the fountain of heaven's happiness to supply and fill and satisfy all, and there is in all respects enough for the happiness of all.

—Jonathan Edwards

In my Father's house are many rooms.

—John 14:2

Let all be thus exhorted to seek admittance to a room in heaven.[63] If those enjoy a high privilege who have seats in kings' courts or in apartments in kings' palaces—especially those who have dwellings there equal in quality to the king's children—then how great a privilege will it be to have a room assigned to us as God's children in his heavenly palace! How great is their glory and honor that are admitted to the household of God!

And seeing there are many rooms there, rooms enough for us all, our folly will be the greater if we neglect to seek a place in heaven, having our minds foolishly taken up about the worthless, fading things of this world.

Consider how little a while you have any place of abode in this world. [Here] you have a dwelling amongst the living, a house or room of your own, or at least one that is at present for your use. But in a very little while, the place that now knows you in this world will know you no more. The residence you have here will be empty of you; you will be carried dead out of it or will die at a distance from it and never enter it anymore—or any other dwelling in this world. Your room or dwelling place in this world, however convenient or comfortable it may be, is only a tent that will soon be taken down. Your stay is as it were but for a night. Your body itself is only a house of clay that will quickly decay and tumble down, and you will have no other dwelling here in this world but the grave.

Therefore, take warning, and don't be such fools as to neglect seeking a place and room in heaven. Let it be your main care to secure an everlasting dwelling for hereafter.

Consider that when you die, if you have no room in the house of God in heaven, you must have your place in the dwelling of devils. There is no middle place between them, and when you go from here, you must go to one or the other of these. Consider how miserable those must be who shall dwell with devils to all eternity. Devils are foul spirits, God's great enemies. Their dwelling is a place of darkness, utmost filthiness, abomination, darkness, disgrace, and torment. O, how would you rather ten thousand times have no place of abode at all, have no being, than to have [such] a place!

—Jonathan Edwards

In my Father's house are many rooms.

—John 14:2

Heaven is God's house.[64] A house of public worship is a house where God's people meet and is called God's house. The temple of Solomon was called God's house. God was represented as dwelling there. There he had his throne in the holy of holies.

Sometimes the whole universe is represented in Scripture as God's house, built one story above another. But the highest heaven is represented in Scripture as the house of God, reserved for himself for his own dwelling. The heavens are the Lord's, [thus], though he is everywhere present, God is represented both in Old Testament and New as being in heaven in a special and peculiar manner. Heaven is the temple of God. Solomon's temple was a foreshadow of heaven. The epistle to the Hebrews calls heaven the holy of holies, the place of God's most immediate residence. Houses where assemblies of Christians worship God are in some respects figures of this house of God above. When God is worshipped in them in spirit and truth, they become the outworks of heaven and, as it were, its gates.

Heaven is represented in Scripture as God's dwelling: "I lift up my eyes to you, to you whose throne is in heaven" (Ps. 123:1). Heaven is God's palace. 'Tis the house of the great King of the universe; there he has his throne, which is therefore represented as his house or temple: "The LORD is in his holy temple; the LORD is on his heavenly throne" (Ps. 11:4).

God is represented as a householder or head of a family, and heaven is his house. The saints, being the children of God, are said to be of the household of God (Eph. 2:19). Heaven is the place that God has built for himself and his children. And though some of this family are now on earth, all are going home. God has many children, and the place designed for them is heaven.

Heaven is the house not only where God has his throne, but also where he keeps his table, where his children sit down with him and where they are feasted in a royal manner becoming the children of so great a King (Luke 22:30).

God is the King of Kings, and heaven is the place where he keeps his court. There are his angels and archangels that, as the nobles of his court, attend him.

—Jonathan Edwards

In my Father's house are many rooms.
—John 14:2

There are sufficient and suitable accommodations for all sorts of persons: for persons of all nations and all conditions and circumstances, for those who have been great sinners as well as for moral livers; for weak saints and babes in Christ as well as for those who are stronger and more grown in grace.[65] There is in heaven enough for the happiness of everyone, an accommodation for everyone who will hearken to the calls of the gospel.

The disciples were very different from Christ: he was the Shepherd and they the sheep; he was the glorious, holy Son of God, they were poor, sinful, corrupt people. But Christ encourages them that there will be room in heaven for them, for there were many rooms there. As in a king's palace there is not only a room of state built for the king himself and for his eldest son and heir, but there are many rooms, for all his children, attendants, and servants.

When God made heaven in the beginning of the world, he intended it for an everlasting dwelling for a vast and innumerable multitude. When heaven was made, it was intended and prepared for all those particular persons whom God had from eternity designed to save. And that is a very great and innumerable multitude. Heaven was built so as most conveniently to accommodate all this multitude, as a house that is built for a great family is built large and with many rooms in it; as a palace that is built for a great king is built very large with a great many apartments; as a house of public worship that is built for a great congregation is built very large with many seats in it.

Here is encouragement for sinners who are concerned for the salvation of their souls, such as are afraid that they will never be admitted to any dwelling there and are aware that they are until now in a sad state because they are out of Christ and so have no right to any inheritance in heaven but are in danger of going to hell and having their eternal dwelling fixed there. You may be encouraged by what has been said to earnestly seek heaven, for there is room enough there. Let your case be what it will, there is suitable provision there for you, and if you come to Christ, he'll see to it that you will be well accommodated in heaven.

—Jonathan Edwards

In my Father's house are many rooms.

—John 14:2

This means that there are seats of various dignity and different degrees and circumstances of honor and happiness.[66] Though they are all seats of great honor and blessedness, yet some are greater than others.

This is how a palace is built. Though every part of the palace is magnificent, some apartments are more stately and costly than others. One apartment is the king's chamber, other apartments [are] for the heir to the crown, others for other children, others for their attendants and the great officers of the household.

Another image of this was in Solomon's temple. There were many rooms of different degrees of honor and dignity. There was the holy of holies, where the ark was, the place of God's residence, where the high priest alone might enter. There was another apartment called the holy place, where the other priests might enter. Next to that was the inner court of the temple, where the Levites were admitted, and [wherein were] lodgings for the priests. Next to that was the court of Israel where the people of Israel might enter. Next to that was the court of the Gentiles, where the Gentiles might enter.

Not that we are to understand the words of Christ so much in a literal sense, that every saint in heaven is to have a certain seat or room or dwelling where he or she is locally fixed. But we are to understand what Christ says chiefly in a spiritual sense. People will have different degrees of honor and glory in heaven, aptly represented as different seats of honor. Some will be nearer the throne than others. Some will be next to Christ.

When Christ was going to heaven and the disciples were sorrowful at parting with their Lord, he let them know that there are rooms of various degrees of honor in his Father's house, that there was not only one for him, the head of the church, but also for those who were his disciples and younger brothers and sisters.

Christ also may mean not only degrees of glory in heaven but different activities. We know their activities in general—some may be set in one place for one kind of work and others in another. God has set everyone in the body as it has pleased him; one is the eye, another the ear, another the head, and so on.

—Jonathan Edwards

My Father is always at his work to this very day, and I,
too, am working.

—John 5:17

It is characteristic of the Christian gospel that its Savior should be a worker.[67] In the old world, work was a thing for slaves and serfs, not for freeborn people. Thus work and greatness rarely went together, and nothing was more alien to paganism than a toiling God. Jesus has changed all that. It was a revolution when Jesus taught "God loves." But it was hardly less revolutionary when he taught "God works."

And he not only taught it, he lived it too. People saw in Christ a life of endless toil. Jesus stooped to the very humblest tasks, and he has left us an example, that we should follow in his steps.

What is striking about the work of Jesus is the magnitude of his aim compared with the ordinariness of his methods.

It is a great thing to command an army or to be a minister of state guiding a people toward their national destiny. But the aims of general or of diplomat seem almost insignificant when compared with the purposes of Jesus. He claims a universal sovereignty and runs it out to every sphere. He is to be the test in moral questions. He is to shape our law and mold our literature. He is the conqueror of death. The purposes of Jesus [are] far more stupendous than humanity had ever dreamed of.

And it is the apparent ordinariness of his methods that strikes us. Had he a pen of fire? He never wrote a line, except in the sand. Was unlimited wealth at his command? "Foxes have holes and birds of the air have nests, but the Son of Man has no place to lay his head" (Matt. 8:20). Were his first followers people of influence? Simon and Andrew were fishers. Or would he use the sword like Mohammed? "Put your sword back in its place, . . . for all who draw the sword will die by the sword" (26:52). It seems impossible that in such ways Christ would achieve his purpose.

It is a simple lesson for every man and woman who seeks to serve in the true Christian spirit. Surrounded by the ordinary, we should be facing heavenward. Poorly equipped in all things else, we should be mightily equipped in noble hope. If I am Christ's, I cannot measure possibilities by methods. If I am Christ's, I cherish the loftiest hope, and I am content to work for it in lowliest ways.

—George H. Morrison

They went about in sheepskins and goatskins, destitute,
persecuted and mistreated—the world was not worthy of
them. They wandered in deserts and mountains, and in
caves and holes in the ground.
—Hebrews 11:37–38

We have not even in dreams experienced the things among which those men and women spent their whole lives, always doing rightly and yet always afflicted.[68]

They had not even clothing, no city, no lodging place—the same as Christ, who had no place to lay his head. Not even when they had gained the wilderness were they at rest. Even there, they were driven out of even that which was uninhabitable. Wandering like exiles and outcasts, they found no refuge but must always be flying, seeking hiding places, always in terror.

What then is the reward?

They have not yet received it but are still waiting, and after thus dying in such great tribulation. They gained their victory so many ages ago and have not yet received it. And you who are yet in the conflict, are you vexed?

How great a thing it is that Abraham should be sitting, and the apostle Paul, waiting till you have been perfected, that then they may receive their reward. For the Savior has told them that unless we also are present, he will not give it to them. And are you vexed that you have not yet received the reward? What then will Abel do, who is sitting uncrowned? And Noah? And they who lived in those times, seeing that they wait for you and those after you?

For "God had planned something better for us." In order that they might not seem to have the advantage over us from being crowned before us, he appointed one time of crowning for all, and those who gained the victory so many years before receive their crowns with you. See his tender carefulness?

"That only together with us would they be made perfect." They were before us as regards the conflicts but are not before us as regards the crowns. He didn't wrong them, but he honored us. For if we are all one body, the pleasure becomes greater to this body when it is crowned altogether. The righteous are worthy of admiration in this, that they rejoice in our welfare as in their own. So this is their wish, to be crowned along with their own members. To be glorified all together is a great delight.

—John Chrysostom

Strike the shepherd, and the sheep will be scattered.
—Zechariah 13:7

What [caused the disciples to scatter]?[69] They were not accustomed to do so. They never did so afterwards. They would not have done so now had there been influences from heaven on them. But how then would Christ's sorrows have been extreme, without succor, if they had stuck to him in his troubles? No, Christ must not have the least comfort, and therefore the Lord for a time withholds his encouraging influences from them, and then they were as weak as other people.

As God permitted it, so the effectiveness of that temptation was much greater than ordinary, it was an hour when darkness reigned. Never had the disciples met with such a storm before. The Devil would have sifted and separated them so that their faith utterly failed, had Christ not secured it by his prayer for them. So it was an extraordinary trial that was on them.

That which contributed to their relapse, as a special cause of it, was the remaining corruptions that were in their hearts. Their knowledge was but little and their faith not much.

Do not censure them in your thoughts nor despise them for their weakness. Neither say in your heart, *Had I been there, I would never have done as they did.* They thought as little of doing what they did, and their souls detested it as much. But here you may see where a soul that fears God may be carried, if its corruptions are irritated by strong temptation, and God withholds usual influences.

[But] the outcome of their apostasy ended far better than it began—the morning was overcast, but the evening was clear.

Peter repents of his denial of Christ and never denied him more. All the rest likewise returned to Christ and never abandoned him anymore. And they who dared not acknowledge Christ afterwards confessed him openly before councils and rejoiced that they were counted worthy to suffer for his sake. Those who started at every sound became as bold as lions and did not fear any danger but sealed their confession of Christ with their blood. For though they abandoned him, it was not voluntarily, but by surprisal. Though they abandoned him, they still loved him; though they fled from him, there still remained a gracious principle in them; the root of the matter was still in them, which recovered them again.

—John Flavel

Do not be arrogant, but be afraid.

—Romans 11:20

Did the disciples forsake Christ, though they had such strong resolutions never to do it?[70] Then we see that self-confidence is a sin too likely to the best of people. They little thought their hearts would have proved so cowardly when they were tried. "Even if all fall away," said Peter, "I will not" (Mark 14:29). Good man; he resolved honestly, but he did not know what a feather he would be in the wind of temptation, if God once left him to his own fears.

Little reason have the best of saints to depend on their inherent grace, let their stock be as large as it will. Every merit without the prop of divine preservation is but a weight that tends to a fall. What becomes of the stream if the fountain supply it not? The best people will show themselves but human if God leave them. He who has set them up must also keep them. It is safer to be a humble worm than a proud angel. Adam had more favorable opportunity to maintain his station than any of you. For though he were left to the liberty of his own will and though he was created upright and had no inherent corruption to endanger him, yet he fell.

And shall we be self-confident, after such instances of human frailty! "Do not be arrogant, but be afraid," when you have considered well the examples of Noah, Lot, David, and Hezekiah, men famous and renowned in their generations who all fell by temptations, and when you would think they had never been better provided to cope with them. Lot fell soon after the Lord had thrust him out of Sodom and his eyes had seen hell, as it were, rained on them out of heaven; Noah, immediately after God's wonderful preservation of him in the ark when he saw a world of men and women perishing in the floods for their sins; David, after the Lord had settled the kingdom on him, which for sin he took from Saul, and given him rest in his house. Hezekiah was just up from a great sickness in which the Lord wrought a wonderful salvation for him. Did such people and at such times, when one would think no temptations should have prevailed, fall, and fall so dishonorably? Then, "if you think you are standing firm, be careful that you don't fall" (1 Cor. 10:12). O do not be arrogant, but be afraid.

—John Flavel

"Awake, O sword, against my shepherd, against the man who is close to me!" declares the LORD Almighty. "Strike the shepherd, and the sheep will be scattered."
—Zechariah 13:7

Did Christ stand his ground and go through with his work of suffering, when all who had followed him abandoned him?[71] Then a resolved adherence to God and duty, though left alone without company or encouragement, is Christlike and truly excellent.

Paul complains, "At my first defense, no one came to my support, but everyone deserted me. . . . But the Lord stood at my side" (2 Tim. 4:16–17). And as the Lord stood by him, so he stood by his God, alone, without any aids or support from people. How great an argument of integrity is this! To be faithful to God when abandoned by people, to be a Lot in Sodom, a Noah in a corrupted generation—how excellent it is! It is sweet to travel over this earth to heaven in the company of the saints who are going there with us, but if we meet no company, we must not be discouraged to go on. It is likely that before you have gone many steps farther, you may have cause to say, Never less alone than when alone.

Did the disciples thus forsake Christ and yet were all recovered at last? Then believers, though backsliding, are secured from final apostasy and ruin. Saints may fall, but they shall rise again. The highest resolution may ebb, but saving grace is "a spring of water welling up to eternal life" (John 4:14). God's unchangeable election, the frame and constitution of the New Covenant, the intercession of Jesus Christ, give the believer abundant security against the danger of a total and final defection. None of those souls who are within the blessed clasp and bond of [that security] can possibly be lost. It is settled on unchangeable things— and we know all things are as their foundations are.

And as the fear of God in our hearts pleads in us against sin, so our potent intercessor in the heavens pleads for us with the Father, and for that reason we cannot finally miscarry. What shall separate us from the love of God? Understand it either of God's love to us—as Calvin, Beza, and Martyr do—or of our love to God, as Ambrose and Augustine do. It is true in both senses—and a most comforting truth.

—John Flavel

> *"Awake, O sword, against my shepherd, against the man*
> *who is close to me!" declares the* LORD *Almighty. "Strike the*
> *shepherd, and the sheep will be scattered."*
> —Zechariah 13:7

Did the sheep fly when the shepherd was struck?[72] How sad a thing it is to be left to our own carnal fears in a day of temptation. "Fear of man will prove to be a snare" (Prov. 29:25). In that snare these good souls were taken and for a time held fast.

Isn't it a shame to Christians to see themselves outdone by a heathen? The emperor Vespasian had commanded Fluidius Priscus not to come to the senate or, if he did, to speak nothing but what he would have him. The senator returned this brave and noble answer, that as he was a senator it was fit he should be at the senate and if, being there, he were required to give his advice, he would speak freely that which his conscience commanded him. The emperor threatening that then he would die, he returned thus, "Do what you will, and I will do what I ought. It is in your power to put me to death unjustly and in me to die faithfully." Learn to trust God with your lives, liberties, and comforts in the way of your duty, and when you are afraid, trust in him, and do not magnify poor dust and ashes as to be scared from your God and your duty by their threat.

We may differ from ourselves, according as the Lord is with us or withdrawn from us. Yes, the difference between myself and myself is as great as if I were not the same person. Sometimes bold and courageous, despising dangers, bearing down all discouragement in the strength of zeal and love to God; at another time faint, feeble, and discouraged at every petty thing. From where is this except from the different administrations of the Spirit, who sometimes gives forth more and sometimes less of his gracious influence. These very men who flinched now, when the Spirit was more abundantly poured out on them could boldly own Christ before the council and despised all dangers for his sake.

We are strong or weak according to the degrees of assisting grace. As we cannot take the just measure of Christians by single acts, so neither must we judge them by what they sometimes feel.

But when their spirits are low and their hearts discouraged, they should rather say to their souls, Hope in God, for I will yet praise him; it is low with me now, but it will be better.

—John Flavel

> "Awake, O sword, against my shepherd, against the man
> who is close to me!" declares the LORD Almighty. "Strike the
> shepherd, and the sheep will be scattered."
> —Zechariah 13:7

Was the sword drawn against the Shepherd, and he left alone to receive the mortal strokes of it?[73] How should all adore both the justice and mercy of God so illustriously displayed in this! Here is the triumph of divine justice—and the highest triumph that it ever had—to single forth the chief Shepherd, the man that is God's equal, and sheathe its sword in his breast for satisfaction. No wonder it is drawn and brandished with such a triumph: Awake, O sword, against my Shepherd! For in this blood shed by it is more glory than if the blood of all the men and women in the world had been shed.

And the mercy and goodness of God is no less shown in giving the sword a commission against his equal, rather than against us. Why did he not rather say, Awake, O sword, against the people who are my enemies; shed the blood of those who have sinned against me? Blessed be God, that the dreadful sword was not drawn and brandished against our souls, that God did not set it to our breasts, that he did not make it fat with our flesh and bathe it in our blood—that his friend was abused so that his enemies might be spared. O what manner of love was this! Blessed be God therefore for Jesus Christ, who received the fatal stroke himself and has now so sheathed that sword in its scabbard that it will never be drawn any more against any that believe in him.

Were the sheep scattered when the Shepherd was beaten? Learn from this that the best of us do not know our own strength till we come to the trial. Little did these holy men imagine such a cowardly spirit had been in them till temptation put it to the proof. Let this therefore be a caution forever to the people of God. You resolve never to forsake Christ, you do well, but so did these and yet were scattered from him. You can never take a just measure of your own strength till temptation has tried it. It is said that God led the people so many years in the wilderness to prove them and to know them—that is, to make them know— what was in their hearts. Little did they think such unbelief, murmuring, discontent, and a spirit bent to backsliding had been in them, until their straits in the wilderness gave them the sad experience of these things.

—John Flavel

> *"Awake, O sword, against my shepherd, against the man*
> *who is close to me!" declares the* LORD *Almighty. "Strike the*
> *shepherd, and the sheep will be scattered."*
> —Zechariah 13:7

Did the sword of divine justice smite the Shepherd, and at the same time [remove] all his outward comforts?[74] Then learn that the holiest people have no reason to despond though God should at once strip them of all their outward and inward comforts. In one day Christ loses both heavenly and earthly comforts. Now as God dealt with Christ, he may at one time or other deal with his people. You have your comforts from heaven; so had Christ. He had comforts from his little flock; you have your comforts from the society of the saints, comfortable relations, and so on. Yet none of these are so firmly settled on you that you may not be left destitute of them all in one day. God took all comfort from Christ, both outward and inward—and are we greater than he?

Should the Lord deal thus with any of you, the following considerations will be seasonable and relieving.

First, though the Lord deal thus with you, yet this is no new thing; he has so dealt with others, yes, with Jesus Christ who was his equal. How little reason have we to complain?

Secondly, this befell Jesus Christ so that the similar condition might be sanctified to you when you are brought into it. Jesus Christ passed through such conditions on purpose that he might take away the curse and leave a blessing in those conditions, in preparation for the time that you would come into them.

Thirdly, though inward and outward comforts were both removed from Christ in one day, yet he did not lack support: "You will leave me all alone. Yet I am not alone, for my Father is with me" (John 16:32)—with me by way of support when not by way of comfort. Your God can in like manner support you when all tangible comforts shrink away from your soul and body in one day.

Remark that this comfortless, forsaken condition of Christ immediately preceded the day of his greatest glory and comfort. It was so with Christ, it may be so with you. Therefore act your faith on this, that the most glorious light usually follows the thickest darkness. The louder your groans are now, the louder your triumphs hereafter will be. The horror of your present will but add to the luster of your future state.

—John Flavel

*Peter got down out of the boat, walked on the water and
came toward Jesus. But when he saw the wind, he was
afraid and, beginning to sink, cried out, "Lord, save me!"*
—Matthew 14:29–30

The first thought to force itself on me is that it was Peter's temperament that put him in this danger.[75] He began to sink not because he was wicked—he began to sink because he was Simon Peter. The other disciples were all safe and sound. It never occurred to them to leave the vessel. They were men of wisdom and common sense and knew the difference between land and water. But Peter was reckless, headstrong, and impetuous, acting on the impulse of the moment. Peter followed the dictate of his heart and never waited for his laggard reason. In a sense, that was the glory of his character. It made him do what no one else would do. It gave him the charm of daring and enthusiasm that always fascinates.

But those very qualities, which in the hand of Christ were to go to the upbuilding of the church, sometimes brought him to the verge of ruin. It was only Peter who would begin to walk, and it was only Peter who would begin to sink. He was led into peril on these stormy waters because of what was self-forgetful in him. And it may be you have not sunk yet, but are beginning to sink because you have a temperament like that. Our perils do not always reach us through our worst. Our perils sometimes reach us through our best, through what is charming in us and delightful and self-forgetful and enthusiastic. And so, like Peter, we begin to do what the cold and calculating would never do, and then, like Peter, we begin to sink. That is why we all need to be saved not only from sin but from ourselves. That is why God, in his holy love, to save us gave us not a message but a Man. For our brightest social qualities may wreck us. A touch of genius may be our ruin. For all that is implied in that word *temperament,* we need the keeping of the Lord Jesus Christ.

—George H. Morrison

*Peter got down out of the boat, walked on the water and
came toward Jesus. But when he saw the wind, he was
afraid and, beginning to sink, cried out, "Lord, save me!"*
—Matthew 14:29–30

Peter began to sink when he began to fear.[76] And Scripture tells when he began to fear: it was when he took his eyes off his Lord. There is not a trace that the wind had grown more fierce while the disciple was walking on the water. It had been just as fierce, and the waves had been just as boisterous when he had sprung from the gunwale of the boat. But then he had thought of nothing but the Master and had eyes for nobody except the Master; as long as that continued he was safe. Looking to Christ he could go anywhere. The very sea was as a pavement to him. Looking away from Christ he was as other people, and the perils that surrounded him were terrible. And then he regretted the rashness of his venture and saw nothing around him but the seething waters, and so Peter began to be afraid and beginning to be afraid, began to sink.

That is true of every kind of life. It is true especially of spiritual life. In the perilous calling of the spiritual life, to lose heart is to lose everything. And that is why the Lord is always saying to us, "Give me your heart," for only in his keeping is it safe. It is a simple message—looking to Jesus—yet it is the message of salvation. To trust in him and to keep the eye on him is the one secret of all Christian victory. When we have failed to do so in the stress of life, as all of us, like Simon Peter, fail, then there is nothing left but to cry with Peter, Lord, save me.

And so I close by saying that when Peter began to sink, his Savior was not far away. Immediately, he put out his hand and grasped him. My brother or sister, just beginning to sink, will you remember that Christ is at your side? All human help may seem very far away; remember that he is not very far away. He is near you now, near you where you sit. You need him greatly and he is there for you. Cry out now, "Lord, save me," and he will do it, completely, for you!

—George H. Morrison

For the transgression of my people he was stricken.
—Isaiah 53:8

Those who meditate aright on the suffering of Christ become terror stricken in heart, and their consciences at once sink in despair.[77] This terror should spring forth so that you see the severe wrath and the unchangeable earnestness of God in regard to sin and sinners, in that he was unwilling that his only and dearly loved Son should set sinners free unless he paid the costly ransom for them—an earnestness so inexpressible and unbearable that a person so immeasurably great goes to meet and suffers and dies for it. If you reflect on it deeply, that God's Son, the eternal wisdom of the Father, himself suffers, you will indeed be terror stricken, and the more you reflect the deeper will be the impression.

You meditate on the suffering of Christ aright if you deeply believe and never doubt the least that you are the one who thus martyred Christ. For your sins most surely did it. Thus Saint Peter struck and terrified the Jews as with a thunderbolt in Acts 2:36–37, when he spoke to them all in common: "Jesus, whom you crucified," so that three thousand were terror stricken the same day and tremblingly cried to the apostles, "Brothers, what shall we do?" Therefore, when you view the nails piercing through his hands, firmly believe it is your work. Do you see his crown of thorns? Believe the thorns are your wicked thoughts and your other sins.

Now see where one thorn pierces Christ, there more than a thousand thorns should pierce you, yes, eternally should they thus and even more painfully pierce you. Where one nail is driven through his hands and feet, you should eternally suffer such and even more painful nails—as will be also visited on those who let Christ's sufferings be lost and fruitless as far as they are concerned. For this earnest mirror, Christ, will neither lie nor mock; whatever he says must be fully realized.

Saint Bernard was so terror stricken by Christ's sufferings that he said, "I imagined I was secure and I knew nothing of the eternal judgment passed on me in heaven, until I saw that the eternal Son of God took mercy on me, stepped forward and offered himself on my behalf in the same judgment. Ah, it does not become me still to play and remain secure when such earnestness is behind those sufferings."

—Martin Luther

For the transgression of my people he was stricken.
—Isaiah 53:8

The benefit of Christ's sufferings depends almost entirely on people coming to a true knowledge of themselves.[78] Where people do not come to this point, the sufferings of Christ have no benefit to them. For the characteristic, natural work of Christ's sufferings is that they make all people equal and alike, so that as Christ was horribly martyred, we must also be martyred in our consciences by our sins. This does not take place by means of words but by means of deep thoughts and a profound realization of our sins.

Take an illustration: If an evildoer were judged because he or she had murdered the child of a monarch, and someone convinced you that you had enabled the wicked person to do the act—then you would be in the greatest straits, especially if your conscience also revolted against you. Much more anxious than this you should be when you consider Christ's sufferings. For you are truly the one who strangled and crucified the Son of God through your sins.

Whoever perceive themselves to be so hard that they are not terror stricken by Christ's sufferings and led to a knowledge of him, they should fear and tremble. For it cannot be otherwise; you must become like the picture and sufferings of Christ, whether in life or in hell. You must at the time of death, if not sooner, fall into terror, tremble, quake, and experience all Christ suffered on the cross. It is truly terrible to attend to this on your deathbed; therefore you should pray God to soften your heart and permit you fruitfully to meditate on Christ's suffering. For it is impossible for us profoundly to meditate on the sufferings of Christ of ourselves unless God sink them into our hearts. But first you are to seek and long for the grace of God, that you may accomplish it through God's grace and not through your own power. Some people never treat the sufferings of Christ aright, for they never call on God for that purpose but devise out of their own ability their own way and treat those sufferings entirely in a human and an unfruitful manner.

Such a meditation changes a person's character, and almost as in baptism he or she is born anew. Then Christ's suffering accomplishes its true and noble work; it slays the old Adam, banishes all lust, pleasure, and security that one may obtain from God's creatures, just like Christ was forsaken by all, even by God.

—Martin Luther

For the transgression of my people he was stricken.
—Isaiah 53:8

When you are completely terror stricken in conscience, you must be on your guard that your sins do not thus remain in your conscience and nothing but pure doubt certainly come out of it.[79]

Then cast your sins from yourself on Christ. Believe that your sins are his wounds and sufferings, that he carries them and makes satisfaction for them, as Saint Peter says in his first epistle: "He himself bore our sins in his body on the tree" (2:24). On these and like passages you must rely with all your weight, and so much the more the harder your conscience martyrs you. For if you do not take this course but miss the opportunity of stilling your heart, then you will never secure peace and must finally despair in doubt. For if we deal with our sins in our consciences and let them continue in us and be cherished in our hearts, they become much too strong for us to manage, and they will live forever. But when we see that they are laid on Christ and he has triumphed over them by his resurrection, and we believe it, then they are dead and have become as nothing. Thus Saint Paul speaks, in Romans 4:25, that Christ was delivered over to death for our sins and was raised to life for our justification; that is, by his resurrection he makes us righteous and free from all sin, even if we believe differently.

Now if you are not able to believe, then you should pray to God for faith. For this is a matter in the hands of God that is entirely free and is also bestowed alike at times knowingly, at times secretly.

Look on Christ's sufferings no longer, for they have already done their work and terrified you, but press through all difficulties and see how full of love is his heart toward you—love that compelled him to bear the heavy load of your conscience and your sin. Thus will your heart be loving and sweet toward him and the assurance of your faith be strengthened. Then ascend higher through the heart of Christ to the heart of God, and see that Christ would not have been able to love you if God had not willed it. Be thus drawn to the Father through Christ. That means to know God aright, if we understand him by his goodness and love, there our faith and confidence can then stand unmovable. A person is truly thus born anew in God.

—Martin Luther

For the transgression of my people he was stricken.
—Isaiah 53:8

When your heart is thus established in Christ and you are an enemy of sin—out of love and not out of fear of punishment—Christ's sufferings should also be an example for your whole life, and you should meditate on them in a different way.[80] For until now we have considered Christ's passion as a sacrament that works in us and we suffer; now we consider that we also work, namely thus: if a day of sorrow or sickness weighs you down, think how trifling that is compared with the thorns and nails of Christ. If you must do or leave undone what is distasteful to you, think how Christ was led here and there, bound and a captive. Does pride attack you? See how your Lord was mocked and disgraced with murderers. Do unchastity and lust thrust themselves against you? Think how bitter it was for Christ to have his tender flesh torn, pierced, and beaten again and again. Do hatred and envy war against you, or do you seek vengeance? Remember how Christ, with many tears and cries, prayed for you and all his enemies—he who indeed had more reason to seek revenge. If trouble or whatever adversity of body or soul afflict you, strengthen your heart and say, "Ah, why then shouldn't I also suffer a little since my Lord sweat blood in the garden because of anxiety and grief?" That would be a lazy, disgraceful servant who would wish to lie in bed while the Lord was compelled to battle with the pangs of death.

See, you can thus find in Christ strength and comfort against all vice and bad habits. That is the right observance of Christ's suffering, and that is the fruit of his suffering. And they are called true Christians who incorporate the life and name of Christ into their own lives, as Saint Paul says in Galatians 5:24: "Those who belong to Christ Jesus have crucified the sinful nature with its passions and desires." For Christ's suffering must be dealt with not in words and a show but in our lives and in truth. Thus Hebrews 12:3: "Consider him who endured such opposition from sinful men, so that you will not grow weary and lose heart"; and 1 Peter 4:1: "Since Christ suffered in his body, arm yourselves also with the same attitude."

—Martin Luther

How great is God—beyond our understanding!
—Job 36:26

God is the unknown and the unknowable.[81] What it is possible to know, it must be possible to explain—to put into words that sum themselves into the exact measure of the thing that is known.

What can be known may, of course, be contained by the faculty that knows it. [For] whatever I can know is, by the very fact that I can know it, less than I am. The vessel is of necessity larger than its contents. If, then, any faculty of mine knows God, that faculty contains God and is in that sense larger than God, which is impossible and absurd.

Say this God was dreamed by human genius. What then? The person who dreamed such a God must be the author of some other work of equal or approximate importance. Produce it! That is the sensible reply to so bold a blasphemy.

A man says he kindled the sun, and when asked for his proof, he strikes a match that the wind blows out! Is the evidence sufficient? Or a woman says that she has covered the earth with all the green and gold of summer, and when challenged to prove it, she produces a wax flower that melts in her hand! Is the proof convincing? The God of the Bible calls for the production of other gods—gods wooden, gods stony, gods ill-bred, gods well-shaped and done up skillfully for market uses. From his heaven he laughs at them, and from his high throne he holds them in derision.

He is not afraid of competitive gods. They try to climb to his grandeur but only get high enough to break their necks in a sharp fall. Again and again I demand that the second effort of human genius bear some obvious relation to the first. The sculptor accepts the challenge, so does the painter, so does the musician; why should the Jehovah-dreamer be an exception to the common rule of confirmation and proof?

We wait for the evidence! We insist on having it. Then, so we don't waste our time in idle expectancy, we can meanwhile call on God, saying, "Our Father in heaven, hallowed be your name, your kingdom come, your will by done on earth as it is in heaven"! (Matt. 6:9–10).

—Joseph Parker

> *How great is God—beyond our understanding!*
> —Job 36:26

I am tired of the known and the knowable, tired of saying this star is fifty millions of miles in circumference, and yonder planet is five million times larger than the earth.[82] It is mere gossip in polysyllables, getting importance by hugeness.

It is in this manner that people want to make God pronounceable in words! Failing this, they suppose they have destroyed him by saying he is Unknowable and Unknown.

Human soul, if you would truly *see*—see the boundless, see the possible, see God—go into the dark when and where the darkness is thickest. The light is vulgar in some uses. It shows the mean and vexing detail of space and life with too gross a palpableness, and it frets the sensitivity of the eyes. I must find the healing darkness.

Deus absconditus. God hides himself, most often in the light; he touches the soul in the gloom and vastness of night, and the soul, being true in its intent and wish, answers the touch without a shudder or a blush. It is even so that God comes to me.

God does not come through human argument, a flash of human wit, a sudden and audacious answer to an infinite enigma. His path is through the pathless darkness—without a footprint to show where he stepped; through the forest of the night he comes, and when he comes the brightness is all within!

My God—unknown and unknowable—cannot be chained as a prisoner of logic or delivered into the custody of a theological proposition. Shame be the portion of those who have given him a setting within the points of the compass, who have robed him in cloth of their own weaving and surnamed him at the bidding of their cold and narrow fancy!

For myself, I know that I cannot know him, that I have a joy wider than knowledge, a conception that domes itself above my best thinking, as the sky domes itself in infinite pomp and luster above the earth whose beauty it creates.

God? God! God! Best defined when undefined; a fire that may not be touched; a life too great for shape of image; a love for which there is no equal name. Who is he? God. What is he? God. Of whom begotten? God. He is at once the question and the answer, the self-balance, the All.

—Joseph Parker

> *How great is God—beyond our understanding!*
> —Job 36:26

Define God?[83] We have called him Creator, Sovereign, Father; then Infinite Creator, Eternal Sovereign, Gracious Father, as if we could build up our word-bricks to heaven and surprise the unknown and the unknowable in his solitude and look on him face-to-face.

Our words! Words that come and go like unstable fashions. Words that die of age, that cannot be accepted unanimously even by two people in all their suggestions and relations. Into these words we have invited God, and because he cannot come into them but as a devouring fire, we have stood back in offense and unbelief.

God! God! God! Ever hidden, ever present, ever distant, ever near, making the knees knock in terror, filling all space yet leaving room for all his creatures; a terror, a hope—undefinable, unknowable, irresistible, immeasurable.

We have chosen the very worst word in our haste, and we have needlessly humbled ourselves in doing so. Instead of unknowable, invisible, and incomprehensible, say superknowable, supervisible, and supercomprehensible. Then the mystery is made luminous.

From the unknowable I turn away humiliated and discouraged; from the superknowable I return humbled yet inspired. The unknowable says, "Fool, why knock at granite as if it were a door that could be opened?" The superknowable says, "There is something larger than your intelligence; a secret, a force, a beginning, a God!" The difficulty is always in the lame word and not in the solemn truth. We make no progress in religion while we keep to our crippled feet, picking over such stones as unknown, unknowable, invisible, and incomprehensible, and we finish our toilsome journey exactly where we began it.

In its higher aspects and questionings [religion] is not a road to walk on, it is an open expanse of the heavens to fly in. Enthusiasm sees God. Love sees God. But we have built our prudent religion on the sand. On the sand! So we walk around it and measure it and break it up into propositions and placard it on church walls.

My soul, amid all unknowableness, hold fast to the faith that you can know God. You cannot know *about* him by intellectual art or theological craft. By love and pureness, know him.

—Joseph Parker

> *How great is God—beyond our understanding!*
> —Job 36:26

Invisible![84] The invisibleness of God is not a scientific discovery; it is a biblical revelation: "No one has ever seen God" (John 1:18). This is the difficulty of all life, and the higher the life the higher the difficulty. No one can see *oneself* and live! You can see your incarnation, but your very *self*—the pulse that makes you human—you have never seen, you can never see!

Anatomy says it has never found the soul and adds, "Therefore there is no soul." The reasoning overleaps itself and takes away its own life. Has anatomy found *genius?* Or has anatomy laid its finger on imagination and held it up, saying, "Look, the mighty wizard"?

But if there is no soul simply because anatomy has never found one, then there is no genius, no imagination, because the surgeon's knife has failed to come upon them!

Anatomize the dead poet and the dead ass, and you will find as much genius in one as in the other; therefore there is no genius! Who that valued his or her life would set foot on such a bridge as the rickety "therefore"? But some people will venture on any bridge that leads away from God—because they do not like to retain God in their hearts (Rom. 1:28). It is not because of intellectual superiority but because of moral distaste, an invincible aversion.

Yes, God is unknown and unknowable. But that does not make him unusable and unprofitable. If scientists avow that they have not developed a theory of magnetism, do they therefore ignore it or decline to inquire into its uses? Do they write its name with a big M and run away from it, shaken and whitened by fear? Indeed they are not such fools. They actually use what they do not understand.

Bring their example to bear on the religious life. I do not scientifically know God. The term does not come within the analysis that is available to me. God is great, and I know him not; yet the term has its practical uses in life, and into those broad and obvious uses all people may inquire. What part does the God of the Bible play in the life of the person who accepts him? Any creed that does not come down easily into the daily life to purify and direct it is imperfect and useless.

—Joseph Parker

How great is God—beyond our understanding!
—Job 36:26

I cannot read the Bible without seeing that God has moved his believers in the direction of *courage* and *sacrifice*.[85]

In the direction of courage, this is not mere animal courage, for then the argument might be matched by many gods whose names are spelled without capitals. No, this is moral courage, noble heroism, fierce rebuke of personal and national corruption, lofty and inspiring judgment of all good and all evil.

The God idea made mean people valiant soldier-prophets; it broadened the piping voice of the timid inquirer into the thunder of the national teacher and leader. For brass it brought gold; for iron, silver; for wood, brass; and for stones, iron. Instead of the thorn it brought up the fir tree and instead of the brier the myrtle tree, and it made the bush burn with fire.

Wherever the God idea took complete possession of the mind, every faculty was lifted up to a new capacity and borne on to heroic attempts and conquests. The saints who received it conquered kingdoms, administered justice, gained what was promised, shut the mouths of lions, quenched the fury of the flames. Their weakness was turned to strength, they became powerful in battle, they routed foreign armies.

Any idea that inspired life and hope in humankind is to be examined with reverent care. The quality of the courage determines its value and the value of the idea that excited and sustained it.

What is true of the courage is true also of the sacrifice, which has ever followed the acceptance of the God idea. This is not the showy and fanatical sacrifice of mere bloodletting. Many a juggernaut, great and small, drinks the blood of its devotees.

But spiritual discipline, self-renunciation, the esteeming of others better than one's self, the suppression of selfishness—these are the practical uses of the God idea. It is not a barren sentiment.

It arouses courage. It necessitates self-sacrifice. It touches the imagination as with fire. It deepens every thought. It sanctifies the universe. It makes heaven possible. Unknown, unknowable. Yes, but not therefore unusable or unprofitable.

—Joseph Parker

So Abraham called that place The Lord Will Provide.
—Genesis 22:14

As Abraham and Isaac traveled up the hill, the son bearing the wood and the father the knife, the boy said, "Where is the lamb?" (Gen. 22:7), and Abraham, steadying his voice, said, "God himself will provide the lamb" (v. 8).[86] When the wonderful outcome of the trial was plain before him and he looked back on it, the one thought that rose to his mind was of how, beyond his meaning, his words had been true. So he named that place by a name that spoke nothing of his trial but everything of God's provision.

It is true that we may cast all our anxiety about all outward things on him in the assurance that he who feeds the ravens will feed us and that if lilies can blossom into beauty without care, we will be held by our Father of more value than these. But there is a deeper meaning to the provision spoken of here. What was it that God provided for Abraham? What is it that God provides for us? A way to discharge duties that seem impossible for us and which, the nearer we come to them, look the more dreadful and seem the more impossible.

And yet, when the heart has yielded itself in obedience and we are ready to do the thing that is enjoined, there opens up before us a possibility provided by God, and strength comes equal to our day. Some unexpected gift is put into our hands that enables us to do the thing of which nature said, "My heart will break before I can do it," and in regard to which even Grace doubted whether it was possible for us to carry it through. If our hearts are set in obedience, the farther we go on the path of obedience, the easier the command will appear, and to try to do it is to ensure that God will help us to do it.

This is the main provision that God makes, and it is the highest provision that he can make, for there is nothing in this life that we need so much as to do the will our Father in heaven. All outward needs are poor compared with that. The one thing worth living for, the one thing that in being secured we are blessed, and being missed we are miserable, is compliance in heart with the commandment of our Father and the compliance wrought out in life. So, of all gifts that he bestows on us and of all the abundant provision out of his rich storehouses, is not this the best, that we are made ready for any required service?

—Alexander Maclaren

So Abraham called that place The Lord Will Provide.

—Genesis 22:14

"The Lord Will Provide."[87] Provide what? The lamb for the burnt offering that he has commanded. We see in the fact that God provided the ram that became the appointed sacrifice, through which Isaac's life was preserved, a dim revelation of the great truth that the only sacrifice that God accepts for the world's sin is the sacrifice that he himself has provided.

This is the meaning of all the sacrificial worship—God himself will provide a Lamb. The world had built altars, and Israel, by divine appointment, had its altar too. All these express the lack that none of them can satisfy. They show that humanity needed a sacrifice, and that sacrifice God has provided. He asked from Abraham less than he gives to us. Abraham's devotion was sealed and certified because he did not withhold his son from God. And God's love is sealed because he has not withheld his only-begotten Son from us.

So this name that came from Abraham's grateful and wondering lips holds true in all regions of our wants. On the lowest level, the outward supply of outward needs; on a higher, the means of discharging hard duties and a path through sharp trials; and, on the highest of all, the spotless sacrifice that alone avails for the world's sins—these are the things that God provides.

If we wish to have our outward needs supplied, our outward weaknesses strengthened, power and energy sufficient for duty, wisdom for perplexity, a share in the sacrifice that takes away the sins of the world, we receive them all on the condition that we are found in the place where all God's provision is treasured. If someone chooses to sit outside the baker's shop, that person may starve on its threshold. And if we will not ascend to the hill of the Lord and stand in his holy place by simple faith, God's amplest provision is nothing to us, and we are empty in the midst of affluence.

Get near to God if you would partake of what he has prepared. If you would drink from his fullness, live in fellowship with him by simple love and often meditate on him,. And be sure of this, that however within his house the stores are heaped and the treasury full, you will have neither part nor lot in the matter unless you are children of the house.

—Alexander Maclaren

So Abraham called that place The LORD Will Provide.
—Genesis 22:14

Note what we are to do with the provision when we get it.[88]

Abraham christened the anonymous mountaintop, not by a name that reminded him or others of his trial, but by a name that proclaimed God's deliverance. He did not say anything about his agony or about his obedience. God spoke about that, not Abraham. Abraham did not want these to be remembered, but what he desired to hand on to later generations was what God had done for him. Oh, dear friends, is that the way in which we look back on life? Many a bare, bald mountaintop in your career and mine we have names for. Are they names that commemorate our sufferings—or God's blessings? When we look back on the past, what do we see? Times of trial or times of deliverance?

This name enshrines the duty of commemoration—yes! and the duty of expectation. "The Lord Will Provide." How do you know that, Abraham? And his answer is, "Because the Lord did provide." That is a shaky argument if we use it about one another. Our resources may give out, our patience may weary. If we go to a storehouse, all the corn in it will be eaten up some day, but if we go to some boundless plain that grows it, we can be sure that there will be a harvest next year as there has been a harvest last.

So think of God not as a storehouse but as the soil from which there comes forth, year by year and generation after generation, the same crop of rich blessings for the needs and the hungers of every soul.

"You have been with me in six troubles, and in seven you will not forsake me," is a bad conclusion to draw about one another, but it is the right conclusion to draw about God.

And so, as we look back on our past lives and see many a peak gleaming in the magic light of memory, let us name them all by names that will throw a radiance of hope on the unknown and unclimbed difficulties before us and say, as the patriarch did when he went down from the mount of his trial and deliverance, "The Lord Will Provide."

—Alexander Maclaren

I beseech you therefore, brethren, by the mercies of God,
that ye present your bodies a living sacrifice, holy, accept-
able unto God, which is your reasonable service.

—Romans 12:1 KJV

[Paul] discourses at large on the love of God toward us and points out God's concern for us and [his] goodness, which cannot even be traced out.[89] He next persuades those who have received the benefit to exhibit a way of life worthy of the gift. He beseeches them—not for any enjoyment he was likely to get himself but for what they would gain.

And no wonder he beseeches when he puts God's mercies before them. For since, he means, it is from the mercies of God you have those numberless blessings, reverence them, be moved to compassion by them, that you would show no conduct unworthy of them. I entreat you then, he means, by the very things through which you were saved to "present your bodies a living sacrifice, holy, acceptable unto God, which is your reasonable service" (KJV). When he said "sacrifice," to prevent any from thinking he bade them kill themselves, he at once added (Greek order) "living." Then to distinguish it from the Jewish [sacrifice], he calls it "holy, acceptable unto God"—for theirs was a material one, and not very acceptable, either. So Paul also here bids us present our bodies as living sacrifices.

And how is the body to become a sacrifice? Let your eye look on no evil thing, and it has become a sacrifice; let your tongue speak nothing filthy, and it has become an offering; let your hand do no lawless deed, and it has become a whole burnt offering. Or rather, this is not enough, but we must have good works also: let the hand give gifts for the poor, the mouth bless them that curse you, and the hearing find leisure evermore for lessons taught from Scripture.

Let us then from our hands and feet and mouth and all other members yield a firstfruit to God. Such a sacrifice is well pleasing—as that of the Jews was even unclean. Not so ours. That presented the thing sacrificed dead; this makes the thing sacrificed to be living. For the law of this sacrifice is new, and so the sort of fire is a marvelous one. For it needs no wood under it, but our fire lives of itself and does not burn up the victim but rather makes it live. This was the sacrifice that God sought of old.

—John Chrysostom

I beseech you therefore, brethren, by the mercies of God,
that ye present your bodies a living sacrifice, holy, accept-
able unto God, which is your reasonable service.

—Romans 12:1 KJV

Observe the exactness with which [Paul] uses each word. For he does not say, offer your bodies as a sacrifice, but "present" them, as if he had said, Never again have any interest in them.[90] You have given them up to another. For even they that *furnish* (same word) the warhorses have no further interest in them. And you too have presented your members for the war against the Devil and for that dread battle array. Do not let them down to selfish use.

And he shows another thing also from this, that you must make them approved. For it is not to any mortal being that we present them, but to God, the King of the universe. Since then it is both to be presented (that is, as for a king's use) and is a sacrifice, rid it of every spot, since if it has a spot, it will no longer be a sacrifice. For neither can the eye that looks lecherously be sacrificed nor the hand be presented that is greedy nor the feet that go to playhouses nor the belly that is self-indulgent nor the heart that has rage in it nor the tongue that utters filthy things.

Thus we must spy out the spots on our bodies. For if those who offered the sacrifices of old were commanded to look on every side and were not permitted to offer "the blind, the injured or the maimed, or anything with warts or festering or running sores" (Lev. 22:22), much more must we, who offer ourselves, be pure in all respects. For if when Elijah offered the visible sacrifice, a flame that came down from above consumed the whole—water, wood, and stones—much more will this be done upon you.

And if you have anything in you relaxed and secular, and yet offer the sacrifice with a good intention, the fire of the Spirit will wear away that worldliness and perfect (or "carry up") the whole sacrifice.

But what is "reasonable service"? It means spiritual ministry, a way of life according to Christ. And this will be so if every day you bring [to] him yourself as a sacrifice and become the priest of your own body and of the virtue of your soul, offering soberness, relief for the poor, and goodness and moral strength. For in doing this you offer "a reasonable service" (or worship).

—John Chrysostom

Do not conform any longer to the pattern of this world, but
be transformed by the renewing of your mind.

—Romans 12:2

Having shown that each of us is a priest of our own flesh by our way of life, [Paul] mentions also the way we may accomplish all this.[91] What then is the way?

Do not be fashioned after this world, for the pattern of this world is groveling and worthless and only temporary, neither does it have anything of loftiness or lastingness or straightforwardness but is wholly perverted. If then you would walk upright (or aright), do not pattern yourself after the fashion of this present life. For in it there is nothing abiding or stable. For speak of riches, glory, beauty of person, luxury, or of whatever other of its seemingly great things you will, it is a fashion only, not reality, a show and a mask, not any abiding substance. But you, he says, do not conform, but be transformed, by the renewing of your mind. Virtue's not an appearance but a kind of real form, with a natural beauty of its own, not the trickeries and fashions of outward things, which no sooner appear than they go to nothing. For all these things, even before they come to light, are dissolving. If then you throw the appearance aside, you will speedily come to the form. For nothing is more strengthless than vice, nothing so easily wears old. Then since it is likely that being human his hearers would sin every day, he consoles them by saying, renew yourself from day to day. This is what we do with houses, we keep constantly repairing them as they wear old, and so you do to yourself. Have you sinned today? Have you made your soul old? Do not despair, do not despond, but renew it by repentance and tears and confession and by doing good things. And never stop doing this.

—John Chrysostom

For by the grace given me I say to every one of you: Do not
think of yourself more highly than you ought, but rather
think of yourself with sober judgment, in accordance with
the measure of faith God has given you.

—Romans 12:3

After saying, "I urge you, brothers, in view of God's mercy," here [Paul] says again, "by the grace."[92] Observe the teacher's lowliness of mind. He means to say that he is in no respect worthy to be trusted in such an exhortation and counsel. But at one time he takes the mercies of God along with him, at another his grace. It is not my word, he would say, that I am speaking, but one from God. "To every one of you." Not to this person and to that merely, but to the governor and to the governed, to the slave and to the free, to the unlearned and to the wise, to the woman and to the man, to the young and to the old. And by this he also makes his language inoffensive, setting the lessons he gives to all, even to such as do not come under them, that those who do come under them may with more willingness accept such a reproof and correction. And what do you say? Let me hear. "Do not think of yourself more highly than you ought." Here he is bringing before us the mother of good deeds, which is lowliness of mind, in imitation of his own Master. For as Jesus, when he went up into the mountain and was going to give a teaching of moral precepts, took this for his first beginning and made this the foundation, in the words, "Blessed are the poor in spirit" (Matt. 5:3), so Paul too, as he has now passed from the doctrinal parts to those of a more practical kind, has taught us virtue in general terms by requiring of us the admirable sacrifice. And being on the point of giving a more particular portrait of it, he begins from lowliness of mind as from the head and tells us not to think more highly of ourselves than we ought to think but to think of ourselves with sober judgment. We have received wisdom not that we should use it to make us arrogant but to make us sober-minded. And he does not say in order to be lowly in mind, but in order to sobriety, meaning by sobriety here not that virtue which contrasts with lewdness nor the being free from intemperance, but being sensible and healthful in mind. And the Greek name of it means keeping the mind safe.

—John Chrysostom

PART FOUR

Autumn

Summers pleasures they are gone like to visions every one
And the cloudy days of autumn and of winter cometh on
I tried to call them back but unbidden they are gone.
—John Clare in "Remembrances"

For man, autumn is a time of harvest, of gathering together. For nature,
it is a time of sowing, of scattering abroad.
—Edwin Way Teale
(quoted in *Reader's Digest*, September 1997)

No spring, nor summer beauty hath such grace
As I have seen in one autumnal face.
—John Donne

The summer has ended.

—Jeremiah 8:20

The soul of the intelligent Christian reflects the natural.[1] The year is a temple of praise on whose altar, as an offering, spring puts its blossoms and summer its grain and autumn its fruits, while winter stands at the altar praising God with psalm of snow and hail and tempest.

Summer is the perfection of the year, the season of beauty. But that wave of summer beauty is receding. The sap of the tree is halting in its upward current. The night is fast conquering the day.

In the latter part of October or the first of November is a season called Indian summer. It is the gem of the year—a haziness in the atmosphere, but everything pleasant and mild. And I see before me tonight some who have come to that season. A haziness is on their vision, but the sweetness of heaven has melted into their souls. I congratulate those who have come to the Indian summer of their lives. Their grandchildren climb on the back of the chair and run their fingers along the wrinkles that time has furrowed there. Blessed is old age, if found in the way of righteousness!

But my text is appropriate for all those whose fortunes have perished. If you lose your property at thirty or forty years of age, it is only a sharp discipline, generally, by which later you come to larger success. It is folly to sit down in midlife discouraged. Though the meridian of life has passed with you, and you have been routed in many a conflict, do not give up in discouragement. There are victories yet for you to gain.

But sometimes monetary disaster comes when there is something in your age or in your health or in your surroundings that makes you know that you will never get up again. Leaves of worldly property all scattered—the daybook, the ledger, and the money. But you have more remaining than you have lost.

Sons and daughters of God, do not mourn when your property goes. The world is yours, and life, death, immortality, thrones of grandeur, rivers of gladness, and shining mansions are yours, and God is yours! The eternal God has sworn it, and every time you doubt it, you charge the King of heaven and earth with perjury. Instead of complaining how hard you have it, go home tonight, take up your Bible full of promises, get down on your knees before God, and thank him for what you have, instead of spending so much time complaining about what you do not have.

—T. DeWitt Talmage

By the breath of God frost is given.

—Job 37:10 KJV

The leaves are down.[2] The warmth has gone out of the air. The birds have winged southward. The landscape has been scarred by the autumnal equinox. Another element now comes to bless and adorn and instruct the world. It is the frost. The palaces of this king are far up in the Arctic, glittering winter palaces of ice, [and] from those hard, white, portals King Frost descends and waves his silvery scepter over our temperate zone. You already feel his breath in the night wind. By most considered an enemy, the frost is a friend, charged with lessons potent and tremendous.

There are passages of Scripture that once were enigmas and impossible for you to understand, but the frosts of trouble after awhile exposed the full meaning to your soul. You said, "I do not see why David keeps rolling over in his psalms the story of how he was pursued and persecuted." He describes himself as surrounded by bees. You think, *What an exaggeration for him to exclaim, "Out of the depths I cry to you, O Lord"* (Ps. 130:1). There is so much lamentation in his writings you think he overdoes it. But after awhile the frost comes upon you in the shape of persecution, and you are pierced with censure, wounded with defamation, and stung with lies in swarms [that] are buzzing about your ears, and at last you understand what David meant.

For a long while a disproportionate amount of the Bible seemed given to consolation. Why page after page and chapter after chapter taken up with comforts [and] consolations? The Book seems like an apothecary, one-half of the shelves occupied with soothing salves. But after a while, bankruptcy, sickness, and bereavement. Now the consolatory parts of the Bible do not seem disproportionate. You want something off almost all the shelves of that sacred dispensary. What has uncovered to you the usefulness of so much of the Bible that was hidden before? The frosts have been fulfilling their mission.

Thank God for frosts. What helped make Milton the greatest of poets? The frost of blindness. What helped make Washington the greatest of generals? The frost of Valley Forge. Special trials fit for special work.

Without complaint, take the hard knocks. It will not take long for God to make up to you in the next world for all you have suffered in this. Trouble comes for beneficial purpose, and on the coldest nights the aurora is brightest in the northern heavens.

—T. DeWitt Talmage

*Whoever watches the wind will not plant; whoever looks at
the clouds will not reap.*

—Ecclesiastes 11:4

The language in which this proverb is couched is taken from the harvest field and is therefore peculiarly applicable at this season.[3] That does not mean, of course, that the way to succeed in farming is entirely to disregard the weather. But it means that if farmers will not work except when all the conditions for their work are perfect, if they are always doubting and fearing and forecasting rain, worrying and fretting instead of making the best of things, then probably they will neither sow nor reap and are little likely to make successful farmers. Just as a person may fail through too much zeal, so may a person fail through too much prudence.

In the first place, I like to apply our text to the important matter of our bodily health. If people are always thinking of their health, the chances are they will have a sorry harvest. That we must be reasonably careful of our bodies we all know; it is one of the plainest of our Christian duties. By the coming of the Son of God in our flesh and by making the body the temple of the Spirit, by the great doctrine of the resurrection, when what is sown in weakness will be raised in glory, the gospel of Christ has glorified the body in a way that even the Greeks had never dreamed of. But I am not speaking of reasonable care; I am speaking of morbid and worrying anxiety. Why, you can hardly drink a glass of milk today but some newspaper will warn you that you may be poisoned. And what I want you to feel is that that alarmist attitude, which will scarce allow you to breathe in this glad world, is the kind of thing that is denounced by Solomon in the memorable proverb of this verse. Lean on the Keeper of Israel and go forward.

—George H. Morrison

Whoever watches the wind will not plant; whoever looks at the clouds will not reap.

—Ecclesiastes 11:4

I like to apply our text to the difficulties that beset our daily work, for we may so fix our eyes on these difficulties that all the strength is taken from the arm.[4] A person may ruin any work by rashness, as Simon Peter would have ruined the work of Jesus, but remember that if the rash have their perils, there are also perils for the overcautious. Do you remember the parable of the talents? Do you remember why the person with the one talent failed? He said, "I knew that you are a hard man. . . . So I was afraid and went out and hid your talent in the ground" (Matt. 25:24–25). The other servants took the common risks in giving out their money to the changers, but this man would risk absolutely nothing, and, willing to risk nothing, he lost all. Do you imagine it is just a chance that this individual had the one talent? We talk about the perils of genius, but our Savior talked of those of mediocrity. Great men and women have their glow and inspiration; things are worth doing when you can do them greatly. Genius is prodigal and scatters its pearls abroad; genius, like childhood, is equal to its problem. It is those of the one talent and mediocre minds who are tempted to the sin of being over-cautious. I have known so many average people who failed because they were waiting for an impossible perfection. They said, "Tomorrow—by and by—I'll be ready; I'll have all the information in ten years"—and the ten years hurried by, and they did nothing, except to wish that they had started earlier. Do you think we ministers could ever preach to you if we watched the wind and looked at the clouds? If we waited for inspiration and a glowing brain, could we ever face the inevitable Sunday? The hours will come, and come to everyone, when taskwork quivers and palpitates with life, but perhaps they only come because we have been faithful, with a certain grimness, through the days of gloom. Let people hold to their lifework through mood and melancholy. Let them hold to it through headache and through heartache. For whoever watches the wind will never plant, and whoever looks at the clouds will never reap.

—George H. Morrison

Whoever watches the wind will not plant; whoever looks at
the clouds will not reap.

—Ecclesiastes 11:4

Just as a person may fail through too much zeal, so may a person fail through too much caution.[5]

Our text has notable application in the great work of national reform. A certain disregard of obvious difficulties and of all that would discourage lesser spirits has ever been one mark of great reformers, whether in the church or in the state. When told that Duke George of Saxony was lying in wait for him, "I would go," said Luther, "if it rained Duke Georges." The winds were bitter and the clouds black as midnight, and Luther planted and reaped because he disregarded them. It is an easy thing to sneer at fanatics and to say that they are the ruin of their cause. It is an easy thing to make fun of the enthusiasts who are so terribly in earnest that they are not wise. But I will tell you those who are a thousand times more fatal to any cause than the enthusiasts are those who always eye the clouds and spend their days in shrinking from the wind. It is better to try and fail than to do nothing. We snatch our triumphs from the brink of failure. It is so easy to stand aside and criticize and magnify difficulties and raise objections. But we are here to plant and we are here to reap, as Luther knew and as every brave woman and man knows. Whoever watches the wind will never plant, and whoever looks at the clouds will never reap.

Then, I want you to apply our text to the great matter of decision for Christ Jesus. I want you to go away thinking of Peter when he walked on the sea to get to Christ. "Lord, if it's you, tell me come to you," and Jesus across the water cried to Peter, "Come"; whereupon Peter leaped out of the ship and walked on the water to his Lord. Then he regarded the clouds—how the wild rack was flying! He observed the wind—how boisterous it was—and, observing them, he began to sink and had to cry, "Lord, save me." Isn't Christ saying "Come" to someone here tonight? Isn't there someone like Peter who has heard his call? In such an hour the one thing that is fatal is to give heed to the uproar of the storm. O you of little faith, why do you doubt? He is mighty to save and powerful to keep. Disregard everything except the beckoning Savior, and by and by you will reap a hundred times what you planted.

—George H. Morrison

And Mary said: "My soul glorifies the Lord and my spirit rejoices in God my Savior."

—Luke 1:46–47

Mary's Magnificat was a song of faith.[6] Have you ever realized the difficulties under which this hymn was composed and sung? If not, permit me to remind you that the wondrous birth, which had been promised to her, had not then been accomplished, and in her mind there must have been a consciousness that many would doubt her statements. The visitation of the angel and all its consequences would seem to be ridiculous and even impossible to many to whom she might venture to mention the circumstances—no, more than that—would subject her to many cruel insinuations, which would scandalize her character. That which conferred on her the highest honor that ever fell to woman would, in the judgment of many, bring on her the greatest possible dishonor. We know what suspicions even Joseph had and that it was only a revelation from God that could remove them. Mary must have been sorely troubled if she had been influenced by her natural feelings and had been swayed by external circumstances.

It was only her wondrous faith—in some respects, her matchless faith, for no other woman had ever had such a blessed trial of faith as she had—only her matchless faith that she would be the mother of the holy child, Jesus, sustained her. Even before there was an accomplishment of the things that were told her by the angel, she could sing, "My soul glorifies the Lord and my spirit rejoices in God my Savior." Unbelief would have said, "Wait." Fear would have said, "Be silent." But faith could not wait and could not be silent; she must sing, and sing she did most sweetly. I call your attention to this fact because when we ourselves have a song to sing to the Lord, we may perhaps be tempted not to sing it until our hopes are accomplished and our faith has been exchanged for fact. Do not wait, for your song will spoil if you do. There is another song to be sung for the accomplished mercy, but there is a song to be sung now for the promised mercy; therefore, do not let the present hour lose the song that is due to it.

—C. H. Spurgeon

*And Mary said: "My soul glorifies the Lord and my spirit
rejoices in God my Savior."*

—Luke 1:46–47

Let us sing, first, because singing is the natural language of joy.[7] Are the jubilant songs all made for the ungodly and the dirges for us? Are they to lift high the festive strain and we to be satisfied with the "Dead March" or some such melancholy music as that? No, friends, if they have joy, much more have we. Their joy is like the crackling of thorns under a pot, but ours is the shining of a star that never will be quenched. Let us sing then, for our joy abounds and abides. When warriors win victories, they shout; haven't we won victories through Jesus Christ our Lord? When people celebrate their festivals, they sing; are there any festivals equal to ours—our paschal supper, our passage of the Red Sea, our jubilee, our expectation of the coronation of our King, our hymn of victory over all the host of hell? Oh, surely, if the children of earth sing, the children of heaven ought to sing far more often, far more loudly, far more harmoniously than they do.

Let us sing, too, because singing is the language of heaven. It's thus that they express themselves up yonder. Many of the songs and other sounds of earth never penetrate beyond the clouds. Sighs and groans and clamors have never reached those regions of serenity and purity, but they do sing there. Heaven is the home of sacred song, and we are the children of heaven. Heaven's light is in us; heaven's smile is on us; heaven's all belongs to us.

Let us also sing because singing is sweet to the ear of God. I venture to say that even the song of birds is sweet to him, for in Psalm 104 where it is written, "May the LORD rejoice in his works" (v. 31), it is also mentioned the birds "sing among the branches" (v. 12). Is there anything sweeter in this world than to wake up about four or five o'clock in the morning, just at this time of the year, and hear the birds singing as if they would burst their little throats and pouring out, in a contest of sweetness, their little hearts in joyous song? I believe that, in the wild places of the earth where no human foot has ever defiled the soil, God loves to walk. When I have been alone among the fir trees, inhaling their fragrance, or have wandered up the hill where the loudest voice could not be answered by another voice for no one was there, I have felt that God was there and that he loved to listen to the song of birds that he had created. Yes, even the harshly croaking ravens he hears when they cry.

—C. H. *Spurgeon*

*And Mary said: "My soul glorifies the Lord and my spirit
rejoices in God my Savior."*

—Luke 1:46–47

He loves to hear us sing when we sing his praises from our hearts.[8] Don't you delight to hear your own children sing, and is there anything sweeter than a song from a child? And God loves to hear his children sing. Even your discords, so long as they do not affect your heart but are only of sound and not of soul, will please him. What a beautiful simile is used in Psalm 22: "O thou that inhabitest the praises of Israel" (KJV)! Just as God's ancient people, during the feast of tabernacles, dwelt under booths made from the boughs of trees, so Jehovah is represented as having made for himself a tabernacle out of the praises of his people. They are only like fading boughs that soon turn brown, yet the great Lord of all condescends to sit beneath them, and as we each bring a new bough plucked from the tree of mercy, we help to make a new tabernacle for the Most High to dwell in.

Mary praised God with personal devotion. Notice how intensely personal her song is. We should join with other Christians in their songs of praise, but always mind that your personal note is not omitted, "*My* soul glorifies the Lord." Don't you think that some of you too often forget this? You come to hear sermons, and sometimes you do not come to the assembly as much as you ought for the purpose of directly and distinctly praising God in your own personality and individuality. The music is delightful to us as it rises from thousands of voices, but to God it can be pleasant only as it comes from each heart. "My soul"—for I have a personal indebtedness to you, my God, and there is a personal union between you and me; I love you, and you love me; therefore, even if all other souls are dumb, my soul glorifies the Lord. In this fashion, have a song to yourself, and mind that it is thoroughly your own.

In Mary's song we see great spirituality. She is far from being content with mere lip service. Her language is poetic, but she is not satisfied with her language. But she speaks of "my soul" and "my spirit." Let us never be satisfied with any kind of worship that does not take up the whole of the inner and higher nature. It is what you are within that you really are before the living God. It is quite a secondary matter how loud the chant may be or how sweet the tone of your hymn or how delightfully you join in it, unless your spirit, your soul, truly praises the Lord.

—C. H. Spurgeon

And Mary said: "My soul glorifies the Lord and my spirit
rejoices in God my Savior."
—Luke 1:46–47

Let us think of his greatness; it will be really praising him if we thus think of him.[9] You need not speak, but just ponder, weigh, consider, contemplate, meditate on the character of the Most High. Begin with his mercy if you cannot begin with his holiness, but take his attributes one by one and think about them. As you think of any one of them, it will delight you and carry you away. You will be lost in wonder, love, and praise as you consider it; you will be astonished and amazed as you plunge into its wondrous depths, and everything else will vanish from your vision. That is one way of making God great—by often thinking about him.

The next way to make God great is by often drinking him into yourself. The lilies stand and worship God simply by being beautiful—by drinking in the sunlight and the dewdrops. Stand before the Lord and drink him in; do you understand what I mean by this expression? You go down to the seaside when you are sickly; there is a delightful breeze coming up from the sea; you feel as if it came in at every pore of your body and you seem to be drinking in health at every breath you breathe. Do just like that in a spiritual sense with God; go down to the great sea of Godhead; magnify it by thinking how great it is, and then take it into your very soul. God cannot be greater than he is, but he can be greater in you than he is at present. He cannot increase; there cannot be more of God than there is, but there may be more of God in you. More of his great love, more of his perfect holiness, more of his divine power may be manifested in you, and more of his likeness and light may be revealed through you. Therefore, make him great in that respect.

And when you have done that, by his help, then try to make him great by what you give forth, even as the rose: when it has satisfied itself with the sweet shower, no sooner does the clear shining come after the rain than it deluges the garden all around with its delicious perfume. Do the same; first drink in all you can of the deity, and then exhale him; breathe out again in your praise, in your holy living, in your prayers, in your earnest zeal, and in your devout spirit the God whom you have breathed in. You cannot make more of God than he is, but you can make God more consciously present to the minds of others and make them think more highly of God by what you say and what you do.

—C. H. Spurgeon

And Mary said: "My soul glorifies the Lord and my spirit
rejoices in God my Savior."

—Luke 1:46–47

Is there any true praise without joy?[10] Isn't praise the twin to joy? And do not joy and praise always dwell together? Rejoice, then, beloved, in your Savior—in him above everything else. Never let any earthly thing or any person stand higher in your joy than Jesus Christ. Rejoice in him as most surely yours, for, dear believer, Christ is yours. If you are resting in him, he belongs to you, so rejoice in your own Savior, for all of Christ is yours—not half a Savior; not one of his wounds for you and one for me, but all his wounds for you and all for me; not his thoughtful head for you and his loving heart for me, but his head and his heart all for you and all for me—he is my Savior from his feet that were pierced by the nails to his head that was crowned with thorns.

If the fact that Christ is ours involves the bearing of the cross, we are glad to bear it. It may involve suffering and shame and a thousand temptations and trials; if it is so, each true believer can say with Mary, "My spirit rejoices in God my Savior"—in what he is, in what he is to me, in what he is to all his children, in what he is to poor sinners, in what he is to God, in what he will be when he comes again, and in what he will be throughout eternity. Do as much as you can of all good things, but still there must be times for quiet meditation, times for reading, times for praying, and times for praising. There is no waste about such times; they are among the best-spent hours that we ever have. You and I, beloved, are the living to praise God. This is the culmination, the very apex of the pyramid of existence, pointing straight up to heaven—that we praise God with all our hearts and souls.

Prayer and praise are two of the sure signs of a true-born heir of heaven. If you never praise God, my friend, you can never go to heaven. Until the Lord has taken out of you the praise of other things and the love of other things and given you the grace to love him and praise him, you cannot enter his glory. Begin now to praise that God who freely forgives the greatest sin and who is willing to cleanse the very worst sinner, for he has given Christ to die, the just for the unjust, that he may bring them to God. Oh, begin to glorify him and rejoice in him now, and you will never want to leave off doing so, world without end.

—C. H. Spurgeon

A woman in the crowd called out, "Blessed is the mother who gave you birth and nursed you." He replied, "Blessed rather are those who hear the word of God and obey it."
—Luke 11:27–28

The wonder is not that this woman spoke as she did but that people who hear the teaching of Jesus do not more often speak in his praise.[11] Of our blessed Lord his enemies said, "No one ever spoke the way this man does" (John 7:46). His very tone was melody, and his language was truth set to music. The doctrines that he taught were more than golden, they were light to the head and joy to the heart. He revealed the inmost heart of God and taught as never prophet or sage had before.

This earnest woman did not mean, in the first place, to praise Christ's mother. In the East, if they want to insult a man, they speak vilely of his mother; if they wish to honor him, they laud his mother to the skies.

It was a brave speech for her to make, for the Savior had been confronted by persons of authority. They had spoken ill words of him. They had even dared to say that he cast out devils through Beelzebub, the prince of devils. When he had answered them wisely, this woman proclaimed his victory. If there is a time when not only enthusiasm suggests, but when affection compels us to speak for Christ, it is when others are opposing his name and cause. We cannot be silent when he is discredited. O Woman—your courage deserves our praise and our imitation! Oh, that we had a fire in our hearts burning as it did in yours, then would it consume the bonds that hold our tongues. Let us believe that when the current of thought around us runs in a wrong direction, such is the power of enthusiasm that one earnest, impassioned voice may turn it, and our Lord may yet win glory where now he is despised.

To hear the Word of God and obey it is a blessing preferable to having been the mother of our Lord. We are sure of this because Jesus himself adjusts the scales of blessedness. We believe, on his authority, that though Mary was greatly blessed, yet even more emphatically are those blessed who hear the Word of God and obey it. This preference so truly given by the Master puts the highest blessedness within the reach of all of us.

Notice that this preferable blessing is found in a very simple manner. "Blessed rather are those who hear the word of God and obey it." The process is stripped of all ambiguity or mystery. There is nothing about it that is hard or difficult: Hear the word and obey it; that is all.

—C. H. Spurgeon

And Mary said: "My soul glorifies the Lord and my spirit rejoices in God my Savior."

—Luke 1:46–47

Mary sings.[12] When God shows himself, what music will suffice for the grand psalm of adoring wonder? In the Incarnation, it is the divine person who is revealed, wrapped in a veil of our lesser clay. Worthy of peerless music is the fact that "the Word became flesh and made his dwelling among us" (John 1:14). There is no longer a great gulf fixed between God and his people; the humanity of Christ has bridged it. We can no longer think that God sits on high, indifferent to our wants and woes, for God has come down to our humble state. No longer need we lament that we can never participate in the moral glory and purity of God. Let us dream no longer in somber sadness that we cannot draw near to God, so that he will really hear our prayers and pity our necessities, since Jesus has become bone of our bone and flesh of our flesh, born a babe as we are born, living as human as we must live, bearing the same infirmities and sorrows, and bowing his head to the same death. O can't we come with confidence by this new and living way to the throne of the heavenly grace, when Jesus meets us as Immanuel—God with us?

The stress of the Virgin's canticle is laid on God's special grace to her. Those little words, the personal pronouns, tell us that it was truly a personal affair with her. *My* soul glorifies the Lord and *my* spirit rejoices in God *my* Savior. The Savior was, in a special sense, hers. You can never know the joy of Mary unless Christ becomes truly and really yours. But, oh! when he is yours, yours within, reigning in your heart, changing your nature, subduing your corruptions—yours within, an inexpressible and glorious joy—oh! then who can restrain your tongue?

The natural conception of the Savior's holy body was not one-tenth so fitting a theme for congratulation as the spiritual conception of the holy Jesus within your heart when he will be in you the hope of glory. My dear friend, if Christ is yours, there is no song on earth too high, too holy for you to sing. No, there is no song that thrills from angelic lips, no note that thrills archangel's tongue, in which you may not join. Even this day, the holiest, the happiest, the most glorious of words and thoughts and emotions belong to you. Use them! God help you to enjoy them. His be the praise while yours is the comfort evermore. Amen.

—C. H. Spurgeon

For your sakes he became poor.

—2 Corinthians 8:9

Christ humbled himself in his birth.[13] The humiliation of the birth of Christ consists mainly in its humble state. There were indeed notable flashes of his glory attending his birth by which God testified that he was the Messiah. But his birth itself was accompanied with an awe-inspiring humility, as he abased himself through it. He was born for us, and so he was born in a condition appropriate to our need. He showed in his birth what sin had made us. There are a few things we may take notice of as properly belonging to his humiliation:

1. *He was born under a sentence of condemnation.* As soon as he put on our nature, he stood under the doom of the Law. He was born to die and was adjudged by it as soon as he was human. We are all born children of wrath in our natural state, and he put himself in our place, and therefore came to *fulfill the Law* (Matt. 5:17), and this is the main article of it. He intended to be made a sacrifice; God prepared him a body for this (Heb. 12:5). Justice took hold on him as soon as he came into the world and did not discharge him until it had taken its satisfaction of him, and he lived in view of it all his days and spoke of it frequently.

2. *He was born of a sinful woman.* It was a particular condescension of the Son of God to be born of any of Adam's sinful children. True honor in God's account consists in holiness, and sin is to him the vilest disgrace. Original sin in Christ's mother had made her more contemptible and ignoble than anything else could; had she been an empress, it would yet have been to Christ a degrading of himself to derive his humanity from her. As it is a disgrace to have a traitor as one's father, so it is no less to have a sinner for one's mother. Thus Christ, though without sin, would be intimately related to sinners, for whose sake he came into the world.

3. *Joseph and Mary were very poor and wretched.* Mary was his true mother, as really as any other mother is the mother of her children. And Joseph, though not really his father, was commonly accepted so, and the honor or contempt of his father's condition reflected on him. They were indeed descendants of King David, but they were reduced to an inferior condition, little to be regarded among rich and wealthy neighbors. Joseph was a carpenter, a laborious calling that was not very profitable.

—Samuel Willard

For your sakes he became poor.
—2 Corinthians 8:9

There are a few [more] things we may take notice of as properly belonging to Christ's humiliation:[14]

4. *The time of his birth is very important.* There was a time when [Israel] enjoyed its liberty. But he was born when the nation was in slavery to the Roman Empire, when, in witness of his slavery, there was a proclamation of a tax, and everyone was required to appear at his city to submit. Therefore even in the circumstances of his birth, he not only took on himself human form, but the *nature of a servant* (Phil. 2:7), because we by sin have become slaves, brought under the most cruel bondage.

5. *The place and circumstances of his birth further set forth its humble condition.* When we hear the report that the King of the world is to be born, we would picture the greatest preparations imaginable to be made for the occasion. But how far is it from this? Instead of a palace, he is content with a stable; for attendants, he is born among the beasts; for apparel, either some rags obtained by charity or whatever his poor parents could afford. Instead of a cradle richly prepared, he had a manger, with some hay for a pillow. The best attendants at this solemn occasion was a company of poor folks, who had better places to lodge than Joseph's. Thus he came silently into the world; no bells rung, no bonfires, no proclamations inviting the world to come and pay homage. This was because we had turned ourselves out of all and forfeited our right to every blessing.

Learn from this how low sin had laid us and how much Christ has loved us. Truly everything Christ suffered in his humiliation points to this lesson. When we consider what Christ made himself, it shows us what we had made of ourselves by sin. When we reflect on the fact that he did it for us, it declares his unspeakable kindness to us. He is the Lord of heaven and earth, entering into his dominion in the lowest and most obscure situation imaginable. He who made both heaven and earth not accommodated with so much as a house to be born in but turned out among the beasts. And why? Our sins procured it; we lost our right to all, we deserved poverty and misery, we deserved to be turned out of house and home. We were under this curse. It was for this reason he was born. Wasn't this condescension a disclosure of his great love? Let this stable and manger make him exceedingly precious to us.

—Samuel Willard

Search me, O God, and know my heart; test me and know
my anxious thoughts. See if there is any offensive way in
me, and lead me in the way everlasting.
—Psalm 139:23–24

What is implied in the sincere petition contained in the text?[15]

First, it implies the realization of the omniscience of God. The psalmist was under a deep impression of the omnipresence and omniscience of God, that God understands our real hearts and is able to search us.

Second, it implies a sense of the moral purity or holiness of God. Observe, he prays to be searched—that his whole being may be exposed—to see if there was any offense in him. It is plainly implied that he had such a sense of the purity of God as to be convinced that God is infinitely opposed to all iniquity.

This petition implies a thorough wakefulness of mind to one's moral or spiritual state. [The psalmist] is in an honest, searching state of mind—thoroughly in earnest to know all about himself; he is wide awake to his own spiritual condition and desires that all his errors may be rectified.

It implies an intense anxiety to be perfect as God would have him to be—conformed to the holy will of God. Observe, he prays to be led in the way everlasting, which plainly implies that he was willing to be led to abandon all iniquity.

Such a petition implies the assumption on the part of the petitioner that he or she needs to be deeply tried—penetrated with the light of truth to the deepest recesses of the soul. When we offer such a petition, we assume that there may be things about us that we have overlooked, and we ask for the scrutiny of God's eye to search them out and to apply tests so that we may see them.

Such a petition implies a willingness to be subjected to any process of searching that God may see to be needed. [The psalmist] does not point out any particular way in which he desires to be searched and tried, but he leaves that to the divine discretion—he only asks that it may be done. When we ask to be searched—without any real design to be searched—there is an inclination to dictate the way in which it will be done, but this is not an acceptable way of offering such a petition.

An acceptable offering of such a petition implies of course that we are really willing to have it answered and will not resist any process through which God causes us to pass as the means by which it is answered.

—Charles G. Finney

Search me, O God, and know my heart; test me and know
my anxious thoughts. See if there is any offensive way in
me, and lead me in the way everlasting.
—Psalm 139:23–24

What are some of the ways in which God answers requests of this kind?[16]

By his Spirit and by the application of his truth, light often shines into the mind to give people a view of themselves that without this searching they never would have had. But while it is true that God often searches in this way and has done so in all ages, yet it is by no means the *only* way in which he searches the human mind. No, it is certain that he much more frequently searches us in other ways. Notice, God's object in searching is not to inform himself about us but to reveal us to ourselves, for he knows well the state of our minds, our spiritual latitude and longitude, what we are in our present state, and what sort of characters we would develop under any and all circumstances. Consequently, God, in bringing us out to our own view, must apply tests to us that let us see ourselves as he himself sees us. In order to do this, he answers such petitions by means of his *providence outside us* and by his *Spirit inside us.* God brings us into various conditions and circumstances for the demonstration of character and then comes by his Spirit and presents it to our minds when it is demonstrated.

For example, he often allows things to occur that really will show to us—and to those around us—what sort of tempers we have. When we pray to be searched, often God allows us to be maligned and criticized. [This] shows whether we possess the virtue of meekness or whether we will say that we have a right to be angry. Now, perhaps, some of you have had such a test as this applied to you this very day. Did it demonstrate the meekness and gentleness of Christ, or did it make you angry?

God often arranges matters so that we are treated with neglect—perhaps, sinfully so—by those around us. God does not prevent this but allows it to be done. Did it make you angry and show an unholy temper, or otherwise? Perhaps God allows you to be treated with unmistakable injustice, and, when thus tried, do you show the Spirit of Christ? Do you find working in you the temper that was shown by Christ on such occasions? Remember that it is written, "If anyone does not have the Spirit of Christ, he does not belong to Christ" (Rom. 8:9). We would be exceedingly ignorant of ourselves if none of these tests were applied.

—Charles G. Finney

*Search me, O God, and know my heart; test me and know
my anxious thoughts. See if there is any offensive way in
me, and lead me in the way everlasting.*
—Psalm 139:23–24

I will mention some [more] ways in which God answers these petitions.[17]

When people have nothing to try them, they are in great danger of deceiving themselves. Has injustice been done you—has someone refused you honest wages or refused to pay a just debt? Well, under these painful circumstances, what spirit did you manifest? Did you find the Spirit of Christ in you? Perhaps you have been misunderstood and misrepresented; well, how have you borne it? Perhaps you have been treated disrespectfully by those who are under particular obligations to you; well, how did you bear it? Did your indignation rise—did you manifest an un-Christlike spirit? Or did you find the Spirit of Christ was in you? You prayed to be searched, and in answer to your prayer, your children or employees or those related to you, who are under particular obligations to you, treated you in a very improper manner—directly the reverse of what you had a right to expect from them. Though all this was very wrong and very provoking, what has been the effect on you? What has it taught you? And what has it taught those who witnessed the demonstration? Has it brought out your state of mind? Doubtless it has, and if it was not outwardly shown, what were your feelings within? Someone, perhaps, has contradicted you! Can you bear contradiction? Do you bear it well? Were you patient under it? Did you act as Christ would have acted under the circumstances—or did you behave un-Christlike? These things never occur by accident; God designs that every one of them should demonstrate our characters—that they should try us and show what there is in us and reveal to us the springs of action in us. Now when these tests of your character and disposition have been applied, what has been the result? Did you find that you were nothing but the same old sinner yet? that instead of finding Christ in you and his temper demonstrating itself, you found the old self with its deceitful desires?
—Charles G. Finney

Search me, O God, and know my heart; test me and know
my anxious thoughts. See if there is any offensive way in
me, and lead me in the way everlasting.
—Psalm 139:23–24

I will mention some [more] ways in which God answers these petitions.[18]

How often when individuals pray to be searched and tried, God gives them opportunities to prove if they love their neighbors as themselves—to see if they will share the profits where there is money to be made, or whether they will dip their hands into their neighbors' pockets. These are golden opportunities for us to know ourselves and are designed to search us to the bottoms of our hearts.

Often, God so arranges it that [you] can take advantage of others without danger to [your] own reputation. Now is the time of trial—see whether it is the love of God or the fear of society that motivates you. Suppose that someone has, at your store, paid too much, and it is never likely to be found out, or suppose you have found something in the street, and you can keep it or restore it as you please. These are searchings from God, and how completely such circumstances show your true character! Now suppose that instead of finding the Spirit of Christ exhibiting himself, you demonstrate the opposite spirit and resort to some selfish reasonings to quiet your conscience. Well, it is written upon you, *Mene, Mene, Tekel*—weighed on the scales and found wanting (see Dan. 5:25, 27).

God often allows people to accumulate property that they may have an opportunity to extend the cause of truth and righteousness in the earth. Those who profess Christianity acknowledge themselves to be only stewards for God—that everything they possess is his and, consequently, is at his disposal. Now [do] these people act in harmony with their professions? Well, God often tries them to see if they are acting the hypocrite or not.

God in his providence often causes us to suffer losses by some means, just to see whether we will regard these losses as God's or our own. Look at someone who once had large property to manage and by some means lost it all, and that person goes about saying, I have sustained such and such great losses. We may profess that it belongs to God and even deceive ourselves into the belief that we are sincere, but when a loss occurs, it often shows us that we did not regard it as God's but our own.

—Charles G. Finney

*Search me, O God, and know my heart; test me and know
my anxious thoughts. See if there is any offensive way in
me, and lead me in the way everlasting.*

—Psalm 139:23–24

I will mention some [more] ways in which God answers these petitions.[19]

He will lay open our temper to us and enable us to see whether we are impatient or otherwise, and he will show us whether we are ambitious—whether we desire to climb and scramble up some height from which we can look down with scorn or contempt on others.

God often gives us opportunities to show off, and, on the other hand, he often denies us such opportunities, to see if we will murmur and be envious of those who have them. Many people will be found often speaking against ostentation—when they do not have the means to indulge in it. They will be very loud in their censures on others who ride in their coaches and furnish their houses in a superior style. But give these sermonizers the means of doing the same, and see what they will do—see if they will not imitate and, perhaps, act more extravagantly than those whom they before condemned.

Sometimes God will deny you many things, to see if you will be satisfied with his provision. Do you bear poverty well, or are you envious at the rich? Are you, in your poverty, what Christ would have been in your circumstances? Thus riches and poverty, sickness and health, and a thousand other things are sent to try us and prove to us, and to those around us, what our real state is.

God often tests us to show if we are self-willed—to show if our wills are ready to submit to his will or whether we will make ourselves unhappy and wretched because God wills so concerning us. How often is it the case that people do not know they are self-willed; so long as the providence of God seems to favor them they are very pious and can talk about submission with the greatest apparent sincerity. But let God just drive across their path, lay his hand on them, blow their schemes to the winds of heaven, and see whether they will talk of submission then; see whether they are self-willed or whether they will instantly submit. How have [such things] affected you? What was the state of mind that you discovered in yourselves? God was searching you, applying the tests that would, without fail, show what was the working in your minds.

—Charles G. Finney

*Search me, O God, and know my heart; test me and know
my anxious thoughts. See if there is any offensive way in
me, and lead me in the way everlasting.*
— Psalm 139:23–24

Saints who ask to be searched must be willing to submit to anything that God sees fit to lay on them.[20]

Saints should be prepared to receive answers to prayer in their own persons. Perhaps God lets them fall ill just when they had some very great object in view. Well, it is intended for their good, therefore they ought not to brood or murmur but receive with thankfulness the good that is intended for them.

It is necessary that these trials should be awarded us, for it will not do that God should always feed his children on sweets. We need severe discipline; it makes us good soldiers. A mere silken religion that passes through no trials has little productiveness in it. These providential trials take away the dross and tin and make us strong in the Lord. How lovely is the character of the Christian who has patiently endured the trials through which she or he has had to pass. These individuals quiet themselves under all the dispensations of providence; they receive everything as bestowed on them from their Father. The more holy Christians become, the more necessary they find it to lay their whole hearts before him and ask him that he may search them and purify them, until he is satisfied with his own work. Christians, are you in the habit of asking the Lord to satisfy himself, to do that which will bring you into a condition that will please him? Don't you long for the pruning knife to be applied, to be purged of all your selfishness and everything that is offensive to God, so that you may stand before him in meekness and love, while he looks on you and says, this is my handiwork, and it is very good. Ask God to search you, then, and do not be afraid to have it done. Look on all the trials of life as coming from your heavenly Father, in order that if you are really self-deceived you may know it, and if you are not, that you may grow up into the likeness of the Son of God.

— Charles G. Finney

None of the rulers of this age understood it, for if they had,
they would not have crucified the Lord of glory.
—1 Corinthians 2:8

Whatever else is to be made of it, everyone feels that the cross stands out as a hideous tragedy, a dreadful fact black as a splash of ink on our human records.[21] They "have crucified the Lord of glory"! gasps Paul in horror. And as often as it comes in sight of Calvary, the human heart echoes that shuddering cry, stands rooted to the spot, staring incredulously at what can't be true, yet there it really is!

How did it happen, this appalling thing? What sudden orgy of insanity overwhelmed for one mad day the kindly human nature that we know so well and swept it headlong into this? For we feel hotly that it must have been something monstrous, inexplicable, blown in from the darkness round us that was guilty of that horror. Yet the last haunting terror of it is that it was brought about by ordinary mortals like us, kind and likable in many ways, no doubt. Their children ran with happy shouts to father that day he came home from Calvary, well satisfied, as he kept telling his wife as he played with his little one, with the day's admirable work—it was not something unthinkable and gross and obviously devilish that was responsible for our Lord's cross, but it was set up by the quite ordinary, decent, and respectable little sins of decent and respectable people, by the kind of thing into which we are all apt to drift every other day. Let us remember that with a great shivering awe, lest in our lives, too, there rings out that sound of hammering as the nails run home.

"The past throws light on the future," says Guicciardini, "because the world was ever on the same make, and all that is or will be in another day has already been, and the same things return, only with different names and colors. It is not everyone who knows them under the new face, but the wise know them." And age by age the Lord Christ is crucified. And we too have crowded eagerly to Calvary and nailed him to his cross and laughed up into his face and watched him die and gone our way well pleased and much relieved that we have hustled him out of the way—yes, even we.

—Arthur John Gossip

None of the rulers of this age understood it, for if they had,
they would not have crucified the Lord of glory.
—1 Corinthians 2:8

Who brought this infamy about?[22] To begin with, there were the Pharisees. They disliked Christ, and they said so. They resented the intrusion of this layperson—and an ill-educated man at that—into their domain. His teaching, or much of it, seemed to them sheer blasphemy. His habits they thought disgusting. You can always tell people by the company they keep, they sneered, and glanced scornfully at the rabble with whom Christ was not ashamed to mingle. Yet they were zealously religious people, keen churchgoing folk, as we would say, more keen and zealous by far than we are. They prayed, they fasted, they disciplined themselves along lines that might well make us much ashamed. They were good people in their way, devout and desperately in earnest, so far as they saw.

But they made two mistakes. They were apt, as Jesus told them bluntly, to keep their lives and their religion in separate compartments. To pray and fast and keep their multitudinous rules was hard but, after all, a good deal easier than to be kind and unselfish when that clashed with their desires. They hoped and felt that it might do instead. They prayed long and ardently, but it had small effect on their characters. Their temper remained uncurbed, their animosities hardly checked, nor did that seem to vex them or to make them feel that something was wrong somewhere. That that was the goal of religion had not struck them. And so, while praying and thronging to the temple day by day, they planned Calvary and worked it out into a fact of history.

This is a warning for us all. For Jesus tells us that his experience has taught him this—people can be eagerly, even fussily religious, and yet nothing may come of it in their characters. He pursues us in this matter with blunt, pertinacious questions, difficult to face. These prayers of yours, he asks, what are they doing in you? Do they end with themselves? Are they really making you more like God, or do you run them up as a cheap substitute for worthy living? [Regarding] your knowledge of the Father and of the human community—is the [former] forcing you to live your life in God's way? Is the [latter] making your conscience more acute to things about you, so that you can't pass by, now, on the other side, happy in your own comforts, until these wrongs are righted?

—Arthur John Gossip

None of the rulers of this age understood it, for if they had,
they would not have crucified the Lord of glory.
—1 Corinthians 2:8

The Pharisees' other error proved the more tragic.[23] They stood for the old ways and the accepted forms of things, and they were simply inhospitable to new light, incredulous that there was any more to find. Their fathers had been given amazing spiritual experiences, and they not only remembered them with gratitude and founded on them, as was fitting, but took it for granted that the way God acted then must be the way he would act now. They forgot that God was alive in their day too. They had no expectation of any further news bursting in to them from God. When rumors of that reached them, at once and without examination they discredited them as impossible and unauthentic. Boldly they laid it down that their poor, passing conceptions were a perfect reflection of God's thoughts. Their theories were not simply theories but the eternal facts, which must not be altered. Moses said this! Moses did that! they said, and for them that was final. And when Jesus stood forth and said, "No doubt he did, but I now tell you something wholly different and vastly better," they clapped horrified hands over their outraged ears and would not listen. They resolved that this appalling person must be hustled out of the way. For if these notions of his spread abroad, why, plainly, there is an end of religion!

[Christ] looked with compassion at these dull, angry souls, shut into their corner of a world, mistaking their dim, smoky rushlights for God's sun. The prophets grow quite fierce over that habit of either looking back wistfully to the days when God really was God and things really happened, whereas now our lot is cast; or else assuming that what they have is all that they can have.

But Christ is very gentle. No one, he says, prefers new wine to old, and to be satisfied with the familiar is all but universal. He did not think it strange that many did not take to him at once, and he was content to wait. Nonetheless, he urges us to keep our minds open and our hearts expectant—on the lookout for God. Not to do so, he indicates, is a moral failure that may have tragic consequences. For it was no hideous and ugly sin but just a narrowness of mind, an unwillingness to credit or even consider what was new and unaccustomed, a dislike of being jostled out of their settled lines of thought—that set up Christ's cross on Calvary!

—Arthur John Gossip

> *None of the rulers of this age understood it, for if they had,*
> *they would not have crucified the Lord of glory.*
> —1 Corinthians 2:8

When one hears people—passionate in their dislike of any innovation in theology or in religious thinking, declaring it is loyalty to Christ that makes them take their stand, the fact stares at us that it was such people—in their day quite sure that they too were right and working for God's honor—who crucified our Lord.[24] In every age since then, they have continued doing it—old, angry, ill-conditioned Prejudice—with his deaf ears and his inhospitable heart.

Are our hands clean? It is easy to lose the gallant spirit that follows truth unflinchingly wherever truth may lead.

In the New Testament, however high the writers pitched their thoughts of Christ, they found these thoughts couldn't meet the facts from their own experience, that they must make their thinking of him ampler still, and they kept doing it joyously. And it is a poor tribute to Christ to say that we have come to the end of him and know everything in him there is to know.

Suppose in our time a young man suddenly emerged out of an obscure village, a trades worker who had never been much out of his own valley and, talking in that provincial accent of his, told us that our accredited teachers were in many ways wrong and our religion largely obsolete, that he had come to show us a more excellent way, a truer faith—would we listen to him any more than they did then? Do we listen when he does send his messengers to us with some new light? "Christ," said Tertullian, "did not call himself the custom, but the truth." And while we are all loyal worshipers of custom, truth has few real disciples. Always it has had to fight its way to victory through hostile minds, distrustful and suspicious.

"I observe," wrote Jonathan Edwards in his diary, "that old men seldom have any advantage of new discoveries, because these discoveries are beside a way of thinking they have long been used to. If ever I live to years I will be impartial to all pretended discoveries and receive them, if rational, how long soever I have been used to another way of thinking." Such an entry in the diary of Caiaphas or Annas, lived out, would have saved us the Cross. Glancing up awestruck at what sins like ours can do, let us, too, pledge ourselves to that, praying God for the open mind that recognizes Jesus when he comes.

—Arthur John Gossip

None of the rulers of this age understood it, for if they had,
they would not have crucified the Lord of glory.
—1 Corinthians 2:8

The Sadducees held all the high places in the church, yet they had lost all spirituality and all belief in it.[25] Religion was all very well, they said, but really, to get things done, you must look only to politics. The axioms of pious people were unprovable and almost certainly untrue. There was no resurrection—no rewards and punishments hereafter; this brief life of ours was really all. A soul? No doubt there was a soul. But don't brood over that. Give us practical measures of reform for this life here, and the soul will take care of itself. And this [Jesus] was becoming troublesome with his insistence on secondary things and was breeding trouble where they wanted peace and quiet. Yes, they felt, he were better away, and in the council they, too, voted death.

We [today] also are not worrying about immortality, hardly believe in it, or at least are not sure. We, too, have limited ourselves to this dust-speck of time, leaving unclaimed the vast inheritance of which Christ told us. We, too, are putting all our passion and enthusiasm into things of this earth—material things—quite certain that that is the only road to progress and that this chatter about the soul is quite beside the point.

People are so certain, so often animated by lofty motives, so sure that there is no need for Christ. Given a particular panacea, the world will manage very well. To talk about Christ and changing people's hearts and making us new creatures is to lose precious time and wander from the practical into daydreaming.

Today, too, there is a great shouting for Barabbas, for the man of action; we, too, believe in politics and economics—but religion? Set their circumstances right, and people will need no savior, will soon show that they can take care of themselves! "If . . . the light within you is darkness, how great is that darkness!" (Matt. 6:23). If the cures and remedies of an age touch none of the roots of the disease, what then? And still Christ holds to it—as he did in his own day, full as ours is now of social sores and economic problems—that in the last resort nothing can save the world but a new race of men and women, with new aims and likings and a new ardor of self-sacrifice. And still that angers people, and they rise up and cast him out. We are all members of the council before which he is tried. And how does your heart vote?

—Arthur John Gossip

None of the rulers of this age understood it, for if they had,
they would not have crucified the Lord of glory.
—1 Corinthians 2:8

In thinking of [Judas] we must start from this, that Christ loved Judas.[26] Christ believed in Judas, Christ chose Judas, with prayer and deliberation, as one of the Twelve whom he loved best to have beside him and of whom he hoped the most. Judas was a great soul—or had the makings. And when we come upon that horror, scarcely human, lying mangled there at the cliff foot, we look up and, with a shudder, see how high he once walked and from what he fell.

The gospel writers are, frankly, not fair to their fallen colleague. Always that ghastly end of his is there before their eyes, and from the very first they find it difficult to mention him without adding, "who betrayed him" (Matt. 10:4).

So doing, unconsciously they leave the impression that [Judas] was chosen for the traitor's part, as an actor is cast to be the villain and is marked villain from the start. But it was far more terrible than that. It is a most noble nature that we watch crumble to ruin. How did it happen and Christ's confident dreams and hopes for him go out in such a starless night?

Some say that Judas's sin was rather this—that Christ's prolonged delay amazed him—set his mind arguing, "Isn't there here a lack of nerve? Doesn't he see the tide is at the full, and he must launch out now? That it is turning, that if anything is ever to be done, then it must be at once?" And still Christ let chance after chance, as Judas judged, go by and waited—and for what? Things were not growing better but much worse. The opposition of the leaders had been given time to harden. The people had lost much of that first passion of enthusiasm with which, had it been seized at once and rightly used, anything might have been done. Christ was drifting, Judas felt, straight on the rocks. But vigorous action even yet might save the situation, and he planned to bring Christ to a test that he could not evade, to place him in a position that would lay compulsion on him to take action. He had lost patience with Christ, thought his plans were bungling and crude and clumsy and by far too slow. Judas was looking for a shortcut; he thought that he had found it; he took it—and it ended in that horror and the cross!

—Arthur John Gossip

None of the rulers of this age understood it, for if they had,
they would not have crucified the Lord of glory.
—1 Corinthians 2:8

If Judas in [his] blundering way meant well, thinking that he knew better than his Master and—because he could not wait for him and his unhurried ways—sought to force his hand, God pity us![27] For are we not all apt to do just that? Is the church ever quite free from a half-bewildered, half-fretful impatience that can't trust to the steady drip, drip of the weekly services soaking into people's souls; that is irritated by the seeming lack of results of his appointed methods; that must have the kingdom break in with a rush and a loud noise and all people taking note of it; that keeps seeking for a swift, immediate revival not at God's time but now, in ours? Devising desperate expedients, trying to whistle up the winds of God! And they won't come. And these futilities we thought so wise and good and clever end in nothing except robbing people of their hopes and so delaying what was in God's mind to give us, what was coming and might have been here by now, had we not rushed in with our silly nothings, our machine-made revivals, our grotesque improvings on Christ.

It is not this way that real revivals rise, but, says Christ, like the winds. We hear the sound of them but cannot tell from where they come or where they go. A miner coming home from work is greeted in a courteous fashion by a friendly stranger, and somehow there on the road there rises up in his heart a passion of affection for other people that makes him give his life for them and sweeps them by the thousands into the kingdom!

God works in his own time, in his own ways. And if we try to dictate, to demand it must be now and in this fashion, only confusion comes of that. If we would cease our cunning engineering, our hot organizing, our continual talking and conferring, of which nothing ever seems to come but more conferring, if we would sit quiet and reverent in God's presence and worship him and wait and give his voice a chance of reaching people—instead of ours—how much more we might see! For does our fussiness and cleverness do anything except this? Like Judas, we get in Christ's way and hinder him, we who had meant to help were so sure we could help and had found the very way to do it! It was impatience with his methods, it was thinking he knew better than his Master, it was running on ahead of him, that, think some, was the sin of Judas, and that brought Christ to his cross. And who of us is not guilty of that?

—Arthur John Gossip

None of the rulers of this age understood it, for if they had,
they would not have crucified the Lord of glory.
—1 *Corinthians* 2:8

Pilate [was] as pathetic a figure as [exists] in human history.[28] A Roman, with a Roman's sense of justice, he knew at once that these charges against Christ were faked. With a question or two, he had the poor, bribed, muddled witnesses tripping over their own stories or contradicting one another at all points, quite evidently twisting innocent words into sinister meanings that they did not carry in the accused's mouth. *Tools,* thought the man on the judgment seat, and looked contemptuously at the hot faces showing through the doors, shouting and bawling, half beside themselves with rage, though they would come no further into a Gentile court, these holy men on this holy day, lest they might be polluted! How he despised and hated them! Being quite clear that there was nothing against the strange, silent prisoner, he tried hard to get him off. And yet he signed the order for the crucifixion and goes down in history hooted and pelted with the infamy of every race. Why didn't he leap to his feet and cry, "This is mere malice and not a substantial charge. The prisoner is acquitted! And as for you, be off with you, for fear that you stand in his place!" Why, like a noble creature caught in a trap, does he only snarl and show his teeth and struggle and long to hurl himself at his taunting enemies, yet cannot break free?

They say old sins troubled him, past failures that made things difficult for him now. He had been too hectoring and domineering—at least these impossible people said so—though he himself denied it. At all events, protesting to Rome, they had won the emperor's ear and humbled their governor. And that must not happen again. Ah, me! is not life a fearsome thing? Take care! take care! For if you sin a sin, be sure that somehow you will pay for it. And it may be a hideous price! So Pilate found in his day; so you, too, will find in ours.

Our acts follow us from afar,
And what we have been makes us what we are.

Pilate was curt and domineering to the Jews one day. And because of that, months later, his unwilling hands set up the cross of Christ; unwilling—but they did it. Take care! For sin is merciless. If you have had the sweet, sin will see to it that you drink the bitter—to the very dregs. Think, think, and take care!

—Arthur John Gossip

None of the rulers of this age understood it, for if they had,
they would not have crucified the Lord of glory.
—1 Corinthians 2:8

Fitz-James Stephen thought that Pilate's report of Christ's trial would make, could it be found, one of the most arresting state papers in history.[29] And this is not only because of the prisoner's personality, but because of the strong case that Pilate could make out for himself. There had been trouble before; there was always trouble with these pestilent Jews, with their mad hearts and touchy patriotism, quick to read offense in just nothing at all, and so unyielding about even their smallest rights. And Rome had laid it down that they must not be irritated. And yet here out of nowhere the old trouble was breaking out once more—and at the worst possible time in the whole year, when the city was thronged and overflowing far into the country on every side with multitudes of the fanatical creatures, two million of them, it is said, only too ready and willing to be inflamed. These wretched priests would soon have this inflammable mass ablaze, and once more the gutters would be running blood. And that was not to be. The orders given him were strict that bloodshed was to be avoided and that peace must be kept unbroken. Thus, looking at it from Pilate's standpoint, it comes down to this, that it was to keep peace Christ's cross was set up on Calvary.

"It is better for you that one man die for the people" (John 11:50), Caiaphas announced. And Pilate, put in a cruel dilemma, came at last to think that of it too. The man was innocent. But if he set him free, far worse was bound to happen; lives by the score would be sacrificed, and who could say where it would end? We must have peace. That was the one fixed point. And yet he hesitated, was unwilling. If only this had happened any other time! But with these Passover crowds about I cannot risk it. Peace we must have, and he must die. Quite plainly Pilate was impressed by Christ. Yet no doubt there is something in what Luther says. "Pilate took our Savior Christ to be a simple, honest, ignorant man, one perchance come out of a wilderness; a simple fellow, a hermit who knew or understood nothing of the world or of government." Yes, it was a pity, but he must die.

—Arthur John Gossip

None of the rulers of this age understood it, for if they had,
they would not have crucified the Lord of glory.
—1 Corinthians 2:8

It is easy to say that if the man was innocent, then let the heavens fall, but let justice be done.[30] Yet not so long ago, in our own empire, a mob gathered where they had been forbidden, a shot was fired, several shots, and a thrill of horror swept us. But when those in authority stated that not to have fired meant an uprising and ugly massacres over a widespread area, we settled down again, reflecting that it was a dreadful position in which they were placed, and no doubt they did what was best where nothing could be good—and said no more about it. They must judge, there on the spot. Pilate, too, had to judge on the spot. And, looking long at Jesus, slowly he brought himself to vote for peace.

And we had better think of that. For today we are all agog for peace—must have it. And it is little wonder, for those who have once seen war have no desire to see it again. The thing is an insanity. For, quite obviously, to hurl chunks of metal at each other can prove nothing regarding the original dispute. And we do well to labor zealously to make it a bad dream and a forgotten horror. For no one can imagine what another war, with all the devilments of science thrown in, would be.

Yet we can go too far in our pursuit of peace. Is our zeal for it altogether pure or that of a tired world that is not going to make any further sacrifices? Peace! Peace! we cry. Yet what about righteousness? Was Pilate right? And are we not beginning to slip into his mood? Two little nations snarl at each other. And we are very bold. Be off, we say, and they slink away, making faces at each other. But a great power bullies a little one and announces it will brook no interference, that this touches its national honor. And we all gaze the other way. We must have peace. What about righteousness? Was Pilate right? Ekken, a great Japanese philosopher, remarks that "if a man will not give his life for righteousness he does not know the relative values of righteousness and life."

Pilate, too, tried to dodge trouble. But you can't. Are we, too, trying that? Are we, too, sinking to that level? What if a day comes when you can't have peace and righteousness? What if the gutters must just run with blood and our homes again be broken—and our hearts—or Christ be led to Calvary? What then?

—Arthur John Gossip

*None of the rulers of this age understood it, for if they had,
they would not have crucified the Lord of glory.*
—1 Corinthians 2:8

[What was] the role of the people, the decent, foolish, likable, thoughtless people?[31] It was they who did it, for they could have stopped it. When Pilate left it to them, no doubt he was quite certain he had found the way to free Christ. For he must have known of the enthusiasm for him in the streets. There could be no doubt about the popular verdict. And he was plainly disconcerted when there came that long shout for Barabbas and not a single voice for Christ.

It was only a little gathering, of course. But where were the others, those on whom Pilate had relied? They must have heard of Christ's arrest and trial, yet they who could have saved him were not there. There were the usual excuses. After all, it was no affair of theirs. They were busy sight-seeing, for it was not often they were up in the capital. They had friends to look up, and these had detained them. Or they were worshiping in the temple. Or they felt there was no need for them to hurry to the court. Christ could not be in any pressing danger. He would be all right. The others would be there to shout for him. There was no lack of voices yesterday. They need not bother running through the heat. And so, because everyone felt there was no need to be there, Christ died—a perfectly unnecessary death, if only even a few had done their part.

Let us remember that. For isn't it just this way that things the world cries for get delayed and frustrated? It isn't through ill-will nor through hostility but because people can't be bothered voting or are made to feel that they make no difference that changes are not made. Yet we can all do something that would help. Not much perhaps, yet yours and yours and yours and mine, added together, would be quite enough. And it is because these littles we could offer are lacking that nothing happens, and the shame goes on. We are not hostile, we are not indifferent, we are not against it. But we are not there. And so again Christ dies.

So true it is that we, too, you and I, have crucified the Lord of glory and subjected him to public disgrace. It was not something gross, unthinkable, obscene, that brought Christ to his cross, but little decent sins of ordinary decent people, such as we sin every day. Look at your hands, and make sure you do not have Christ's blood on them even now!

—Arthur John Gossip

> *God is spirit, and his worshipers must*
> *worship in spirit and in truth.*
>
> —John 4:24

Why should we worship God?[32] [First,] because it is due to him.

Robert Hall said that the idea of God subordinates to itself all that is great, borrows splendor from all that is fair, and sits enthroned on the riches of the universe. More than that is true. All that exalts our souls ought to lift them up toward God.

Especially we ought to adore the holiness of God. There is not a human heart that does not somehow, sometimes, love goodness. Find the most wicked in your city, and there are times when they admire goodness. I imagine there are times when they hope that they may yet be good themselves. When someone we love has died, we are prone to exaggerate in our funeral discourse, in our inscriptions on tombstones. We seldom exaggerate in speaking of a person's talents or learning or possessions or influence, but we are ready to exaggerate her or his goodness. We feel that goodness is the great thing for someone who has gone into the unseen world. Long ago, a prophet saw the Lord seated high on a throne in the temple, with flowing robes of majesty, and on either side adoring seraphs bent and worshiped, and what was the theme of their worship?: "Holy, holy, holy is the LORD Almighty; the whole earth is full of his glory" (Isa. 6:3). And there do come times when we want to adore the holiness of God.

Then think of his love and mercy! He hates sin. And yet he loves sinners! How he yearns over the sinful! How he longs to save them! God so loved the world that he gave his one and only Son, that whoever will have it so, might through him be saved.

Holiness and redemption! We ought to adore if we had nothing to do with it, for we have a moral nature to appreciate it. And are we uninvolved spectators? That most wonderful demonstration of God's mercy and love has been made toward us. And if the angels find their highest theme of praise in what the gracious God has done for us, how should we feel about it? Yes, there is a sense in which, amid the infirmities of earth, we can pay God a worship that the angels cannot offer.

And sinful beings out of grateful hearts for sins forgiven may strike a note of praise to God that will pierce through all the high anthems of the skies and enter into the ear of the Lord God Almighty.

—John A. Broadus

*God is spirit, and his worshipers must
worship in spirit and in truth.*

—John 4:24

Why should we worship God?[33] Not only because it is due to him but, [second,] because it is good for us.

If you look on the glory of the autumn woods; if you gaze on the splendor of the night sky; if you stand in awe before the great mountains, snow-clad and towering; if you gaze on the rush of the river or stand by the seashore and hear the rolling waters, there swells in the breast something that wants God for its crown and for its completeness. There are yearnings in these strange natures of ours that only God can satisfy. Our thinking is a mutilated fragment without God, and our hearts can never rest unless they rest in him.

Sometimes only worship can soothe our sorrows and our anxieties. There come times with all of us when everything else fails us; there come times when we go to speak with sorrowing friends and feel that all our themes are weak and empty. You went to visit a friend who had lost a child or husband or wife, and as you sat by your friend and wanted to say something comforting, you felt that everything else was useless but to point the sorrowing heart to God—and you felt ashamed of yourself that you did not dare to do that. How often have devout hearts found comfort in sorrow, found support in anxiety, by the worship of God, by the thought of submission to God and trust in God, a belief that God knows what he is doing, that God sees the end from the beginning, that in all things God works for the good of those who love him!

Further, the worship of God nourishes the root of morality—individual and social. Morality cannot live on mere ideas of expediency and utility. The root of morality is the sentiment of moral obligation. What does it mean when your child first begins to say "I ought to do this" and "I shouldn't do that"? What does it mean? "I ought." It is the glory of being human. It makes us in the image of the one who made us. And what is to nourish and keep alive and make strong that sentiment of moral obligation in our souls? It is the recognition that there is a God who gave us this high, moral, spiritual being, who made us for himself, to whom we belong. Our worship of him nourishes in us the highest and best. How can I tell the reasons why we should worship God? They are as high as heaven, as vast as the universe; all existence and all conception—everything is a reason why we should worship God.

—John A. Broadus

As the offering began, singing to the Lord began also.
—2 Chronicles 29:27

It is not till the burnt offering begins that we ever hear a single strain of music.[34] Every human life has got its shadow, and every human life has got its cross. It is well to distinguish the shadow from the cross, lest by confusing them we go astray. For the shadow is something into which we enter and out of which we will pass in God's good time. But the cross is something that we must take up, or stumble over into the mouth of hell. Now one of the deepest questions in life is, "In what way do you regard your crosses?" Do you hate them? Do you rebel against them? Would you give anything to fling them from you? Along that road there is no voice of song. Along that road there is the hardening heart. Along that road there is a growing bitterness, the foretaste of the bitterness of death. But take up your cross, as Jesus bids you do—take it up as a mother takes her child. Lay it against your heart and cherish it—say "This, too, like the summer roses, is from God." And so this is how your poor life will become a harmony—and what is harmony but perfect music—and when the burnt offering begins, the song of the Lord will begin also.

—George H. Morrison

This is the name by which he will be called:
The LORD Our Righteousness.

—Jeremiah 23:6

Self-righteousness is the last idol that is rooted out of the heart.[35] And we have contracted such a devilish pride by our fall from God that we would, in part at least, glory in being the cause of our own salvation. It is true we disclaim the doctrine of merit and are ashamed to say we deserve any good at the hands of God. Therefore, as the apostle observes, we seek to establish a righteousness of our own and, like the Pharisees of old, will not wholly submit to God's righteousness that is through Jesus Christ.

The righteousness of Jesus Christ is one of those great mysteries that the angels desire to look into and seems to be one of the first lessons that God taught people after the Fall. For what were the garments that God made to put on our first parents but types of the application of the merits of the righteousness of Jesus Christ to believers' hearts? We are told that those garments were made of skins of beasts, and as beasts were not then human food, we may fairly infer that those beasts were killed in sacrifice, in commemoration of the great sacrifice, Jesus Christ, to be offered later. And the skins of those beasts thus killed being put on Adam and Eve, they were by this taught how their nakedness was to be covered with the righteousness of the Lamb of God.

This is what is meant when we are told Abraham believed God, and it was credited to him as righteousness. In short, this is it of which both the law and all the prophets have spoken, especially Jeremiah in the words of the text: "The LORD Our Righteousness."

The person mentioned in the text under the character of Lord is Jesus Christ. By "righteous Branch" (Jer. 23:5), all agree that we are to understand Jesus Christ. He it is who is called "the LORD" in our text. If there were no other text in the Bible to prove the divinity of Christ, that is sufficient. For if the word *Lord* may properly belong to Jesus Christ, he must be God. For as you have it in the margins of your Bibles, the word *Lord* is in the original *Jehovah,* which is the essential title of God himself. It is plain that by the word *Lord* we are to understand the Lord Jesus Christ who here takes to himself the title of *Jehovah* and therefore must be very God of very God, or, as the apostle devoutly expresses it, God over all, forever praised.

—George Whitefield

This is the name by which he will be called:
The Lord *Our Righteousness.*

—Jeremiah 23:6

The Lord is our righteousness by *imputation.*[36] For it pleased God, after he had made all things, to create the human race in his own image. And so infinite was the condescension of the one who lives forever that, although he might have insisted on the everlasting obedience of Adam and his posterity, he obliged himself by a covenant made with his own creatures, on condition of obedience, to give them eternal life. For when it is said, "For when you eat of it you will surely die" (Gen. 2:17), we may infer that as long as they continued obedient and did not eat of it, they would surely live. Genesis 3 gives us a full account of how our first parents broke this covenant and therefore stood in need of a better righteousness than their own in order to procure their future acceptance with God.

Here then opens the scene of divine philanthropy—God's love to humanity. For what we could not do, Jesus Christ undertakes for us. And that God might be just and the one who justifies those who have faith in Jesus, he took the nature of a servant, even human nature. In that nature he obeyed and thereby fulfilled the whole moral law in our stead; he also died on the cross and by that became a curse for, or instead of, those whom the Father had given him. As God and human in one person, he satisfied at the same time that he obeyed and worked out a full and perfect righteousness for all to whom it was to be imputed.

Here then we see the meaning of the word *righteousness.* It implies the active as well as passive obedience of the Lord Jesus Christ. Generally, when talking of the merits of Christ we only mention the latter—his death—whereas his life and active obedience are equally necessary. Christ is not the Savior we need unless we join both together. Christ not only died but lived; not only suffered but obeyed for, or instead of, sinners. And both these jointly make up that complete righteousness that is to be imputed to us, as the disobedience of our first parents was made ours by imputation. This is what [Paul] elsewhere terms our becoming in Christ the righteousness of God. This is the sense in which the prophet would have us understand the words of the text—the church itself "will be called," having this righteousness imputed to her, "the Lord Our Righteousness" (Jer. 33:16). A passage, I think, worthy of the profoundest meditation of all the descendants of Adam.

—George Whitefield

This is the name by which he will be called:
The LORD Our Righteousness.

—Jeremiah 23:6

If we deny this doctrine of salvation by grace, we turn the truth—the Word of God—into a lie.[37] We subvert all Scripture that says we have been saved by grace, not by works, so that no one can boast—that salvation is God's free gift. For if the whole personal righteousness of Jesus Christ is not the sole cause of my acceptance with God, if any work done by me was in the least looked on by God as a cause for acquitting my soul from guilt, then I have something for which I may boast. Now boasting is excluded in the great work of our redemption. But that cannot be if we are enemies to the doctrine of an imputed righteousness. It would be endless to enumerate how many texts of Scripture must be false if this doctrine is not true. Let it suffice to affirm that if we deny imputed righteousness, we may as well deny divine revelation.

Can you say, *The Lord our righteousness?* For entertaining this doctrine in your heads, without receiving the Lord Jesus Christ by a living faith into your hearts, will only increase your damnation. An unapplied Christ is no Christ at all.

Is Christ your sanctification as well as your outward righteousness? For the word "righteousness" in the text not only implies Christ's personal righteousness imputed to us, but also holiness of heart worked in us. These two God has joined together. He never will separate them. If you are justified by the blood, you are also sanctified by the Spirit of the Lord. Were you ever made to detest yourselves for your actual and original sins and to loathe your own righteous acts as filthy rags? Were you ever made to see and admire the all-sufficiency of Christ's righteousness and excited by the Spirit of God to be thirsty for the righteousness of Christ?

And after these inward conflicts, were you ever enabled to reach out the arm of faith and embrace Jesus in your souls, so that you could say, *My lover is mine and I am his?* If so, fear not. The Lord Christ, the everlasting God, is your righteousness. Christ has justified you.

Think on the love of Christ in dying for you! If the Lord is your righteousness, let the righteousness of your Lord be continually in your mouth. Talk of and recommend the righteousness of Christ. Think of the greatness of the gift as well as the giver.

—George Whitefield

> *Remember those earlier days after you had received the light, when you stood your ground in a great contest in the face of suffering.*
>
> —Hebrews 10:32

No blessing is nobler than illumination.[38] It tells of the benediction of the light, of a life that has arisen from darkness and moved into the sun. After illumination—a great joy? We would have looked for some conclusion such as that. After illumination, liberty and peace that the world cannot take away? Scripture does not deny these blessed consequences, but in its fidelity to all experience it says that after illumination may come battle.

Think, then, of the illumination of the intellect and of all that follows on the light of knowledge. That is not always liberty and power; it is sometimes conflict. When Eve ate of the tree of the knowledge of good and evil, her eyes were opened, and she was illuminated, yet that light did not bring peace to Eve nor gladness nor any rest of the heart, but only the sorrow of struggle. The more we know the more we want to know. The more we know the more we cannot know. And doubts are born and much that once seemed certain grows unstable, until at last, wearied and in perplexity, not through the power of darkness but of light, we realize how grim is the struggle that follows illumination.

There are those here who can recall the struggle that followed the light. Here for instance is a young man, a student, who has been trained in a pious home. There he accepted without questioning the faith of his father and mother. Their character commended it to him—he saw it lived and therefore felt it true—and in a faith that never had been shaken, he joined in worship and in prayer. There are many who never lose that childhood faith. But often, with that light of knowledge that the years bring to most of us today, there falls a different story. Illumination comes by what we read: it flashes on us in our college lectures. And the world is different, and God and humanity are different. And then begins that time of stress and strain, so bitter and yet so infinitely blessed, through which people must fight their way, alone, to faith and peace and character and God. There is a strife that is nobler than repose. There is a battle more blessed than tranquility. There is a stress and strain that comes when God arises and cries to a young heart "Let there be light." All which, so modern that it seems of yesterday, is yet so old that Scripture understands it.

—George H. Morrison

*Remember those earlier days after you had received the
light, when you stood your ground in a great contest in the
face of suffering.*

—Hebrews 10:32

It may be we have been groping in the darkness, not seeing clearly what our duty was.[39] And choice was difficult, so much depended on it—there was so much to win, so much to lose. And then it may be in one radiant hour, never to be forgotten throughout the years, we heard, as it were, a voice behind us saying, "This is the way; walk in it." Perhaps by some word from friendly lips or by some providence or disappointment, clear as the sun shining in midheavens we saw what for us must be the path of duty. Such hours of high and resolute decision are among the greatest hours of human life. There is not a power or faculty we have that is not illuminated by the glory of them. And yet the struggle and torment that preceded them, when we were stumbling and groping toward decision, may not be half so terrible and searching as the struggle and the strain that follow after. Never do things renounced appeal to us so sweetly and so subtly and so secretly as in the season when we have turned our backs on them and set our faces bravely to the morn. The most difficult task in life is not to win. The most difficult task is to keep what we have won—never to falter, when the shadows deepen, from the verdict of our high and radiant hours; never to go back on our decisions; never to listen again to any voices that in our worthiest and purest moments we knew to be the voices of the Enemy. That is the reason why great decisions ought to be reinforced by prayer. There is no weapon on earth like prayer for helping us to keep what we have won. For prayer unites us to the living Christ and touches the vilest of us with the touch of heaven and brings to our aid that power of perfect living which was witnessed long ago in Galilee. In the gloomiest day you may lift your heart up and draw for your need out of the grace of Jesus. And so the highest comes back to us once more, and we see it and love it again, for all our faltering.

—George H. Morrison

Remember those earlier days after you had received the light, when you stood your ground in a great contest in the face of suffering.

—Hebrews 10:32

The illumination of the heart is love.[40] Just as the light of the intellect is truth, so the light of every heart is love. Without love the heart is always dark, and with love the heart is always light. The most common dwelling becomes a palace with it, and there is sunshine for the dreariest day. And all the wealth of Ormus and of Ind and all the joy of fame and whirl of fashion can never irradiate these hearts of ours like love. Whoever dwells in love dwells in God, and whoever dwells in God is in the light. The luster of the heart is always there, but it is unlighted until love comes in. And now remember the former days in which, after you were illuminated, you endured a great fight of afflictions. Long years ago some of you mothers here gathered you firstborn child into your arms, and there was such gladness in these eyes of yours that every neighbor saw your life illuminated. And now as you look back on it all and think of all that has come and gone since then, you know the sorrows that have followed love. What sleepless nights—what hours of weary watching—what seasons of agony when death was near! What struggle to do what was hard to do, when wills were rebellious and lips untruthful. All this followed the illumination that came when the love of motherhood was born, and all this is the anguish of the light. Let people love their work, and in that light they will be led to many a weary wrestling. Let people love their land, and in that light they will take up burdens that are not easily borne. Let people love their risen and living Savior, and in that light their lives will be a battlefield, as they struggle daily not against flesh and blood but against the rulers and the powers of this dark world. Love has its triumphs, but it has its tortures. Love has its paradise and it has its purgatory. Love has its mountains of transfiguration and its love gardens where the sweat is blood. Love is the secret of the sweetest song that ever was uttered by human lips, and love is the secret of the keenest suffering that ever pierced the heart.

—George H. Morrison

Then he said to Thomas, "Put your finger here; see my
hands. Reach out your hand and put it into my side.
Stop doubting and believe."

—John 20:27

We are born questioners.[41] Look at the wonderment in a little child's eyes before it can speak. The child's great word when it begins to speak is "Why?" Every child is full of questions about everything that moves and shines and changes in the little world in which he or she lives.

That is the commencement of doubt in human nature. Respect doubt for its origin. It is an inevitable thing. It is not a thing to be crushed. It is a part of humanity as God made us. Heresy is truth in the making, and doubt is the prelude of knowledge.

Further, the world is a Sphinx—an unfathomable mystery—and on every side there is temptation to questioning. In every leaf, in every cell of every leaf, there are a hundred problems. Someone spends ten years investigating what is in a leaf and five years more investigating the things that are in the things that are in the leaf. God planned the world to incite us to intellectual activity.

But the instrument with which we investigate truth is impaired. Some say it fell, and the glass is broken. Some say prejudice, heredity, or sin has spoiled its sight and has blinded our eyes and deadened our ears. In any case, the instruments with which we work on truth, even in the strongest people, are feeble and inadequate to their task.

And all religious truths are doubtable. There is no absolute proof for any one of them. Even the fundamental truth—the existence of a God—no one can prove by reason. The ordinary proof for the existence of God involves either an assumption, an argument in a circle, or a contradiction. The impression of God is kept up by experience, not by logic. And thus when the experience of religion of an individual, of a community, or of a nation wanes—their idea of God grows indistinct, and that individual, community, or nation becomes infidel.

This brief account of the origin of doubt teaches us intellectual humility. It teaches us sympathy and toleration with all who venture after truth to find their own paths. Let us never think evil of those who do not see as we do. Let us pity them and take them by the hand and spend time and thought over them and try to lead them to the true light.

—Henry Drummond

Then he said to Thomas, "Put your finger here; see my hands. Reach out your hand and put it into my side. Stop doubting and believe."

—John 20:27

What has been the church's treatment of doubt?[42] It has been very simple. "Burn the heretic!"

We have got past that physically; have we got past it morally? What does the modern church say to [the] skeptical? Not "Burn them!" but "Brand them!" Perhaps that is the treatment we are inclined to give to those who cannot see the truths of Christianity as we see them.

Contrast Christ's treatment of doubt. [Consider] his partiality for outsiders—for the scattered heretics up and down the country, of the care with which he dealt with them and of the respect in which he held their intellectual difficulties. Christ never failed to distinguish between doubt and unbelief. Doubt is *can't* believe, unbelief is *won't* believe. Doubt is looking for light, unbelief is content with darkness. Loving darkness rather than light—that is what Christ attacked. But for the intellectual questioning of Thomas, Philip, Nicodemus, and the many others who came to him to have their problems solved, he was respectful and generous and tolerant.

And how did he meet their doubts? "Teach them." Thomas came to him and denied his very resurrection and stood before him waiting for scathing words for his unbelief. They never came! Christ gave him facts—facts! No one can go around facts. Christ said, "Look at my hands and my feet" (Luke 24:39). The great god of science is a fact. Its cry is, "Give me facts. Base anything you like on facts, and we will believe it." The spirit of Christ was the scientific spirit. He founded his religion on facts, and he asked all people to found their religion on facts.

Take people to the facts. Theologies are human versions of divine truths and hence the varieties and inconsistencies of them. Allow people to select whichever version of this truth they like afterward, but ask them to begin with no version but go back to the facts and base their Christian lives on these.

That is the great lesson of Christ's treatment of doubt. It is not "Brand them!" but teach them. Faith is never opposed to reason in the New Testament; it is opposed to sight. You will find that a principle worth thinking over.

—Henry Drummond

Then he said to Thomas, "Put your finger here; see my
hands. Reach out your hand and put it into my side.
Stop doubting and believe."

—John 20:27

How are we to deal with those who are in intellectual difficulty?[43]

First, we make all the concessions to them that we conscientiously can. When doubters first encounter you, they pour out a deluge of abuse of churches and ministers and creeds and Christians. Nine-tenths of what they say is probably true. Make concessions. Agree with them. It does them good to unburden themselves of these things, and they are startled to find a Christian who almost entirely agrees with them. We are of course not responsible for everything that is said in the name of Christianity—a person does not give up medicine because there are quack doctors, and people do not have a right to give up their Christianity because there are spurious or inconsistent Christians. We ask them to accept Christ and the facts about Christ and the words of Christ. These people are in revolt against the kind of religion that we exhibit to the world—against the cant that is taught in the name of Christianity. And if they have never seen the real thing—if you could show them that, they would receive it as eagerly as you do.

Second, beg them to set aside, by an act of will, all unsolved problems such as the origin of evil, the problem of the Trinity, and so on—problems that have been investigated for thousands of years without result—as insoluble. In the meantime, just as a person who is studying mathematics may be asked to set aside the problem of squaring the circle, let them go on with what can be done and what has been done and leave out of sight the impossible. That will relieve the skeptic's mind of a great deal of unnecessary cargo that has been in the way.

Third, talking about difficulties only aggravates them. Entire satisfaction to the intellect about any of the greater problems is unattainable, and if you try to get to the bottom, there is no bottom there; therefore you make the matter worse. Say what is known and what can be honestly, philosophically, and scientifically said about one or two of the difficulties that doubters raise, just to show that you are not merely groping in the dark yourself, but you have found whatever basis is possible. It would be a pity if all these problems could be solved. The joy of the intellectual life would be largely gone, and the whole intellectual world would be stale and unprofitable if we knew everything.

—Henry Drummond

*Then he said to Thomas, "Put your finger here; see my
hands. Reach out your hand and put it into my side.
Stop doubting and believe."*

—John 20:27

How [else] are we to deal with those who are in intellectual difficulty?[44] Turn away from the reason and open a new door into the practical side of human nature. Entreat doubters not to postpone their usefulness until they have settled the problems of the universe. Tell them those problems will never all be settled, that their lives will be done before they have begun to settle them, and ask them what they are doing with their lives meantime. Invite them to deal with the moral and practical difficulties of the world and leave the intellectual difficulties as they go along. To spend time on these is to prove the less important before the more important, and as the French say, The good is the enemy of the best. It is a good thing to think; it is a better thing to work—it is a better thing to do good. And you have them there. They can't get beyond that. Tell them, in fact, that there are two organs of knowledge, the one reason, the other obedience. And now tell them, since they have tried the first and found the little in it, just for a moment try the second. And when they ask whom they are to obey, tell them there is but one, and lead them to the historical figure who calls all people to him, the one perfect life, the Savior of humankind, the one Light of the world. Ask them to begin to obey Christ, and, doing his will, they will know whether his teaching comes from God.

That is about the only thing you can do with people, to get them into practical contact with the needs of the world and to let them lose their intellectual difficulties meantime. Don't ask them to give them up altogether. Tell them to solve them afterward one by one if they can, but meantime to give their lives to Christ and their time to the kingdom of God. You fetch them completely around when you do that. You have taken them away from the false side of their natures, and for the first time in their lives perhaps, they put things in their true place. They put their natures in the relations in which they ought to be, and they then only begin to live. By obedience they will soon become learners—Christ will teach them things. And they will find whatever problems are solvable gradually solved as they go along the path of practical duty.

—Henry Drummond

When he opened his eyes he could see nothing.

—Acts 9:8

There was a young man once, in Old Testament times, who was sorely frightened by an Assyrian army.[45] And the prophet, in pity for him, prayed to God, "Lord, open the young man's eyes that he may see." And when the eyes of that young man were opened, he saw a sight to make any coward brave, for the mountain was full of the chariots of the Lord. That is the fitting consequence of vision. It reveals to us what we never saw before. It shows us in common hearts unlooked-for things and in common scenes an undiscovered glory.

Suppose we think of the little frets of life, of the little pinpricks and unkindnesses that most people experience as they journey. There are folk who brood on such things as these until they practically see nothing else. They tend and water all their little grievances until their blossoms would take prizes at a show. And what I have noticed of such folk is that when through the mercy of God their eyes are opened, of all these little pinpricks they see nothing. Their eyes have been opened to what real suffering is. They were only playing before at being miserable. Their eyes have been opened to that larger life that is always given us in Christ. And the beautiful thing about that life is that worries that were overwhelming yesterday somehow have vanished so that we cannot see them in the love demonstrated on the cross. Every rock and ridge is clear and glistening in the Highland brook when it is low. But when the summer rain falls or the winter snow, then they become invisible. And I have found it so in many people's lives when a new tide of being has possessed them. Things that were sharp and hard and hurt yesterday, somehow have become invisible today.

—George H. Morrison

When he opened his eyes he could see nothing.
—Acts 9:8

Our text, as it seems to me, applies to many of those messages with which the world is ringing.[46] There are faiths and philosophies that vanish when you see. When the sun is shining on you and the world is beautiful, you go, for instance, to hear a certain preacher. You have never been plunged into the depths yet and have never felt your utter need of Christ. And the man is artistic or he is intellectual or he has the fire and passion of the orator, and you feel as if you would never want another message. If the sun were always shining, it may be that such a message would be sufficient. But this is a strange, grim world with lightning flashes and storms that cry havoc and waves that cruelly beat. And when these days come, and you feel your need of Christ and of an arm to lean on and a hand to save you, no charm of speech—no intellect or artistry—can reach and grip and satisfy the soul. You want a power to hold you out of hell. You want a love that goes to the limit. You want a heart on which to lean securely though the whole universe should fall in ruin. And whenever through trial and suffering and sorrow your eyes have been opened to see that, then in the fine, artistic preaching you see nothing. Nothing to pluck you from the miry clay. Nothing commensurate with sin and hell. Nothing that can be heard across the battle, like the voice of the trumpet summoning to victory. That is why the old and chastened saints who have suffered and struggled, battled, conquered, and fallen feel sometimes that there is not a word for them in preaching that may be exquisite as music.

In the case of Paul and in the case of many people since Paul, this is what happens when through the Holy Spirit our eyes are opened to see that we are sinners. There was a Pharisee once who came up to the temple, and he thanked God he was not as others. He fasted and was an exemplary person; he was proud of all he was and all he did. In that same temple was a publican whose eyes had been opened by the grace of God, and when his eyes were opened, he saw nothing. Nothing of all his fasting and his tithing, nothing of all he had ever striven to do. His best was sinful. His life had been a failure. "God, have mercy on me, a sinner." When you see nothing, you see Christ. When you see that your best is rags, you see his riches. When you see at last that you have nothing to plead, you are ready for all the gladness of his grace.

—*George* H. *Morrison*

> *"The Lion of the tribe of Judah, the Root of David, has*
> *triumphed. He is able to open the scroll and its seven*
> *seals." Then I saw a Lamb, looking as if it had been slain,*
> *standing in the center of the throne.*
>
> —*Revelation 5:5–6*

Notice the two distinct names here given to Christ.[47]

He is called a Lion, the Lion of the tribe of Judah in allusion [perhaps] to what Jacob said in his blessing on his deathbed, when he compared Judah to a lion. It is much on account of the valiant acts of David that the tribe of Judah, of which David was, is in Jacob's prophetic blessing compared to a lion, but more especially with an eye to Jesus Christ, who also was of that tribe and was descended from David and is in our text called "the Root of David."

He is called a Lamb. John was told of a Lion that had prevailed to open the book and probably expected to see a lion in his vision, but a lamb appears to open the book, a very different kind of creature from a lion! A lion is a devourer, accustomed to make terrible slaughter of others, and no creature more easily falls a prey to him than a lamb. And Christ is here represented not only as a lamb, but a lamb as if it had been slain, that is, with the marks of its deadly wounds.

There is a coming together of admirable virtues in Jesus Christ. The lion and the lamb, though very different, yet have their peculiar virtues. The lion excels in strength and in the majesty of its appearance and voice; the lamb excels in meekness and patience, besides [being] good for food and yielding [wool] for clothing and being suitable to be offered in sacrifice to God. But we see that Christ is in the text compared to both, because the different virtues of both wonderfully meet in him.

From this doctrine we may learn one reason why Christ is called by such a variety of names and held forth under such a variety of representations in Scripture. It is the better to signify and exhibit to us the variety of virtues that meet together in him. Many names are mentioned together in one verse: "For to us a child is born, to us a son is given. . . . And he will be called Wonderful Counselor, Mighty God, Everlasting Father, Prince of Peace" (Isa. 9:6). It shows a wonderful conjunction of virtues, that the same person should be a son, born and given, and yet be the everlasting Father; that he should be a child and yet be he whose name is Counselor and Mighty God. And well may his name, in whom such things are brought together, be called Wonderful.

—Jonathan Edwards

Love and faithfulness meet together; righteousness and
peace kiss each other.

—Psalm 85:10

Such different virtues are expressed in [Christ] toward us that otherwise would have seemed impossible, particularly these three: justice, mercy, and truth.[48]

The strict *justice* of God, and even his revenging justice, against human sins never was so gloriously displayed as in Christ. He showed an infinite regard to God's justice in that, when he had a mind to save sinners, he was willing to undergo such extreme sufferings rather than that their salvation should injure the honor of [God's justice]. And as he is the judge of the world, he himself exercises strict justice; "he does not leave the guilty unpunished" (Exod. 34:7).

Yet how wonderfully is *mercy* toward sinners displayed in him! And what grace and love have been and are exercised by him toward sinful people! Though he is the judge of a sinful world, yet he is also the Savior of the world. Though he is a consuming fire to sin, yet he is the light and life of sinners: "God presented him as a sacrifice of atonement, through faith in his blood. He did this to demonstrate his justice, because in his forbearance he had left the sins committed beforehand unpunished—he did it to demonstrate his justice at the present time, so as to be just and the one who justifies those who have faith in Jesus" (Rom. 3:25–26).

So the changeless *truth* of God in the punishments threatened in his law against human sins was never so displayed as it is in Jesus Christ, for there never was any greater trial of the unchangeableness of the truth of God as when sin was charged to his own Son. And then in Christ has been seen already an actual, complete accomplishment of those threats, which never has been nor will be seen in any other instance, because the eternity that will be taken up in fulfilling those threats on others never will be finished. Christ showed an infinite regard to this truth of God in his sufferings. And, in his judging the world, he makes the covenant of works that contains those dreadful threats his rule of judgment. He will see to it that it is not infringed in the least jot or tittle: he will do nothing contrary to the threats of the law and their complete fulfillment. And yet in him we have many great and precious promises, promises of perfect deliverance from the penalty of the law. And this is what he promised us—eternal life. And in him all the promises of God are *Yes* and *Amen.*

—Jonathan Edwards

"See, the Lion of the tribe of Judah . . . has triumphed. . . ."
Then I saw a Lamb, looking as if it had been slain.
—Revelation 5:5–6

There meet in Jesus Christ infinite highness and infinite condescension.[49]

Christ, as God, is infinitely great and high above all. He is higher than the kings of the earth, for he is King of Kings. He is so high that he is infinitely above any need of us, above our reach that we cannot be profitable to him, and above our conceptions that we cannot comprehend him. Christ is the Creator and great possessor of heaven and earth. He rules over the whole universe and does whatever pleases him. His knowledge is without bound. His wisdom is perfect and what none can circumvent. His power is infinite, and none can resist him. His riches are immense and inexhaustible. His majesty is infinitely awful.

Yet none are so low or inferior but Christ takes notice of them. He lowers himself not only to the angels, humbling himself to view the things that are done in heaven, but he also stoops to such poor creatures as the human—not only to take notice of rulers and great ones but of those who are lowest, the "poor in the eyes of the world" (James 2:5). Those commonly despised by others Christ does not despise: "He chose the lowly things of this world and the despised" (1 Cor. 1:28). He takes notice of little children: "Let the little children to come to me" (Matt. 19:14). Yes, which is more, he takes notice of the most unworthy, sinful creatures, those who deserve no good and those who deserve infinite ill.

He becomes their friend, their companion, unites their souls to him in spiritual marriage. He takes their nature on him, becomes one of them, that he may be one with them. He descends yet lower for them, even to expose himself to shame and spitting; yes, to yield himself to an ignominious death for them. And what greater act of self-abasement can be conceived of? Yet such an act as this has he yielded to.

Such a coming together of infinite highness and low condescension in the same person is admirable. In many people, a high standing has a tendency to make them quite contrary. If one worm is a little exalted above another, having more dust or a bigger dunghill, how much does it make of itself! What a distance it keeps from those below! Christ stoops to wash our feet, but great men and women (or, rather, the bigger worms!) consider themselves debased by acts far less humble!

—Jonathan Edwards

> *"See, the Lion of the tribe of Judah . . . has triumphed. . . ."*
> *Then I saw a Lamb, looking as if it had been slain.*
> —*Revelation 5:5–6*

There meet in the person of Christ diverse qualities that would have been thought utterly incompatible in the same person.[50] These are brought together in no other person, either divine, human, or angelic.

Infinite glory and lowest humility. Infinite glory and the virtue of humility meet in no other person but Christ. They meet in no created person, for no created person has infinite glory, and they meet in no other divine person but Christ. For though the divine nature is infinitely abhorrent to pride, yet humility is not properly attributed to God the Father and the Holy Spirit, who exist only in the divine nature, because [humility] is a proper quality only of a created nature.

But in Jesus Christ, who is both God and human, those two diverse qualities are united. He is a person infinitely exalted in glory and dignity. There is equal honor due to him with the Father. God himself says to him, "Your throne, O God, will last for ever and ever" (Heb. 1:8). And the same respect and worship is paid to him by the angels of heaven as to God the Father: "Let all God's angels worship him" (v. 6).

But however he is thus above all, yet he is lowest of all in humility. None ever was so aware of the distance between God and him or had a heart so humble before God as the man Jesus (Matt. 11:29). When he was here on earth, what humility appeared in him, in all his behavior: in his contentment in his inferior outward condition, living in the family of Joseph the carpenter and Mary, his mother, for thirty years together and afterwards choosing outward commonness, poverty, and contempt rather than earthly greatness; in his washing his disciples' feet and in all his speeches and behavior toward them; in his cheerfully taking the nature of a servant through his whole life and submitting to such immense humiliation at death!

Self-sufficiency and entire trust and reliance on God. As he is a divine person, he is self-sufficient, standing in need of nothing. All creatures are dependent on him; he is dependent on none but is absolutely independent.

Yet Christ entirely trusted in God—his enemies say that of him, "He trusts in God. Let God rescue him now if he wants him" (Matt. 27:43). And the apostle testifies, "He entrusted himself to him who judges justly" (1 Peter 2:23).

—Jonathan Edwards

> *"See, the Lion of the tribe of Judah. . . ." Then I saw a*
> *Lamb, looking as if it had been slain.*
> —Revelation 5:5–6

There meet in the person of Christ [other] diverse qualities that would have been thought incompatible in the same person.[51]

Infinite majesty and transcendent meekness. These again are two qualities that meet together in no other person but Christ. Meekness is a virtue proper only to the creature, for by it seems to be signified calmness and quietness arising from humility in changeable beings [who] are naturally liable to be put into a ruffle by the assaults of an injurious world. But Christ, being both God and human, has both majesty and meekness.

Christ was a person of infinite majesty. It is he who is spoken of in Psalm 45:3: "Gird your sword upon your side, O mighty one; clothe yourself with splendor and majesty." It is he who is mighty, "who rides on the clouds" (68:4). It is he who is awesome in his sanctuary (68:35), who is "mightier than the breakers of the sea" (93:4), before whom a "fire goes . . . and consumes his foes on every side" (97:3); at whose presence the earth quakes and the hills melt (Nah. 1:5); who sits "above the circle of the earth, and its people are like grasshoppers" (Isa. 40:22); who rebukes the sea and makes it dry (50:2); whose eyes are "like blazing fire" (Rev. 1:14); from whose presence and from whose power the wicked will be punished with everlasting destruction; who is "the blessed and only Ruler, the King of kings" (1 Tim. 6:15); whose "kingdom is an everlasting kingdom, and [whose] dominion endures through all generations" (Ps. 145:13).

And yet he was the most marvelous instance of meekness and humble quietness of spirit that ever was, agreeing with the prophecies of him: "See, your king comes to you, gentle and riding on a donkey" (Matt. 21:5). And, agreeing with what Christ declares of himself: "I am gentle and humble in heart" (Matt. 11:29). And agreeing with what was seen in his behavior, for there never was such an instance seen on earth of a meek behavior under injuries and reproaches and toward enemies; "when they hurled their insults at him, he did not retaliate; when he suffered, he made no threats" (1 Peter 2:23). He had a wonderful spirit of forgiveness, was ready to forgive his worst enemies and [even] prayed for them. With what meekness he appeared in the ring of soldiers [who] were scorning and mocking him; he was silent and "was led like a lamb to the slaughter" (Isa. 53:7). Thus is Christ a lion in majesty and a lamb in meekness.

—Jonathan Edwards

> *"See, the Lion of the tribe of Judah. . . ." Then I saw a*
> *Lamb, looking as if it had been slain.*
> —Revelation 5:5–6

There meet in the person of Christ [other] diverse qualities that would have been thought incompatible in the same person.[52]

The deepest reverence toward God and equality with God. Christ, when on earth, appeared full of holy reverence toward the Father. He paid worship to him, praying to him with postures of reverence: He "knelt down and prayed" (Luke 22:41). This became Christ as one who had taken on him the human nature, but at the same time he existed in the divine nature, so that his person was in every way equal to the person of the Father. God the Father has no attribute or perfection that the Son has not, in equal degree and equal glory.

Infinite worthiness of good and the greatest patience under sufferings of evil. He was perfectly innocent and deserved no suffering. He deserved nothing from God by any guilt of his own, and he deserved no ill from human beings. Yes, he was not only undeserving of suffering, but he was infinitely worthy—worthy of the infinite love of the Father, worthy of infinite and eternal happiness, and infinitely worthy of all possible esteem, love, and service from all peoples.

And yet he was perfectly patient under the greatest sufferings that ever were endured in this world: He "endured the cross, scorning its shame" (Heb. 12:2). He suffered nothing from his Father for his faults but for ours, and he suffered from humans not for his faults but for those things for which he was infinitely worthy of their love and honor, which made his patience the more wonderful and the more glorious: "How is it to your credit if you receive a beating for doing wrong and endure it? But if you suffer for doing good and you endure it, this is commendable before God. To this you were called, because Christ suffered for you, leaving you an example, that you should follow in his steps. 'He committed no sin, and no deceit was found in his mouth.' When they hurled their insults at him, he did not retaliate; when he suffered, he made no threats. Instead, he entrusted himself to him who judges justly. He himself bore our sins in his body on the tree, so that we might die to sins and live for righteousness; by his wounds you have been healed" (1 Peter 2:20–24). There is no such coming together of innocence, worthiness, and patience under sufferings as in the person of Christ.

—Jonathan Edwards

"See, the Lion of the tribe of Judah. . . ." Then *I saw a
Lamb, looking as if it had been slain.*
—Revelation 5:5–6

There meet in the person of Christ [other] diverse qualities that would have been thought incompatible in the same subject.[53]

Supreme obedience with supreme dominion over heaven and earth. Christ is the Lord of all things in two respects: as God-man and Mediator, his dominion is appointed, having it by delegation from God. But he is Lord of all things in another respect; since he is (by his original nature) God, he is by natural right the Lord of all and supreme over all as much as the Father. Thus, he has dominion over the world in his own right.

And yet in the same person is found the greatest obedience in the universe to the commands of God: "I do exactly what my Father commanded me" (John 14:31). Never anyone received commands from God of such difficulty and that were so great a trial of obedience as Jesus Christ. One of God's commands to him was that he should yield himself to those dreadful sufferings that he underwent. And Christ was thoroughly obedient to this command of God: "He humbled himself and became obedient to death—even death on a cross" (Phil. 2:8). Never was there such an instance of obedience in human or angel as this, though he was at the same time supreme Lord of both angels and humans.

Absolute sovereignty and perfect submission. Christ, as he is God, is the absolute sovereign of the world, the sovereign disposer of all events. The decrees of God are all his sovereign decrees, and the work of creation and all God's works of providence are his sovereign works. It is he who works out everything in conformity with the purpose of his will.

Yet Christ was the most wonderful instance of submission that ever appeared in the world. He was absolutely and perfectly submissive when he had a near and immediate prospect of his terrible sufferings and the dreadful cup that he was to drink. The idea and expectation of this made his soul sorrowful even unto death, putting him into such agony that his sweat was like drops of blood, falling to the ground. But in such circumstances he was wholly submissive to the will of God: "My Father, if it is possible, may this cup be taken from me. Yet not as I will, but as you will" (Matt. 26:39); "My Father, if it is not possible for this cup to be taken away unless I drink it, may your will be done" (v. 42).

—Jonathan Edwards

*"See, the Lion of the tribe of Judah. . . ." Then I saw a
Lamb, looking as if it had been slain.*
—Revelation 5:5–6

As there is such an admirable meeting of diverse virtues in Christ, so there is everything in him to render him worthy of your love and choice and to win and engage it.[54] Whatever there is or can be desirable in a friend is in Christ and that to the highest degree that can be desired.

Would you choose for a friend a person of great dignity? [People like] to have those for their friends who are much above them, because they look on themselves honored by the friendship of such. Christ is infinitely above you and above all the princes of the earth, for he is the King of Kings. So honorable a person as this offers himself to you in the nearest and dearest friendship.

And would you choose to have a friend not only great but good? In Christ infinite greatness and infinite goodness meet together and receive luster and glory from one another. His greatness is rendered lovely by his goodness. And how glorious is the sight, to see him who is the great Creator and supreme Lord of heaven and earth, full of condescension, tender pity, and mercy toward the degraded and unworthy! His almighty power and infinite majesty and self-sufficiency render his great love and grace the more surprising. And his condescension and compassion endear his majesty, power, and dominion and render those attributes pleasant that would otherwise be only terrible.

Would you choose not only that the infinite greatness and majesty of your friend would be tempered and sweetened with condescension and grace, but would you also desire to have your friend brought nearer to you? Would you choose a friend far above you and yet on a level with you too? Thus is Christ. Though he is the great God, yet he has brought himself down to be on a level with you, to become human as you are, that he might not only be your Lord but your brother and that he might be the more fit to be a companion for such a worm of the dust. This is one purpose of Christ's taking on him human nature, that his people might have the advantage of more familiar dealings with him than the infinite distance of the divine nature would allow. One design of God in the gospel is to bring us to make God the object of our undivided respect, that he may engross our regard every way, that whatever natural inclination there is in our souls, he may be the center of it, that God may be all in all.

—Jonathan Edwards

*"Do not weep! See, the Lion of the tribe of Judah. . . ." Then
I saw a Lamb, looking as if it had been slain, standing in
the center of the throne.*

—Revelation 5:5–6

There is an inclination in the creature not only to the adoration of a Lord and Sovereign, but to love and delight in someone as a friend and companion.[55] And God has so contrived that a divine person may be the object of this inclination. Such a one has taken our nature, has become one of us, and calls himself our friend, brother, and companion.

Would you want him to be a person of meekness and humility? Why, such is Christ! He has not only become human, but is by far the meekest and most humble of all, the greatest instance of these virtues that ever was or will be. And he has all other human virtues in perfection. These, indeed, are no proper addition to his divine virtues. Christ has no more excellence since his incarnation than he had before, for divine excellence is infinite and cannot be added to. Yet his human virtues are additional displays to us of his glory and excellence and are additional recommendations to our esteem and love. The glory of Christ in his human nature appears to us in virtues that invite our acquaintance and draw our affection. The glory of Christ as it shows in his divinity, though far brighter, more dazzles our eyes and exceeds the strength of our sight or our comprehension, but as it shines in the human virtues of Christ, it is brought more to a level with our conceptions and is more suitable to our nature and manner, yet retaining a semblance of the divine beauty and a savor of the divine sweetness. It tends to endear the divine majesty and holiness of Christ to us that these are attributes of one in our nature, one of us, who is our brother and is the meekest and humblest of our kind. How much more glorious and surprising do the meekness, the humility, obedience, resignation, and other human virtues of Christ appear when we consider that they are in so great a person as the eternal Son of God, the Lord of heaven and earth!

By your choosing Christ for your friend and portion, you will obtain these two infinite benefits: Christ will give himself to you, with all those various virtues that meet in him, to your full and everlasting enjoyment. He will ever after treat you as his dear friend. And you will before long be where he is and will see his glory and dwell with him, in most free and intimate communion and enjoyment.

—Jonathan Edwards

Then I saw a Lamb, looking as if it had been slain, standing in the center of the throne, encircled by the four living creatures and the elders.

—Revelation 5:6

When the saints get to heaven, they will not merely see Christ and have to do with him as subjects and servants of a glorious and gracious Lord and Sovereign, but Christ will entertain them as friends and family.[56] This we may learn from the manner of Christ's conversing with his disciples here on earth: though he was their Sovereign Lord and did not refuse but required their supreme respect and adoration, yet he did not treat them as earthly sovereigns are accustomed to do their subjects. He did not keep them at an awful distance but all along conversed with them with the most friendly familiarity, as a father amongst a company of children, yes, as with family. So he did with the Twelve, and so he did with Mary, Martha, and Lazarus. He told his disciples that he did not call them servants but friends, and we read of one of them that leaned on his bosom—and doubtless he will not treat his disciples with less freedom and endearment in heaven. He will not keep them at a greater distance for his being in a state of exaltation, but he will rather take them into a state of exaltation with him.

This will be the increase Christ will make of his own glory, to make his beloved friends partakers with him, to glorify them in his glory, as he says to his Father: "I have given them the glory that you gave me, that they may be one as we are one: I in them and you in me" (John 17:22–23). We are to consider that though Christ is greatly exalted, yet he is exalted not as a private person for himself only, but as his people's head; he is exalted in their name and on their account as the firstfruits and as representing the whole harvest. He is not exalted that he may be at a greater distance from them but that they may be exalted with him. Instead of the distance being greater, the union will be nearer and more perfect.

When believers get to heaven, Christ will conform them to himself; as he is set down in his Father's throne, so they shall sit down with him on his throne and shall in their measure be made like him.

—Jonathan Edwards

Do not weep! See, the Lion of the tribe of Judah, the Root of
David, has triumphed.

—Revelation 5:5

When Christ was going to heaven, he comforted his disciples.[57] After a while he would come again and take them to him. And we are not to suppose that when the disciples got to heaven, they found him keeping a greater distance than he used to do. No, doubtless, he embraced them and welcomed them to his and their Father's house and to his and their glory. Those who had been his friends in this world, who had been together with him and had shared in sorrows and troubles were welcomed by him to rest and to share in glory with him. He led them into his chambers and showed them all his glory: "Father, I want those you have given me to be with me where I am, and to see my glory" (John 17:24). And he led them to his living fountains of waters and made them partake of his delights: "That they may have the full measure of my joy within them" (John 17:13). He sat them with him at his table in his kingdom and made them eat and drink with him, according to his promise (Luke 22:30), and led them into his banqueting house and gave them new wine to drink with him in the kingdom of his Father, as he foretold them when he instituted the Lord's supper (Matt. 26:29).

Yes, the saints' conversation with Christ in heaven will not only be as intimate and their access to him as free as of the disciples on earth, but in many respects much more so, for in heaven that union will be perfect which is very imperfect here. While the saints are in this world, sin and darkness disunite them from Christ, which will then all be removed.

When the saints see Christ's glory in heaven, it will indeed possess their hearts with greater admiration and respect, but it will not awe them into separation. It will serve only to heighten their surprise and joy when they find Christ condescending to admit them to such intimate access, freely and fully communicating himself to them. So if we choose Christ for our friend and portion, we will hereafter be so received to him that nothing will hinder the fullest enjoyment of him, the satisfying of the utmost cravings of our souls. Christ will then say, as in Song of Songs 5:1: "Eat, O friends, and drink; drink your fill, O lovers." There will never be any end of this happiness or anything to interrupt our enjoyment of it or in the least to molest us in it.

—Jonathan Edwards

Do not weep! See, the Lion of the tribe of Judah, the Root of David, has triumphed.

—*Revelation 5:5*

By your being united to Christ, you will have a more glorious union with and enjoyment of God the Father than otherwise could be.[58] For by this the saints' relation to God becomes much nearer; they are the children of God in a higher manner than otherwise could be. For, being members of God's own Son, they are partakers of his relationship to the Father: they are not only children of God by regeneration, but by communion in the sonship of the eternal Son. The church is the daughter of God not only as he has begotten her by his word and Spirit, but as she is the spouse of his eternal Son.

So we, as members of the Son, are partakers in our share of the Father's love of the Son and pleasure in him: "You . . . have loved them even as you have loved me" (John 17:23). So we will take part in the Son's enjoyment of God and have his joy fulfilled in us. And by this means we will come to a higher, more intimate, and full enjoyment of God than otherwise could have been. For there is doubtless an infinite intimacy between the Father and the Son, which is expressed as his being "in the bosom of the Father" (John 1:18 KJV). And saints being in him will take part with him in it and of the blessedness of it.

And by our redemption we are brought to an immensely more exalted kind of union with God and enjoyment of him, both the Father and the Son, than otherwise could have been. For Christ being united to the human nature, we have the advantage of a more free and full enjoyment of him than we could have had if he had remained only in the divine nature. So we, being united to a divine person, as his members, can have a more intimate union and communion with God the Father, who is only in the divine nature, than otherwise could be. Christ, by taking our nature on him, descends from the infinite distance and height above us and is brought near us, so we have the advantage of fully enjoying him. And, on the other hand, we, by being in Christ ascend up to God through the infinite distance and have the advantage of fully enjoying him also.

This was the design of Christ, that he and his Father and his people might all be united. Christ has brought it to pass that those whom the Father has given him would be brought into the household of God, that he and his Father and his people should be as one family—that the church would be admitted into the society of the blessed Trinity.

—Jonathan Edwards

Do not be afraid, little flock, for your Father has been
pleased to give you the kingdom.

—Luke 12:32

The prophet Isaiah foretold the appearance of Jesus in the character of a shepherd: "The Sovereign LORD . . . tends his flock like a shepherd: He gathers the lambs in his arms and carries them close to his heart; he gently leads those that have young" (Isa. 40:10–11).[59] Accordingly, when our Lord appeared in human nature, he said, "I am the good shepherd" (John 10:14). Jesus feeds his flock with truth and consolation. They have many powerful enemies, but he is an all-powerful friend.

Sheep are striking emblems of true Christians. Like them, the Christian is harmless, meek, and inoffensive. The malignant and violent dispositions [of our] natural beings are brought into subjection by Scriptural conversion. Thus, the lion becomes a gentle lamb; arrogant, mischievous, and turbulent human dispositions become humble, useful, meek, and gentle. A society of such people may be compared to a flock of sheep because they love to dwell together and to feed in the same pastures. In times of danger, they form themselves into a close body and look up for protection to the great Shepherd of the sheep.

The followers of Jesus are a little flock. One would have supposed from the purity of Jesus' conduct, the wisdom displayed in his discourses, and his mighty works that the whole Jewish nation would have received him as their shepherd. This, however, was so far from being the case that he had only a few obscure individuals in his flock.

The number of genuine Christians has been very small when compared with the great mass of humanity. It does not follow that this will always be the case. There can be no doubt that Jesus will finally conquer his enemies.

The flock of Jesus are not to be afraid. Every follower of Jesus has the promise of a kingdom. With that prospect, who can yield to doubts and fears? "He who did not spare his own Son, but gave him up for us all—how will he not . . . graciously give us all things?" (Rom. 8:32). What God gives is given with pleasure. He takes delight in making us happy, and our happiness and his glory are inseparably connected.

Therefore, commit yourselves to his pastoral care. You will soon be conducted to his heavenly fold. There all his sheep will spend a blessed eternity with their heavenly Shepherd.

—Jonathan Edmondson

Is any one of you in trouble? He should pray.

—James 5:13

Prayer in trouble implies of sense our impotence, an acknowledgment of God's power, and dependence on him for help.[60] These considerations reveal the suitability of this duty and the probability of success, if we pray in a right spirit.

When we are troubled, let us pray for pardon. Perhaps some crime may be the cause of our suffering, which must be pardoned before we can obtain deliverance: "Is any one of you sick? He should call the elders of the church to pray over him . . . and the prayer offered in faith will make the sick person well; the Lord will raise him up. If he has sinned, he will be forgiven" (James 5:14–15).

In troubles we should pray for counsel. "If any of you lacks wisdom, he should ask God, . . . and it will be given to him" (James 1:5). While clouds and darkness roll round us, we know not which way to go, but when we acknowledge God in the duty of prayer, he directs our steps.

We should pray for a sanctified use of trouble. When trouble is sanctified, it promotes our good, the good of others, and the glory of God. God neither troubles in vain nor willingly grieves us. After an affliction is over, it is pleasing to reflect that, like silver in the furnace, we have lost nothing but dross. In this way, and for this very purpose, God often afflicts his children.

It is lawful in our troubles to pray for deliverance. When the Israelites wandered in a solitary way and when their soul fainted with hunger and thirst, "Then they cried out to the LORD in their trouble, and he delivered them from their distress" (Ps. 107:6).

Those in trouble should ask others to join with them in prayer. United petitions are powerful. The prayers of saints ascend before the throne of God like holy incense, and speedy answers are sent down. Hurry, then, to call in the pious, and set great value on their prayers.

But prayer in troubles does not set aside the use of other means. Every means that prudence may dictate should be used, but all should be mixed with prayer, that God may give his blessing, without which all our endeavors will prove useless.

The character of the divine Being is an encouragement to pray in troubles. He is full of compassion and waits to do his needy creatures good. He pities people in their troubles, and his arm is stretched out to help and deliver.

—Jonathan Edmondson

Diligently study the Scriptures.

—John 5:39

The Sadducees came to our blessed Lord and put to him the question, whose wife that woman should be in the next life who had seven husbands in this.[61] He told them they erred, not knowing the Scriptures. And if we would know what first caused all the errors that have overspread the church of Christ, we would find that, in a great measure, they flowed from the same fountain, ignorance of the Word of God.

Had the human race continued in a state of innocence, we would not need an outward revelation, because the law of God was written on the human heart. But having eaten the forbidden fruit, [Adam] incurred the displeasure of God and lost the divine image and, therefore, without an external revelation, could never tell how God would be reconciled to him or how he should be saved from the misery and darkness of his fallen nature.

That these truths are so I need not refer you to any other book than your own hearts. For unless we are fallen creatures, of what origin those corruptions that daily arise in our hearts? We could not come thus corrupt out of the hands of our Maker, because he, being goodness, could make nothing but what is like himself—holy, just, and good. And that we want to be delivered from the disorders of our nature is evident, because we are unwilling to admit that we are depraved, and we strive to appear of a quite different frame and temper of mind.

God in his written word shows you how you are fallen into darkness and misery. And, at the same time, he points the way to what you desire, even how you may be redeemed by believing in and copying after the Son of his love.

On these two truths rest all divine revelation: It is given to show [both] our misery and our happiness, our fall and our recovery.

From this cause, then, arises the necessity of searching the Scriptures. Since they are nothing else but the grand charter of our salvation, the revelation of a covenant made by God with people in Christ, and a light to guide us into the way of peace, it follows that all are obliged to read and search them, because all are equally fallen from God. All equally stand in need of being informed how they must be restored to him and again united with him.

—George Whitefield

Diligently study the Scriptures.

—John 5:39

I will lay down some directions for you to study the Scriptures with benefit.[62]

First, have always in view the purpose for which the Scriptures were written—to show us the way of salvation by Jesus Christ. "These are the Scriptures that testify about me," says our Lord. Look, therefore, always for Christ in the Scripture. He is the treasure hidden in the field, both of the Old and New Testaments. In the Old, you will find him under prophesies, types, sacrifices, and shadows; in the New, revealed in a body to become a propitiation for our sins as a priest, and as a prophet to reveal the whole will of his heavenly Father.

Have Christ, then, always in view when you are reading the Word of God, and this, like the star in the east, will guide you to the Messiah, will serve as a key to everything that is obscure, and will unlock to you the wisdom and riches of all the mysteries of the kingdom of God.

Second, search the Scriptures humbly—childlike. God hides the sense of them from those who are wise in their own eyes and reveals them only to babes in Christ, who hunger and thirst for righteousness and crave pure spiritual milk, so that they may grow by it.

Imagine yourselves, therefore, when you are searching the Scriptures, especially the New Testament, to be with Mary sitting at the feet of Jesus. And be as willing to learn what God will teach you as Samuel was, when he said, "Speak, Lord, for your servant hears."

Third, search the Scriptures with a sincere intention to put in practice what you read. A desire to *do* the will of God is the only way to *know* it. To those who desire to know from his Word who he is, that they may believe on and live by and to him, he will reveal himself as clearly as he did to the woman of Samaria, when he said, "I who speak to you am he."

Fourth, in order to search the Scriptures still more effectively, make an application of everything you read to your own hearts. For whatever was written in the book of God was written for our learning. And what Christ said to those before, we must look on as spoken to us also, for since the Holy Scriptures are nothing but a revelation from God how fallen humanity is to be restored by Jesus Christ, all the precepts, threats, and promises belong to us and to our children, as well as to those to whom they were immediately made known.

—George Whitefield

Diligently study the Scriptures.

—John 5:39

I will lay down some [further] directions for you to study the Scriptures with benefit.[63]

Fifth, labor to attain that Spirit by which they were written. The Scriptures have been compared to the cloud that went before the Israelites. They are dark and hard to be understood by the natural self, as the cloud appeared dark to the Egyptians. But they are light to Christians, as that same cloud, which seemed dark to Pharaoh and his house, appeared bright and altogether glorious to the Israel of God.

How could it be otherwise? For God, being spirit, cannot communicate himself any other way than in a spiritual manner to human hearts, and consequently if we are strangers to his Spirit, we must continue strangers to his Word, because it is altogether like him, spiritual. Labor therefore earnestly to attain this blessed Spirit; otherwise, your minds will never be opened to understand the Scriptures aright, and remember, prayer is one of the most immediate means to get this Holy Spirit.

Therefore, sixth, before you read the Scriptures, pray that Christ, according to his promise, would send his Spirit to guide you into all truth. Intersperse short interjections while you are engaged in reading. Pray over every word and verse, if possible, and when you close the book, most earnestly implore God that the words that you have read may be engrafted into your hearts and bring forth in you the fruits of a good life.

Do this, and you will, with a holy violence, draw down God's Holy Spirit into your hearts. You will experience his gracious influence and feel him enlightening, reviving, and inflaming your souls by the Word of God. You will then not only read, but observe, learn, and digest what you read—and the word of God will be food and drink to your souls.

Seventh, read the Scripture consistently, or, to use our Savior's expression, "Diligently study the Scriptures." Dig in them as for hidden treasure, for here is an allusion to those who dig in mines, and our Savior would by it teach us that we must take as much pains in constantly reading his word, if we would grow wise by it, as those who dig for gold and silver. The Scriptures contain the deep things of God and therefore can never be sufficiently searched by a careless, superficial, cursory reading, but by an industrious, close, and humble application.

—George Whitefield

Diligently study the Scriptures.

—John 5:39

Perhaps you have no taste for this despised book.[64] Perhaps plays, romances, and books of polite entertainment suit your taste better. If this is your case, give me leave to tell you your taste is impaired, and, unless corrected by the Spirit and Word of God, you will never enter his heavenly kingdom, for unless you delight in God here, how will you be made fit to dwell with him hereafter? Is it a sin then, you will say, to read useless, impertinent books? I answer, Yes, and for the same reason that it is a sin to indulge in useless conversation, because both tend to grieve and quench that Spirit by whom alone we can be sealed to the day of redemption. You may reply, How will we know this? Why, put in practice the precept in the text; study the Scripture in the manner that has been recommended, and then you will be convinced of the danger, sinfulness, and unsatisfactoriness of reading any others than the book of God, or such as are written in the same spirit. Then you will say, when I was a child and ignorant of the excellence of the Word of God, I read what the world calls harmless books, but now that I have tasted the good word of life and have come to a more mature knowledge of Christ Jesus my Lord, I put away these childish, trifling things and am determined to read no other books but what lead me to a knowledge of myself and of Christ Jesus.

Study diligently, therefore, the Scriptures, my dear brothers and sisters. Taste and see how good the Word of God is, and then you will never leave that heavenly manna, that angel's food, to feed on dry husks, that light bread, those trifling, sinful compositions in which people of false taste delight themselves. No, you will then disdain such poor entertainment and blush that you yourselves once were fond of it. The Word of God will then be sweeter to you than honey and the honeycomb and dearer than gold and silver; your souls by reading it will be filled "as with the richest of foods" (Ps. 63:5) and your hearts gradually molded into the spirit of its blessed Author. In short, you will be guided by God's wisdom here and conducted by the light of his divine word into glory hereafter.

—George Whitefield

*When the hour came, Jesus and his apostles
reclined at the table.*

—Luke 22:14

We see the Master sitting down at the table to eat and drink with his twelve apostles—what did this make them?[65]

They were convinced that he was the Messiah, and they, therefore, began with *following* him. This is where we must begin. The most important way of following him is to trust him and imitate his example. This is a good beginning and will end well, for those who walk with him today will dwell with him hereafter; those who tread in his footsteps will sit on his throne.

Being his followers, they next became his *disciples.* To explain, to clear away doubts, and to make truth intelligible is the office of a teacher among his disciples. It was a blessed thing to become disciples, but still disciples are not necessarily so intimate with their master as to sit and eat with him. There is something beyond.

The chosen ones next rose to become his *servants.* Servants have some strength, receive some measure of training, and render something in return. Their Master gave them power to preach the gospel and to execute commissions, and happy were they to wait on such a Master and aid in setting up his kingdom. Yet is there something beyond.

Toward the close of his life, our Master revealed the yet nearer relationship with his disciples: "I no longer call you servants, because a servant does not know his master's business. Instead, I have called you *friends,* for everything that I learned from my Father I have made known to you" (John 15:15). The friend is told what the servant need not know, enjoys a communion that the servant, disciple, or follower has not attained.

On the night before his passion, our Lord led his friends a step beyond ordinary friendship. Here the Lord Jesus lifted up his chosen ones to sit with him at the same table, to eat of the same bread and drink of the same cup with him. From that position he has never degraded them; they were representatives, and where the Lord placed them, he has placed all his saints. All the Lord's believing people are sitting at the same table with Jesus, for truly, our fellowship is with the Father and with his Son, Jesus Christ. We are his table companions and will eat bread with him in the kingdom of God.

Table companions, then—that is the answer to the question, "What did this festival make the apostles?"

—C. H. *Spurgeon*

When the hour came, Jesus and his apostles
reclined at the table.

—Luke 22:14

What did this table companionship imply?[66]

It implied, first, *mutual fidelity.* This eating and drinking together was a pledge of faithfulness to one another. Know, then, that your Master would not ask you to his table if he intended to desert you. He has received you as his honored guests and fed you on his choicest food, and by this he says to you, "I will never leave you, come what may, and in all times of trial, depression, and temptation I will be at your right hand."

But you do not understand this supper unless you are also reminded of the faithfulness that is due from you to your Lord, for the pledge is mutual. In eating with him, you plight your troth to the Crucified. May the Holy Spirit work in our souls a fidelity that will not permit our hearts to wander from him nor our zeal for his glory to decline!

There is, too, in this solemn eating and drinking together a pledge of fidelity between the disciples themselves. Judas would have been a traitor if he had betrayed Peter, John, or James; so, when you come to the one table, you must from this time on be true to one another. All bickering and jealousy must cease, and a generous and affectionate spirit must rule in every bosom. If you hear any speak against those you have communed with, reckon that you are bound to defend their reputations. Reckon their characters are as dear as your own. Drinking from the same cup, eating the same bread, you set forth before the world a token that I trust is not meant to be a lie. As it truly shows Christ's faithfulness to you, so let it as truly typify your faithfulness to Christ and to one another.

Eating and drinking together was also a token of *mutual confidence,* for when they were told that one of them would betray their Lord, they did not suspect each other, but each one said, "Surely not I, Lord?" (Matt. 26:22). They were a trustful company who sat at that supper table. Now, beloved, when you gather around this table, come in the spirit of implicit trustfulness in the Lord Jesus. If you are suffering, do not doubt his love, but believe that he works all things for your good. If you are vexed with cares, prove your confidence by leaving them entirely in your Redeemer's hands. It will not be a festival of communion to you if you come here with suspicions about your Master. No, show your confidence as you eat bread with him. Let there also be a friendly confidence in each other.

—C. H. Spurgeon

*When the hour came, Jesus and his apostles
reclined at the table.*

—Luke 22:14

What [else] did this table companionship imply?[67]

A third meaning of the assembling around the table is *camaraderie.* Our Lord showed himself one with them, a brother indeed. We do not read that there was any order of priority by which their seats were arranged.

You have no right to come to that table unless those who are washed in Jesus' blood have a claim on your love and on your benevolence. Are you to live together forever in heaven, and will you show no affection for one another here below? It is your Master's new command that you love one another; will you disregard it? He has given this as the badge of Christians: "By this all men will know that you are my disciples"—not if you wear a gold cross, but—"if you love one another" (John 13:35).

But this table means more yet: it signifies *common enjoyment.* Jesus eats, and they eat, the same bread. He drinks, and they drink, the same cup. There is no distinction in the provisions. What means this? The very joy that delights Christ is that which he prepares for his people. You, if you are a true believer, have part in Christ's joy, you delight to see his kingdom come, the truth advanced, sinners saved, grace glorified, holiness promoted, God exalted; this also is his delight. But are you certain that the mainstay of your life is the same as his, namely, to do the will of the heavenly Father? If it is, may you joy in him as he joys in you, and so may your fellowship be sweet!

The feast at the one table indicated *familiar affection.* It is the child's place to sit at the table with its parents, for there affection rules. People at the table often reveal their minds more fully than elsewhere. Now, the Lord Jesus Christ sat at the table with his disciples. 'Twas a meal of a simple kind; intimate exchange ruled the hour. Oh, brothers and sisters, I am afraid we have come to this table sometimes and gone away again without having had communion with Christ, and then it has been an empty formality and nothing more. Do pray the Lord to reveal himself to you. Ask that it may not be a dead form to you but that now in very deed you may give to Christ your heart, while he will show you his hands and his side and make known to you his agonies and death, with which he redeemed you from the coming wrath. All this, and vastly more, is the teaching of the table at which Jesus sat with the Twelve.

—C. H. Spurgeon

When the hour came, Jesus and his apostles
reclined at the table.

—Luke 22:14

What further may be inferred from this sitting of Christ with his disciples at the table?[68]

First, there may be inferred from it *the equality of all the saints.* There were twelve apostles here. When the Lord's supper was celebrated after all the apostles had gone to heaven, was there to be any alteration because the apostles had gone? Not at all. Believers are to do this in remembrance of their Lord *until he comes.*

It is only in the church of God that the words *liberty, equality,* and *fraternity* can ever be any more than a dream. You have them where Jesus is—not in a republic but in the kingdom of our Lord, where all rule and dominion are vested in him, all of us willingly acknowledge him as our glorious head, and we all are brothers and sisters. Do not think that what the Lord worked in the early saints cannot be worked in you. The grace of God sustained the apostles; that grace is not less today than it was then. There is the same table for you, and the same food is there in emblem, and grace can make you like those holy men, for you are bought with the same blood and made alive by the same Spirit.

Another inference is that *the needs of the church in all ages will be the same, and the supplies for the church's needs will never vary.* There will be the table still, with the same provisions—bread still, nothing more than bread for food; wine still, nothing less than wine for drink. The church will always need the same food, the same Christ, the same gospel.

Lastly, there is in this truth a prophecy that *this will be the portion of all his people forever.* In heaven there cannot be less of privilege than on earth. It cannot be that in the celestial state believers will be degraded from what they have been below. What were they, then, below? Table companions. What will they be in heaven above? Table companions still, and blessed are they who will eat bread in the kingdom of God. And the Lord Jesus will be at the head of the table. Now, what will his table of joy be? Set your imagination to work, and think what will be his festival of soul when his reward will be all before him and his triumph all achieved. Can you imagine it? Whatever it is, you will share in it.

In the anticipation of the joy that will be yours, forget your present troubles, rise to the difficulties of the hour, and if you cannot rejoice in the present, yet rejoice in the future, which shall so soon be your own.

—C. H. Spurgeon

When the hour came, Jesus and his apostles
reclined at the table.

—Luke 22:14

The Lord's supper, like believers' baptism, is simplicity itself.[69] It consists of bread broken and wine poured out, these provisions being eaten and drunk at a festival—a delightful picture of the sufferings of Christ for us and of the communion that the saints have with one another and with him.

We now ask you in contemplation to gaze on the first celebration of the Lord's supper. You perceive at once that there was no altar in that large upper room. There was a table, a table with bread and wine on it. Jesus did not kneel, there is no sign of that, but he sat in the Oriental way, by a partial reclining. He sat down with his apostles. Now, he who ordained this supper knew how it ought to be observed, and as the first celebration of it was the model for all others, we may be assured that the right way of coming to this communion is to assemble around a table and to sit or recline while we eat bread and drink wine together in remembrance of our Lord.

There are some of you who must not come to the table of communion because you do not love Christ. You have not trusted him; you have no part in him. There is no salvation in sacraments. Believe me, they are but delusions to those who do not come to Christ with their hearts. You must not come to the outward sign if you have not the thing signified. Here is the way of salvation: believe in the Lord Jesus Christ, and you will be saved. To believe in him is to trust him; to use an old word, it is *recumbency;* it is leaning on him, resting on him. Here I lean, I rest my whole weight on this support before me; do so with Christ in a spiritual sense; lean on him. You have a load of sin, lean on him, sin and all. You are unworthy and weak and perhaps miserable; then cast on him the weakness, the unworthiness, the misery, and all. Take him to be all in all to you, and when you have thus trusted him, you will have become his follower; go on by humility to be his disciple, by obedience to be his servant, by love to be his friend, and by communion to be his table companion.

The Lord so lead you, for Jesus' sake! Amen.

—C. H. Spurgeon

*Faith is being sure of what we hope for and certain of what
we do not see.*

—Hebrews 11:1

You see something [so] that you may believe something and from what you see may believe what you see not.[70] Do not be ungrateful to him who has made you see so that you may be able to believe what as yet you cannot see. God has given you eyes in the body, reason in the heart; arouse the reason of the heart, wake up the inhabitant of your eyes, let it take to its windows, examine the creature of God. God has made you a rational animal, set you over the cattle, formed you in his own image. Ought you to use your eyes as the cattle do, only to see what to add to your belly, not to your soul? Stir up the eye of reason, use your eyes as a human being should, consider the heaven and earth, the fruitfulness of the earth, the flight of the birds, the swimming of the fish, the goodness of the seeds; consider the works, and seek for the author. Look at what you see, and seek him whom you see not. Believe in him you do not see because of these things that you see. If you think that it is with my own words that I have exhorted you, hear the Apostle: "For since the creation of the world God's invisible qualities . . . have been clearly seen, being understood from what has been made" (Rom. 1:20).

These things you saw and disregarded. God's daily miracles were disesteemed not for their easiness but their constant repetition. For what is more difficult to understand than death and birth, that one who existed should depart into darkness and that one who was not, should come forth to light? What else is as marvelous? But with God easily done. Marvel at *these* things! Are his unusual works greater than those that you are accustomed to see? People wondered that our Lord Jesus filled so many thousands with five loaves, yet they do not wonder that through a few grains the whole earth is filled with crops. When the water was made wine, people were amazed; isn't this what takes place with the rain along the root of the vine? He did the one, he does the other; both are wonderful, for both are the works of God. You see unusual things and wonder; of what origin are you yourself who wonders? You wonder at other things when you, the wonderer, are yourself a great wonder. From where then are these things that you see but from him whom you see not? But because you disesteemed these things, he came himself to do unusual things, that in these usual ones too you might acknowledge your Creator.

—Augustine of Hippo

In the beginning was the Word, and the Word was with
God, and the Word was God.

—John 1:1

He came, to whom it is said, "Show signs"; to whom it is said, "Show forth your marvelous mercies"; for dispensing them he ever was; he dispensed them, and no one marveled.[71] Therefore he came a little one to the little, he came a physician to the sick—he who was able to come when he would, to return when he would, to do whatever he would, to judge as he would.

These things he did, yet he was despised by the many, who did not consider so much what great things he did as how small he was, as though they said to themselves, *These are divine things, but he is human.* You see then two things: divine works and a human being. If divine works cannot be done except by God, take heed for fear that in this man God lies concealed. Pay attention to what you see; believe what you do not see. He who has called you to believe has not abandoned you; though he enjoins you to believe that which you cannot see, he has given you something to see by which you may be able to believe what you do not see. Is the creation itself a small indication of the Creator? You could not see God; so God became human, that in one being you might have both something to see and something to believe. "In the beginning was the Word, and the Word was with God, and the Word was God" (John 1:1). He who made man and woman comes forth from a woman. He who made man and woman was not made by man and woman. In this very birth there are at once two things, one you may see and another you may not see, so that by what you see you may believe what you do not see. You had begun to despise, because you see him who was born; believe what you do not see—that he was born of a virgin. "How trifling a person," you say, "is one who is born!" But how great is he who was of a virgin born! And he who was born of a virgin brought you a temporal miracle—he was not born of a father, of any man, yet he was born of the flesh. But let it not seem impossible to you that he, who made a man before father and mother, was born by his mother only.

He brought you then a temporal miracle, that you may seek and admire him who is eternal. He is coeternal with the Father, he it is who "in the beginning was the Word, and the Word was with God, and the Word was God." He did for you that by which you might be cured, that you might be able to see what you did not see.

—Augustine of Hippo

I have spoken openly to the world. . . .
I said nothing in secret.

—John 18:20

In our text our Lord lays claim to a great openness, and it is a claim that cannot be disputed.[72] The whole impression made by the life of Jesus is that of a teacher who was frank and bold; of one who would not hesitate to speak, whatever the consequences to himself might be.

Of course this candor of our Lord and Master was always at the service of his love. It was the instrument of a pure and perfect sympathy that knew that there were seasons to be silent. The perfect candor of our Redeemer's talk was ever subservient to that noblest love which dares to speak when other lips are silent and to be silent when other voices speak. There is a candor that is the child of ignorance, for fools rush in where angels fear to tread. There is a candor that betrays the bitter heart, for it speaks the truth—but does not speak in love. But the candor of Jesus goes hand in hand with reticence, and both look up to catch their inspiration from the most loving and sympathetic eyes that ever beamed on a sinful world.

Now there are times in every life when it takes a certain courage to be quiet. To every man and woman there come seasons when the path of duty is the path of silence. All that is basest in us bids us speak, for there is a candor that is the child of hell; but all that is noblest in us checks our speech, lest to someone we do irreparable harm. But remember if it takes courage to be quiet, it also may call for courage to be frank.

—George H. Morrison

Look, the Lamb of God, who
takes away the sin of the world!

—John 1:29

Look at what he takes away: "the sin of the world."[73] Not "sins," but "sin"; sin with which not some individual but the whole world is charged. None but God can number the sins that have been committed since the world was, that will be committed while the world lasts. But though the sins are many and the sinners who commit them many, a unity binds all the sin of the world together. "The sin of the world," of which the various sins are so many branches and displays, is the world's apostasy and alienation from the living God. "Everyone who sins breaks the law; in fact, sin is lawlessness" (1 John 3:4). And the law of God is one; multitudes of commandments, but one in its principle—its principle being love to God and love to all created beings for God's sake. It is one, as flowing all from the same essential purity, justice, and universal moral good of the divine nature. Sin has a unity contrary to this.

What is a world's sin, the sin of a race that for six thousand years has been sinning? What is the amount of actual sin?

It's "the sin of the world." It involves me, it involves you, it involves each individual. We as individuals have our sins and as an integral part and portion of Adam's posterity are connected thus with the whole amount of the sin of the world.

Now if we look through the world we will not find anything to take away its sin or even to lessen and restrain its sin—nothing there to make amends for it in whole or in part, nothing to subdue it. It is only capable of growing worse and worse. Isn't this a pitiable world!

But, "Look, the Lamb of God, who takes away the sin of the world!" He was in the world, but he was not of the world. He comes into this world from the God against whom this world transgressed. And what may the world expect he comes to do? On what other errand could it be but to condemn the world? Ah no! "God did not send his Son into the world to condemn the world, but to save the world through him" (John 3:17). O what a visitor! How rightly might John point to him, how rightly may we all listen to John's short but pithy declaration, "Look, the Lamb of God, who takes away the sin of the world!"

—John Duncan

Look, the Lamb of God, who
takes away the sin of the world!

—John 1:29

There is a reference here to the purity of the Lord Jesus Christ—holy, separate from sinners.[74] But there is special reference to sacrifice, a reference exhibited in two cases. First, when God commanded Abraham to offer his son Isaac, the ram caught in the thicket was sacrificed; Isaac was spared, a type of our salvation by the substitution of the Lord Jesus. The other reference is to the lamb of the Passover. What did God teach there? That the destroying angel will not find Israel better than the Egyptians, but God would spare his people whom he had set apart for himself. And so the destroying angel did not destroy the firstborn of Israel.

Now here is God's lamb—the Lamb he has provided for a burnt offering—not typically but actually, not the shadow but the reality. The world did not have a lamb to make amends for its sin—not to speak of the necessity of a divine Person to atone for sin, for—infinite evil of it—the world had no innocent person. But God provided a lamb. 'Twas Jehovah's own finding—and what was his provision? We read that he who is called the Lamb of God is the Word of God, who in the beginning was with God and was God, the Creator of all things, by whom all things were made—God's own Son, the only begotten of the Father, the kindred and equal of the Lord of Hosts, and the exact representation of his being.

When we consider the Lamb of God, we consider him as God and human—Immanuel—which he was from all eternity but, when the time had come, by actual unveiling. We are sent to Bethlehem to see this great thing, to see the child born, the Son given, whose name is the Mighty God! "Since the children have flesh and blood, he too shared in their humanity" (Heb. 2:14), that he might be a kinsman-redeemer, that satisfaction might be given to divine justice in the same nature that had offended. His deity gave infinite value and effectiveness to his obedience and atonement. He is the Lamb of God, pure and spotless—for such alone could bear away sin.

The Lord has accepted his offering—the Lamb whom God, having provided and accepted, now exhibits to us sinners. He says of him—for we have greater testimony than that of John—"This is my Son, whom I love; with him I am well pleased."

—John Duncan

Look, the Lamb of God, who
takes away the sin of the world!

—John 1:29

O wondrous transaction this, that God's lamb takes away the world's sin![75] He takes away the world's sin, first, by *substitution.* The first and original transference of our sin, if we could see it, is not either in the day of our pardon or in the day of atonement but in the day of the everlasting covenant, when Christ pledged to substitute himself for sinners given to him by the Father, when he put his soul in their souls' stead and had their guilt transferred to him and laid on him. The Son of God, having become answerable for sin and having it thus on him in the way of obligation to bear it, it came on him in the way of actual demand; God came and laid the iniquities on him. What then does sin deserve? The whole amount of all sin that has been or will ever be forgiven, the whole sin of all who have been and will be saved—who would have borne them with the rest of the world down to everlasting destruction—that was inflicted on the Lamb of God. He was able to bear it. He was willing to bear it. "It was the Lord's will to crush him and cause him to suffer" (Isa. 53:10). Then, Christ by bearing sin thus bears sin away; like the one of the goats that was lead out to bear the sin of Israel away, the Lamb of God bears away the sin of the world. There is "redemption through his blood, the forgiveness of sins, in accordance with the riches of God's grace" (Eph. 1:7). He "has authority on earth to forgive sins" (Matt. 9:6; Mark 2:10). He bears sin away, actually takes it off the shoulders of individuals in the day of regeneration, conversion, and justification. And we must remark that he bears, or takes, away not only the guilt but actually the sin. The direct purpose of his atonement, indeed, is expiation of the guilt of sin, but the result of expiation is consecration and obedience, by his sprinkled blood—the blood that, shed makes atonement to God, the same applied to sinners purges them and consecrates them to be a royal priesthood and a people belonging to God. Christ washes us from our sin in his own blood.

—John Duncan

Look, the Lamb of God, who
takes away the sin of the world!

—John 1:29

The Lamb of God is not only set before us this day in the preached gospel, he is about to be set before us also in sacramental symbol.[76] God is saying at his table, "Look, the Lamb of God, who takes away the sin of the world!" Oh, of what use is the gospel when we only hear the words—human words—and of what use are sacraments when we see only the bread and wine? God clothes eternal realities in human words, formed by human breath and written by human hands, and he connects them also with outward and visible signs in the sacraments. The Word is nothing without the Spirit, the symbols nothing unless we see Jesus. Oh, what need, then, we have of the Spirit of God, that we may see Christ in the Word, in the sacraments!

We are by nature, all of us, of the world; we are all in the world's sin. We have been speaking about the world's sin, but oh, friends, it's *my* sin. I am one of this world, and I am in its sin. You and I, then, being sinners and in the world's sin, need to be looking at the Lamb of God; to feel our own sin, that we may find what has to be taken away and look to him who takes sin away—not so sin may be slight in our esteem but the Lamb of God more precious. Oh, in prospect of the table of the Lord, be trying to get hold of this text! And if you ask me how, it is not by adding anything about myself to the gospel held forth to me as an individual sinner but by taking hold of the whole gospel in that word which touches me, that word *sin*. I cannot get near the Lamb of God, it may be—but sin, I am near it—and I will just go and confess my sin before God, with my finger on that word *sin,* keeping it there before the eyes of God and of the Lamb. "Here is a trustworthy saying that deserves full acceptance: Christ Jesus came into the world to save sinners" (1 Tim. 1:15). Sinners—that's it; that's the point in the text that God is holding out to me, that I may get hold of the whole text. "The Son of Man came to seek and to save what was lost." Lost—that is the word. Take it individually, and if you cannot put your finger on Christ, put it on sin in a text where God has put sin and Christ together. Let me exhort you to take possession of faith.

—John Duncan

*God did this so that men would seek him and perhaps
reach out for him and find him, though he is not far from
each one of us.*

—Acts 17:27

That there is much more near us than we understand or know, that we are every hour on the brink of doing things and being things that we never do or are gives life a restlessness and inspiration.[77] We seem to ourselves, sometimes, like people who walk in the dark up and down a large, richly furnished house.

There comes in life to most people a sense of fumbling, a consciousness of this vague living in the dark. And out of it there come the universal characteristics of the human race—the unquenched hope, the sense that nothing is quite impossible, the self-pity and pathos with which people regard their own lives when they are thoughtful, the self-reproach that lies in wait just under the surface of our complacent vanity. All of these come from people vaguely knowing that they are always missing the things that they need most, things lying in the dark that they cannot see.

And suppose it were possible for a being with a sight that could see through the darkness to watch our fumbling. What would his feeling be about this humanity forever missing helps and chances it needed, often only by a finger's breadth? How solemn his sight of us would be! He saw how hearts came and went in this world, always just touching on, just missing, the great comforting truths of a personal immortality, till Christ with his gospel brought it to light. He has seen how souls have gone through life burdened, distressed, perplexed, when the river flowed so close that it seemed as if they could not move without finding their hot and tired souls bathed in its rich waters—the faith they wanted, the Water of Life that their deaths were crying out for.

What must be the feeling of such a being about human life? Pity and awe. A blended sense of the vast endowment humanity has and, at the same time, of the terrible thing it is to miss so much. There is not merely pity for the sinner who can be so wicked, but reverence for the child of God who might be so good, blended into that perfect unity of saving love with which Jesus stoops to lift even the vilest and most insignificant of us out of our sin.

—Phillips Brooks

God did this so that men would seek him and perhaps
reach out for him and find him, though he is not far from
each one of us.

—Acts 17:27

Over all the history of our race's acquaintance with God, all the religions, all the theologies, it seems so plain.[78] God has been forever desiring, forever trying to give knowledge of himself to human beings. Always God has been trying to make us understand him. Never has he turned and gone away in anger and left us in our ignorance. He has hovered about the human mind with an unbroken presence. Thus people in every age, in every condition, even in their own despite, have learned that God is just, that God is merciful, that he governs the world in obedience to his own perfect nature, that he therefore must punish, and that he must reward. These are not guesses about God. They are not beliefs about him that people have reasoned out from their own natures. They are the truths about him that God has been able to press into the human understanding, even through every veil that humanity drew between itself and God.

There is no one so ignorant, so careless, so indifferent about what God is and what God is doing that God is not all the time pressing on that individual life and crowding into it all the knowledge of himself that it will take. As the air crowds on everything, on the solidest and hardest stone and on the softest and most porous earth, and into each presses what measure of itself each will receive, so God limits the revelation of himself by nothing but the capacity of every person to take and hold his revelation.

God is teaching you always just as much truth as you can learn. If you are in sorrow at your ignorance, still you must not despair. Be capable of more knowledge and it will be given to you. What hinders you from knowing God perfectly is not God's unwillingness but your imperfection. Grow better and purer, and diviner wisdom will come to you—not given as wages, as reward, but simply admitted into a nature grown more capable of receiving it. "If anyone chooses to do God's will, he will find out whether my teaching comes from God" (John 7:17). Here is Christ's old promise again: "Here I am! I stand at the door and knock. If anyone hears my voice and opens the door, I will come in and eat with him" (Rev. 3:20).

—Phillips Brooks

*God did this so that men would seek him and perhaps
reach out for him and find him, though he is not far from
each one of us.*

—Acts 17:27

Two people are in deep suffering; the same great woe has fallen on each of them.[79]
They need, with their poor bruised and mangled souls, some healing, some
strength that they cannot make for themselves. Why does one of them seem to
get it and the other fail? Why does one lift up the head and go looking at the
stars, while the other bends and stoops and goes with eyes on the ground? Is one
God's favorite more than the other? Is God near to one and far from the other?
We imagine such unreal discriminations and favoritisms! We think that one soul
is held in the great warm hands, while the other is cast out on the cold ground!
But then comes in our truth: "He is not far from each one of us." The difference,
then, cannot be in God and in his willingness; it must be in the souls.

What, then, can we say to anyone who seems to be left comfortless when others all around are gathering in plentiful comfort? We may say this: God is comforting and helping you even when you do not know it. Do not for a moment
imagine that God's help is limited by what you can feel and recognize. If you are
looking to God for help, he is sending you help although you do not feel it. Feeling is not the test. Your soul is feeding on it, though your eyes may not see it, any
more than they can see the sweet and wholesome air by which you live.

In something that you are, not in anything that God is, must be the secret of
the darkness of your soul. Do not let yourself for one moment think or feel that
God has turned his back on you, that he has gone away from you and left you to
your fate. Don't ask yourself, If he had, who are you that you should call him
back? Who is he that he should turn round at your calling? That way lies despair.
No, "He is not far from each one of us." He is not far from you. You must turn
to him, and when you turn, his light is already shining full on you. What a great
truth it is, how full of courage, this truth that we may go away from God, but
God cannot go away from us! How God loves his own great character of faithfulness! He cannot turn his back on his child. If his face is not shining on you, it
must be that your back is turned on him. And if you have turned away from
him, you can turn back to him again. That is the courage which always comes to
one who takes all the blame of life on himself or on herself and does not cast it
on God. In humility there is always comfort and strength.

—Phillips Brooks

God did this so that men would seek him and perhaps
reach out for him and find him, though he is not far from
each one of us.

—Acts 17:27

Where is the God who brings the spiritual salvation?[80] Is he near to each person, ready to help, always trying to help all people to be deeply and spiritually good? Many people find it harder to believe this than that the God of wisdom or comfort is near his children.

As soon as people get below the surface and come to real study of their own spiritual lives, they find nothing so meets the story of their lives, nothing so explains themselves to themselves, as this: the hypothesis of God present with and working on our souls, to make them pure, strong, true, brave. Unseen by us, but always close to us, and always working, always hindered by our ignorance, our obstinacy, our wickedness, but never discouraged, never turning away, doing all that omnipotent love can do upon unwilling souls to make them live to him.

If that were true, what would our lives be? Think how you would live, how you would feel, ever touched and pressed on by a God you did not see, trying to persuade you to holiness, trying to convict you of sin. Run back over your life ever since you can remember. Restless, self-accusing, dreaming of goodness that you never reached; trying tasks that your experience told you were impossible; haunted by wishes that you dared to laugh at but did not dare to chase away; with two sets of standards about right and wrong, one that you kept for the world, the other that you hid deep in your heart and were more than half ashamed of— what does all that correspond to but the life surrounded and pressed on by an unseen God? God-haunted our lives are, until they give themselves to God, as the brains of sleepers are haunted by the daylight until they open their eyes and give themselves to the morning.

Or a beast lies tangled in a net. Some kind hands try to unsnarl the cords and let it go. The creature feels them tugging at the strings and writhes and struggles all the more and twists itself into a yet more inextricable snarl. But by and by it catches in its dull soul the meaning of the tugs and pulls that it feels, and it enters into sympathy with its deliverers. It lies still while they unbind it or moves only so as to help their efforts, and so at last is free. That is the way in which God sets a soul free from its sins. And in this the soul freed from its sins sees the explanation of all its struggles that have gone before.

—Phillips Brooks

God did this so that men would seek him and perhaps
reach out for him and find him, though he is not far from
each one of us.

—Acts 17:27

This, then, is the story of the present God.[81] What is the meaning of the Incarnation? We picture Christ coming from far, down through the ranks of angels, down from the battlements of heaven; far, far beyond the sun we picture him leaving his eternal seat and "coming down" to save the world. Then we picture Christ's departure. Back by the way he came, beyond the sun again, once more through the shining hosts, until he takes his everlasting seat at the right hand of God. There is truth in such pictures. But haven't we caught more of the spirit of the Incarnation if we think of it not as the bringing to us of a God who had been far away, but as the showing to us of a God who had been hidden? It is as if the cloud parted and the tired and thirsty traveler saw a brook of clear, sweet water running along close by the road traveled. Then the cloud closed again, but the traveler who had once seen the brook never could be faint with thirst again but must always know where to find it and drink of it. Christ was not a God coming out of absence. He was the ever-present God revealing how near he always was.

And so of the new life of Christ in people. It is not something strange and foreign, brought from far away. It is the deepest human sensibility, revealed and made actual. When you stand at last complete in Christ, it is not some rare adornments that he has lent from his divinity to clothe your humanity with. Those graces are the signs of your humanity. They are the flower of your human life, drawn out into luxuriance by the sunlight of the divine love. You take them as your own and wear them as the angels wear their wings.

This is what belief means, then. Not the far-off search for a distant God, but the turning, the looking, the trusting to a God who has been always present, who is present now. This is what belief means. "Believe in the Lord Jesus, and you will be saved" (Acts 16:31).

—Phillips Brooks

So whether you eat or drink or whatever you do,
do it all for the glory of God.

—1 Corinthians 10:31

To glorify is to make glorious or to declare to be glorious.[82] God glorifies, that is, makes angels or people glorious, but we cannot make God glorious, for he is not capable of additional glory, being infinitely glorious. So God gets no advantage to himself by our best works. God is glorified, then, when his glory is declared. This is done by the inanimate creation—the heavens declare the glory of God (Ps. 19:1). Humanity declares his glory actively.

And this we ought to do *by our hearts:* "Glorify God . . . in your spirit" (1 Cor. 6:20 KJV). Honoring God with the lips and not with the heart is lame and unacceptable. He ought to be glorified by our understanding, esteemed in the glory that the Scripture reveals him in. So, they that know him not can never glorify him, and they that esteem any person or thing more than or as much as him dishonor him. We glorify him by our wills, choosing him as our portion and our chief good; by our affections, loving him and rejoicing and delighting in him above every other.

By our lips: "He who sacrifices thank offerings honors me" (Ps. 50:23). The human tongue is our glory not only because it serves us for speech, which exalts us above the brutes, but because it is a proper instrument for speaking forth the glory of God. So it is a strange perverting of the tongue to let it loose to the dishonor of God and fetter it as to his glory.

By our lives: "Let your light shine before men, that they may see your good deeds and praise your Father in heaven" (Matt. 5:16). A holy life is a shining light to let a blind world see the glory of God. Sin darkens the glory of God, draws a veil over it. The holy life says, "God is holy," just as a well-ordered family tells what the head of it is like.

O how much God is dishonored by our hearts, lips, and lives! O what self-seeking mixes itself with our best actions! How eagerly do we pursue created things and how faintly the enjoyment of God! How dishonorable to a holy God! It is saying that God is not the chief good, that he is not a suitable portion for the soul, and that the creature is better than God. How we should be ashamed of ourselves on this account and labor earnestly to make God the chief and ultimate end of all our actions and the enjoyment of him our chief happiness!

—Thomas Boston

> *Whom have I in heaven but you? And earth has nothing I*
> *desire besides you. My flesh and my heart may fail, but*
> *God is the strength of my heart and my portion forever.*
> —Psalm 73:25–26

God's glory is our purpose.[83]

His glory is the purpose that God aimed at when he made the human race. "The LORD works out everything for his own ends" (Prov. 16:4); "For from him and through him and to him are all things" (Rom. 11:36). Every rational being sets itself a purpose in working. Now God is the most perfect Being and his glory the noblest purpose. God is not actively glorified by all people, but he designed to have glory from them, either by them or on them, and so it will be. Happy are those who glorify him by their actions, that they may not glorify him by their eternal sufferings.

It is the purpose of humanity as God's work. People were made fit for glorifying God. "God made mankind upright" (Eccl. 7:29), as a well-tuned instrument or as a house built for convenience.

It is that which we should aim at, the mark to which we should direct all we do. "Whether you eat or drink or whatever you do, do it all for the glory of God" (1 Cor. 10:31). This is what we should continually have in our eye, the grand design we should be carrying on in the world. "I have set the LORD always before me," says David (Ps. 16:8).

God's glory is our *chief* purpose.

His glory is that which God chiefly aimed at, the chief purpose of humankind as God's work, and that which people should chiefly aim at. God made the human race for other purposes, as to govern, use, and dispose of other creatures in the earth, sea, and air, wisely, soberly, and mercifully (Gen. 1:26). We were fitted for these purposes, and we may propose them lawfully to ourselves, seeing God has set them before us, but still these are only subordinate means to his glory. There are some goals that people propose to themselves that are simply unlawful, such as to satisfy their revenge, their lust, their covetousness, and so on. These are not capable of subordination to the glory of God. But there are other intents that are indeed in themselves lawful yet become sinful if they are not set in their due place, that is, subordinate to the glory of God.

—Thomas Boston

Whom have I in heaven but you? And earth has nothing I
desire besides you. My flesh and my heart may fail, but
God is the strength of my heart and my portion forever.
—Psalm 73:25–26

God's glory is made our chief purpose when three things concur:[84]

1. When the glory of God is one of our purposes in acting. If the nourishment of our bodies is the only intent of our eating and drinking, it is sinful and out of the due order.

2. When God's glory is not only our purpose, but is our main and principal purpose, our chief intent. But when, on the contrary, someone eats and drinks (for instance) more for the nourishment of the body than for God's glory, it is plain that God's glory is not the chief purpose of the individual in that action. Hence we read of some that are "lovers of pleasures more than lovers of God" (2 Tim. 3:4 KJV).

3. When it is the ultimate purpose, the top and perfection of what we design, beyond which we have no more view and to which all other intents are made subservient and as means to that end. Thus we should eat that our bodies may be refreshed; we should desire that our bodies may be refreshed that we may be the more capable to serve and glorify God in our stations. Thus we are obliged to seek salvation that God may be glorified and not to seek God's glory only that we may be saved, for that is to make the glory of God a stepping-stone to our own safety.

See the excellence of the human above other creatures on earth! We are made for a noble purpose—to glorify and enjoy God, while other creatures were made for us. How sad it is that people should thus forget their dignity and turn slaves to those creatures that were made to serve them! And how deplorable and lamentable is it that people, in place of making God their ultimate purpose and placing their chief happiness in him, should make their appetites, their lusts, and idols their gods and place their chief felicity in the gratification of sensual and brutish pleasures. Our hearts by nature are set on the earth that we tread on, and our desires reach up to those things that we should make stepping-stones of. Let us earnestly implore divine grace to cure this disorder of our hearts and give them a bias to more excellent things and the enjoyment of that which will survive the grave and not perish with the wrecks of time and the dissolution of the world.

—Thomas Boston

So whether you eat or drink or whatever you do,
do it all for the glory of God.
—1 Corinthians 10:31

Regard for the glory of God is as salt that must be served up with every dish.[85]
The great work of our lives is to glorify him.

This must be the purpose *of our natural actions* (1 Cor. 10:31), eating, sleeping, walking, and the like. We are under a law as to these things. We may not eat and drink as we please, any more than pray as we please. All must be done in subordination to God, that we may live and, living, may glorify God.

This must be the purpose *of our civil actions,* our work, buying and selling, and so on (Eph. 6:7). One of the sins of the old world was that they were eating (Matt. 24:38); the word is properly used of beasts eating their food—they had no higher purpose in it than beasts; and in marrying, no eye to God.

This must be the purpose *of our moral and religious actions* (Zech. 7:5). We must pray, fast, and the like, for God's glory. This is such a necessary ingredient in our actions that none of them are truly good and acceptable to God without it. Do what we will, it cannot be pleasing service to God if we do not make him our purpose. We should always design to glorify God. And that is done

- when the course of our lives is directed to the glory of God;
- when we live according to God's Word, taking heed that we swerve not in anything from it;
- when God's will is the reason as well as the rule of our actions—when we believe a truth because God has said it and do a duty because God has commanded it.

If we do not so, God loses his glory, and we lose our labor.

God is the fountain of our being, and seeing we are of him, we should be to him (Rom. 11:36). God is our creator, preserver, and benefactor. Your being or mine is only a borrowed being from him. Whatever perfection we have is from him, and it is at his cost that we live. As when the waters come from the sea to the earth and go back again by brooks and rivers, so all that we receive and enjoy comes from God and ought to go back to him by being used for his glory. To make ourselves our chief purpose is to make ourselves a god to ourselves; for a creature to be a center to itself and God a means to that end is to blaspheme.

—Thomas Boston

> *[Saul] asked him for letters to the synagogues in Dam-*
> *ascus, so that if he found any there who belonged to the*
> *Way, . . . he might take them as prisoners. . . . Saul grew*
> *more and more powerful and baffled the Jews living in*
> *Damascus by proving that Jesus is the Christ.*
>
> —Acts 9:2, 22

What wonderful contrasts in the character of Saul of Tarsus![86] Contrasts so sharp as almost to make him into another person. Saul, who went out to persecute, remained to pray. His breath was a fierce blast; in a little time his face is turned upward in prayer. Have any of us passed from fierceness to gentleness, from darkness to light, from blasphemy to worship? This is precisely the work that Christianity undertakes, to cool your breath, to subdue your rancor and your malignity, and to clasp your hands in prayer at your Father's feet. The religion of Jesus Christ would have nothing to do if this were not to be accomplished.

A second contrast is quite as remarkable. When Saul was a Pharisee he persecuted; when he became a Christian he proved. How many miles of the moral kind lie between? Let this miracle stand as an argument invincible and complete. Standing with the Scriptures open before him, he reasons and mightily contends; he becomes a luminous speaker of Christian truth. Has all the persecuting temper gone? Yes, every bit of it. Christianity is a plea, a persuasion, an address to reason, conscience, heart, and to everything that makes us human. Christianity uses no force and asks for no force to be used on its behalf.

How far is it from persecuting to praying? From threatening and slaughter to proving? That distance Christ took Saul, who only meant to go from Jerusalem to Damascus, some 136 miles. Christ made him accomplish the entire journey that lies between persecution and prayer, slaughter and argument. It is thus that Jesus Christ makes us do more than we intended. He meets us on the way of our own choice and graciously takes us on a way of his own.

Christianity does not merely alter a person's views or prejudices. Christianity never makes a little alteration in a person's thinking and action. Christianity makes new hearts, new creatures. This Redeemer, who bought us with his own blood, does not make a little difference in our attitudes and our purposes. He wants us to be born again. "If anyone is in Christ, he is a new creation; the old has gone, the new has come!" (2 Cor. 5:17). Scales drop from our eyes, and with pure hearts, we see a pure God.

—Joseph Parker

*Everyone brings out the choice wine first and then the
cheaper wine after the guests have had too much to drink;
but you have saved the best till now.*

—John 2:10

Wherever God in Christ is working, the best wine is kept until the end.[87]

Think first for a moment of Creation.

First there was chaos and the formless deep, then light and the ingathering of the waters, then the first dawn of life in lowliest form, mounting into the power of bird and beast. And always, under the working of that wisdom to which a thousand years are as a day, the path was upward from dull and shapeless horror to what was better, richer, and more beautiful. And then at last, not at the first, came Adam, capable of communion with his Maker, greater, by that spark of God within him, than sun and moon and all the host of heaven. And it is in human beings, so noble though so fallen, so touched with heaven although so soiled with hell, that we discover it is the way of God to keep the best wine until the end.

Isn't this true also of our Christian calling? The path of the righteous is like the first gleam of dawn, shining ever brighter till the full light of day. Not all at once does Christ reveal himself, when we go forward determined to be his. The old life still struggles for the mastery, and we are in heaviness through manifold temptations. But the difference between Christ and the Devil is just this, that the Devil's tomorrow is worse than his today; but the morrow of Christ, for everyone who trusts him, is always brighter and better than his yesterday. Every act of obedience that we do gives us a new vision of his love. Sorrow and trial reveal his might of sympathy, as the darkness of the night reveals the stars. And when at last the wrestling is over, and like tired children we lie down to sleep, and when we waken and see his face in the land where there is no more weariness, I think we will look back on it all and find new meanings in every hour of it, but I think also we will cry adoringly, "You have kept the best wine until now."

—George H. Morrison

*Everyone brings out the choice wine first and then the
cheaper wine after the guests have had too much to drink;
but you have saved the best till now.*

—John 2:10

Wherever God in Christ is working, the best wine is kept until the end.[88] Think how true this is of sin. It is indeed the masterpiece of evil. It is the token and the triumph of all sin that it always gives the best wine at the start. That is why people of open and generous natures are often those most bitterly assailed. They do not calculate nor look ahead nor reckon seriously with the morrow. And sin is so fair and pleasant at the outset and hides its *afterward* with such consummate mastery that the reckless heart becomes an easy prey. Don't you think that, now, if all the miseries of drunkenness were to meet one who is on the verge of drinking—don't you think that person would cry out for help and turn from the accursed vice and flee? But drunkenness does not begin like that. It begins in the social hour and happy comradeship; only afterward there are the blighted prospects and the shattered body and the ruined home. But sin is cunning and conceals all that; it sets on the table a delicious vintage and only afterward—but *always* afterward— that which is worse. If sin conceals the worse behind tomorrow, may it not conceal the worst behind the grave?

—George H. Morrison

Grow in the grace and knowledge of our
Lord and Savior Jesus Christ.

—2 Peter 3:18

By *grace* we must understand the principle of new life, implanted in regeneration.[89] It is as if the apostle had said, Increase in holiness or advance in piety.

But grace is not a plant. It is of heavenly origin. By nature we are all "objects of wrath" (Eph. 2:3), conceived in sin, and totally destitute of holiness. None, therefore, but the truly regenerated soul is capable of growth in grace. We have, it is true, a rational nature and a moral constitution and are accountable, free agents, but in relation to spiritual exercises, we are dead: "dead in . . . transgressions and sins" (v. 1).

A seed that possesses life, although it has lain dormant for a thousand years, yet when placed in a congenial soil and subjected to heat, air, and moisture, will readily sprout and grow until it arrives at maturity. But if the vital principle is lost, it will never give any indications of life, and all human skill and power can never cause it to vegetate. Yet, this seed may appear to have no defect in its internal structure. It may possess the perfect organization of seeds of the same species, but its life has fled, and no power on earth can restore it.

Analogous to this is the condition of the human soul. Possessed of all the faculties with which it was created, it has lost the image of God. The principle of spiritual life with which it was animated has become extinct. And as the communication of life is the prerogative of God, so is the regeneration of the soul, and as this work requires the exertion of the same power that first caused light to shine out of darkness, it is denominated "a new creation" (2 Cor. 5:17), and, as there is in it some analogy to raising a dead body from the grave, it is called a resurrection (see Eph. 2:6). But as this divine power is exerted without any consideration of merit in the creature, it is called *grace.*

Although grace does not exist in anyone by nature, yet it may be received at any period of our existence in this world, from infancy to old age, and we read of some who were sanctified from the womb. But the number of such is very small. Piety is seldom observed to exist with the first dawning of reason and moral feeling. Most persons, therefore, who become the subjects of grace, can remember the time when they were alienated from God and have some knowledge of the change that took place in their views and affections.

—Archibald Alexander

Grow in the grace and knowledge of our
Lord and Savior Jesus Christ.

—2 Peter 3:18

Another thing implied in the exhortation of our text is that grace in its commencement is imperfect and that its progress to maturity is gradual, for if it were perfect there could be no room for growth.[90] Although in different individuals the vigor of spiritual life is different in degree, yet in most cases grace is, in its infancy, feeble. The indications of its existence may be clear, and though its action is lively, this is nothing more than the vivacity and strength of a healthy babe in Christ. For in young converts the knowledge of spiritual things, generally, is indistinct and limited, and the faith wavering. When their feelings are joyful, they can exercise confidence in God, but when a cloud overshadows them, they are cast down and sometimes driven to distrust the mercy and faithfulness of the Redeemer. Their pious affections also are unsteady and, though apparently strong, are nevertheless mingled with gross animal feelings and alloyed with selfishness.

Also, piety is subject to diseases [that] retard its progress and cause it, for a season, to decline. These declensions are so common that some have supposed that all Christians make a retrograde motion and lose something of the ground already gained. But there seems to be no just foundation for this opinion. In some saints, both those whose lives are recorded in Scripture and those who fall under our own observation, there is no evidence of backsliding, but there are very few who have professed piety who have not reason to confess that they have at some time forsaken their first love and become remiss in vigilance and, of course, unfruitful in their lives. And not infrequently, while in this feeble state, they are overcome by some temptation, so as not only to contract a sense of guilt, but also to bring reproach on the profession they have made. This frequency of spiritual decays is one of the chief causes that so few Christians rise to eminence in piety. A fall may, indeed, make a person more cautious ever afterwards, but one purchases experience at a dear rate who pays for it with a broken bone or a joint out of place.

The tendency of the heart, even in the best, to depart from God furnishes powerful reason for the exhortation to grow in grace, for in religion, there is no such thing as standing still. A Christian who makes no advancement is going backward. The only course of safety, therefore, as well as comfort, is to make vigorous efforts to grow in grace.

—Archibald Alexander

Grow in the grace and knowledge of our
Lord and Savior Jesus Christ.

—2 Peter 3:18

Growth in grace is a gradual increase of those virtues that make up holiness and is necessarily accompanied with a decrease of the power of sin.[91] A real growth in grace includes also an advancement in spiritual knowledge, especially in the knowledge of our own depravity and helplessness, and of the Lord Jesus Christ as our Mediator. The apostle, therefore, joins these two things together and exhorts, "Grow in the grace and knowledge of our Lord and Savior Jesus Christ."

An *increase of faith* is part of growth in grace. The belief of the reality of divine things becomes more firm and constant, more reliance is placed on the promises of God, and the soul is enabled to commit all its concerns to the care of a covenant-keeping God.

But there is nothing more essential in this progress than the growing fervor and constancy of love to God, [which] strikes its roots deeper in the heart and becomes more and more purified from the alloy with which it was at first mingled. Growth in divine love manifests itself in reverence for the moral attributes of God, in meditating on his holiness and goodness, and in gratitude for his love and mercy toward us and others. It is accompanied also with a more ardent desire to please God, to enjoy communion with him, and to advance his glory in the world.

Progress in piety includes also an increase of humility. The more true knowledge believers acquire, the more penetrating is our view of the sin that secretly works within us. Those who suppose that they are near perfection and yet are not abased before God, under a sense of their own vileness, only deceive themselves.

Resignation to the will of God is an important part of that grace in the heart that growth affirms. The more uniformly and sincerely we can say under even the most afflictive circumstances, "Your will be done," the more strength has grace acquired. And as genuine progress in piety is the growth of the whole spiritual being, so our love to the children of God and our sincere good will to all humanity will bear a just proportion to our piety to God.

And if piety flourishes in the inner being, it will show itself by its fruits. [Loving], active, universal obedience to God and love to other people and will demonstrate that we are thriving Christians.

—Archibald Alexander

Endnotes

Part 1: Winter

1. Arthur John Gossip, "But When Life Tumbles In, What Then?" in *Classic Sermons on Suffering,* comp. Warren W. Wiersbe (Grand Rapids: Kregel, 1984), 11–20; originally published in *The Hero in Thy Soul* (Edinburgh, Scotland: T. & T. Clark, 1928).

2. George H. Morrison, "The Untrodden Way," in *Highways of the Heart* (London: Hodder and Stoughton, 1926; reprint, Grand Rapids: Kregel, 1994), 17–19.

3. George H. Morrison, "The Higher Offices of Winter," in *Highways of the Heart* (London: Hodder and Stoughton, 1926; reprint, Grand Rapids: Kregel, 1994), 185–87.

4. George H. Morrison, "The Race Not to the Swift," in *The Wings of the Morning* (New York: Hodder and Stoughton, n.d.; reprint, Grand Rapids: Kregel, 1994), 52–56.

5. George H. Morrison, "The Net Mender," in *The Weaving of Glory* (London: Hodder and Stoughton, n.d.; reprint, Grand Rapids: Kregel, 1994), 51–57.

6. George H. Morrison, "The Failure of the Brook," in *The Wings of the Morning* (New York: Hodder and Stoughton, n.d.; reprint, Grand Rapids: Kregel, 1994), 72–77.

7. Ibid.

8. Ibid.

9. John A. Broadus, "The Habit of Thankfulness," downloaded from the Web site of Blessed Hope Ministries of Shiloh Church, Gainesville, Georgia, at members.aol.com/blesshope, accessed Aug. 21, 2001.

10. Ibid.

11. Ibid.

12. Ibid.

13. George H. Morrison, "Unconscious Ministries," in *Wind on the Heath* (original title: *The Afterglow of God,* London: Hodder and Stoughton, 1912; reprint, Grand Rapids: Kregel, 1994), 18–22.

14. George H. Morrison, "The Jealousy of God," in *Wind on the Heath* (original title: *The Afterglow of God,* London: Hodder and Stoughton, 1912; reprint, Grand Rapids: Kregel, 1994), 57–62.

15. Ibid.

16. George H. Morrison, "The Separating Power of Things Present," in *Highways of the Heart* (London: Hodder and Stoughton, 1926; reprint, Grand Rapids: Kregel, 1994), 176–78.

17. George H. Morrison, "Just There," in *Highways of the Heart* (London: Hodder and Stoughton, 1926; reprint, Grand Rapids: Kregel, 1994), 140–41.

18. Alexander Maclaren, "A Prisoner's Dying Thoughts," in *Classic Sermons on the Apostle Paul,* comp. Warren W. Wiersbe (Grand Rapids: Kregel, 1996), 116–17.

19. John Ker, "The Heavenly Home," in *Classic Sermons on Heaven and Hell,* comp. Warren W. Wiersbe (Grand Rapids: Kregel, 1994), 58–60.

20. Ibid., 66–67.

21. Ibid., 67–68.

22. Ibid., 68–69.

23. Ibid., 69–70.

24. C. H. Spurgeon, "Our Great Shepherd Finding the Sheep," in *Spurgeon's Sermons on Soulwinning* (Grand Rapids: Kregel, 1995), 124–27.

25. Ibid.

26. Ibid., 129–30.

27. Ibid.

28. George W. Truett, "The Threefold Secret of a Great Life," in *Classic Sermons on the Apostle Paul,* comp. Warren W. Wiersbe (Grand Rapids: Kregel, 1996), 127–29.

29. Ibid., 130–35.

30. Henry Drummond, "The Greatest Thing in the World," in *The World's Great Sermons,* vol. 10, comp. Grenville Kleiser (New York: Funk & Wagnalls, 1908) 3–35.

31. Ibid., 3–35.

32. William E. Sangster, "The Homesickness of the Soul," in *Classic Sermons on Heaven and Hell,* comp. Warren W. Wiersbe (Grand Rapids: Kregel, 1994), 47–53.

33. Clovis Gillham Chappell, "A Glimpse of the Afterlife," in *Classic Sermons on Heaven and Hell,* comp. Warren W. Wiersbe (Grand Rapids: Kregel, 1994), 100–2, 104.

34. Gossip, "But When Life Tumbles In, What Then?" 11–20.

35. Ibid.

36. Ibid.

37. Ibid.

38. C. H. Spurgeon, "The Centurion's Faith and Humility," in *New Testament Men,* bk. 2 (Grand Rapids: Kregel, 1996), 61–63.

39. Ibid.

40. George H. Morrison, "The Springs of Endurance," in *Highways of the Heart* (London: Hodder and Stoughton, 1926; reprint, Grand Rapids: Kregel, 1994), 35–37.

41. George H. Morrison, "The Lonely People of the Gospels," in *Wind on the Heath* (original title: *The Afterglow of God,* London: Hodder and Stoughton, 1912; reprint, Grand Rapids: Kregel, 1994), 23–24.

42. Ibid., 24–25.

43. Ibid., 25–26.

44. Ibid., 26–27.

45. Ibid., 27–28.

46. George H. Morrison, "Folk Who Are a Comfort to Us," in *Highways of the Heart* (London: Hodder and Stoughton, 1926; reprint, Grand Rapids: Kregel, 1994), 29–31.

47. George H. Morrison, "Homesickness of the Soul," in *Sun-Rise: Addresses from a City Pulpit* (n.d.; reprint, with an introduction by Ralph G. Turnbull, Grand Rapids: Baker, 1971), 1–7.

48. Ibid., 7–11.
49. C. H. Spurgeon, "Peter's Restoration," *Spurgeon's Sermons on New Testament Men,* bk. 2 (Grand Rapids: Kregel, 1996), 94.
50. C. H. Spurgeon, "Joseph of Arimathea," *Spurgeon's Sermons on New Testament Men,* bk. 2 (Grand Rapids: Kregel, 1996), 79.
51. C. H. Spurgeon, "Peter After His Restoration," *New Testament Men,* bk. 2 (Grand Rapids: Kregel, 1996), 103–5.
52. Ibid., 100–1.
53. George H. Morrison, "Love and Grief," in *The Wings of the Morning* (New York: Hodder and Stoughton, n.d.; reprint, Grand Rapids: Kregel, 1994), 67–71.
54. H. P. Liddon, "The Divine Indwelling a Motive to Holiness," in *Sermons Preached Before the University of Oxford, Chiefly During the Years 1863–1868* (New York: E. P. Dutton and Co., 1869), 347–53.
55. François de Salignac de la Mothe-Fénelon, "The Saints Converse with God," in *The World's Great Sermons,* vol. 2, comp. Grenville Kleiser (New York: Funk & Wagnalls, 1908), 206–7, 210–11.
56. C. H. Spurgeon, "Paul—His Cloak and His Books," in *Spurgeon's Sermons on New Testament Men,* bk. 2 (Grand Rapids: Kregel, 1996), 144–45.
57. Stephen Charnock, "A Discourse of Delight in Prayer," ed. William Symington, *Fire and Ice: Puritan and Reformed Writings* at www.puritansermons.com, accessed Aug. 20, 2001.
58. Ibid.
59. C. H. Spurgeon, "God's Fatherly Pity," sermon 1,650 in *The Metropolitan Tabernacle Pulpit* series, preached on Thursday evening March 2, 1882, at the Metropolitan Tabernacle, Newington; downloaded from *Fire and Ice: Puritan and Reformed Sermons,* at http://ourworld.compuserve.com/homepages/WCarson/.
60. Ibid.
61. Ibid.
62. Ibid.
63. Ibid.
64. Ibid.
65. Ibid.
66. Ibid.
67. Ibid.
68. Ibid.
69. Ibid.
70. Charles G. Finney, "On Trusting in the Mercy of God," in *Sermons on Gospel Themes* (New York: Revell, 1876), 19–22.
71. Augustine of Hippo, "Homily 4," *Nicene and Post-Nicene Fathers,* series 1, vol. 7, downloaded from the http://ccel.wheaton.edu, Christian Classics Ethereal Library server, at http://www.wheaton.edu/">Wheaton College.
72. Ibid.
73. Jonathan Edwards, "True Saints, When Absent from the Body, Are Present with the Lord," preached October 12, 1747, the day of the funeral of the Rev. Mr. David Brainerd. Sermon 6, downloaded from Christian Classics Ethereal Library server at Wheaton College, http://ccel.wheaton.edu. Scanned and edited by Harry Plantinga, whp@wheaton.edu. This text is in public domain.
74. G. Campbell Morgan, "Worship, Beauty, Holiness," downloaded from Tom Garner's Web page; previously published in *The Westminster Pulpit,* vol. 2 (Westwood, N.J.:Revell, 1954)
75. Ibid.

76. John Flavel, "Of Christ's Humiliation unto Death, in His First Preparative Act for It," sermon 20 in a series, The Fountain of Life Opened Up, from *The Works of John Flavel*, vol. 1 (1820; reprint, Carlisle, Pa.: Banner of Truth Trust, 1968), 1982; downloaded from the Electronic Public Library, http://www.iclnet.org/pub/resources/text/ipb-e/epl-09: flafn-20.txt.

77. Ibid.

78. Ibid.

79. Ibid.

80. Ibid.

81. Ibid.

82. Ibid.

83. Ibid.

84. Ibid.

85. Ibid.

86. G. Campbell Morgan, "Songs in Prison," in *Classic Sermons on the Apostle Paul,* comp. Warren W. Wiersbe (Grand Rapids: Kregel, 1996), 67–69.

87. Albert Barnes, "Development of the Christian Character," in *The American National Preacher* 7, no. 1 (June 1832); sermon 125, downloaded from Gems in the Attic, www.iserv.net/~bettysul/attic.htm.

88. Ibid.

89. Ibid.

90. Ibid.

91. Ibid.

92. Ibid.

Part 2: Spring

1. George H. Morrison, "A Sermon for Springtime," in *The Wings of the Morning* (New York: Hodder and Stoughton, n.d.; reprint, Grand Rapids: Kregel, 1994), 100–4.

2. Ibid.

3. William E. Sangster, "He Rises Again," in *Classic Sermons on the Resurrection of Christ,* comp. Warren W. Wiersbe (Grand Rapids: Kregel, 1991), 149–54; originally in William E. Sangster, *Westminster Sermons,* vol. 2 (London: Epworth, 1961).

4. Ibid.

5. Walter A. Maier, "The Most Magnificent Thing in the World," in *Classic Sermons on the Grace of God,* comp. Warren W. Wiersbe (Grand Rapids: Kregel, 1998), 39–46.

6. Charles H. Spurgeon, "The Cause and Cure of a Wounded Spirit," in *Twelve Sermons for the Troubled and Tried* (reprint, Grand Rapids: Baker, 1975), 113–23.

7. Ibid.

8. Ibid.

9. Ibid.

10. Ibid.

11. Phillips Brooks, "The Sea of Glass Mingled with Fire," in *Classic Sermons on Suffering,* comp. Warren W. Wiersbe (Grand Rapids: Kregel, 1984), 171–82; originally published in Phillips Brooks, *Twenty Sermons* (London: Macmillan, 1886).

12. Ibid.

13. Ibid.

14. Ibid.

15. George H. Morrison, "The Problem of Pain," in *Classic Sermons on Suffering,* comp.

Warren W. Wiersbe (Grand Rapids: Kregel, 1984), 145–52; originally in George H. Morrison, *The Afterglow of God* (London: Hodder & Stoughton, 1912).

16. Ibid.

17. Ibid.

18. George W. Truett, "The Ministry of Suffering," in *Classic Sermons on Suffering*, comp. Warren W. Wiersbe (Grand Rapids: Kregel, 1984), 131–43; originally published in George W. Truett, *A Quest for Souls* (1917; reprint, New York: Douglas, Doran & Co., 1928).

19. Ibid.

20. Ibid.

21. Hugh Black, "The Heroism of Endurance," in *Classic Sermons on Suffering*, comp. Warren W. Wiersbe (Grand Rapids: Kregel, 1984), 123–29; originally published in Hugh Black, *Edinburgh Sermons* (London: Hodder & Stoughton, 1906).

22. Ibid.

23. William E. Sangster, "How to Be Saved," in *Classic Sermons on the Grace of God* (Grand Rapids: Kregel, 1996), 135–41; originally published in *Evangelical Sermons of Our Day*, comp. Andrew W. Blackwood (New York: Harper & Brothers, 1959).

24. Ibid.

25. C. H. Spurgeon, "Paul—His Cloak and His Books," in *Spurgeon's Sermons on New Testament Men*, bk. 2 (Grand Rapids: Kregel, 1996), 140–41.

26. Jonathan Edwards, "Great Guilt No Obstacle to the Pardon of the Returning Sinner," in *Classic Sermons on the Grace of God*, comp. Warren W. Wiersbe (Grand Rapids: Kregel, 1997), 63–74; previously published in *The Works of Jonathan Edwards*, vol. 2 (Banner of Truth Trust, 1976).

27. Ibid.

28. Ibid.

29. George H. Morrison, "The Lowly Duty of Fidelity," in *Highways of the Heart* (London: Hodder and Stoughton, 1926; reprint, Grand Rapids: Kregel, 1994), 191–93.

30. C. H. Spurgeon, "The Sympathy of the Two Worlds," in *Classic Sermons on Angels*, comp. Warren W. Wiersbe (Grand Rapids: Kregel, 1998), 67–71.

31. Ibid., 71–73.

32. Ibid., 74–77.

33. Ibid.

34. George H. Morrison, "The Immanence of God," in *The Wings of the Morning* (New York: Hodder and Stoughton, n.d.; reprint, Grand Rapids: Kregel, 1994), 110–16.

35. Ibid.

36. Ibid.

37. John Bunyan, "The Heavenly Footman," in *The World's Great Sermons*, vol. 2, comp. Grenville Kleiser (New York: Funk & Wagnalls, 1908), 106, 116–19.

38. C. H. Spurgeon, "The Child of Light Walking in Darkness," in *Twelve Sermons for the Troubled and Tried* (reprint, Grand Rapids: Baker, 1975), 54–64.

39. Ibid.

40. Ibid.

41. George H. Morrison, "Drink from the Depths," in *Wings of the Morning* (New York: Hodder and Stoughton, n.d.; reprint, Grand Rapids: Kregel, 1994), 117–20.

42. Ibid.

43. George H. Morrison, "Christ and the Imagination," in *The Return of the Angels*, 2d ed. (London: Hodder and Stoughton, 1909), 178–89.

44. Ibid.

45. John Henry Jowett, "The Energy of Grace," in *Classic Sermons on the Grace of God* (Grand Rapids: Kregel, 1996), 29–37.

46. Ibid.

47. Samuel Cox, "Ruth's *Menuchah,*" in *The Book of Ruth: A Devotional Commentary* (1876; reprint, London: Religious Tract Society, 1922), 81–86.

48. Samuel Cox, "Ruth's *Goel*" and "Christ the True *Goel* of Men," in *The Book of Ruth: A Devotional Commentary* (1876; reprint, London: Religious Tract Society, 1922), 91–94, 146–55.

49. Ibid.

50. Hugh Black, "The Attraction of the Present," in *Modern Sermons by World Scholars,* vol. 1, *Abbott to Bosworth,* ed. Robert Scott and William C. Stiles, (New York: Funk & Wagnalls, 1909), 131–39.

51. Ibid.

52. H. P. Liddon, "The Divine Indwelling a Motive to Holiness," in *Sermons Preached Before the University of Oxford, Chiefly During the Years 1863–1868* New York: E. P. Dutton and Company, 1869, 343–46.

53. Ibid., 353–64.

54. Joseph Barber Lightfoot, "Christ's Gift of Peace," in *Sermons in St. Paul's Cathedral* (London and New York: Macmillan, 1893), 141–49.

55. William James Dawson, "Christ Among the Common Things of Life," in *The World's Great Sermons,* vol. 10, comp. Grenville Kleiser (New York: Funk & Wagnalls, 1908), 82–88.

56. Ibid.

57. Ibid.

58. Joseph Barber Lightfoot, "Christ's Gift of Peace," in *Sermons in St. Paul's Cathedral* (London and New York: Macmillan, 1893), 141–49.

59. J. D. Jones, "Our Father," in *The Model Prayer: A Series of Expositions on The Lord's Prayer* (London: James Clarke, n.d.), 25–34, 43.

60. Ibid., 25–34, 43.

61. J. D. Jones, "Hallowed Be Thy Name," in *The Model Prayer: A Series of Expositions on The Lord's Prayer* (London: James Clarke, n.d.), 44–61.

62. J. D. Jones, "The Second Petition," in *The Model Prayer: A Series of Expositions on The Lord's Prayer* (London: James Clarke, n.d.), 62–75.

63. J. D. Jones, "Peter," in *Classic Sermons on the Apostle Peter,* comp. Warren W. Wiersbe (Grand Rapids: Kregel, 1995), 33–44.

64. Ibid.

65. C. H. Spurgeon, "The Two Appearings and the Discipline of Grace," in *Classic Sermons on the Grace of God,* comp. Warren W. Wiersbe (Grand Rapids: Kregel, 1996), 9–11.

66. Ibid., 12–14.

67. Ibid., 25–26.

68. William G. T. Shedd, "Religious Meditation," in *Sermons to the Spiritual Man,* comp. Warren W. Wiersbe (1884; reprint, London: Banner of Truth Trust, 1972), 13–18.

69. Ibid.

70. James S. Stewart, "The Burden of the Mystery," in *Classic Sermons on Suffering,* comp. Warren W. Wiersbe (Grand Rapids: Kregel, 1984), 63–72.

71. James S. Stewart, "Lights in the Darkness," in *Classic Sermons on Suffering,* comp. Warren W. Wiersbe (Grand Rapids: Kregel, 1984), 75–84.

72. Ibid.

73. James S. Stewart, "Wearing the Thorns as a Crown," in *Classic Sermons on Suffering,* comp.

Warren W. Wiersbe (Grand Rapids: Kregel, 1984), 87–97; originally published in *The Strong Name* (Edinburgh: T. & T. Clark, 1940).

74. Ibid.
75. James S. Stewart, "The Cross of Victory," in *Classic Sermons on Suffering,* comp. Warren W. Wiersbe (Grand Rapids: Kregel, 1984), 99–107. Taken from *The Strong Name* (Edinburgh: T. & T. Clark, 1940).
76. Stewart, "Lights in the Darkness," 75–84.
77. Ibid.
78. Joseph Barber Lightfoot, "The Triumph of Failure," in *Sermons in St. Paul's Cathedral* (London and New York: Macmillan, 1893), 122–35.
79. Joseph Barber Lightfoot, "The One Taken and the Other Left," in *Sermons in St. Paul's Cathedral* (London and New York: Macmillan, 1893), 114–21.
80. Ibid.
81. Joseph Barber Lightfoot, "The Fall of Judas," in *Sermons Preached in St. Paul's Cathedral* (London and New York: Macmillan, 1893), 58.
82. Ibid.
83. C. H. Spurgeon, "The Unconquerable King," in *Classic Sermons on the Sovereignty of God,* comp. Warren W. Wiersbe (Grand Rapids: Kregel, 1994), 32–42.
84. George Whitefield, "Christ the Best Husband: Or an Earnest Invitation to Young Women to Come and See Christ," preached to a Society of Young Women in Fetter-Lane. Sermon 5, downloaded from Christian Classics Ethereal Library of Calvin College, ccel.org/w/whitefield/sermons.
85. G. Campbell Morgan, "Jehovah of Hosts—The God of Jacob," in *Classic Sermons on the Names of God,* comp. Warren W. Wiersbe (Grand Rapids: Kregel, 1993), 29–40.
86. Ibid.
87. Clarence E. Macartney, "Heaven," in *The Faith Once Delivered* (Grand Rapids: Kregel, 1995), 135–44.
88. G. Campbell Morgan, "Worship, Beauty, Holiness," *The Westminster Pulpit,* vol. 2, (Westwood, N.J.: Revell, 1954).
89. George H. Morrison, "The Offense of the Cross," from G. H. Morrison's page provided by Tom Garner, www.txdirect.net/~tgarner/ghmor2.htm, accessed Aug. 21, 2001.
90. Ibid.
91. Ibid..
92. C. H. Spurgeon, "Jehovah Rophi," in *Classic Sermons on the Names of God,* comp. Warren W. Wiersbe (Grand Rapids: Kregel, 1993), 83–100.
93. Ibid.

Part 3: Summer

1. George H. Morrison, "The League with the Stones," in *The Unlighted Lustre: Addresses from a Glasgow Pulpit* (London: Hodder and Stoughton, 1910), 10–19.
2. Ibid.
3. Ralph Erskine, "God's Great Name, the Ground and Reason of Saving Great Sinners," preached at Carnock, July 18, 1730, before the administration of the sacrament of the Lord's Supper, downloaded from *Fire and Ice, Puritan and Reformed Writings,* at www.puritansermons.com, accessed Aug. 21, 2001.
4. Ibid.
5. Ibid.
6. Ibid.

7. Ibid.

8. Ibid.

9. Ibid.

10. Ibid.

11. Ibid.

12. George H. Morrison, "The Dedication of the Will," in *The Wings of the Morning* (New York: Hodder and Stoughton, n.d.; reprint, Grand Rapids: Kregel, 1994), 95–99.

13. John A. Broadus, "Come unto Me," downloaded from the Web site of Blessed Hope Ministries of Shiloh Church, Gainesville, Georgia, at members.aol.com/blesshope, accessed Aug. 21, 2001.

14. Ibid.

15. Ibid.

16. Ibid.

17. Ibid.

18. Ibid.

19. Horatius Bonar, "Divine Philosophy," sermon 5, from *Christ the Healer,* downloaded from Rare Book Room, The Museum of Pilgrims, Gems in the Attic, at www.members.nbci.johnowen/ctwog.htm, accessed Aug. 21, 2001.

20. Ibid.

21. Ibid.

22. Thomas Brooks, "Christ's Love to Poor Sinners," downloaded from Web site *Fire and Ice, Puritan and Reformed Writings,* at www.puritansermons.com, accessed Aug. 21, 2001.

23. Ibid.

24. Thomas Brooks, "Love the Lord Jesus Christ!" downloaded from *Fire and Ice, Puritan and Reformed Writings,* at www.puritansermons.com, accessed Aug. 21, 2001.

25. Stephen Charnock, "A Discourse of Delight in Prayer," ed. William Symington, *Fire and Ice, Puritan and Reformed Writings,* at www.puritansermons.com, accessed Aug. 21, 2001.

26. Ibid.

27. Ibid.

28. Ibid.

29. Ibid.

30. Ibid.

31. Arthur John Gossip, "A Message for Gray Days," in *Classic Sermons on Hope,* compiled by Warren W. Wiersbe (Grand Rapids: Kregel, 1994), 11–16.

32. Ibid., 17–18.

33. Thomas Watson, "Mystic Union Between Christ and the Saints," downloaded from *Fire and Ice, Puritan and Reformed Writings,* at www.puritansermons.com, accessed Aug. 21, 2001.

34. Ibid.

35. Ibid.

36. Ibid.

37. Ibid.

38. Ibid.

39. Ibid.

40. C. H. Spurgeon, "Andrew: Everyday Usefulness," *New Testament Men,* bk. 2 (Grand Rapids: Kregel, 1996), 16–17.

41. Augustine, "Sermon X. [LX. Ben.]," *Nicene and Post-Nicene Fathers,* series 1, vol. 6, downloaded from the Christian Classics Ethereal Library at www.ccel.org, accessed Aug. 21,

2001. On the words of the gospel, Matt. 6:19, "Lay not up for yourselves treasures upon earth," etc., an exhortation to alms deeds.

42. Ibid.

43. John Chrysostom, "Homily 26," from Christian Classics Ethereal Library, *Nicene and Post-Nicene Fathers,* series 1, vol. 14, at www.ccel.org, accessed Aug. 21, 2001.

44. Ibid.

45. John A. Broadus, "The Saviour Praying for Us," downloaded from the Blessed Hope Ministries of Shiloh Baptist Church, Gainesville, Ga. at members.aol.com/blesshope, accessed Aug. 21, 2001.

46. Ibid.

47. Ibid.

48. Ibid.

49. Ralph Erskine, "Heaven's Grand Repository," downloaded from Web site *Fire and Ice, Puritan and Reformed Writings,* at www.puritansermons.com, accessed Aug. 21, 2001.

50. Ibid.

51. Ibid.

52. Ibid.

53. Ibid.

54. Ibid.

55. Phillips Brooks, "The Nearness of God," downloaded from the Web site The Unofficial Episcopal Preaching Resource Page, at www.edola.org/clergy/episcopalpreaching.html, accessed Aug. 21, 2001.

56. Ibid.

57. Thomas Boston, "Of God and His Perfections," downloaded from The Boston Homepage at www.geocities.com/~thomasboston, accessed Aug. 21, 2001.

58. Ibid.

59. Ibid.

60. George H. Morrison, "The Renascence of Wonder," in *Wind on the Heath* (original title: *The Afterglow of God,* London: Hodder and Stoughton, 1912; reprint, Grand Rapids: Kregel, 1994), 46–51.

61. Ibid.

62. Jonathan Edwards, "Many Mansions," on the Sabbath after the seating of the new meeting house, December 25, 1737; from Jonathan Edwards.com Web site, at www.jonathanedwards.com, accessed Aug. 21, 2001.

63. Ibid.

64. Ibid.

65. Ibid.

66. Ibid.

67. George H. Morrison, "Some Features of Christ's Working," source document downloaded from Web site of Tom Garner, www.txdirect.net/~tgarner/ghmor2.htm, accessed Aug. 21, 2001.

68. John Chrysostom, "Homily 28," downloaded from *Nicene and Post-Nicene Fathers,* series 1, vol. 14, from the Christian Classics Ethereal Library, www.ccel.org, accessed Aug. 21, 2001.

69. John Flavel, "Of the Manner of Christ's Death, in Respect to the Solitariness Thereof," sermon 28 in a series, The Fountain of Life Opened Up, from *The Works of John Flavel,* vol. 1 (London: Banner of Truth Trust, 1968).

70. Ibid.

71. Ibid.

72. Ibid.

73. Ibid.

74. Ibid.

75. George H. Morrison, "Beginning to Sink," in *Wind on the Heath* (original title: *The Afterglow of God*, London: Hodder and Stoughton, 1912; reprint, Grand Rapids: Kregel, 1994), 40–45.

76. Ibid.

77. Martin Luther (1483–1546), "The True and the False Views of Christ's Sufferings," in *The Precious and Sacred Writings of Martin Luther*, vol. 11 (Minneapolis: Lutherans in All Lands, 1906); preached by Luther c. 1519–1521; reprinted as "Christ's Holy Sufferings," in *The Sermons of Martin Luther*, edited by Eugene F. A. Klug (Grand Rapids: Baker, 1996).

78. Ibid.

79. Ibid.

80. Ibid.

81. Joseph Parker (1830–1902), "The Unknowable God," downloaded from a Web site of Tom Garner, at www.txdirect.net/~tgarner/ghmor2.htm, accessed Aug. 21, 2001.

82. Ibid.

83. Ibid.

84. Ibid.

85. Ibid.

86. Alexander Maclaren, "Jehovah Jireh," in *Classic Sermons on the Names of God* (Grand Rapids: Kregel, 1993), 103–8; originally published in Alexander Maclaren, *Expositions of Holy Scripture*, vol. 1 (Grand Rapids: Baker, 1974).

87. Ibid.

88. Ibid.

89. John Chrysostom, "Homily 20," in the *Nicene and Post-Nicene Fathers*, series 1, vol. 11, from the Christian Classics Ethereal Library, at www.ccel.org, accessed Aug. 21, 2001.

90. Ibid.

91. Ibid.

92. Ibid.

Part 4: Autumn

1. T. DeWitt Talmage, "The Arrival of Autumn," in *Old Wells Dug Out* (New York: Harper & Brothers, 1876).

2. T. DeWitt Talmage, "The Mission of the Frost," in *500 Selected Sermons* (1900; reprint, Grand Rapids: Baker, 1956), 375–87.

3. George H. Morrison, "The Fault of Over-Prudence," in *The Wings of the Morning* (New York: Hodder and Stoughton, n.d.; reprint, Grand Rapids: Kregel, 1994), 121–25.

4. Ibid.

5. Ibid.

6. C. H. Spurgeon, "Mary's Magnificat," in *Spurgeon's Sermons on New Testament Women*, bk. 1 (Grand Rapids: Kregel, 1994), 9–20.

7. Ibid.

8. Ibid.

9. Ibid.

10. Ibid.

11. C. H. Spurgeon, "Believers as Blessed as the Blessed Virgin," in *Spurgeon's Sermons on New Testament Women,* bk. 2 (Grand Rapids: Kregel, 1996), 7–8.

12. C. H. Spurgeon, "Mary's Song," in *Spurgeon's Sermons on New Testament Women,* bk. 2 (Grand Rapids: Kregel, 1996), 19–32.

13. Samuel Willard, "Christ Humbled Himself," preached May 12, 1696, the second in a series of twelve sermons on this question from the *Westminster Shorter Catechism;* downloaded from *Fire and Ice, Puritan and Reformed Writings,* at www.puritansermons.com, accessed Aug. 21, 2001.

14. Ibid.

15. Charles G. Finney, "Heart Searching," preached November 27, 1849, at the Borough Road Chapel, Southwark; downloaded from The Gospel Truth Web site, at www.gospeltruth.net/cgfworks.htm, accessed Aug. 21, 2001.

16. Ibid.

17. Ibid.

18. Ibid.

19. Ibid.

20. Ibid.

21. Arthur John Gossip (1873–1954), "What Brought Christ to the Cross?" in *The Galilean Accent* (Edinburgh: T. & T. Clark, 1926).

22. Ibid.

23. Ibid.

24. Ibid.

25. Ibid.

26. Ibid.

27. Ibid.

28. Ibid.

29. Ibid.

30. Ibid.

31. Ibid.

32. John A. Broadus, "Worship," in *Sermons of John A. Broadus,* downloaded from the Web site of Blessed Hope Ministries of Shiloh Baptist Church, Gainesville, Ga., at members.aol.com/blesshope, accessed Aug. 21, 2001.

33. Ibid.

34. George H. Morrison, "Sacrifice and Song," in *Classic Sermons on Praise,* comp. Warren W. Wiersbe (Grand Rapids: Kregel, 1994), 78–79.

35. George Whitefield, "The Lord Our Righteousness," in *Classic Sermons on the Names of God,* comp. Warren W. Wiersbe (Grand Rapids: Kregel, 1993), 111–29.

36. Ibid.

37. Ibid.

38. George H. Morrison, "The Anguish of the Light," in *The Weaving of Glory* (London: Hodder and Stoughton, n.d.; reprint, Grand Rapids: Kregel, 1994), 79–81.

39. Ibid., 81–83.

40. Ibid., 81.

41. Henry Drummond, "Dealing with Doubt," in *Classic Sermons on Faith and Doubt,* comp. Warren W. Wiersbe (Grand Rapids: Kregel, 1991), 25–32.

42. Ibid.

43. Ibid.

44. Ibid.

45. George H. Morrison, "The Blindness of Vision," in *Wind on the Heath* (original title:

The Afterglow of God, London: Hodder and Stoughton, 1912; reprint, Grand Rapids: Kregel, 1994), 52–56.

46. Ibid.
47. Jonathan Edwards, "The Excellency of Christ," downloaded from the Christian Classics Ethereal Library, at www.ccel.org, accessed Aug. 21, 2001.
48. Ibid.
49. Ibid.
50. Ibid.
51. Ibid.
52. Ibid.
53. Ibid.
54. Ibid.
55. Ibid.
56. Ibid.
57. Ibid.
58. Ibid.
59. Jonathan Edmondson, "The Little Flock of Christ Encouraged," taken from the book *Short Sermons on Important Subjects,* Shiloh Online Library, downloaded from the Web site of Blessed Hope Ministries of Shiloh Baptist Church, Gainesville, Ga., at www.shilohonline.org, accessed Aug. 21, 2001.
60. Jonathan Edmondson, "Prayer in Affliction," taken from the book *Short Sermons on Important Subjects,* Shiloh Online Library, downloaded from the Web site of Blessed Hope Ministries of Shiloh Baptist Church, Gainesville, Ga., at www.shilohonline.org, accessed Aug. 21, 2001.
61. George Whitefiled, Sermon 37 "The Duty of Searching the Scriptures," downloaded from the Christian Classics Ethereal Library, at www.ccel.org, accessed Aug. 21, 2001.
62. Ibid.
63. Ibid.
64. Ibid.
65. C. H. Spurgeon, "Christ and His Table-Companions," in *Till He Come* (1896; reprint, Pasadena, Tex.: Pilgrim Publications, 1971), 263–82; electronic version from the HtmlResAnchor Christian Classics Ethereal Library at HtmlResAnchor Calvin College, ccel.wheaton.edu/spurgeon/till_he_come/tblecmp.html.
66. Ibid.
67. Ibid.
68. Ibid.
69. Ibid.
70. Augustine of Hippo, "Sermon on John 5:19," downloaded from a Web site of Tom Garner, at www.txdirect.net/~tgarner/ghmor2.htm, accessed Aug. 21, 2001.
71. Ibid.
72. George H. Morrison, "The Candor of Christ," in *The Wings of the Morning* (New York: Hodder and Stoughton, n.d.; reprint, Grand Rapids: Kregel, 1994), 47–51.
73. John Duncan, "Behold the Lamb of God," preached on October 25, 1840, at Milton Church, Glasgow, Scotland; downloaded from *The Westminster Presbyterian,* a Web site of the Presbyterian Reformed Church of Metropolitan Washington, at members.aol.com/rsich/grace.html, accessed Aug. 21, 2001.
74. Ibid.
75. Ibid.
76. Ibid.

77. Phillips Brooks, "The Nearness of God," downloaded from the Web site The Unofficial Episcopal Preaching Resource Page, at www.edola.org/clergy/episcopalpreaching.html, accessed Aug. 21, 2001.
78. Ibid.
79. Ibid.
80. Ibid.
81. Ibid.
82. Thomas Boston, "Of Man's Chief End and Happiness," downloaded from The Boston Homepage, at www.geocities.com/~thomasboston, accessed Aug. 21, 2001.
83. Ibid.
84. Ibid.
85. Ibid.
86. Joseph Parker, "Saul Self-Contrasted," in *Classic Sermons on the Apostle Paul,* comp. Warren W. Wiersbe (Grand Rapids: Kregel, 1996), 39–44.
87. George H. Morrison, "The Best Wine Last," in *The Wings of the Morning* (New York: Hodder and Stoughton, n.d.; reprint, Grand Rapids: Kregel, 1994), 19–24.
88. Ibid.
89. Archibald Alexander, "The Nature and Means of Growth in Grace," in *National Preacher* 3, no. 8 (January 1829), downloaded from the Web site Gems in the Attic, www.iserv.net/~bettysul/attic.htm.
90. Ibid.
91. Ibid.

Thumbnail Biographies
of the Preachers

Alexander, Archibald (1772–1851) Presbyterian minister, professor, and first president of Princeton Seminary (1812), b. Tidewater country of Virginia. Short in stature and notable for his gray, uncombed hair, Alexander demonstrated a preaching style influenced by his contemporary Patrick Henry. Alexander preached in a voice that was "lively and penetrative," powerful enough to be heard even in a large room.

Augustine (354–430) Bishop of Hippo in North Africa, b. North Africa. Converted at age 32, Augustine became one of the most important preachers and teachers of the post-New Testament era until the Reformation. A professor of rhetoric, Augustine wrote the first textbook on the art of preaching. He preached without notes, and his sermons were logical, often using alliteration and rhyme.

Barnes, Albert (1798–1870) New School Presbyterian pastor and preacher in Philadelphia during the Second Great Awakening (1800–1835), b. U.S. Seeking a new interpretation of the essential Christian truths, Barnes sought to adapt Christianity to the spirit of freedom that was burgeoning in the period between the American Revolution and the Civil War. He was charged with heresy for denying original sin but, nonetheless, retained his pastorate. His preaching style was conversational, never loud.

Black, Hugh (1869–1953) Presbyterian minister and author, b. Scotland. For a time, Black shared in ministry with Alexander Whyte in Edinburgh, where it was said Whyte painted the congregation black in the morning and Black painted them white in the evening. Black became a professor of practical theology at Union Theological Seminary in New York.

Bonar, Horatius (1808–1889) Presbyterian minister, writer, and hymn writer, b. Scotland. Some hundred of Bonar's hymns are in common use today, including "Blessing and Honor"; "Glory Be to God the Father"; "Here, O Lord, I See Thee"; "I Heard the Voice of Jesus Say";

"I Lay My Sins on Jesus." Bonar participated in the "Disruption" in 1843, when 451 ministers left the Presbyterian Church and established the Free Church of Scotland. Bonar was well acquainted with personal sorrow—five of his children died young. He had a strong physique and a powerful intellect, combined with a gentle, sympathetic nature.

Boston, Thomas (1676–1732) Presbyterian pastor, preacher, theologian, author, and Hebrew scholar, b. Scotland. As a child, Boston often sat outside the prison where his nonconformist father was imprisoned; as an adult he led in resisting the hyper-Calvinism of his day to preach the gospel to all. He was skilled in making high teaching accessible to the comprehension of common people. He exercised care in creating every sermon, writing them out ahead of time, and preached them with "majestic energy."

Broadus, John A. (1827–1895) Baptist preacher, taught New Testament interpretation and homiletics at the Southern Baptist Theological Seminary in Greenville, South Carolina, b. U.S. Broadus was a pastor in Virginia, and during the Civil War he served as a chaplain to Lee's Army of Northern Virginia. After the war, the seminary was moved to Louisville, where Broadus became its second president. Broadus's preaching appeared extempore but did not flow from extempore thinking. Rather, he demonstrated a free delivery after careful preparation. Studious care, Bible exposition, simplicity, clarity of thought and expression intended to convince and persuade, and a warm, contagious faith characterized his preaching.

Brooks, Phillips (1835–1893) Episcopalian minister and writer of the hymn "O Little Town of Bethlehem," b. Boston. Pastor in Philadelphia and later at Trinity Church in Boston, theologically, Brooks is called a liberal and is criticized for blunting the sharp edges in Protestant tradition, preaching a "bland religion of reassurance." Nonetheless, he preached Christ crucified. When he preached he spoke rapidly because he thought rapidly. While in Philadelphia, Brooks and Albert Barnes were among those ministers who volunteered to work on the trenches and fortifications around the city when Lee's army invaded Pennsylvania in 1863. Brooks was six-feet-four and three hundred pounds—a large man with a large soul—mentally, morally, and spiritually intense.

Brooks, Thomas (1608–1680) Nonconformist, Congregationalist preacher, b. England. Brooks was born into a Puritan family who was still part of the Church of England, the state church, but he became a Congregationalist. Brooks served as a chaplain in the English Civil War and afterwards ministered in London from 1648 until 1660, when he was ejected as the monarchy was restored. He continued to minister secretly, however, working in London during the Great Plague and the Great Fire. Eventually, though, Brooks obtained a license to preach again. During his career he wrote numerous devotional books.

Bunyan, John (1628–1688) Nonconformist, Puritan preacher, and author, b. England. At sixteen, Bunyan joined Cromwell's Parliamentary Army in the English Civil War. After serving in the army he settled down to a trade as a tinker and married at age twenty. After his conversion, Bunyan became a popular preacher in the Puritan Free Church. When the monarchy was restored in 1660, Bunyan refused to stop preaching and was jailed for more than twelve years. His preaching was earnest and direct, picturesque, simple, and clear in style, delivered with tenderness and warmth. His renowned works—the more remarkable because at the time Bunyan was converted he couldn't read or write—include *Grace Abounding to the Chief of Sinners* and *The Pilgrim's Progress.*

Chappell, Clovis G. (1882–1972) Methodist minister, b. Tennessee. Pastoring in several cities across the South, Chappell demonstrated an insight into human character and a vivid imagination. For that reason his sermons on Bible personalities remain memorable. His preaching was biblical and evangelistic but gentle.

Charnock, Stephen (1628–1680) Presbyterian, Puritan preacher, b. England. Chaplain to the governor of Ireland under Cromwell's Protectorate, Charnock, after the monarchy was restored, joined a Presbyterian ministry in London. A master of Greek and Hebrew scriptural texts, Charnock's preaching demonstrated great knowledge and warm piety, characteristics that, contrary to modern stereotypes, were reflected in Puritan preaching.

Chrysostom, John (c. 343–407) *Chrysostom,* meaning "Of the Golden Mouth," was an appellation given a century and a half after his death. John of Antioch (his original name) was an ascetic youth who became a deacon and later a presbyter and preacher. He was kidnapped and made the bishop of Constantinople. He died during his second exile after brave, although in this case tactless, criticism of the empress and of sin in the imperial court. Of note in his preaching was a focus on the literal and historical meaning of the Scripture text.

Cox, Samuel (1826–1893) Little-known nonconformist preacher, editor of *The Expositor,* b. England. Though an evangelical, Cox held and taught "the larger hope"—universal salvation. Many of his expositions of Scripture and sermons were meant to throw light on misunderstood and difficult passages. He also published sermons for children.

Dawson, William James (1854–1923) Congregationalist, writer, and literary critic, b. England. Dawson trained for the ministry of Wesleyan Methodist churches, pastored in London, Glasgow, and Newark, New Jersey, and his preaching style was that of the orator. He deeply loved literature and quoted Shelley, Browning, Blake, and others.

Drummond, Henry (1851–1897) Evangelist and author, b. Scotland. A professor at New College, Edinburgh, Drummond lectured on the relation of science and religion. He maintained an effective outreach ministry to university students in Scotland and was involved in the Moody-Sankey crusade of 1873–75, during which he became a personal friend to D. L. Moody. Drummond is criticized, however, as making some concessions to biblical criticism. He traveled widely, to the U.S., Africa, Australia, and the South Seas, and was also well-read. Drummond's preaching voice was rich and his vocabulary extensive.

Duncan, John (1796–1870) Presbyterian preacher, b. Scotland. Because of his ability in the Hebrew language, Duncan was commissioned to a ministry among the Jews in Hungary. He returned from Hungary to teach Hebrew and Old Testament at New College, Edinburgh. He was gifted—but absentminded. His students called him "Rabbi," or "Rab," because of his long white beard. It is noteworthy that, throughout his life, Duncan battled depression.

Edmondson, Jonathan (1766–1842) Wesleyan Methodist minister, b. England. Edmondson emphasized practical godliness and holiness. He carried on an itinerant circuit ministry for fifty years until ill health forced him into retirement.

Edwards, Jonathan (1703–1758) Congregational minister, b. New England. Considered one of the greatest preachers of his age, Edwards's preaching was logical, simple, and plain, using little illustration and nothing personal. He did, however, use poetry, symbols, and metaphors. In 1734–35, the Great Awakening began in Edwards's church in Northampton, Massachusetts. Controversy eventually deprived him of his church, after which he worked as a missionary to the Native Americans. A few months prior to his death he was made president of Princeton.

Erskine, Ralph (1685–1752) Pastor, scholar, and theologian, b. Scotland. Erskine was fond of music and proficient on the violin. With his elder brother, Ebenezer, and a few others, he was an active participant in the secession from the Church of Scotland.

Fénelon, François de Salignac de la Mothe (1651–1715) Catholic, Archbishop of Cambrai, b. south of France. Born into a noble family, Fénelon became a court favorite of Louis XIV and tutored the Duke of Burgundy, the heir apparent to the French throne. Preaching at the French court was often ornate, called French-lacquer style because of its elegance, and Fénelon is known not only for his eloquence but for his deep spirituality. Fénelon was more tolerant of Protestants than most other court preachers.

Finney, Charles G. (1792–1875) Revivalist and for several years an itinerant preacher, b. U.S. Finney was often involved in theological controversy—some could not tolerate his strong preaching on hell; others criticized that in regard to salvation he emphasized human responsibility rather than the grace of God. Neither did Finney eschew political controversy, adopting a public stand against slavery. Finney's preaching was logical and clear as well as dramatic; he used brief, simple language. Many remarked on his large, blue eyes, which could be mild as a spring sky or cold and penetrating as steel.

Flavel, John (c. 1627–1691) Nonconformist, pastor, and theologian, b. England. While Flavel was the minister at Dartmouth, the Acts of Uniformity ejected nonconformist ministers from their churches. Flavel had to leave the Dartmouth pulpit and hold services in secret in private homes and elsewhere, even in the woods. During part of this period he was under house arrest, and his parents were imprisoned as nonconformists and died from pestilence contracted while in prison. Flavel's first wife died in childbirth, as did their child; he outlived two more wives but was outlived by the fourth.

Gossip, Arthur John (1873–1954) Presbyterian minister, professor of practical theology at Trinity College, Glasgow, b. Scotland. Gossip ministered in England and Scotland and served as an army chaplain in World War I. Not possessing a good speaking voice, Gossip preached without notes, in a heavy accent, using awkward gestures. Notwithstanding, he was very pastoral and caring, and was known for his sermons for children.

Jones, J. D. (1865–1942) Congregationalist minister, b. Wales. Jones was raised in Calvinistic Methodism. A short, burly figure with white hair even in his prime, Jones preached in the same church for forty years. His wife died in 1917, and their only son was gassed and wounded in France. The son recovered but was later killed in Africa. Jones was a warm pastor who gave a sympathetic ear and practical help. His preaching style was calm rather than fiery and dramatic, with a note of strength and comfort. He took great care in preparing his written sermons and used his manuscript in the pulpit.

Jowett, John H. (1864–1923) Congregational minister and author, b. Yorkshire, England. Jowett and his wife enjoyed a successful ministry to children. He studied words as a hobby and carefully polished his sermons, delivering them in a great speaking voice with graceful gestures. He pastored in New York for a time at the Fifth Avenue Presbyterian Church. But at the end of World War I, he returned to England, where he preached an Armistice service to the king and queen at the Royal Albert Hall, London. Although he appeared frail and was bald, Jowett was meticulous about his appearance.

Ker, John (1819–1886) United Presbyterian preacher, professor of preaching and pastoral work at the United Free Church Seminary in Glasgow, b. Scotland. Ker preached without notes but took great care in composing and mastering the material ahead of time so that he spoke with an air of ease and spontaneity. Physically frail and homely in appearance, he was sparing of gesture but had a clear, melodious delivery.

Liddon, H. P. (1829–1890) High Church Anglican minister and a canon at St. Paul's, London, b. England. Liddon was outspoken against higher criticism and willingly engaged in controversy. He was associated, too, with the Oxford Movement, which pulled the Anglican Church toward the Roman Catholic beliefs in apostolic succession and the authority of tradition. It is a note of personal interest that Liddon had a lifelong fondness for cats.

Lightfoot, J. B. (1828–1889) Anglican, Bible expositor, historian, professor at Cambridge, b. England. Lightfoot worked on the committee for the English Revised Version of the New Testament, which gives a more correct and consistent rendering of the original Greek than does the King James Version. (The English Revised Version is the basis for the American Standard Version of 1901.) Lightfoot left Cambridge to become bishop of Durham and trained men for Holy Orders in the Anglican Church.

Luther, Martin (1483–1546) Teacher, leader of the Protestant Reformation, author, Bible translator, hymn writer, b. Germany. Luther's studies—especially of Psalms, Romans, and Galatians—contributed to his conversion. Until the Reformation, anyone outside the clergy had little or no access to the Bible. Luther saw the need for people to have the Scriptures in their language, thus, while an outlaw, he translated the New Testament into German. His high view of Scripture led to a high view of preaching, built on the text alone, with converting the hearers the object. Although not as systematic a thinker as Calvin, Luther was a feeling preacher, but in submission to the text. Earthy, courageous, and gifted, Luther married a former nun.

Macartney, Clarence E. (1879–1957) Presbyterian minister, b. U.S. In the fundamentalist-modernist controversy of the 1920s, Macartney denounced Fosdick's views as contrary to Presbyterian doctrine and a departure from the historic Christian faith. His extensive reading in history and biography became sermon material. His preaching was topical rather than expository, including few but fitting gestures. He had a strong voice and used only subdued humor. Macartney was one of the most important scholars of Abraham Lincoln in the country.

Maclaren, Alexander (1826–1910) Baptist preacher, b. Scotland. Maclaren was dedicated to exegesis of the original Hebrew and Greek texts of Scripture. He refused most invitations to preach outside his own flock but visited his church families two nights a week. His voice was rich and musical, clear and penetrating, with a pleasant brogue.

Maier, Walter A. (1893–1950) Lutheran preacher and professor of Old Testament and of Semitic languages at Concordia Seminary in St. Louis, b. U.S. Maier worked in inner-city ministry in St. Louis. Known around the world as the speaker on *The Lutheran Hour,* Maier defended the reliability of Scripture. His voice was strong rather than melodious, and he gestured vigorously even when preaching on the radio.

Morgan, G. Campbell (1863–1945) Congregational preacher, teacher, and author, b. England. A pastor of both English and American churches, Morgan studied and preached a verse or a book in the context of the whole Scripture. His forte was in Bible exposition, and in his preaching Morgan used few illustrations outside the Bible itself. He refrained from much application, believing that application is the work of the Holy Spirit. He preached his first public sermon at age thirteen and later taught for three years at a Jewish school for boys. Tall, almost gaunt, Morgan had a deep, strong voice.

Morrison, George H. (1866–1928) Presbyterian pastor and preacher, b. Scotland. As a young man, Morrison assisted in the preparation of the Oxford English Dictionary. The pastor of Wellington Church, Glasgow, for twenty-six years, Morrison made use of visits, postcards, and letters for any in his care who were sick or in sorrow or trouble. He was never idle. He did not serve on committees, preferring to spend his time on what he considered were his greatest responsibilities to his church—mornings in study, afternoons in visiting his congregation. Quiet and genial in his preaching style, after a complete study of his text, Morrison strove to present it simply, so that all who heard him, from bishops to laborers, received help along the way. Morrison's son was killed in World War I.

Parker, Joseph (1830–1902) Popular Congregationalist preacher and writer, b. England. Mostly self-educated, Parker pastored London's City Temple from 1869 until his death in 1902. He published the *People's Bible,* a collection of notes on sermons, with prayers, that he had preached through the entire Bible. Described as a "massive figure [with] leonine head," Parker's style in the pulpit was lively, imaginative, and intense.

Sangster, William E. (1900–1960) Methodist pastor, evangelist, and author, b. England. Sangster served in the army at the end of World War I, and during World War II he pastored a London church, managed an air-raid shelter in its basement, ministered to the homeless of central London, and studied for his Ph.D. It is said that his greatest sermon was the one he preached over the many months during which he was dying from an incurable disease. He was tall and, prior to his illness, strong, talking incessantly with his hands.

Shedd, William G. T. (1820–1894) Presbyterian, university and seminary professor, b. U.S. Shedd was professor of biblical literature and then of systematic theology at Union Theological Seminary in New York. Regarding his theology as Augustinian and Calvinistic, Shedd opposed the higher criticism becoming popular in the late nineteenth century. Although thin, he was not severe in appearance.

Spurgeon, C. H. (1834–1892) Baptist-Calvinist preacher, b. England. Spurgeon preached to huge audiences, even by today's standards. His delivery was enthusiastic, humorous, sincere, intense, and loving, "a long bright river of silver speech." And what he preached he published. Physically, Spurgeon was very heavy, a lifelong smoker with kidney problems and rheumatic gout.

Stewart, James S. (1896–1990) Pastor, writer, and professor of theology and New Testament at New College, Edinburgh, b. Scotland. Stewart served as chaplain of a local soccer club, preached regularly at a rescue mission, and lectured around the world. Though highly educated, he was not intellectually isolated but engaged with the Bible and the world around him.

Talmage, T. DeWitt (1832–1901) Reformed minister, b. U.S. Ministering in Philadelphia, then in Brooklyn, Talmage attracted large audiences—as well as criticism for his theatrical style. His preaching was, however, invincibly optimistic. Talmage thought and spoke in colorful word pictures accompanied by dramatic movements, and his sermons were published regularly in many newspapers. Tall, slightly stooped, broad shouldered, and bony, Talmage had a square jaw and sandy sideburns, with a massive head that was bald on top. The death of his first wife in a boating accident devastated Talmage, but he recovered from the tragedy.

Truett, George W. (1867–1944) Baptist pastor-evangelist, b. North Carolina. Pastor of the First Baptist Church of Dallas, Texas, for forty-seven years. Truett preached to troops in Europe before and after the armistice of World War I. He served terms as president of the Southern

Baptist Convention and the Baptist World Alliance. A tall man with blue-gray eyes, Truett preached his sermons in simple language with a forceful delivery and few gestures. In a hunting accident, Truett killed his best friend, an event that shattered him and nearly drove him from the ministry. Compassion was a characteristic focus of his sermons.

Watson, Thomas (c.1620–c.1689) Puritan and nonconformist preacher, b. England. Watson protested the beheading of King Charles and was briefly imprisoned for his part in a plot to bring Charles II to the throne. But after the restoration of the monarchy, he was ejected from the churches as were other nonconformist ministers. He continued private preaching until the Acts of Indulgence permitted a return to public ministry. His most famous work is *Body of Practical Divinity*, a series of 176 sermons on the catechism that served to train ordinary people in doctrine. Spurgeon wrote of Watson, "There is a happy union of sound doctrine, heart-searching experience and practical wisdom throughout all his works."

Whitefield, George (1714–1770) Evangelist of the Revival and leader of Calvinistic Methodists, b. England. Whitefield preached throughout England, Wales, Scotland, and the United States, and in his early visits to the U.S. he established orphanages and schools in Georgia. When Anglican pulpits in Britain were closed to him, he preached in the open air. Whitefield was associated with the Wesleys, but a break came between them over disagreement in regard to the elect—Whitefield believed the elect are so because God chooses them; the Wesleys believe that God chooses the elect because he foresees who will believe. Whitefield died while in the U.S. on a preaching tour.

Willard, Samuel (1640–1707) Second-generation New England Puritan and prolific writer, b. America. One of Massachusetts Bay Colony's major theologians, Willard's first ministry ended when Indians killed some townspeople and burned down the settlement where Willard pastored. Soon he was preaching in Boston and was installed as the teacher at Boston's South Church. His *Compleat Body of Divinity*, published posthumously, was a series of 250 lectures on the Shorter Catechism. Willard, a thoughtful and wise man, was influential in halting the Salem witch trials in 1692.

Information about many of these preachers is from David L. Larsen's *The Company of the Preachers: A History of Biblical Preaching from the Old Testament to the Modern Era* (Grand Rapids, Kregel, 1998). Other helpful resources are *Eerdmans' Handbook to the History of Christianity* (Herts, England: Lion Publishing, 1977; First American edition 1977); and Ralph G. Turnbull, *A History of Preaching, Volume III* (Grand Rapids, Baker, 1974).